PANDA GUIDES

THINK CHINA THINK PANDA

SHANGHAI

THIS EDITION WAS RESEARCHED AND WRITTEN BY

Brendan P. O'Reilly
Trey Archer
Sam Gusway
Ansel Klusmire

How to Use this Book

1. **Overview** – The Overview is the place to start. Here you can learn about the history and culture of Shanghai, and decide which season is best for your trip and which festivals are going on during your visit. There are plenty of fun facts as well, including the Shanghai reading and movie list.

2. **Hot Topics** – Mentally prepare with Hot Topics. Everything you need to know about how to travel with kids, protect yourself against pollution, stay safe and healthy, and more is touched on in this chapter. There are also a few sample itineraries to help with planning your trip.

3. **Getting Prepared** – Pack those bags, get your visa and buy a ticket through the help of our user-friendly Getting Prepared section.

4. **Top Attractions & Other Attractions** – Learn about Shanghai's many world-class attractions through vivid descriptions, histories and vibrant full-color pictures. If your trip is limited in time, the hardest part will be narrowing down the list! It's also a good idea to bring this guidebook to these sites to stay fresh on their details – it's certainly cheaper than hiring an overpriced tour guide.

5. **Side Trips** – If you have time to spare after seeing your desired sights, go for one (or a few) of our Side Trips. Whether it's a rugged hike up one of the most beautiful mountains in the world at Mt Huangshan, a relaxing retreat at the glorious canal town of Suzhou, a history lesson through the museums of the former capital of Nanjing, or a spiritual walk around Hangzhou's West Lake, we have options for every kind of traveler.

6. **Sleeping** – Book the perfect lodging using the Sleeping chapter. You can even use the pull-out city map to ensure your hotel or hostel is close to all of your desired sights. To save cash, choose a place with a Panda Partnership. Each location with the blue ribbon `10% OFF` offers discounts when you flash this Panda Guides guidebook.

7. **Eating and Drinking & Nightlife** – Reserve a five-star restaurant or do as the locals do and chow down at a hole-in-the wall using our comprehensive restaurant list. Then paint the town red at the city's hottest bars, clubs and live music venues. Be sure to see which ones offer discounts for showing your Panda Guides book (look for the blue discount ribbon). It'll save you a pretty penny.

8. **Distractions** – When you need a break from all the sightseeing, flip through Distractions to see which massage parlor wants to spoil you. Perhaps ice-skating, a show or a cooking class is calling your name? We have tons of relaxing activities to "distract" you along the way.

9. **Travel Resources** – Lost your passport and need a new one? Decided to continue traveling and need visas for other countries? Want to live like a local and check out the expat websites, news and events happening during your stay? Travel Resources can be your best friend and a lifesaver if a problem arises.

10. **Mandarin Phrasebook** – By speaking the local lingo and learning more about one of the world's oldest and most fascinating languages, not only will you enlighten your soul, but you'll also find traversing the town a lot easier. Get started in our Mandarin Phrasebook.

Table of Contents

Shanghai Overview

Shanghai is the most populated city in China (and by some estimates, the largest in the world), but it wasn't always that way. Considering China's vast and ancient history, the development of Shanghai as an economic powerhouse is fairly recent. When other cities were home to dynasties and empires thousands of years ago, Shanghai was just a quiet fishing village with little importance to the nation.

It became a market town in the 12th century, and by 1292 it was a regional hub. Things grew slowly for a few hundred years, with a few temples being constructed and more business being done within the city walls. Starting in the 1800s, though, things hit hyper-speed for this once-sleepy town.

In 1842, at the height of the First Opium War, the British captured Shanghai and never looked back. When the war ended a few months later with the signing of the Treaty of Nanking, the Qing government allowed foreigners to do unlimited business in China for the first time ever. Shanghai was one of five Chinese cities that opened up to foreign trade, and land concessions were granted to a number of international world powers. Each nation-state policed their own territory based on their national law, so their judiciary systems always favored their fellow countrymen and discriminated against local Chinese. For example, any crime a foreigner committed inside of his concession against a Chinese person usually resulted in a "not guilty" verdict.

Foreigners were long intrigued by the mysteries of the East, and the Opium Wars blew the gates of China wide open, allowing them to enter freely. Internationals began pouring into Shanghai, and it was difficult for many businesses to imagine doing trade without this "Pearl of the Orient." Soon after its grand opening, Shanghai was considered the most lucrative of all Chinese cities, but

with great wealth came great competition.

By 1853, foreigners were building fortunes within the borders of their concessions, but at the same time the Chinese-controlled section of the city was under attack from the Small Swords Society, a group aligned with the Taiping Rebellion (1851-1864). Hong Xiuquan, founder of the Taiping (Heavenly Peace) movement, had started a Chinese Christian crusade after claiming to be the younger brother of Jesus Christ. Soon, the grassroots rebellion spread like wildfire throughout most of the eastern part of the country.

Things intensified when a handful of British and American troops went mercenary and joined the rebels, while the French supported the Qing government. Ultimately, however, all foreign governments agreed to back the Qing, and though the Small Swords rebels controlled the city for two years, the Qing government finally defeated them and restored order. Peace didn't last long, within a decade the official Taiping army was making invasion attempts on the city of Shanghai.

This time, foreign armies were actively involved in the defense of the city, using modern artillery and machine guns to inflict heavy damage on the fanatical Taiping troops. Over the course of almost two years, the rebels only captured Pudong, and in September 1862, the allied forces finally managed to drive them out of the city completely. In the end, the rebellion took nearly 30 million lives and is therefore considered the bloodiest in world history.

The next 50 years saw unprecedented growth, and by the 1920s Shanghai had swelled to become the fifth largest city on the planet. One of the world's true international cities, Shanghai at the time was home to people from all across the globe who came in search of a more exotic and better life. It was also a safe haven for thousands of refugees who streamed out of Russia during the 1917 revolution, and many Jews arrived as well fleeing persecution.

For many Chinese too, the city became a beacon of hope, a place where the streets were paved with proverbial gold. Legions swarmed in from all provinces, looking to shake off the dust of their mountain or farming towns and make something special out of themselves under the bright lights of the big city. More foreigners flocked in as well, and under a business friendly, internationally open Kuomintang (KMT) government, a golden age dawned in the burgeoning city.

Of course, in a place with so much money changing hands between so many people, it was only a matter of time before a criminal underworld emerged. Du Yuesheng, or Big-Eared Du – as he was known to foreigners – was the city's Godfather, running nearly every illegal activity under the sun (and with great success). While the Sicilian mobs of New York and Chicago controlled everything in their respective cities, the same scenario was unfolding in Shanghai with Chinese gangsters.

But Du's "Green Gang" wasn't the only underground movement that developed in Shanghai. In 1921, a young Mao Zedong met with a handful of other left-wing sympathizers for the founding and first meeting of the Chinese Communist Party (CCP).

Right from the start, there was trouble from the organized crime community, who were often paid by wealthy business owners to "take care of" troublesome communists. (Du ultimately backed the wrong pony by showing support for the Kuomintang instead of the Communists, who would eventually take power.) By the 1930s the KMT and the Communist Party were involved in a brutal power struggle defined by a gruesome civil war.

In 1932, however, a much larger threat arose as Japanese troops amassed in Shanghai and began attacking various targets around the Chinese sections of the city, all while leaving the concessions unscathed to avoid making new enemies. Despite the best efforts of the League of Nations, fighting raged across the city. Eventually Japan reluctantly signed a

ceasefire agreement, though it was barely acknowledged, and skirmishes continued for the next five years as Japan slowly gobbled up pieces of China.

By 1937, things reached a boiling point, and following another skirmish near Beijing at the Marco Polo Bridge, the Second Sino-Japanese War was in full swing. Despite their most courageous efforts, the out-gunned, out-trained and out-numbered Chinese could not handle the maniacal Japanese army. The only reason Chiang Kai-shek – the Kuomintang's leader at the time – held off on abandoning the city was because he realized that he could attract foreign attention to his cause if he defended Shanghai for as long as possible.

After suffering a few months of brutal war tactics by the Japanese, the Chinese army found themselves in full retreat and were forced to surrender their most industrious city to the Japanese. When Japan brought the US into the war with the bombing of Pearl Harbor in December 1941, they also took control of the international settlements in Shanghai, ending the era of Shanghai's cosmopolitan society. Japan would rule the city with an iron fist until the bombings of Hiroshima and Nagasaki finally bought an end to both the Second World War and the Second Sino-Japanese War.

Though Mao's Communists and Chiang Kai-shek's Nationalists had called a truce to form a united front against Japan, the Chinese Civil War erupted again between the two in 1945 after Japan's surrender. After years of horrific combat, the Communists finally came out on top, and Mao Zedong brought the country in a radical new direction with the announcement of the founding of the People's Republic of China on October 1, 1949.

Almost overnight, Shanghai entered a new phase in its history. Private enterprise was outlawed and deemed anti-revolutionary, and Shanghai fell to the bottom almost as quickly as it had risen to the top.

Mao's vision of a socialist utopia didn't quite take off as he had imagined. The country was slipping into the depths of poverty, and the economy sputtered along under collective farms and inefficient governmental reforms. This largely prompted Mao to implement the Cultural Revolution (1966-1976) to eliminate the culture of the past and pave the way for his vision of a bright and prosperous future.

In reality, the Cultural Revolution lead to even more turmoil and left its own horrible scars on Shanghai and the nation as thousands of executions were carried out against intellectuals and dissidents who opposed the Party. Those lucky enough to escape a death sentence were often exiled to tiny backwater towns in the middle of nowhere, where they were forced into grueling manual labor through the "Down to the Countryside" program (basically China's equivalent to the Gulag).

In a sense, the days of Mao were a sobering age for Shanghai. After the Chinese Revolution, the crazy party years of the 1920s were forgotten, and Shanghai simply became the workhorse for the nation, providing wealth to rest of the country through its incredibly high taxes. Industry, not business, became the new hallmark of Shanghai through government reforms.

But just as China was on the brink of economic, social and political collapse as the Cultural Revolution hit its deepest and darkest hours, US President Richard Nixon and Secretary of State Henry Kissinger made a landmark voyage to China to shake hands with Chairman Mao in 1972.

Nixon's trip planted the seeds of New China and Shanghai's phase of "opening up," but it was after the death of Mao in 1976, and the implementation of his successor's new economic policy of Reform and Openness, when things really began to blossom. China's new president, Deng Xiaoping, announced to a socialist China that "To get rich is glorious" and issued a new doctrine to transform the Chinese economy into a financial powerhouse ready to step foot on the global stage. These reforms of the early '80s were extremely successful, so the government allowed them to go into effect in Shanghai in 1991.

Since then, Shanghai has rebounded in a big way. The population has more than doubled and the expat community has risen exponentially. In 20 years, Pudong in particular had gone from being a muddy field on the east banks of the river to a glistening financial powerhouse that dazzles the world with one of the planet's most recognizable skylines. Business is rocketing and Shanghai has ideologically turned a complete 360 back to the heydays of the 1920s.

Today, Shanghai is back and better than ever. It's one of the planet's most exciting international metropolises, standing side by side with the likes of New York, Paris, London, Tokyo and Hong Kong.

Changing Shanghai

More than just Shanghai's skyline has changed over the last centuries. Here's a look at how the styles of China's most fashion-forward metropolis have evolved over the years.

	1920s	1960s	Today
Women's Dresses	Qipao	Green or blue unisex Mao suits	Jeans
Women's Hair	Curled hair with short bangs	Braids or bob/bowl cut	Anything goes
Getting Around Town	Rickshaw or on foot	Bus or old bike	Volkswagen Santana or electric scooter
Men's Hats	Fedora	Mao hat	Cheesy hip-hop ball cap
Popular Books	Dream of the Red Chamber	Mao's Little Red Book	50 Shades of Grey
Beloved Foreign Celebrity	Charlie Chaplin	Fidel Castro	Lebron James
Snack of Choice	Xiaolongbao	Xiaolongbao	Xiaolongbao

The world's most notable cities can all be identified by their globally recognized landmarks: New York has the Statue of Liberty, Paris has the Eiffel Tower, Rio de Janeiro has Christ the Redeemer. For Shanghai, a city that changes faster than the weather, the Bund and its unique view of Pudong's skyline is the most iconic sight in town.

Today, the Bund is a promenade that sees thousands of tourists each day, but in the past it was (mostly) the brick and mortar proof of the big business and unlimited financial potential that Shanghai represented.

Beginning with the Treaty of Nanking, which ended the First Opium War in 1842, Shanghai was open for business, and it didn't take foreign nations long to label it as the Pearl of the Orient. As a port town, it offered an entry point into the seemingly endless wealth of China, and because of this, the British, French and Americans all wholeheartedly began attempts to establish as much of a business base as possible in their respective "concessions."

While the French Concession also boasted a waterfront a little farther south, it was used primarily as a no-nonsense dock for loading and unloading ships. The north end, though, quickly became the highest profile neighborhood in the city, with banks, hotels, and newspapers setting up their headquarters just a stone's throw from the river's edge.

By 1901, the booming economy of Shanghai allowed for the first of the still-standing structures to be built. Within a few decades, the strip became an architect's dream, with stunning new buildings going up every year. As 1930 rolled around, the Bund was beginning to look pretty much as it does today, with all of its iconic art-deco behemoths standing watch over the harbor. Gone was the old muddy road; the streets were paved and double decker buses ferried passengers across the city. Of course, that's if you were looking west. If you turned towards the water, things were very different indeed.

It took about 50 years of random typhoon floods before the Bund's next big change. The local government finally decided to act and constructed a 10 meter-high levee to prevent any further damage to the "colonial relics" that were finally starting to get some appreciation.

The year 1986 saw the beginning of another phase, when Paulus Snoeren was hired to transform the Bund into an esplanade worthy of his native Holland. Since that time, it has been made a little bigger and better each year, with a major overhaul completed in 2010, just in time for the Shanghai World Expo.

Bund in 1945

Bund Today

Throughout most of the Bund's construction, Pudong slept just across the River. It wasn't until economic reforms went into place in the 1990s that construction on an unprecedented scale began. Two decades later, it is now home to over 30 skyscrapers representing the biggest names in banking and hospitality. It provides an incredible image of two distinct eras of international business, with the days of old on the west bank and the new on the east. An old saying goes that the Shanghainese would rather have a bed in Puxi than a home in Pudong" (宁要浦西一张床，不要浦东一幢房), but given how things have changed (as you can see from the before and after pictures below), which would you prefer?

Pudong in the early 1980s

Pudong today

But the Bund and Pudong aren't the only areas of Shanghai that have changed. People's Square, which today represents the cultural and geographic center of downtown Shanghai, was once the site of the city's prestigious racecourse. As far back as 150 years ago, thousands of people would gather here to watch the Grand Festivals of Shanghai, hoping to make their fortune through some good luck with the ponies. While the track is long gone, you can still see its oval shape looping around People's Park and People's Square.

The central street that separates Shanghai into east and west has also seen its share of changes over the years. Originally known as Boulevard de Montigny, it became Tibet

Road before the city government officially Sinicized it as Xizang Lu a few years ago. The street has always been busy, especially near its intersection at "Bubbling Well Road," which eventually became Nanjing West Road.

Park Hotel & surrounding area on Bubbling Well Road (1945)

Park Hotel & surrounding area on Nanjing West Road (2010)

But while the names of these streets might have changed over the years, their position of importance in the city has not. This is the same for "Avenue Joffre," which was home to some of the city's first portrait studios, cinemas and department stores. Today you can still pose for a sitting (in period clothes from any era in Shanghai's history), go to a movie, or shop 'til you drop on the modern Avenue Joffre, now called Huaihai Road.

Avenue Joffre in 1945

Modern Huaihai Road

Jing'an Temple in 1900

Jing'an Temple today

Changes of a more extreme nature have taken place farther west at Jing'an Temple. Though the temple dates back to the year 247 CE, it was moved to its current site in 1216 during the Song Dynasty. Throughout the years it has been upgraded and renovated several times, with the biggest changes happening in 1880. Sadly, in 1972 the temple suffered a huge fire, but it has been faithfully rebuilt in its original image. Back then, there wasn't much around the temple but a few dusty roads and the "Bubbling Well" that gave the street its name. Flash forward to today and the temple still stands in all its gold-plated glory, but now it is surrounded by high-end shopping centers and deluxe hotels. Though it sits atop one of the city's biggest transportation hubs, inside the temple things are pretty much the same as they were in 1880 (except that the monks might be wearing Nikes under their robes).

This is Shanghai!

Politics

Though Shanghai's current mayor, Yang Xiong (杨 雄), holds an extremely prominent position, he is outranked in power by the local Communist Party Chief (officially known as the "Communist Party of China Shanghai Municipal Committee Secretary"), Han Zheng (韩 正). Han's role is the envy of many politicians, as Shanghai is often viewed as a stop-off on the way to the most powerful circle in the nation, the Politburo Standing Committee. In fact, since 1989, when Jiang Zemin became National Party Chief, all but one of Shanghai's Chiefs have made it to this elite level. Zhu Rongji became Premier, Wu Bangguo was named Chairman of the National People's Congress, Huang Ju became Vice Premier, Yu Zhengsheng is Chairman of the National Committee of the Chinese People's Political Consultative Conference... all the way up to Xi Jinping, the current General Secretary of the Party (aka the President of China – the highest ranking official in the entire country). The only one in the last 25 years who didn't make the cut was Chen Liangyu, who was fired in 2006 amidst a storm of corruption accusations (of which he was eventually convicted).

Officials connected to Shanghai are known as the Shanghai Clique, a powerful faction within the national government that often competes against the rival Youth League faction over personnel appointments and policy decisions. Xi Jinping, successor to Hu Jintao as General Secretary and President, was considered a compromise between these two powerful groups, as he had supporters in both camps.

Religion

Thanks to its long history of being a city open to different nations and cultures, Shanghai has a very broad acceptance of different religious viewpoints. The evidence for this can be seen from the religious buildings and institutions around the city.

Taoism, one of China's classic, homegrown philosophies, is represented by several temples, including the City God Temple near Yu Garden, as well a temple dedicated to the Three Kingdoms general Guan Yu. The Wenmiao, meanwhile, is a temple dedicated to Confucius.

Buddhism has also been highly visible in Shanghai since ancient times. Longhua Temple, the largest temple in Shanghai, and Jing'an Temple, were first founded during the Three Kingdoms period (220-280 CE), and the Jade Buddha Temple is another popular site of devotion for Shanghai's Buddhists and tourists alike. Along with the ancient sites, dozens of modern temples have been built throughout the city.

Islam first came into Shanghai more than 700 years ago via Muslim merchants traversing the Silk Road, and a mosque was built in 1295 in the Songjiang District. By 1843, a college was also set up (the Shanghai Muslim Association) in the Xiaotaoyuan Mosque.

Among Western faiths, Shanghai has the highest percentage of Catholics in Mainland China. St Ignatius Cathedral in Xujiahui is one of the largest places of worship, while Sheshan Basilica is the only active pilgrimage site in China. Christianity in Shanghai also includes Eastern Orthodox minorities and, since 1996, registered Christian Protestant churches.

Judaism is the only other officially permitted religion in China, and it has a strong history in Shanghai. During World War II, the city was one of the world's few safe havens for Jews fleeing Hitler's genocide, and they created a strong community near the Ohel Moshe Synagogue until Japan's alliance with Nazi Germany forced them out. The area is still intact and makes for an interesting landmark of Shanghai and world religion.

However, China's tradition of being a land of various religious beliefs has had little effect on the local Han population. Religion and other so-called "superstitions" were nearly all eradicated during Mao's Cultural Revolution, resulting in a massive number of Chinese atheists today. While religion is making a resurgence – as it is throughout most of the former communist world – it's growing at only a snail's pace.

Education

Shanghai is home to some of the highest-ranked universities in China, and in recent years, they have been attracting more and more foreign exchange students who are looking for a side of adventure with their education. In fact, some have been known to register for the student visa just so they can have residence in the country.

The biggest school by far is Fudan University, founded in 1905 and located at the far north end of the city. In fact, most of the "big" schools in Shanghai: East China Normal University, Tongji University, Shanghai University and Shanghai International Studies University (SISU), are located far from downtown. If you are planning a semester abroad and want to stay in the heart of the action, then your best bet is at Jiaotong University, the only major school with a downtown campus (just north of Xujiahui).

Population

According to statistics from 2010, the city's population broke 23 million that year. This doesn't include tourists, who number approximately half a million people at any given time (almost a quarter of tourists to China spend time in Shanghai).

It also doesn't include the huge population of migrant workers – people who live and work in Shanghai but are still legally registered as living in their home provinces. In fact, more than a third of the city's residents (some 9

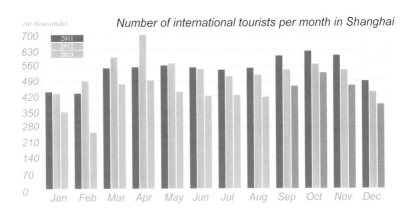

(in thousands) **Number of international tourists per month in Shanghai**

2011 · 2012 · 2013

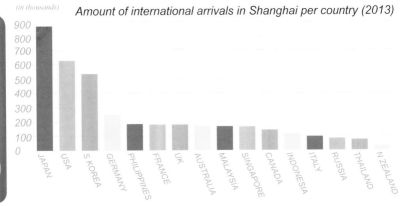

(in thousands) **Amount of international arrivals in Shanghai per country (2013)**

JAPAN · USA · S KOREA · GERMANY · PHILIPPINES · FRANCE · UK · AUSTRALIA · MALAYSIA · SINGAPORE · CANADA · INDONESIA · ITALY · RUSSIA · THAILAND · N ZEALAND

million people) are registered as "long term migrants," meaning they have come for work, but are settled in with no plans on returning to their home provinces anytime soon.

A great number of foreigners (aka expatriates, or expats) also come here for work as China's booming economy has created a demand for Western connections. Though many of the younger expats make a living by teaching English, a large number are hired as foreign experts and work as consultants in import/ export, architecture, tourism and hospitality, and manufacturing.

So where are the expats coming from? Well, Japan leads the way with the highest number of registered foreigners, followed by the USA, South Korea and Germany. There were about 160,000 registered expats living in Shanghai in 2010, but that number doesn't include all the people who arrive as tourists and quietly work under the table. In all, it's estimated that there are more than 200,000 foreigners residing both legally and illegally in Shanghai.

What's more, a large number of the official residents are from Japan, Korea and Singapore (not even counting Taiwanese, who are estimated around 700,000), making them, as we would say in the West, "non-visible minorities" (at least for untrained foreign eyes). This still leaves about 100,000 "visible" foreigners in Shanghai, a good sized city worth of expats. Most of them can be found in Jing'an and Xuhui Districts, and the farther you get from the city center, the fewer you will see.

If you happen to be one of these visible minorities, even though you only make up 0.5% of the population, it doesn't mean you'll be gawked at as you walk down the street or ride the subway. (Although it doesn't mean you won't be either.) Shanghainese are far more accustomed to foreign faces than rural Chinese, and more foreigners have been coming here for much longer than the rest of the country, meaning you will be greeted with far fewer dumbstruck looks than you would in the countryside.

The vast majority of people live downtown (although there are plenty of expat villages: high level compounds in Gubei or Pudong where white collar executives and their families are housed in luxurious surroundings far from the din of the city). Still, the central core has an approximate density of 16,828 people per square kilometer. That's far higher than Tokyo, London or Paris, and yet the city functions peacefully with everybody going about their day at their own pace.

Safety

In regards to crime, Shanghai is extremely safe. This is not to say that life is danger-free though, since crossing a street of chaotic traffic can be deadly, and nearly every day there are new reports of food contamination. But compared to most of China's cities and towns, large or small, violent crime is basically nonexistent here.

Guns are unheard of and highly illegal, and streets full of people mean there are eye witnesses everywhere. Besides this natural crime deterrent, the city is also wired with cameras, but even in the places where there are none, it seems that every citizen between six and 96 has an (possibly fake) iPhone complete with a video recorder.

That being said, keep your wits about you. Make sure your backpacks and purses are zipped up tight, and hold them in front when you're in a crowded place. Watch your pockets while you're compressed into the subway with 10,000 people. And, though this might sound obvious, don't drink so much that you fall down the stairs, crash your bike, or tumble into the gutter. Shanghai is a party city in many aspects, and we all know accidents happen when people are intoxicated, so be sure to pace yourself and always ask the question, "Do I really need another shot right now?"

Another way tourists lose their hard earned cash is through the Tea Scam. Every year, untold numbers of happy-go-lucky foreigners fall for this unfortunate trick, and are often too embarrassed to report it to the police. The scam basically consists of a small group of young Chinese who will approach you on a busy street like Nanjing East Road, or at a crowded market, and strike up a conversation. They say that they are going to drink some tea at a little place not far away, and that they'd like you to come with them. Often (but not always) the group is made up of pretty girls targeting young males, who are more than happy to take part in this cultural event with a troupe of good-looking ladies.

After drinking tea for some time and maybe having a few snacks like watermelon or peanuts, the Chinese gracefully slip out to the bathroom and disappear forever, leaving the gullible foreigner holding an extremely inflated bill, usually into the thousands of RMB. The red-faced expat usually pays the bill and walks out, wondering the whole time what happened. See more scams on page 294.

Shanghai Layout

The Shanghai Municipality has an area of 6,340 sq km (2,450 sq mi) and has 17 county-level divisions (16 districts and the county of Chongming in the north). The Huangpu River slices right through the center of town, separating the financial center of Pudong (east of the river), and Puxi and the Bund (west of the river).

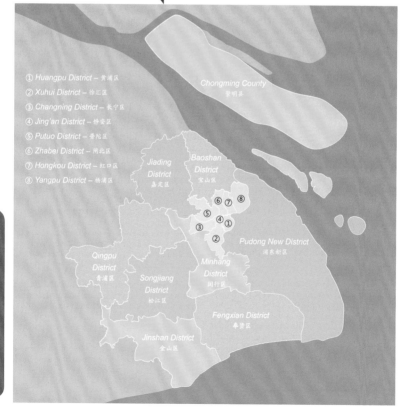

① Huangpu District – 黄浦区
② Xuhui District – 徐汇区
③ Changning District – 长宁区
④ Jing'an District – 静安区
⑤ Putuo District – 普陀区
⑥ Zhabei District – 闸北区
⑦ Hongkou District – 虹口区
⑧ Yangpu District – 杨浦区

Chongming County
崇明县

Jiading District
嘉定区

Baoshan District
宝山区

Pudong New District
浦东新区

Qingpu District
青浦区

Songjiang District
松江区

Minhang District
闵行区

Fengxian District
奉贤区

Jinshan District
金山区

Shanghai is an incredibly easy city to find your way around. Though there are a few twists and turns, the city is primarily built on a simple east-west, north-south grid, and all streets are clearly marked. Every corner will have signs telling you the street name in English and Chinese, along with a helpful reminder of which direction is east, west, north and south. There are even handy numbers on the signs, showing you the range of addresses you can expect to find on that block. You can find enormous blue billboards hanging over busy roads that tell you the next two major streets ahead, as well as the major streets running parallel to the left and right of you.

Taking the subway is just as simple. Though visitors from smaller cities might feel overwhelmed at the thought of 13 metro lines, a quick look at the map will show you that it is all neatly laid out with plenty of interchanges. Once you're in the system, signage is large and clear with English street names right beside the Chinese characters. Exits are clearly numbered and marked too, so it is very easy to meet your friends at a particular exit.

Taxis are of course the easiest (and perhaps most expensive) way to get around town, but sometimes the communication difficulties with taxi drivers can make you wonder. For the record, almost none of the taxi drivers speak any English. Some may be able to muster a poorly pronounced, "thank you" or "OK," but that is the limit for about 99% of the drivers you'll meet. They also cannot read pinyin, so if you have the address written in English, they will not be able to read it. In addition, they are not connected with a constantly squawking radio to dispatch, so they won't be able to ask someone at the office for help translating either. And despite the fact that they all carry cell phones, they never want to call for assistance.

Taxi drivers might seem a little grumpy sometimes, but go easy on them. It's a difficult job and they work hard for 12 hours a day, six or seven a week. Without them the city would come to a standstill, especially after midnight. Though there are a few unscrupulous ones out there (avoid any particularly beaten up or unmarked cabs, especially older vehicles), most will give you a fair ride that will cost less than taking the bus back home, and there's no need to tip. Be sure to ask for a receipt (fāpiào; 发票) as it will come in handy if you end up forgetting your phone or keys in the back of that taxi.

If you want the more scenic way to enjoy the city, you might want to purchase a cheap

Here are a few tips to help you avoid miscommunication:

1. Always carry your Panda Guides book with you and show them the Chinese spellings of addresses.
2. Get the business card of your hotel or hostel, or use your Panda Guides Emergency Card (pg 43), to make it easier to get back home at the end of the night. If you're staying at a friend's, get the business card from a nearby restaurant or business instead.
3. Find the Chinese address info of where you want to go and snap a picture of it on your smart-phone. Show that to the driver.
4. Use the Guanxi telephone service. Simply text the venue name to Guanxi (1066 9588 2929) and when they send you the address, reply "C" to receive it in Chinese. Show it to your driver and you'll be on your way.

bicycle. Shanghai is flat and there are wide bicycle lanes on most streets. True, these are sometimes ignored, and some corners might seem like well-oiled chaos, but there is strength in numbers, so just follow the lead of any of the millions of local cyclists and you should be fine. Keep in mind that there are some major streets that are off limits to bicycles. Most people skirt this law by riding on the sidewalk if they need to, but occasionally a strict traffic monitor might take exception to that.

For more information concerning transportation in and around Shanghai, flip to page 44 for the low down.

Believe it or not, big Shanghai is a great walking city, and you can see a lot of the neighborhoods by taking a stroll. Though you could probably make a good circumference of the city by walking around it for one solid day, you're probably better off actually enjoying the walk by tackling different districts each day. There are 17 in all, but many of them could easily be left off your map. After all, you want to go to where the action is. Here are the best and busiest areas:

Huangpu District (黄浦区) This is the center of it all. Huangpu District covers much of

Puxi (literally meaning "west of the Huangpu River"), from People's Square to the Bund and down south to Old Town – with Yu Garden and the antique streets. It is here that you'll find landmarks like the Nanjing East Road Pedestrian Street (Shanghai's "Times Square"), the Shanghai Art Museum, the MOCA, People's Park and the Shanghai Grand Theater. Huaihai Road cuts through, offering another selection of malls and dining establishments. It is a broad area that covers much of what used to be known as the French Concession (a term that has fallen out of favor with local officials) as well as the broad industrial streets and the waterfront.

Restaurants and bars here include Barbarossa (pg 207), Windows Scoreboard and Garage (pg 200), Xintiandi (pg 84), Lucky Zen (pg 189), and Sinan Mansions (pg 199).

The Bund (Wàitān; 外滩) While technically part of the Huangpu District, the Bund neighborhood has a vibe and attitude of its own, as some of Shanghai's oldest landmarks and newest establishments stand here side by side. A relatively small length of riverfront property, the Bund had a major overhaul in 2010, revitalizing its promenade. It is on the checklist for every tourist in Shanghai – Chinese or foreign – so don't be surprised to see it swarming with families, couples and tour groups shopping for souvenirs and posing for that perfect picture. It is in fact an extremely picturesque spot, offering a front-row view of the Pudong skyline with its multitude of towers on one side, and the old strip of foreign banks and custom houses on the other. Evening is definitely the time to come, when Pudong lights up in sparkles and flashes, while Puxi retains a classic floodlight focused on its art deco architecture.

Restaurants and bars here include Bar Rouge (pg 212), Captain's Bar (pg 203), Mr & Mrs Bund (pg 194).

Jing'an District (静安区) One of the most popular expat neighborhoods in Shanghai, Jing'an is a small district that stretches north from the Yan'an Road overhead expressway to Suzhou Creek. Aside from the flash of Nanjing West Road, Jing'an is home to quieter, narrower streets and a ton of Western owned establishments. It's easy to find your way around, with Jing'an Temple (and its subway station) being on the southern edge of the district.

Restaurants and bars in here include Wuding Rd bar street (pg 199), Bali Laguna (pg 190), Windows Too (pg 201).

Xuhui District (徐汇区) Though centered around Xujiahui (it's the Xu family that gives the entire district its name), Xuhui is probably the most sprawling neighborhood in downtown Shanghai, covering a huge area of the city's coolest spots. Just about every worthwhile location that is south of Yan'an Road and west of People's Square falls into Xuhui District. It also accounts for a fair amount of the former French Concession, so expect to find lots of winding leafy streets and walled compounds, including some foreign consulates. It's home to several parks, including the Yan'an Road Park complex and Xujiahui Park.

Restaurants and bars here include Yongfu Rd bar street (pg 199), Yongkang Rd bar street (pg 199), Zapatas (pg 214), 1001 Nights (pg 190), Geisha (pg 211).

Changning District (长宁区) Things start to cool down a bit just west of Jing'an Temple, but there are still plenty of interesting things to be discovered out in Changning. Based around Zhongshan Park (one of the few parks without a "keep off the grass" policy), there are several streets of shopping and culture to be found here.

Restaurants and bars here include C's (pg 203), Kaiba (pg 202), Yuyintang (pg 214).

Pudong (浦东) Pudong (literally meaning "east of the Huangpu River") is sort of the final frontier for many foreigners and locals alike (even Puxi taxi drivers are often clueless about the streets of Pudong). Though the water is traversed by no less than five subway lines, and it only adds another five or ten minutes to your taxi ride to take a tunnel or bridge over, it is psychologically much farther.

Pudong, or "Pu Jersey" as it is affectionately known, is seen as two things primarily: First, it is the financial district of town, the Wall Street of Shanghai. This small area around Lujiazui accounts for a huge percentage of Shanghai's most recognizable landmarks and a high concentration of some of the world's tallest buildings. Second, it is viewed as a bedroom community for many high level executives. They might commute to Puxi for work, but they return home to their garden villas here at the end of the day. Living even farther out towards the airport is the community of people who have been displaced by Shanghai's constant growth. When a housing district is bulldozed in favor of a shopping mall or a new highway, the residents are relocated to a prime piece of greenery in Pudong (much to their delight, if you believe the city's promotional videos).

Restaurants and bars here include Morton's (pg 194), Big E (pg 215).

Crazy Shanghai

As you make your way through Shanghai, there are things you'll see that are a common part of the city's local and national heritage.

Shikumen: Bejing has hutongs, but in Shanghai the traditional housing is the shíkùmén, a narrow winding lane between a cluster of two to four-story multifamily dwellings. In the old days "dwelling" simply meant "bedroom." Outside in the common courtyard was where you did your cooking, eating and relaxing. It's also where you'd find the communal "restroom" (squatter toilet) and bath.

At one point, 80% of the city's residents lived in shikumen housing, but that number has shrunken drastically as the city has opened up to industry and infrastructure, causing residents to be relocated to tower complexes across the city. While some claim it is a loss of the city's true culture, many people prefer having their own showers and toilets.

Shikumen are still found all around the city however, in various states that range from crumbling and fallen to chic and refurbished, and even the wrecking ball can't silence the influence and appeal of the shikumen. Xintiandi and Tianzifang (pg 84) is a prime example of the spirit of the structure, albeit constructed with new materials and with an entirely new sense of space.

High-rise apartment complexes: This is the new dwelling arrangement in Shanghai, and it makes sense. It would be hard to find room for all 23 million (plus) of the city's residents if it weren't for the highly efficient high-rise compounds across the city. Your typical address in Shanghai will include your street address, your building number and then your apartment number. The complex can range from three towers in a tightly clustered triangle to upwards of 30 buildings of various heights and ages spread out around an entire city block. These mega-compounds might have a population greater than your home town, as each building could be home to 1,000 residents. Many of the complexes will contain a small park with a few benches as well as a small grocery store or other businesses to make your life easier and your Sunday hangover a little less intensive.

Bright lights and surprising darkness:

Scrolling through photos of Shanghai, you are sure to see plenty of shots of Pudong at night, lit up like the 4th of July (or like Spring Festival, as the case here would be), or Nanjing East Road with its billion watts of old school neons mixing with modern LEDs. But it doesn't stop there, all across the city you will come to corners that have more lights blinking and flashing than the Vegas Strip, perhaps advertising nothing more than a questionable KTV or seafood restaurant.

But by 22:30… "click-click," the city goes dark – very dark. Street light coverage that would be cause for worry in most neighborhoods back home is normal here, as the city enters power saving mode. The people don't let the darkness stop them from having a good time, though, and you can find crowds watching a late night poker game on the corner or ballroom dancing in the parks. It's almost as if Bruce Springsteen was singing about them…

Matchmaking: "So, are you seeing anybody?" If you dread hearing these words from your parents, consider yourself lucky. Every Sunday in People's Park, meddling parents converge to form the Marriage Market. On a string of pennants reminiscent of a used car lot, they'll clothespin Xeroxed profiles of their son or daughter in hopes of finding them a significant other. Most profiles will include the person's name, age, height, occupation and hobbies. Men's profiles will often include their salary and women's will have their weight.

Before you judge these old folks too harshly, keep in mind that they are really acting in self-preservation. China's One Child Policy means the parents don't have a lot of options for financial support as they reach old age. If their child is married and has a child, there is a second generation of support for them. Nobody seems to realize that the spouse will also have parents that need looking after as well.

So, take a stroll through the park on a Sunday to experience this cultural phenomenon. Better yet, if you're in the mood for love yourself, then print out your own profile and bring it along to clip up. Be sure to make lots of copies to give to interested parents and potential in-laws.

The doting boyfriend: Shanghai men have it tough, especially since there's a lot more men in this city than women. Even worse, they suffer a negative reputation across China for being weak, spineless and girly. Shanghainese women, on the other hand, have a reputation of being spoiled and demanding. Of course, these are major generalizations, but still, you are bound to see an endless supply of young men carrying their girlfriends' purses down the street while she window shops empty handed. These same men will make the grand gestures of going down on a bent knee to tie her shoelace, and often submit to dressing as a cutesy couple, complete with matching T-shirts or beachwear. As thanks for all this romance, you can often see them being berated on the corner, screamed at on the bus, and slapped on the subway. Ah, young love.

Exercise: The young generation, as its diet changes to Western fast food and ice cream, is getting chubbier, but the adult population in China, for the most part, is very fit. (This is amazing when you consider the health risks involved in eating local food and breathing local air.)

Part of the reason for this spry population is that they stay active and move. In addition to the line dancing that goes on in many courtyards and parks after sunset, all across the city you can find miniature outdoor gyms that have pulleys to move your arms, cross-country ski-style swings, spinning wheels to build up your *qi*, etc. Although none of these machines offer any type of resistance, they keep people moving, which many doctors say is half the battle.

Even outside of these mini-gyms you can see people practicing traditional forms of exercise, including walking backwards and clapping… sometimes at the same time. To really get an idea of the fitness regimen of Shanghai society, though, your best bet is to head to any one of the large city parks at sunrise. There, you'll see hundreds of people practicing kung fu (some with swords) and tai chi, stretching, and even tree slapping, which is often followed up with tree hugging (no joke).

Technology: Take a ride on the subway and you'll quickly see that nobody talks. Those that do are probably talking – often yelling – into a cell phone. The vast majority of riders will be sitting and staring intently at their phones or tablets as they play video poker, Angry Birds, or watch the latest Chinese TV drama. Shanghai is an incredibly wired city, but this shouldn't be a surprise as it has always been on the cutting edge of technology. For example, the first motor car in China was driven in Shanghai and the city has always been at the forefront of cinema, animation and general scientific development.

While many people have internet access in their homes, cyber cafes are still a popular choice for young people, who use them to chat and play games with new friends from around the world. You can usually spot these establishments by the huge murals and billboards out front featuring muscular warriors holding swords bigger than their bodies. If you happen to see one, stop in for a look (you'll need your passport if you actually want to use the internet, though.) Inside, you'll see a huge room densely packed with people hovered over screens that are barking out sound effects of gunfire, explosions, cheap MIDI music and emoticon chimes. Meanwhile, stewardesses roam the aisle with carts hawking Chinese snacks and drinks. The beverage of choice? Red Bull. How else could you level up to Grand Master Wizard at 4:00 in the morning?

Bicycle parking: It might seem like a pretty obvious stereotype that people in China ride bikes, but you can get a better idea of it around the busy corners where people lock up their bikes to jump on the metro or do their shopping. There will be literally hundreds of bicycles in all possible forms of decomposition, from gleaming fresh-from-the-factory ones still with little rubber hairs on the tires, to chunks of ancient machinery that are more rust than steel.

Nowadays, more people are upgrading from the standard cruiser bike. You'll see people with tiny fold-up bicycles (great for taking on the metro or into your office) and electric bikes. These so called e-bikes, along with electric scooters (that look more like small motorcycles or Vespas) are a silent danger, as they can zip up behind you when you step into the crosswalk. There is a benefit to that danger, though, as noise pollution and air pollution dropped significantly when the city banned 2-stroke gas scooters several years ago.

With the extreme popularity of bikes and scooters, you might think that the theft rate of bicycles is high – and you'd be right. Many people double or triple lock their bikes, but there is also an interesting service here of guarded bicycle parking. For a small fee, you can wheel your bike into whichever space it can fit into, and a parking attendant will run a 20-meter communal bike cable through your and everyone else's bike frame. He'll give you a ticket, which you should keep to redeem your bike at the end of the day.

Anarchical traffic: The first thing you'll learn as you make your way through Shanghai is that traffic lights, signs and road markings are an abstract concept. They exists mostly to determine what percentage each party is at fault (Chinese courts routinely put a number on how much each person is to blame in the event of an accident). In spite of this, accidents are surprisingly rare.

True, traffic is far worse in cities like Bangkok or Mumbai, but roads are still packed here, as more than 3.5 million (about 3 million local cars plus 0.5 million outside cars) try to share the roadways. There are now so many licensed vehicles in Shanghai that the city officials often put a daily quota on the streets.

At intersections and even down straight-aways, traffic simply weaves. People just go where they want, when they want (slowly), and everyone just seems to accept this and work around the problem. Driving moves that would give Mother Teresa road rage are all taken in stride every single moment of the day, so try not to get bent out of shape if somebody blocks your taxi or cuts you off in a crosswalk; it's going to happen to you at some point during your visit.

From 7:00 – 19:00 there are cross guards on most corners (who will blow their whistle frantically at you if you jaywalk), but do not rely on them to protect your safety while crossing the street. Constantly look both ways (even if it's your right of way), and never ever expect a bus to stop.

Holidays & Festivals

Public Holidays in the PRC				
Festival	Date	Legal Holidays	2014	2015
New Year's Day	Jan 1	1	Jan 1 – 3	Jan 1 – 3
Spring Festival	Follows the lunar calendar	3	Jan 30 – Feb 5	Feb 18 – Feb 24
Tomb Sweeping Festival (Qingming)	Apr 4 or 5	1	Apr 4 – 6	Apr 4 – 6
May Day	May 1	1	May 1 – 3	May 1 – 3
Dragon Boat Festival	Follows the lunar calendar	1	May 31 – Jun 2	Jun 20 – 22
Mid Autumn Festival	Follows the lunar calendar	1	Sep 6 – 8	Sep 26 – 28
National Day	Oct 1	3	Oct 1 – 7	Oct 1 – 7

Shanghai is a great place to visit year-round, but there are more and more stand-out events that take place each year in addition to the traditional Chinese holidays and festivals.

Spring Festival, or Chinese New Year, is by far the biggest yearly celebration in China. At some point between January and February, the city is festooned in red and covered in cartoon versions of the New Year's zodiac creature.

Since most Chinese people don't get very many holidays each year, the state holidays like Spring Festival, Mid Autumn Festival, and Dragon Boat Festival become huge travel times. People go home to visit their families, and nowadays many people use the time to go on vacation. If you're planning on traveling in China around Spring Festival, you'd better book your tickets long in advance and be prepared for extremely congested airports and train stations. Better yet, avoid coming during Spring Festival altogether.

Otherwise, settle in and enjoy Shanghai's holiday feeling as the streets are packed with celebrating families and local tourists. Join in the fun with feasting and partying and setting off lots of fireworks. You'll see Roman Candles, and hear firecrackers and sonic booms from sunset until the wee hours of the morning, and the next day you'll find the street buried in red papery ashes.

Unique Shanghai Festivals

Lantern Festival: On the 15th day after Chinese New Year, head to Yu Garden to eat glutinous rice dishes and send flaming lanterns into the heavens to make a healthy wish for the new year.

Shanghai International Literary Festival: Occurring in either March or April, hop on over to Glamour Bar to watch speeches by world renowned authors and get your paperbacks autographed.

Longhua Temple Fair: Taking place in late March or in April or May, this temple fair hosts China's largest and most ancient folk gathering with snacks, drinks, music and street entertainment.

Formula 1: The Shanghai International Circuit comes to town in April.

Dragon Boat Festival: Though not a unique Shanghai festival, the Dragon Boat Festival races at Suzhou Creek are phenomenal and some of the best in the country. See the table on the preceeding page for dates.

Shanghai International Film Festival: This international A-category film festival is one of the biggest in all of East Asia. Go to **www. siff.com** for dates and listings.

China Shanghai International Arts Festival: This event takes place in October and November, and even has music, dance, opera, gymnastics and acrobatics.

Music festivals: More and more music festivals are popping up in Shanghai each year. Check out the JZ International Jazz Festival, the Strawberry Fields Festival, the MIDI Festival and the new Sonic Festival (based on the Japanese music festival of the same name).

Kunshan Beer Festival: This festival is not as big, or as well known, as the Qingdao Beer Festival, but it's right in Shanghai's back yard and usually takes place in August.

Shanghai Beer Festival: The chugging usually happens in May, but dates are subject to change, so check **www.shanghaibeerweek. com** for dates and locations.

Dragon Boat Festival

Weather

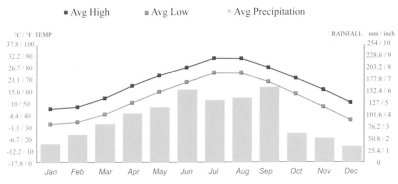

Legend: ■ Avg High   ■ Avg Low   ■ Avg Precipitation

Shanghai Average Temperature & Precipitation

Travelers are often surprised by Shanghai's winters. After all, the city is on the same latitude as Cairo, Egypt and San Diego, California. Sounds like it should be a nice January, right? Wrong. Shanghai is cold (temperatures hover around freezing) and damp all winter. To compound this problem, buildings are poorly insulated and heat is provided by a wall unit that doubles as your air conditioner in the summer. If you're coming in the winter, you'll need a decent jacket – preferably waterproof – as it is often misting or raining very lightly. A scarf and gloves won't hurt, either.

Sometime around November all the women in Shanghai, both local and foreign, seem to simultaneously switch their footwear from heels to boots. Take a page out of their book if you are packing for the trip.

If you'll be here for a while, you might want to adopt the unofficial Shanghai winter uniform: a snazzy set of fleece pajamas and a thick pair of slippers. You'll even see people wearing this attire outside of their home on the streets, and you can buy them almost anywhere during the colder months.

Around April or May the weather starts to warm up a bit, but it can still be uncomfortable as buildings will turn off the

heat in March. Shanghai springs are usually beautiful (if a bit rainy) but notoriously short. Before you know it, summer comes smashing you in the face with maximum heat and humidity.

If you're going to visit between the first of June and the end of September, bring your lightest clothes. Cotton is great, but you will sweat through anything in the time it takes you to dash from your air conditioned cab to the air conditioned shopping center. Shanghai is a very sunny place in the summer, so you might want to bring your own sunscreen as well. If you use the local stuff, you might actually end up a couple of shades lighter as most creams, lotions and sun blocks here contain bleaching agents to cater to an outdated notion of beauty. The Chinese believe white skin is beautiful, and therefore many try to avoid the sun and even use artificial enhancers to keep it white as rice.

Fall is undoubtedly the nicest time of the year; temperatures cool off but rains do not leave the city perpetually soggy. It's also a great time of the year for foodies, as you can experience the highs of the Hairy Crab Festival and the lows of the Moon Cake Festival.

The Arts

Shanghai, unlike old Peking (Beijing) and Canton (Guangzhou), is a relative newcomer to China's grand stage. Therefore, many of China's ancient arts like Peking Opera and Shaolin Kung Fu that can be traced back more than a thousand years are not found here. Nonetheless, this bustling metropolis has always looked more towards the future than the past, so you'll be able to satisfy your artsy side in alternative ways. For the abstract artist, electronic music aficionado and contemporary foreign film buff, Shanghai is your kind of town, and is one of the best places to experience China's budding art scene. But for those who still yearn for the past, don't worry, if you dig deep enough you'll strike gold; there is no shortage of material from Shanghai's golden years of the 1920s.

Art

Shanghai's newly found art scene is growing cautiously under the government censored lights, and it, along with Beijing's radical avant-garde style, is paving the way for the future of Chinese art. There are plenty of galleries across the city (with the most hip being centered around M50, the more traditional found around People's Square, and the most elegant at Three on the Bund), and you can find everything here from Chinese classics to communist propaganda and modern art. Some of the best Shanghai painters today include Huang Yuangqing (abstract), Yang Jianping (sculpture), Yang Fudong (contemporary/realism), Ding Yi (one of the few artists to be born in the '60s who didn't flee), and the wild and at times embarrassing Xu Zhen (do your own personal research on this guy).

Music

There's no grassroots musical movement that rings Shanghai's bells, but the diversity and internationalism of the city more than compensate. About the closest thing Shanghai has to traditional opera is Yueju, which originated from neighboring Zhejiang Province and is extremely popular in eastern China. Western-style symphonies can be heard at the He Luting Concert Hall, while Wanping Theater showcases other traditional Chinese musical art shows, and the Shanghai Oriental Art Center hosts ballet and opera performances. Furthermore, at any given time, big name artists are in town for extravagant concerts.

Though Beijing is often considered China's alternative grunge music capital (with a thriving punk, metal and indie scene), Shanghai isn't too far behind. Live music venues are sprouting up all over the city and becoming more popular among expats and locals. However, given the city's modern futuristic vibe, electro beats seem to dominate the airwaves. Big-name DJs can be found in the city on every weekend, while bars, lounges and clubs blast the latest tunes that you'd hear on a typical night out in London. You're bound to hear American hip-hop, Euro dance mixes, Chinese pop and much more – the big SH has got it all!

Literature

Currently, Shanghai native Han Han—the most popular blogger in China and a best-selling author – is considered one of the country's most esteemed literary artists, and in 2010 he was named by *Time* as one of the top 50 most influential people in the world. Han Han made his fame through critiques and controversies of contemporary life, art and pop culture in China. For an interesting yet critical review on contemporary China, read Han's most famous work *This Generation: Dispatches from China's Most Popular Literary Star (and Race Car Driver)* (2012). This compilation of blog posts and essays from Han during 2007-2012 covers a diverse array of topics: corruption, censorship, youth culture, the government and much more – perfect for anyone trying to get the big picture of New China.

Eileen Chang (1920-1995) is also a Shanghai native who became known as one of the most influential modern Chinese writers. Chang focused on gender roles and love and romance, and she also shed light on the Japanese occupation of China during the 1940s. Some of Chang's most famous works include *Lust, Caution* (1979), which tells the tale of how the Japanese occupied Shanghai in the 1940s, and *Love in a Fallen City* (translated to English in 2006), which describes China's struggle with classical culture and modernism.

For other great reads concerning Shanghai, check out our top editor picks:

Years of Red Dust (2010), Qiu Xiaolong

This fascinating collection of 23 short easy-to-read stories covers all the most important events of Shanghai's captivating past.

The Blue Lotus (1934), Hergé

Hergé researched the politics and society of China thoroughly to create this Tintin adventure (this is the fifth volume of the *Adventures of Tintin*). It's centered on Shanghai at the beginning of Japan's aggressive push for colonization and it is without a doubt one of the most entertaining ways to experience this gruesome time in history. Many scholars widely regard this as Hergé's first masterpiece.

Old Shanghai: Gangsters in Paradise (2011), Lynn Pan

A must for anyone interested in Shanghai's dark past and enthralling underworld.

Shanghai Girls (2009), Lisa See

This is a very popular novel about the relationship between two sisters during the '40s and '50s, following the duo from the the battles of World War II in Shanghai to the Chinatowns of California. See, like Eileen Chang before her, is especially concerned with the social complexities facing women at the time.

Empire of the Sun (1984), JG Ballard

The autobiographical tale of young Ballard speaks about growing up in Shanghai during the years of Japanese occupation.

The Diamond Age (2000), Neal Stephenson

Sticking to Shanghai's forward thinking mentality, this sci-fi novel takes place in Shanghai in the distant, harrowing future. Even if you're not a sci-fi fan, this one is still a page turner.

Wild Swans: Three Daughters of China (1991), Jung Chang

A fascinating introduction to the social changes of the country as a whole, this classic memoir that has sold more than 13 million copies captures the scope of recent Chinese history by following three generations of women in one family as they overcome war, the Cultural Revolution, and the frantic and competitive world of modern China.

Shanghai Flowers (1892), Han Bangqing

This novel was written around the turn of the century when China and Shanghai were undergoing tremendous change. In his work, Han touches on the underground world of prostitution and crime syndicates that controlled the country's most international city.

Film

Where Shanghai lacks in old dusty art, architecture and scrolls, it makes up for on the big screen. Shanghai was the first city in China to jump-start the country's film industry. Although the first movie was shot in Beijing, the nation's first cinema was revealed to the public in 1908 in Shanghai. The industry grew to cover over 140 Shanghai theaters until its flourishing in the 1930s, peaked by *Crossroads* (the 1937 comedy about three unemployed university graduates). However, just when things really began taking off in Shanghai, the Japanese invasion closed the curtain on the Shanghai film industry, with the majority of the artists and directors moving to Hong Kong, Chongqing, or abroad.

After the war, the second golden age of cinema blossomed in Shanghai, starting with *Spring in a Small Town* (1948) and the country's first color film *Remorse at Death* (1948). However, just like the city's first golden age in the 1920s and '30s, the industry was clipped again with the communist takeover in 1949. After the CCP took over the wheel, creative film declined as the government sought to glorify the "socialist utopia" through all means possible: art, film, literature, TV, posters, music, radio... you name it. Film came to a standstill with only eight being produced from 1966-1977.

Nonetheless, just a few years after the death of Chairman Mao, the industry took off again as China embarked on a new era of reform and openness. The rise of the Fourth Generation began in the late '70s, and the ensuing Fifth Generation of the late '80s began gaining international recognition with famous films such as *Red Sorghum* (1987), *Farewell My Concubine* (1993) and *Ju Dou* (1990). Much of the films produced during this time portrayed the darker side of Chinese life and customs, and many were banned by the government.

After a brief crackdown following the

Tian'anmen Square incident on 1989, the Sixth Generation exploded to the scene. Then, in the 2000s, the Post-Sixth Generation continued to climb international ranks with world renowned films such as *Crouching Tiger, Hidden Dragon* (2000), *Hero* (2002) and *Lost in Thailand* (2012) – the Chinese equivalent to America's *The Hangover* (2009).

Nowadays, China is the third largest film industry by the number of feature films produced annually and is predicted to have the largest market in the world by 2018.

Movie List

A great way to get psyched for your Shanghai adventure is to experience it in your living room. Download or rent some of these flicks to learn more about one of the world's coolest cities.

Empire of the Sun (1987), Steven Spielberg

No, this is not a typo. The great Spielberg found Ballard's story so fascinating that he turned it into a film. Of course, it's always better to read the book before watching the movie.

Shanghai Express (1932), Josef von Sternberg

One of the world's top grossing films in the early '30s, this old fashioned black and white classic is considered one of the most famous Shanghai movies ever. It's based on the true story of the kidnapping of foreigners on a hijacked Beijing-Shanghai train.

Shanghai Triad (摇啊摇．摇到外婆桥) (1995), Zhang Yimo

A great film about Shanghai's gangster culture in the turbulent '30s.

Suzhou River (苏州河) (2000), Lou Ye

For a more up-to-date piece on modern Shanghai, this film shows the grim life of Shanghai beneath the glitz and glamour.

Looper (2012), Rian Johnson

A Hollywood sci-fi thriller starring Bruce Willis, *Looper* takes place in Shanghai in the year 2074 when time travel is possible but outlawed, and used by syndicated crime organizations.

TV Series

If you need help killing time on that international flight, download *The Bund* (上海滩) (1980), Chiu Chun-keung. The Bund is a Hong Kong period drama first broadcasted in 1980. It is praised both inside and outside of China as "the Godfather of the East" and spawned several sequels and film adaptations.

(Movie and TV covers from the left to right, up to down)

1. Empire of the Sun   2. Shanghai Express
3. Shanghai Triad   4. Suzhou River
5. Looper   6. The Bund

Mandarin & Shanghaihua

So you study Mandarin, practice calligraphy, and live and breathe Rosetta Stone. Will it help?

Yes and no. There are about ten Chinese languages: Mandarin, Jin, Wu, Hui, Gan, Xiang, Min, Hakka, Yue (or Cantonese) and Ping. These languages vary greatly from one another, but even dialects and regional accents within one particular Chinese language can be so different that Chinese often have hard times communicating.

If a native Cantonese speaker traveled to Taipei and began speaking Cantonese, the locals of Taipei wouldn't understand a word. To make matters even more convoluted, if a native from Chengdu (the capital of Sichuan Province) traveled to the countryside of Sichuan and spoke with their city accent, the villagers with a thick country drawl would have a tough time understanding the Chengdu native due to the enormous gaps in regional accents.

Of the hundreds of dialects and languages that could have been chosen, a form of Beijing's local tongue (of the Mandarin language) is the one that prevailed to become the official language of the country. Though there are other dialects of Mandarin, the official state language is known as *Putonghua* (or simply as Mandarin, especially by foreigners). Who knows? What if the Qing's attempt to make the Nanjing dialect the standard go to language actually worked? Or if Chongqing remained the capital after the Japanese invasion and the government decided to make the Chongqing dialect the lingua franca? Or what if Cantonese rose to prominence instead? Mandarin could have had a very different fate.

In Shanghai, the locals speak Mandarin for official purposes or to communicate with people from other provinces. But when Shanghaiers go home or chat with friends, they use their local Shanghaihua (上 海 话 ; Shanghai language), which is quite different from Mandarin.

Shanghaihua

Shanghaihua is part of the Wu language, which is related to the local speach of nearby Jiangsu and Zhejiang Province. Wu Chinese is the 13th most spoken language in the world with more than 80 million native speakers, and it's mainly concentrated in and around Shanghai. Shanghai's brand of Wu Chinese is mostly similar to Suzhou's and Ningbo's, so locals from these places can use their local Wu to communicate with each other, though there would be some differences in their accents. Shanghaihua begins to differ from other Wu accents around the Jiangsu city of Wuxi and the Zhejiang city of Hangzhou, and even though Shanghaihua and these accents are mutually intelligible, native Wu speakers from different areas would struggle more in a conversation.

Shanghaihua is also very different from Mandarin. About 50% of Shanghaihua and standard Mandarin is the same, but the difference is enough to make the two languages mutually unintelligible, especially since Shanghaihua is rich in pure vowels and has some sounds that Mandarin doesn't. These attributes, along with vocab and pronunciation differences, are some of the factors that set Shanghaihua and other Wu dialects apart from Mandarin and Cantonese.

However, Shanghaihua is somewhat of a dying language. It's been six decades since the PRC made standard Mandarin the official state language required in all schools across the country, a move that weakened Shanghaihua's prominence. In fact, children have often been punished for using Shanghaihua in school. This policy, coupled with the influx of migrants from all over the Middle Kingdom, has increased the city's non-Shanghaihua-speaking population. Thus, standard Mandarin has become the lingua franca on the streets of Shanghai and the official language of Shanghai business and politics.

As Shanghai develops, many locals are returning to their roots and rediscovering their identity. There has been a push by famous Shanghai celebrities, and even Shanghai's former party boss Chen Liangyu, to promote Shanghaihua and begin teaching it in schools again. Whereas in the past schools outlawed Shanghaihua, nowadays some encourage it.

English	Chinese character	Chinese pinyin	Pronunciation	
			Mandarin	Shanghainese
one	一	yī	yee	yep
two	二	èr	arl	lyang
three	三	sān	san	seh
four	四	sì	si	si
five	五	wǔ	woo	ng
six	六	liù	lee-yew	lok
seven	七	qī	chee	ch'ep
eight	八	bā	bar	puh
nine	九	jiǔ	gee-yew	che-ew
Hello	你好	Nǐhǎo	knee-how	nong haw
Goodbye	再见	Zàijiàn	tsai chee-en	tseh way
Thank you	谢谢	Xièxiè	she-eh she-eh	shya shya
Sorry	对不起	Duìbúqǐ	do-eh boo chee	tay ver ch'ee
You're welcome	不客气	Búkèqì	boo ke chee	ver k'uk ch'ee
How much?	多少钱	Duōshǎoqián	dwor shau chien?	jee dee?
too expensive	太贵	tàiguì	tie gway	t'uk jyu
cheap	便宜	piányí	pee-an yee	bee nee
beer	啤酒	píjiǔ	pee gee-ow	bee jew
water	水	shuǐ	shoo-eh	si
tea	茶	chá	char	zoo
settle the bill	买单	mǎidān	my dan	mah teh
bar/pub	酒吧	jiǔbā	gee-ow bar	jew pa
hotel	酒店	jiǔdiàn	gee-ow dee-an	jew tee
restaurant	餐馆	cānguǎn	tsan gwan	veh tee
police	警察	jǐngchá	geen char	jin ts'uh

One local can recognize another through the use of Shanghaihua, which often leads to discounts or better treatment since hometown preference is usually the norm all over the world. Furthermore, in today's China, foreigners who speak Mandarin are a dime a dozen, and locals aren't astonished at a non-Chinese face busting out Mandarin. If you really want to make an impression in Shanghai, try to pick up a few Shanghaihua phrases – that will really blow them out of the water, and it will show that you genuinely have a keen interest in their local culture. Check out the Shanghaihua chart for some of the most common words and phrases.

Shanghai Mandarin

The good news is that if you can speak Mandarin you'll be able to communicate with ease around the city since everyone here speaks it. When Shanghai locals speak standard Mandarin, their accent is very similar to the standard Beijing dialect (which is often taught abroad in foreign countries), but the only major difference is the hard "er" (儿) sound associated with Beijing talk. For example, in Beijing, when a local says "where," he or she will say *na'er* (哪 儿), adding the hard "er" sound to the end of the word. The Shanghai local, on the other hand, would say *nali* (哪里) – using a softer, more pleasant "*li*" rather than a harsh consonant ending. For this reason, and the fact that the Shanghainese speak a little slower and more eloquently, Shanghai accented Mandarin is often seen as more beautiful than its rustic Beijing counterpart, and many universities in the West are starting to teach the Shanghai accent.

If you can't speak Mandarin, don't sweat it – all hope isn't lost. Keep reading for a crash course in one of the world's most interesting languages, and remember that there are also tons of Mandarin schools all across Shanghai that offer intensive classes. If you want to take it more casually, most of Shanghai's social networking sites are filled with ads of locals looking for language exchange partners. Of course, you can always take a leap and just try striking up a conversation with that sexy local you spotted at the café.

Mandarin 101

As you can see from the tables, not one, but TWO Chinese languages are listed as what many linguistic experts perceive as the hardest languages for native English speakers to learn. But why? What makes

Mandarin and Cantonese so difficult? Since Mandarin is the official language of the People's Republic of China, and the world's most widely spoken language with nearly 1 billion native speakers, we will focus on Mandarin. If you would like to learn more about Cantonese, check out Panda Guides *Hong Kong* for more.

Grammar

Let's get the easiest content out of the way, then move on to the harder stuff. Mandarin grammar is surprisingly simple. Unlike many Indo-European languages, there are no verb conjugations, no masculine, feminine or neutral forms, and no cases. In its most basic form, a past tense sentence is formed by adding *le* (了) to a verb or to the end of the sentence. To speak in the future, simply add *hui* (会) before the verb. Apart from a few other words like "already" (yǐjīng; 已经), the past participle "have" (guò; 过) or "going to" (jiāng; 将), there's not much more to basic verb tenses.

Notice below that the character 去 (to go) stays the same in each tense, unlike English where the verb "to go" changes to "went," "gone" and "going to go." In Mandarin, you can transition your sentences to past, present

Example:

I go. – Wǒ qù. – 我去。
I went. – Wǒ qù le. – 我去了。
I have gone. – Wǒ qù guò. – 我去过。
I already went. – Wǒ yǐjīng qù le. – 我已经去了。
I will go. – Wǒ huì qù. – 我会去。
I am going to go. – Wǒ jiāng qù. – 我将去。

and future with ease! But don't get too confident, if the entire language was so easy, everyone would be speaking Mandarin.

Tones

This is that part of Mandarin that is particularly difficult for foreigners because these kinds of tones don't exist in English. And for that matter, not too many other languages out there use tones for word meanings, either. In Mandarin, there are four tones and one neutral tone.

Mandarin is filled with various homophones (words that are pronounced exactly the same but have two different meanings, like "bow" as in ribbon and "bow" as in a bow and arrow) and homonyms (words that sound similar to one another but have different meanings, like "scents" and "sense"). Mandarin has many more homophones and homonyms than English and other Indo-European languages, so using tones is one of the only ways to distinguish what meaning you're actually trying to convey.

For example, "*yánjiū*" is the phonetic pronunciation for the Chinese word "to study" (研 究). However, this homophone sounds almost exactly the same as the word "smoking and drinking" (yānjiǔ, 烟 酒). The only difference between these two very different words are their tones. For studying, yanjiu has *yán* in the second tone and *jiū* in the first tone. For drinking and smoking, yān is in the first tone and jiǔ is in the third tone.

These goofy homophones and homonyms make it easy for a student to nonchalantly tell his or her parents about college. Instead of downplaying the boredom of diligent student life by saying, "eh, studying is studying," with the nimble shift of a tone, the student is actually telling his or her folks that "studying

is drinking and smoking!"

Characters

If the tones, homonyms and homophones weren't already brain-busters, then characters – those 4,000-year-old logograms that were written on tortoise shells back in the day – most certainly are. There are tens of thousands of Chinese characters, but luckily most of these are not used in common written language. Today, you need to memorize more than 3,000 characters to be truly literate, but the average educated Chinese person knows more than 5,000. With so many characters, the pairing of different characters together to make compound words, and some characters having more than one pronunciation, it's no wonder Chinese students cannot fully read a newspaper until their early teens.

Apart from reading, writing is perhaps the most difficult aspect of all. The mere fact that you need to memorize thousands of characters is daunting, but what makes them even harder is that these characters are comprised of multiple strokes. For example, the character for person is *rén* (人) – only two strokes. However, the common word for "to wipe" or "to clean" (cā; 擦) has 17 strokes! And if you mess up, it's wrong, plain and simple, no freebies. Unlike baseball, which gives you three strikes, in Mandarin, it's one "stroke" and you're out!

We could go on and on about the difficulty of Mandarin, but why waste your valuable study time? Go to our phrasebook on page 320 to learn some useful phrases along with some other information about Mandarin, and start speaking like a pro!

Shanghainese in Their Own Words

We've got a lot of great things to say about the Pearl of the Orient, but don't take our word for it. Here's what some of the experts – people who have lived here a long time – had to say:

Jing Jing
32
Shanghainese

Shanghai is amazing! I love it and I am very proud to be Shanghainese. Other cities in China cannot compare to our level of class and sophistication. We have all of the newest fashion and culture, so all the other cities in China wish they were like us.

Jonathan
29
American

I've been living here for a few years now, and while I get homesick occasionally, right now I have no plans to move back to the States. When I finished my degree I spent about a year trying to find a job, but with no luck at all. I had a friend living here who suggested I come out for a visit, and I was working within a month. Love it!

Michel,
23
French

I came to Shanghai for an internship. When I arrived I was thinking I would be very lost and lonely. It is so far away and such a different place than France or Europe, but very quickly I found a lot of good, cool friends here. Some are French, but others are from Germany, Italy, US and Canada. It was a really nice surprise how everybody was so friendly.

Erin
34
Australian

Back home I was working in restaurants most of the time, but I was just so bored with it all. You know Sydney is pretty small, I mean it's our biggest city, but really the scene is just not that big. And I had always heard interesting stories about life in China, so I decided I would go for a tour, and once I got to Shanghai I knew I didn't want to go home. Life here is just too interesting!

Chen Wei
19
Shanghainese

Now I go to school in Canada and I like living there, but I always love coming back to my home town to see my family. Growing up, all my friends and I always admired Western culture (especially our favorite NBA stars), but after having lived in both Shanghai and there, to be honest I don't see much difference between the two. Shanghai is just like Toronto in many ways. I guess that's why everyone says Shanghai is China's most Westernized city.

Felix
27
German

My company was looking for someone to go help set up our offices here and I felt very lucky that they chose me to come. I had always been interested in going to China, but I didn't imagine that one day I would be working in such an environment. Sometimes the office politics is a little different, but the city keeps making me think that it is the city of the future and I am here as it unfolds.

Zhang
64
Beijinger

I moved here with my wife and son about 25 years ago. At that time Shanghai was just starting to open up. People were still working very hard and living good lives, but there were not the same opportunities as today. Now so many companies here are not just from China but from other countries, too. I am happy my son got to finish his school here and live in this city.

Veronica
26
Colombian

I had lived in Taiwan before and learned a little Chinese. I loved it there, but then I got a job offer to work in Shanghai and – wow! This city has so much life! Every day you work, but every night you can really live! You eat, you drink, you party, and you have friends from all over the world. It is really an amazing place to be.

Jordan
35
Canadian

What can I say about Shanghai? Everything happened for me here. I met my wife and started my family. I started my business and it actually worked. I live a life that would be almost impossible for me to have "back home." I mean, that's not even home for me anymore. I've been here nine years now, so this is my home.

Getting Prepared

Before you book:
Imagine your trip and put together an itinerary

Before you spend a single dime or book anything, take the time to let your imagination run wild. What do you want your Shanghai trip to be? A serene and luxurious retreat with mornings spent exploring museums, afternoons whittled away in teahouses, and nights feasting on five-star cuisine? An outdoor experience on a gondola ride through the surrounding canal towns? Or a city-slicker's tour where you shop 'til you drop and hit up some of the city's finest clubs and lounges? Or perhaps you want to do a little bit of everything?

Shanghai has something for everyone, no matter your interest. If you need help getting your imagination going, check out a few local English-language websites to get a good sense of what's going on in town: Shanghai Expat (**shanghaiexpat.com**), eChinaCities (**echinacities. com**), City Weekend (**cityweekend.com.cn**) and Time Out Shanghai (**timeoutshanghai.com**) are four of the most popular. Renting movies about China or giving the latest China bestseller a read are great ways to learn about the place you'll be visiting. Another good way to get psyched is to get in touch with people you know who have visited or lived in China. Just explore and have fun with the idea of your trip before you get down to details.

When you're ready to start planning for real, the first decision you should make is whether or not to use a travel agent or tour company. The internet makes it easy to do everything on your own, book plane tickets and make dinner reservations, so the idea of paying someone to plan your trip might seem outdated or silly. We suggest grabbing your Panda Guides guidebook and thumbing through it to build a trip that's perfectly catered to you at the fraction of the cost of a tour agency.

On that note, we've created some great sample itineraries to help you get the most out of Shanghai. See page 273 to check out our recommendations.

Step 1: Air Ticket & Accommodation	Step 6: Female, Gay, Disabled & Colored Travelers
Step 2: Getting a China Visa	
Step 3: What to Take With You	Step 7: Religious Services in Shanghai
Step 4: Money & Banking	Step 8: Emergency Card
Step 5: Customs Regulations	

1 Air Ticket & Accommodation

Once you know when you want to go, the first step is to book an airline ticket. Your best bet for finding a good deal is to use a website that searches many airlines at once, like Kayak (**kayak.com**), Orbitz (**orbitz.com**) or Expedia (**expedia.com**). Kayak is particularly useful if you have slightly flexible travel days because it allows you to search for a range of departure dates. You can often save hundreds of dollars by leaving on a Tuesday instead of a Monday, for example, and Kayak helps you discover these opportunities.

If you're tempted to buy a one-way ticket and leave the length of your trip flexible, note that when you apply for your Chinese visa you will need to provide proof of a round-trip air ticket to demonstrate your intent to return to your home country. However, if you have a Letter of Invitation from a business, institution, or individual in China, you do not need to show proof of a round-trip ticket. For more on visa application requirements, see the visa section below.

Once you have booked your flights, start thinking about accommodations: what's your budget and where would you like to stay? Most travelers will best maximize their time in Shanghai by staying somewhere around the Bund or People's Square – it's more central and vibrant, and close to many of the main attractions. See Sleeping (pg 158) to get a sense of your options.

If you'd rather not commit to a long stay in one hotel or hostel before you arrive, that's fine. But unless you have a Letter of Invitation, your visa application will need to provide proof of accommodation for at least the first night you're in China. If you're not sure where you want to stay yet, just book an inexpensive hostel online and print out the confirmation for your visa application. You won't have to follow through on the reservation if you don't want to.

2 Getting a China Visa

The following visa procedures are applicable only to citizens of the United States. For details on applying for a China visa from other countries, see our website at **www.pandaguides.com**.

Passport Status

If you don't already have a passport, you'll need to get one as soon as possible. Expedited service takes two to three weeks, while regular processing takes five to six weeks. Add that to the time you'll need for processing your China visa, and you should begin this process at least two months before you plan to leave, and ideally well before that. See **travel.state.gov/passport** for details on how to apply for a passport.

If you already have a passport, check to make sure that it has at least six months of validity remaining before it expires. You won't be granted a visa with less than six months. And if you're applying for a year-long tourist visa, you'll need 18 months of validity remaining.

Visa Application

Once you've got your passport sorted, it's time to apply for a tourist – or L type – visa. But should you do it by yourself, or use a visa service agency? If you live in or near Washington DC, New York, San Francisco, Los Angeles, Houston or Chicago, you have the option of applying for your visa in person at the local Chinese consulate. Go to **www.china-embassy.org/eng/** to find the locations of these processing centers.

If none of those cities are convenient for you, or if you'd rather not go and wait in line, you can hire a visa service agency to do it for you. In that case, you would bring your passport and visa application to them so that they can present it in person at the consulate. There are many reliable and efficient companies to choose from – the China Visa Service Center (**mychinavisa. com**) has a good reputation and an organized website. These agencies invariably charge a fee on top of the cost of the visa. When you apply for a visa, you'll submit your passport and a number of supporting documents. See below for a complete list of the requirements as of the time of research.

How much does a visa cost?

Number of Entries	Visa Validity	2nd or 3rd Day Pickup	4th or 5th Day Pickup
Single Entry	3 months	$160	$140
Double Entry/ Multi-Entry	6 months	$160	$140
Multi-Entry	12 months	$160	$140

As you can see, the cost is the same no matter how many entries you choose, so go ahead and request 12 months multiple-entry, even if your trip will not be that long. You may not always get the longer validity, but it's better to aim high. In the event of unforeseen circumstances it's better to have too long of a visa than to try to negotiate an extension at the last-minute.

What goes into my visa application? – Basic Documents

1) Passport – You should submit your original passport that is valid for at least another six months and a photocopy of the passport's information and photo page. Your passport must also have at least one blank visa page.

2) Visa Application Form – Truthfully and completely fill out the Visa Application Form of the People's Republic of China (V2011A), which is available online at **www.china-embassy.org/eng/**. It's a straightforward form, but be sure to type or print neatly. In the "Itinerary in China" section, if you're planning to travel to the politically sensitive areas of Tibet or Xinjiang, don't include that in your list of intended destinations: no one will check up on it. There is a separate travel permit for Tibet and you must go with an official tour guide, but you need a China visa first, and mentioning Tibet on this application might create a needless red flag.

> There are a few gray areas when it comes to "truthfully" completing your visa application. There is a section that asks you to disclose your criminal record – some US citizens have chosen not to include that information in their application. It's not completely clear what impact your criminal record can have on the status of your application, and it's ultimately a personal choice to disclose or not disclose. Another ambiguity applies to journalists or "staff of media," as the form designates them, who may have a difficult time getting a tourist visa if they disclose their real occupation on the form. Some applicants choose to get around this by writing something else, though again, it's not clear how that choice may affect your application.

3) Photo – Attach one passport-size color photo to your Application Form. The 48 mm x 33 mm photo should be a recent, front view picture taken without a hat or head coverings, and you will need to make sure your ears can be seen (i.e. tuck long hair behind your ears). You can get these photos taken at many national drugstore chains like Walgreens and CVS.

4) Certificate of Name Change – If the name on the new passport is different from a previous one, the official name change certification document should be submitted.

5) One of the following supporting documents is required:

An Invitation Letter for Tourist Group or Invitation Letter for Tourist by a duly Authorized Tourism Unit.

An Invitation Letter issued by a company, corporation, institution or individual in China.

If the Invitation Letter is issued by an individual in China, the photocopy of the ID of the individual is required.

OR

A photocopy of the roundtrip airline ticket and hotel reservation.

If you have a tour group they may provide you with an Invitation Letter, but for most visitors the easiest supporting document to provide is the proof of airline ticket and hotel reservation. However, if you would prefer to submit an invitation letter from a company, group or a friend already in China, the letter must include all of the following:

(A) Personal information of the applicant: name, gender, date of birth, etc.

(B) Information concerning the applicant's visit to China: purpose of the visit, dates of arrival and departure, places to visit, relationship between the applicant and the inviter, and who will bear the cost of the applicant's accommodation in China.

(C) Information of the inviter: name of the business/institute or individual, phone number, address and, if applicable, seal and signature of their legal representative.

(D) The photocopy of the inviter's ID: if they are Chinese, their national ID; if they are a foreigner, their residence permit.

For non-US citizens only, these documents should be included with your application:

Proof of US Residency Status – Third country citizens also need to provide the original and a photocopy of proof of US residency (work or study), proof of residency in the consular district (e.g. ID, water or electricity bills or tenancy agreement, etc) or a valid US visa.

Previous Chinese Visa – Those who have obtained a Chinese visa before, when applying for a visa with a new passport, should submit a photocopy of the original passport's information/photo page and the page containing the previous Chinese visa.

Original Chinese Passport – First-time applicants whose former nationality was Chinese, or who were born in China (including Hong Kong, Macao and Taiwan), need to submit the original Chinese passport and a photocopy of the passport's information/photo page and extension page (if applicable).

It might seem like a lot of documents to assemble, but it's relatively straightforward as long as you leave yourself enough time.

How long will it take to get my visa?

If you submit your application in person, the processing time is usually four business days, or two to three business days if you pay for expedited service. Some consulates have processed same-day applications in the past for an additional fee, but as the volume of applications has increased this is not always an option. When you work with an agency, the same processing times should apply, plus the time it will take to send your application and receive it back in the mail.

3 What to Take With You

What to pack

What you pack is highly personal and depends on the length and season of your trip, not to mention the activities you have planned, so we won't bore you with a detailed universal packing list. But here are some general suggestions, followed by a few recommendations for non-essential items that can make a big difference in your trip.

First and foremost, don't overpack. The hassle of lugging a massive bag through the crowded streets of Shanghai will quickly cancel out the convenience of bringing your entire closet, and if you forget something, you can almost certainly replace it here.

Look up and follow the weather in Shanghai during the weeks leading up to your trip. Winter can be wet and cold, and by the end of May temperatures can exceed 30 °C (86 °F). Try to pack accordingly, though again, don't stress – if later on you find there's something you wish you had packed, buy it here.

Shanghai is not a very formal city, so unless you have a lot of meetings or fancy galas planned, one or two "nice" outfits should be more than enough.

Pack a duffel bag that you can fold up and keep in your luggage – if you buy a lot of souvenirs or hit the clothing markets, you'll have a way of transporting your loot home.

Washing machines are common in China, but driers are not, and it can take more than 24 hours for clothes to air-dry in the humid seasons. Factor that drying time in when you're considering how many outfits to bring.

Check your airline's baggage allowance so you don't get smacked with excess baggage fees.

If you're traveling with kids, packing becomes a bit more complicated: see our section on page 310 for more information on traveling with kids.

 China runs on 220 volts with a variety of plug types. The most common are the two-prong straight plug (USA style; top of photo at left) and three-prong angled (bottom of photo at left). Most laptops, camera chargers, phone chargers, and other electronics will plug into Chinese sockets with no problem. If your devices are not rated for 220V or if you have other plug shapes (including a two-prong straight plug where one plug is slightly larger than the other), you'll need to purchase an adapter. Power strips are widely available for inexpensive purchase in Shanghai, and they can accept just about any plug in the world.

None of the following items are technically essential, but they may come in handy:

E-reader or paper books: Traveling in China often means long bus or train rides, not to mention your long flight here and back. Reading material can turn boring "lost" transit time into a fun and relaxing experience. See our reading list on page 27 for our recommendations.

Earplugs: In a sleeper train or a hotel or hostel, you're bound to hear a lot of sounds that can steal much-needed sleep. Pop some earplugs in and forget all about it.

Ziploc bags: Keep your passport in one to protect against damage. No doubt you'll find many other uses for these throughout the trip.

Pocket-sized dictionary or smart-phone with dictionary app: When you need just a few words of Chinese, a dictionary can be a lifesaver, even if you have to point. For the basics see our Mandarin phrasebook on page 320.

Reusable water bottle: A Nalgene or other hard plastic bottle is a good way of keeping water with you at all times while reducing waste created by disposable plastic bottles. Remember to only fill with boiled or purified water.

Flashlight: Packing or unpacking in the dark, wandering down a dark and charming alley late at night... these are just a few examples of when a flashlight might come in handy.

Money belt: The jury is out on money belts. Some travelers swear by the under-the-clothes variety for protecting their cash, while others think it's a hassle. If you don't have the under-the-clothes type, you might just attract additional attention to your money. Either way, staying alert and keeping your money in a secure location (e.g. in your front pocket instead of your back) is the best way to stay safe.

Camera: It should go without saying, but you might be kicking yourself (and us) if we didn't throw this one in there just in case. If you have a smart-phone, you may not need this. However, keep in mind that China's scenery is extremely photo worthy, so if you have a high-end camera and love photography, you may want to consider bringing it.

Got a smart-phone? There is a grab bag of useful apps that you can throw in your phone to keep you updated on certain useful and important events around town. From giving daily weather and air pollution updates to those covering currency exchange and Chinese language, apps are the future. See page 291 for a list of these apps and how to find them.

Health Insurance

The most important thing you pack might not be in your suitcase. Many people believe that their existing health insurance policy will cover them worldwide, but that's usually not the case. Contact your insurer to confirm what coverage, if any, they provide while you're traveling in China. Some major insurers do have networked providers throughout China, so obtain this information in writing before you depart.

If your regular insurance coverage does not extend overseas, consider purchasing a travel insurance policy. Ask your insurer to recommend one, or check out the policies offered by International SOS (**internationalsos.com/en**).

Some types of travel insurance include emergency evacuation coverage, but do not cover the actual medical costs of treatment. You may need additional medical insurance to cover these situations. Read any potential policy carefully to understand exactly what it covers. Understand if you can use any doctor or if you must use one who is in your network.

Most Chinese hospitals require cash payment. Even if you have medical insurance, you may have to pay first then apply for reimbursement. A few hospitals in major cities may accept credit cards, but don't put all your eggs in one basket. Make sure to get a receipt for all services, or you may not get a reimbursement.

4 Money & Banking

Chinese currency: Renminbi (人民币)

Abbreviated as RMB, *renminbi* means "the people's currency." The main unit of the RMB is the *yuán* (元) – for example, a bottle of water might cost three *yuan*. In Shanghai, the word *yuan* is interchangeable with the word *kuài* (块), and you'll usually hear prices quoted as *kuai* instead of *yuan*. The largest bill in circulation is the red ¥100 (about US$16), followed by ¥50, ¥20, ¥10, ¥5 and ¥1. Below ¥1, there are a series of coins and smaller-sized bills worth ¥0.5 and ¥0.1. These are called *jiǎo* or, more commonly, *máo* (i.e. ¥0.5 is five *mao*).

Though ATMs will only dispense ¥100 bills, you'll find that shop owners and cab drivers sometimes balk at taking one – they may not have enough change. While traveling in China, it's a good idea to keep a supply of ¥100 bills and a good mix of smaller bills.

Australia	AU$1	¥5.7
Canada	CA$1	¥5.9
Euro Zone	€1	¥8.1
Hong Kong	HK$1	¥0.8
New Zealand	NZ$1	¥4.8
Singapore	SG$1	¥4.8
UK	UK£1	¥9.5
USA	US$1	¥6.1
For up-to-date currency exchange rates, see **www.xe.com**		

One Hundred Yuan note

"People's Bank of China" written in five different languages. Clockwise from top: Chinese Pinyin, Tibetan, Zhuang, Uighur, Mongolian.

Credit & debit cards

China is a heavily cash-based economy. Outside of big international hotels and some stores, you shouldn't expect to swipe a credit or debit card. Luckily, almost all foreign ATM cards work in China, though you will incur fees for international withdrawals. If you're concerned, check with your bank. If you plan to use your credit or debit cards while you're abroad, make sure to notify your bank of your travels before you leave so that your purchases do not activate a fraud warning.

Cash

There are a number of ways to get cash during your trip. First, you can bring some of your home currency and exchange it once you arrive at the airport, but the rates will most definitely be inflated. You can also exchange cash at a branch of the Bank of China, though foreigners are restricted to exchanging US$500 worth of currency per day. Second, you can plan to withdraw cash from an ATM once you arrive – ATMs are very common in Shanghai, especially downtown and near tourist attractions.

These can be cashed at international hotels and branches of the Bank of China. Though they do offer more security in the event of theft, the ease of using debit cards to withdraw cash at ATMs has made them less popular in recent years, and you might need to go out of your way to cash them.

5 Customs Regulations

Generally speaking, the customs enforcement at the airport is hands-off. When arriving or departing, you must walk through the "green channel" (nothing to declare) or the "red channel" (something to declare). If you're unsure about declaring something, err on the side of caution and choose the red channel.

What can I bring into China?

400 cigarettes, 1.5 L of alcohol and 50 g of gold or silver are allowed in without any duty. No fresh fruit or meat is permitted. Any amount of foreign currency can be brought in, but more than US$5,000 (or the equivalent) must be declared. Guns, knives, explosives and other weapons are prohibited. Electronics like TVs and computers will need to be declared.

What can I take out?

Pretty much anything, but weapons (obviously), pornography, and produce are forbidden, while pirated DVDs and CDs may be confiscated. Antiques that you bought in China need a certificate and red seal to clear customs. Anything before 1949 is an antique and needs proper documentation, and objects from before 1795 cannot be legally exported, period.

6 Female, Gay, Disabled & Colored Travelers

Female travelers

China is a very safe place for solo female travelers. In addition to its very low crime rate in general, there's much less of a macho alpha-male attitude here than in some other countries. Of course, take the usual precautions, and consider carrying a whistle or other noisemaker in the event of a threatening situation. Try to choose accommodation that is centrally located and well-trafficked. See page 134 for more on solo female travelers.

Gay & lesbian travelers

Homosexuality was only officially decriminalized in China in 1997 and declassified as a mental disorder in 2001. That being said, attitudes toward homosexuality in Shanghai are notably different than in the West, and not always for the worse. When considering others besides friends or family, the basic stance of most Shanghainese on this issue is that it's none of their business. Men being physically affectionate in public may draw attention, but nothing more, and women being affectionate towards each other in public is so common that it won't attract any attention at all. Random harassment or violence against gays, especially foreigners, is basically nonexistent. The area around the southwest end of Huaihai Middle Road is commonly considered the gay neighborhood of Shanghai. Check Utopia's site at **www.utopia-asia.com/tipschin.htm** for more detailed listings (unfortunately, not always up to date), or check below for a few recommendations:

Shanghai Studio – The standby of Shanghai's gay scene is located here at Shanghai Studio in an old bomb shelter. It has a respectable crowd on most weekends, though it's sometimes not as large as the newer options (unless there's a special event, with cover charge in which

case it's reliably packed). The dance floor opens at 23:00.
Phone: 6283 1043
Address: 4, Lane1950, Huaihai Middle Rd (淮海中路 1950 弄 4 号)
Website: www.shanghai-studio.com

Eddie's – Basically at the same intersection as Studio, this bar features slightly older clientele and a lot more style. It's mostly male and more about drinks and conversation than dancing.
Phone: 6282 0521
Address: 1877 Huaihai Middle Rd (淮海中路 1877 号)

390 Shanghai – One of the newer and more youthful bars on the scene; it has many special events and is well-attended, at least for now.
Address: 390 Panyu Rd, near Fahuazhen Rd (番禺路 390 号 . 近法华镇路)
Website: www.390shanghai.com

Travelers with disabilities

Regrettably, Shanghai is not the most convenient place for travelers who are wheelchair-bound or have mobility disabilities. The airport, railway stations, and subway stations are basically barrier-free and up to Western standards, but elsewhere, crowded sidewalks and high curbs make navigating the streets a challenge, and ramps and elevators are not nearly as common as in the West. Crossing large streets can be dangerous if you're a very slow walker, and sidewalks are often clogged with whatever personal property the surrounding residents have put on it. If you bring your own wheelchair, ideally it would be lightweight and collapsible to facilitate fitting it in the trunk of a taxi. Travelers with sight or hearing disabilities should also take extreme caution when crossing the street because cars move fast and rarely yield to pedestrians.

Colored travelers

While the general population of China is quite tolerant of the world's different ethnicities, forms of discrimination can sadly still be found here. While it is rare for black travelers to be discriminated against, there is a small minority of those in China who hold prejudices towards those of African or Middle-Eastern descent. Most of this discrimination comes in the form of difficulties for colored people in finding employment or living spaces, but this descrimination is largely restricted to black or dark-skinned expats and not travelers.

Unfortunately, there is a common misconception among many Chinese that black people are poor and at the bottom barrel of societies, despite the prominent positions and success of countless black men and women throughout the world. You may be asked where you are from, and some may be very surprised and hesitant to believe your answer if it is not an African nation (i.e. some Chinese have been known to be skeptical when a black person says they are from the US or Europe). Take it as naïve ignorance, take a few deep breaths and consider that this might be a good time to educate those around you. When asked about black culture or people, feel free to take the time to kindly explain any discrepancies or misinformation they may have heard, because it is rare for them to get any information from a direct or reliable source.

Most of what you will experience in China if you are a black traveler is curiosity, but Shanghai is one of the country's few mainstream cities where your presence alone will rarely attract special attention. That being said, most of the country is quite ethnically homogenous (around 92% Han Chinese) and you are likely to have at least one instance where a Chinese will want to take a picture of you or with you. For many Chinese and Asians in general, a black person is a rare sight, and their stares simply indicate surprise and curiosity. Some people may also want to touch your hair – so heads up!

7 Religious Services in Shanghai

Bring your passport. This is sometimes required to attend an international service.

Christian

Saint Peter's Catholic Church – This is one of a few places for international Catholic mass and it's centrally located. English mass starts at 17:00 on Saturday and 11:00 Sunday.
Phone: 6467 0199
Email: stpetersintl@gmail.com
Address: 3/F, 270 Chongqing South Rd (重庆南路 270 号 3 楼)

Hengshan Church – It's part of the multi-denominational Christian group called Shanghai Community Fellowship. English services start at 14:00 and 16:00 on Sunday.
Email: info@scfenglish.com
Website: www.shanghaifellowship.org
Address: 53 Hengshan Rd, near Wulumuqi Rd (衡山路 53 号，近乌鲁木齐路)

Jewish

The Shanghai Jewish Center – They offer many different services for the Jewish community, including a kosher mini-market and a synagogue. Chabad-affiliated.
Phone: 6278 0225
Email: info@chinajewish.org
Website: www.chinajewish.org
Address: 89 Shuicheng South Rd, Shang-Mira Garden, Number 1 Villa (水城南路 89 号美丽花园 1 号别墅)
Transport: Subway – Line 10, get off at Shuicheng Rd Station

Muslim

Shanghai Huxi Mosque One of the larger mosques in Shanghai, it serves male and female Muslims.
Phone: 6277 2076
Address: 4, Lane 1328, Changde Rd, near Aomen Rd (常德路 1328 弄 4 号．近澳门路)

8 Emergency Card

It's a good idea to carry an emergency card with you – just in case. We have provided this one which includes Chinese and English, and we encourage you to make copies to suit your needs.

My info	Help
My name 我的名字：	My nationality 我的国籍：
My address 我的地址：	
My phone number 我的电话号码：	
For emergency, please contact 紧急情况请联系：	

Transportation

Airports

Shanghai has two international airports: Hongqiao (虹 桥) and Pudong (浦 东). If you have the choice and there's no cost difference, choose Hongqiao. It's about 10 km (6 mi) from the inner city while Pudong is 30 km (18.5 mi), although the Maglev Train to and from Pudong cuts back on travel time (continue reading for more on the Maglev). If, however, you're staying in the Pudong District, that airport is obviously closer.

Shanghai Hongqiao International Airport (Shànghǎi Hóngqiáo Guójì Jīchǎng; 上 海 虹桥国际机场 *; IATA code: SHA)*

Metro: The inner city is 15 minutes away by metro Line 10 or Line 2. If you're flying out from Hongqiao you should check whether your flight is from Terminal 1 or 2. Each has its own metro station and Line 2 only goes to Terminal 2. The last Line 2 train is at 23:22 and the first is at 6:30. The last Line 10 train is at 23:00 and the first departs at 5:30.

Taxi: Follow the signs to the taxi stand. More taxis will be called if there are many people waiting, but wait times can still be rather long. Don't take a cab from anywhere

but here. Those who approach you in the terminal and ask if you need a taxi are black cabs, which are illegal, unmetered and charge much more (and may raise the price before you get to your destination). Don't worry, there are always official taxis no matter how late it may be since they're specifically called in to handle passengers from late flights. A trip to the center of the city takes about 25 minutes and costs around ¥50.

Bus: Since Hongqiao is so close to the city, all the buses at the station are regular city buses with many stops. Cramming into a city bus with all your luggage and other passengers with all their baggage may not be the most fun introduction to Shanghai, so take the metro or a taxi – you'll be happier in the long run.

Shanghai Pudong International Airport (Shànghǎi Pǔdōng Guójì Jīchǎng; 上海浦东国际机场*; IATA code: PVG)*

Metro: You can get to Shanghai using Line 2, but it will take a while. You'll have to transfer at one point to get onto the regular Line 2, and though the transfer is just a few steps to the other rail, it adds another ten minutes of waiting. All told, it will take a little more than an hour and forty minutes to get to the city center.

Maglev Train: It operates at intervals of 15 minutes and takes another 8 minutes to get to its destination at a charge of ¥50 one way (¥100 for VIP treatment). And for all that, your destination is Line 2 Longyang Metro Station outside of Pudong. Yep, for ¥50 you'll still have to take the metro the rest of the way to the city center, having taken off about 30 minutes from your travel time (so the full trip including the metro will still be more than an hour). But the Maglev moves very fast (top speed: 431 km/h; 268 m/h) and only a few places in the world have them. It's an attraction in and of itself and worth it even if only for one trip. The last metro train leaves at 22:00, the last Maglev leaves at 21:42, and the first Maglev leaves at 6:45. See page 147 for more info about the Maglev.

Taxi: Taxis are more expensive, but probably the quickest option. Get your taxi only from the official taxi stand to avoid the ubiquitous black taxis. A trip to the city center takes about an hour and cost about ¥150. Pray for no traffic. Taxis will definitely be available after late flights; they're the only game in town at that point.

Bus: Buses are actually a pretty good option if you know what stop to get off at. All are special airport routes, meaning that the stops are few and include many hotels (check with your hotel to see if a bus passes their location). Fares are about ¥15-25 depending on where you're getting off, and it'll usually take around an hour without too much traffic. Most buses stop running by 23:00 or earlier and begin service after 6:00.

Travel within Shanghai

Before we get into your transportation options, you should know that although there are many Chinese who speak English in Shanghai, there are far more who do not, so you should never count on finding a taxi driver or passerby who knows English well. And unless you have some experience studying Chinese, don't put too much faith in your ability to pronounce Chinese place names and be understood by the locals. The pinyin romanization of Chinese characters may not get you very far, either. Your best bet is to have the name of the place you want to visit written out in Chinese characters. Location names in this book all have Chinese characters for your convenience, so feel free to point to them when interacting with locals. You can also use apps (see pg 291) on your smart-phone or have someone at your hotel or hostel write the characters out for you.

Shanghai Transportation Card (Shànghǎi Gōnggòng Jiāotōng Kǎ; 上海公共交通卡*)*

If you're planning on taking public transportation a lot, you should get a Jiaotong Card. This is especially true for the metro, where you will have to buy a ticket from a machine each time you take a ride if you don't have it. You can get one at the service counter of any metro station (show them the Chinese word above and they'll know what you want) and you can use it for the metro, all buses and all taxis. You can also refill it easily at any metro station service counter. Every person in your party will have to get a card, because double-swiping at one location isn't registered by the system. Small

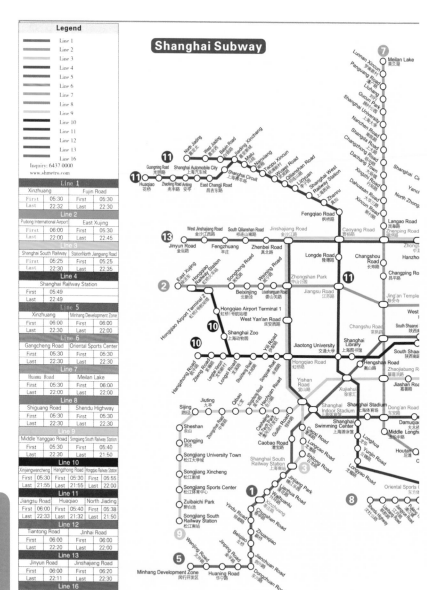

Legend

Line 1
Line 2
Line 3
Line 4
Line 5
Line 6
Line 7
Line 8
Line 9
Line 10
Line 11
Line 12
Line 13
Line 16

Inquiry: 6437 0000
www.shmetro.com

Line 1
Xinzhuang		Fujin Road	
First	05:30	First	05:30
Last	22:32	Last	22:30

Line 2
Pudong International Airport		East Xujing	
First	06:00	First	05:30
Last	22:00	Last	22:45

Line 3
Shanghai South Railway	StationNorth	Jiangyang Road	
First	05:25	First	05:25
Last	22:30	Last	22:35

Line 4
Shanghai Railway Station	
First	05:49
Last	22:49

Line 5
Xinzhuang		Minhang Development Zone	
First	06:00	First	06:00
Last	22:30	Last	22:00

Line 6
Gangcheng Road		Oriental Sports Center	
First	05:30	First	05:30
Last	22:30	Last	22:30

Line 7
Huamu Road		Meilan Lake	
First	05:30	First	06:00
Last	22:00	Last	22:00

Line 8
Shiguang Road		Shendu Highway	
First	05:30	First	05:30
Last	22:30	Last	22:30

Line 9
Middle Yanggao Road		Songjiang South Railway Station	
First	05:30	First	05:40
Last	22:30	Last	21:50

Line 10
Xinjiangwancheng		Hangzhong Road		Hongqiao Railway Station	
First	05:30	First	05:30	First	05:55
Last	21:55	Last	21:55	Last	22:00

Line 11
Jiangsu Road		Huaqiao		North Jiading	
First	06:00	First	05:40	First	05:38
Last	22:33	Last	21:32	Last	21:50

Line 12
Tiantong Road		Jinhai Road	
First	06:00	First	06:00
Last	22:20	Last	22:00

Line 13
Jinyun Road		Jinshajiang Road	
First	06:00	First	06:20
Last	22:11	Last	22:30

Line 16
Luoshan Road		Dishui Lake	
First	06:00	First	06:00
Last	22:00	Last	22:00

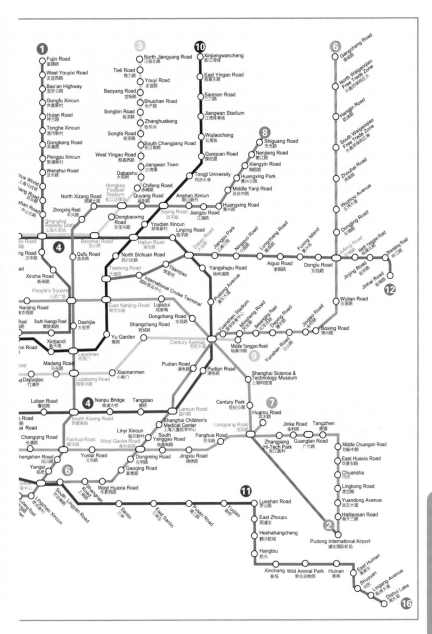

children, however, don't need a card. The official rule is that children under 1.2 m (about 4 ft) ride for free; the unofficial rule is that a kid who can duck under the turnstile without too much effort doesn't need to pay.

There's a ¥20 deposit for the card, so you'll initially have to pay that plus whatever amount you want to put on the card. The deposit will be refunded if you return the card to a designated location, including metro stations Century Avenue and West Nanjing Road, but you have to bring your passport and the original receipt of sale for the card to get the money left on the card back (only if it's over ¥10).

Metro

Shanghai's metro system is all the transportation you'll need if you're willing to walk a bit to your final destination. It's clean and fast, and even during rush hours crowding is not too much of an issue. If taxis weren't so cheap, this would hands down be the best way to travel for any tourist. If you do travel during rush hours (7:00-9:00 and 18:00-20:00), whatever crowding you have to deal with on the metro is definitely preferable to sitting for half an hour in traffic in a taxi or bus.

Fares are distance-based; transfers between lines don't increase the cost. The first 6 km (4 mi) is ¥3, and the next 10 km (6 mi) is ¥4, so ¥3-4 will be the fare for almost anywhere you go within the first ring road. If you take a ride out to the suburbs, the fare will be ¥9 at most. Hours of operation vary by line, but generally trains run between about 5:00 and 23:00. The excellent site **www.exploreshanghai.com** has a clear map of the metro stops in English and shows the times of the first and last trains for each station.

If you don't have a Jiaotong Card you'll need to buy a ticket at a ticket machine, which requires you to first choose your destination via line and station, and then the number of tickets you want. Trust us, it is as tedious as it sounds. Next, insert the ticket into the turnstile slot to go through to the trains. Do not lose the card because you will need to insert it again when leaving your destination station. If you have a Jiaotong Card, you only need to breezily swipe it against the green magnetic area on top of the turnstile.

There are security checkpoints before each turnstile where passengers are supposed to put all bags onto a conveyor belt to be scanned. The city government is currently considering scrapping the system and for good reason. As you'll quickly learn, most people ignore the attendants completely (who themselves couldn't care less) and just walk through with their bags. No one will care if you do so too, but the one time attendants will absolutely insist on passing your belongings through the x-ray is when you have large pieces of luggage.

One efficient and easy way to organize your sightseeing is to simply travel along one line and see all the attractions near its stations. We've compiled a list of the bigger attractions that lie along different subway routes (listed in parenthesis) for your consideration.

Line 1

Hengshan Road (same name of metro station)

Old French Concession (Changshu Road, Shaanxi Road, Huangpi Road)

Shanghai Museum and Shanghai Art Museum (People's Square)

Line 2

Zhongshan Park (same name of metro station)

Jing'an Temple (same name of metro station)

Nanjing West Road (same name of metro station)

Shanghai Museum and Shanghai Art Museum (People's Square)

The Bund (Nanjing East Road)

Oriental Pearl (Lujiazui)

Pudong Skyscraper District and World Fiancial Center (Century Avenue)

Shanghai Science and Technology Museum

Century Park (same name of metro station)

Line 8

Shanghai Museum and Shanghai Art Museum (People's Square)

Shanghai Expo Buildings and Power Station of Art (South Xizang Road)

China Art Palace (ZhonghuaYishu Gong)

Line 9

Songjiang, Sheshan, Happy Valley, Thames

Town (last stops on Line 9)

Tianzifang (Dapuqiao)

Pudong Skyscraper District and World Financial Center (Century Avenue)

Line 10

Shanghai Library (same name of metro station)

Huaihai Middle Road (Shaanxi South Road)

Xintiandi (same name of metro station)

Yu Garden (same name of metro station)

Bus

The bus may seem a bit redundant for tourists willing to take the subway, for unlike the subway, the bus system is designed mostly for the needs of local residents in mind. Sure, you can usually find a stop that's closer to your destination, but figuring out the correct route and transfers involved is no simple task for someone who doesn't read Chinese, since most online resources and route lists at the bus stops are only in Chinese. Although most buses in the city proper have LED screens in front that read out the name of the next stop, you can never be completely sure that there will be an English translation (though often there is), and sometimes the bus driver will simply drive past any stops with no people if no one on the bus looks like they want out, so you have to have a good idea of where you want to go beforehand, or indicate your destination to the driver when getting on. The danger of missing your stop is not small, so it may be best for most travelers to stick to the metro and taxis. If you do decide to take a bus, the fare is ¥2 for city buses, which is reduced to ¥1 if you're transferring within 120 minutes, even from the metro. Just swipe your Jiaotong Card at the front if you have it, or pay in cash (you must get a transfer slip for the discount if you pay in cash).

In some areas farther out from the city, taking the bus is your only option, and this guide has detailed instructions on which routes to take. These buses often charge by how many stops you're taking, so if there's no place to swipe your card in the front, a ticket person on the bus will eventually come by and ask you which stop you're getting off at. You can point to the Chinese characters of the stop printed in this guide and the attendant will tell you the fee. Pay in cash or with your Jiaotong Card, which the ticket person will have a device to swipe it.

Taxi

Taxis are very cheap and abundantly available almost everywhere in the city. A green light on the taxi's dashboard just behind the windshield means it's looking for passengers, and hailing one is as simple as making eye contact and waving your hand. Don't get into a taxi that doesn't have a green light. The light is connected to the taxi's meter, so if it doesn't have one, it's an illegal, unmetered taxi that will surely charge excessive amounts. The fare is ¥14 for the first 3 km (2 mi) and ¥2.4 for every kilometer after that (waiting in traffic is ¥0.5 a minute). After 23:00, the fare rises to ¥18 and ¥3.1 for every kilometer after the first three. Considering most of Shanghai's attractions are within the inner ring road, which makes an area of bout 8 km (5 mi) in diameter, you'll seldom have to pay more than ¥30. Furthermore, since there are always people looking for a taxi, the drivers have little incentive to go the "scenic route" and charge you more.

Passengers usually tell the driver where they want to go by naming the street of their destination and a cross street near it. Each attraction in this guide has all this information listed in Chinese for each attraction, so you can just show it to the driver.

When you get in the taxi, the driver should put down the small sign on the dashboard

with the light, which will start the meter. Don't worry if the driver doesn't put it down immediately, many drivers do it after driving a few seconds. Scamming taxi drivers are extremely rare in Shanghai, so as long as the driver puts it down eventually, don't worry about it (you can point to the sign if you feel the taxi driver is taking too long). When you arrive at your destination, the taxi driver will ask a question to you in Chinese that translates to: "Cash or Jiaotong card?" Show the driver which one you'll use a little before stopping because they will have to press a different button depending on which one. If you use the Jiaotong Card, simply put it on top of the lowered sign on the dashboard when the driver indicates to do so and take it off when he or she says it's OK. Get a receipt (called *fāpiào*) just in case you leave something in the taxi and need to identify which taxi you were in later.

On Foot

Shanghai is big, but its tree-lined streets and many public parks are all very walkable, especially in places with a high concentration of things to do. The following areas are good for walking: 1. Between the Bund and People's Square (the two main roads of interest are Fuzhou Road and Nanjing East Road) 2. Nanjing West Road and Jing'an Temple 3. The old French Concession centered around Huaihai Middle Road (and the area around Huaihai's western terminus) 4. The area between Tianzifang and Xintiandi 5. The Yu Garden area.

Trains

The level of comfort and speed in China's trains varies a lot depending on the type of train you take. The high-speed trains that have been introduced to certain routes are very nice and new – with their smooth, silent

ride, many people prefer them to flying. Each train is identified with a letter and number. Here's what the letters mean:

G – Gāotiě (高铁): Ultra High-Speed Train

C – Chéngjì Lièchē (城 际 列 车): Intercity High-Speed Train

D – Dòngchē (动车): High-Speed Train

Z – Zhídá Tèkuài (直达特快): Direct Express Train

T – Tèkuài (特快): Express Train

K – Kuàichē (快车): Fast Train

Ticket types

For all seat types, smoking is prohibited (except between cars, where the smokers will gather). Lights generally go out around 22:00. Amenities are pretty much limited to a hot-water dispenser and a very basic bathroom.

Soft Sleeper (Ruǎnwò; 软 卧) The most expensive and most comfortable option, soft sleeper tickets get you a bunk in an air-conditioned compartment with three other people. There's a door that can be closed for extra privacy and noise reduction. Tickets for upper berths are slightly cheaper than lower berths.

Hard Sleeper (Yìngwò; 硬卧) For about half the price of a soft sleeper, you can get the most popular ticket type – a bunk in a big, doorless, air-conditioned compartment. The bunks are stacked in threes and slightly less plush than soft sleepers, but the more social atmosphere and cheaper price make up for it.

Seats: Hard Seat (Yìngzuò; 硬 座) and Soft Seat (Ruǎnzuò; 软座). Depending on the train you take, there may be several classes of seats, with the nicest having TVs, outlets, and two-across seating. So-called "hard seats" are the least desirable, not necessarily because the seat is hard, but because the crowding, noise, and less-than-clean surroundings make for a hard trip if you're going far. If tickets have sold out, you may have the option of a standing ticket (Zhànpiào; 站票).

Buying train tickets

Train travel is extremely popular in China, so unless you're going to cities near Shanghai, which have many trains each day, you shouldn't count on being able to get same-day tickets. Most tickets can be booked 10 days in advance of your departure date. For long journeys, sleeper tickets will sell out before seats.

Bring your passport(s)! You can buy as many tickets as you want, as long as you have one passport for each ticket. Each ticket is for one time and one train. If you miss it, you must go back to the ticket office to exchange for another time. Busy periods like Chinese New Year (usually February) and National Day Holiday (the first week of October) set off an all-out free-for-all when it comes to buying tickets, and booking a train then can be downright impossible. Use the excellent site **www.chinatrainguide.com** to find specific trains and times in English for all cities in China.

Ticket counters

You can buy tickets directly at the train station ticket counters for no additional charge. Simply say the name of the city you want and the day you wish to travel on, and the ticket person will show you on their computer screen the specific times and train numbers to choose from. Many ticket counter operators know enough English to handle this (in Shanghai at least), but it would be best to bring a slip of paper with this information written out (pinyin is OK, Chinese characters are better) to ensure that there is no miscommunication. You can also buy tickets at one station for trains departing from another station in Shanghai, but be sure to indicate that information first if you do so. You can use the Chinese names of the stations we've listed, which will also come in handy when taking a train back to Shanghai.

Ticket offices

Instead of going to the train station you can also buy tickets from an official agency. They provide the same services as a train station ticket office with an added ¥5 ticket handling charge. Again, if you don't speak Chinese, have your destination written out. Also, most hotels and hostels provide service for booking train tickets with an extra service fee.

Online

You can book online at **www.chinatripadvisor.com** or **www.china-train-ticket.com**, but be warned that these sites charge a hefty commission that could almost double the price of your ticket. If you're headed to Hong Kong, note that you can order tickets online for face value at **www.mtr.com.hk**.

Railway stations

Shanghai has three railway stations, all with their own metro stop. Remember that there are many more routes available than the ones we have listed, so you may want to check www.chinatrainguide.com for more options and specific times and destinations.

Shanghai Station (Shànghǎi Huǒchē Zhàn; 上海火车站)

Metro: Lines 1, 3, 4; Shanghai Railway Metro Station

From here, trains depart to and arrive from the country's north and west. A word of warning about the station: it's an absolute nightmare of urban planning. The ticket office has been completely cut off from the subway exit and the entrance to the station is by a road that you'll have to walk under. Just keep going east and you'll find the underground walkway.

Shanghai Hongqiao Station (Shànghǎi Hóngqiáo Huǒchē Zhàn; 上海虹桥火车站)

Metro: Lines 2, 10; Hongqiao Railway Metro Station

Handles most of the high speed trains, including those that go to Beijing.

Shanghai South Station (Shànghǎi Nánzhàn; 上海南站)

Metro: Lines 1, 3; Shanghai South Railway Metro Station

The station for most trains departing to and arriving from the south.

Pangda Travel (Pángdà Lǚyóu; 庞大旅游)

Pangda Travel is the first budget airline booking hub for travelers and expats in the Middle Kingdom. While other companies are Chinese owned businesses that target locals, Pangda Travel is a Canadian owned enterprise that knows and understands the needs of foreigners traveling in China. With excellent service, English speaking staff and extremely low prices, Pangda Travel is the preferred agent foreigners turn to when booking domestic and international flights.

Phone: 400 030 7900
Email: pangdatravel@hotmail.com

Getting In & Out

By Plane

Departure – Arrival	Frequency	Duration	Price
Beijing – Shanghai	52 flights daily	2 hr 10 min	¥1,130
Guangzhou – Shanghai	40 flights daily	2 hr 20 min	¥1,280
Shenzhen – Shanghai	45 flights daily	2 hr 10 min	¥1,400
Haikou – Shanghai	10 flights daily	2 hr 40 min	¥1,660
Sanya – Shanghai	16 flights daily	2 hr 50 min	¥1,890
Chongqing – Shanghai	31 flights daily	2 hr 10 min	¥1,490
Kunming – Shanghai	32 flights daily	about 3 hr	¥1,900
Guiyang – Shanghai	25 flights daily	2 hr 20 min	¥1,690
Guiling – Shanghai	11 flights daily	about 2 hr	¥1,300
Nanning – Shanghai	11 flights daily	2 hr 20 min	¥1,660
Chengdu – Shanghai	28 flights daily	2 hr 40 min	¥1,610
Harbin – Shanghai	15 flights daily	2 hr 50 min	¥1,760
Shenyang – Shanghai	19 flights daily	2 hr 10 min	¥1,300
Dalian – Shanghai	19 flights daily	1 hr 50 min	¥1,060
Changchun – Shanghai	17 flights daily	2 hr 30 min	¥1,600
Urumqi – Shanghai	8 flights daily	4 hr 30 min	¥2,800
Hohhot – Shanghai	4 flights daily	2 hr 20 min	¥1,350
Xining – Shanghai	1 flight daily	3 hr 00 min	¥1,850
Lanzhou – Shanghai	3 flights daily	2 hr 30 min	¥1,750
Yinchuan – Shanghai	3 flights daily	2 hr 30 min	¥1,500
Xi'an – Shanghai	25 flights daily	about 2 hr	¥1,260
Changsha – Shanghai	16 flights daily	1 hr 40 min	¥890
Wuhan – Shanghai	19 flights daily	1 hr 30 min	¥980
Nanchang – Shanghai	5 flights daily	1 hr 10 min	¥710

Note: Prices listed above are full prices, but subject to an additional airport construction fee of ¥50 plus a fuel tax of ¥120. However, you can get 10-50% discount if you book the ticket at least one day early.

By Train

Train number	From – To	Departing – Arriving	Duration	Price
G1	Beijing South – Shanghai Hongqiao	09:00 – 13:48	4 hr 48 min	¥553
Note: There are 44 bullet trains from Beijing South to Shanghai Hongqiao daily: departing about every 30 minutes from 7:00 to 17:40.				
G211	Tianjin West – Shanghai Hongqiao	09:31-14:34	5 hr 03 min	¥513.5
Note: There are 23 bullet trains from Tianjin West (or Tianjin South) to Shanghai Hongqiao daily.				
G7003	Nanjing – Shanghai	08:00-09:39	1 hr 39 min	¥139.5
Note: There are 260 bullet trains from Nanjing (or Nanjing South) to Shanghai (or Shanghai Hongqiao, or Shanghai South) daily.				
G7213	Suzhou – Shanghai	09:24 – 10:07	43 min	¥39.5
Note: There are 230 bullet trains from Suzhou (or Suzhou North) to Shanghai (or Shanghai Hongqiao) daily.				
G7201	Wuxi – Shanghai	09:33 – 10:29	56 min	¥59.5
Note: There are 202 bullet trains from Wuxi (or Wuxi East) to Shanghai (or Shanghai Hongqiao) daily.				

Train number	From – To	Departing – Arriving	Duration	Price
D3054/D3051	Changzhou North – Shanghai Hongqiao	14:13 – 15:18	1 hr 05 min	¥49.5
Note: There are 188 bullet trains from Changzhou (or Changzhou North) to Shanghai (or Shanghai Hongqiao) daily.				
G7554	Hangzhou East – Shanghai Hongqiao	08:00 – 09:07	1 hr 07 min	¥73
Note: There are 120 bullet trains from Hangzhou (or Hangzhou East) to Shanghai Hongqiao daily.				
G7532	Ningbo – Shanghai Hongqiao	08:36 – 10:40	2 hr 04 min	¥144
Note: There are 42 bullet trains from Ningbo to Shanghai Hongqiao daily.				
G7504	Wenzhou South – Shanghai Hongqiao	06:35 – 10:15	3 hr 40 min	¥226
Note: There are 27 bullet trains from Wenzhou South to Shanghai Hongqiao daily.				
G177	Ji'nan West – Shanghai Hongqiao	08:06 – 12:14	4 hr 08 min	¥398.5
Note: There are 52 bullet trains from Ji'nan West to Shanghai Hongqiao daily.				
G224/G221	Qingdao – Shanghai Hongqiao	06:57 – 13:36	6 hr 39 min	¥518
Note: There are 3 more bullet trains from Qingdao to Shanghai Hongqiao daily (09:24 – 16:13; 13:53 – 20:45; 16:24 – 23:04).				
D3096/D3093	Hefei – Shanghai Hongqiao	10:51 – 13:58	3 hr 07 min	¥150
Note: There are 53 bullet trains from Hefei to Shanghai (or Shanghai Hongqiao) daily.				
D3122	Fuzhou South – Shanghai Hongqiao	06:50 – 13:20	6 hr 30 min	¥261.5
Note: There are 20 more bullet trains from Fuzhou South to Shanghai Hongqiao daily.				
D3208	Xiamen North – Shanghai Hongqiao	09:03 – 17:07	8 hr 04 min	¥328
Note: There are 13 bullet trains from Xiamen North to Shanghai Hongqiao daily.				
D92	Nanchang – Shanghai Hongqiao	08:10 – 14:27	6 hr 17 min	¥237
Note: There are 15 bullet trains from Nanchang to Shanghai Hongqiao daily.				
D2282	Shenzhen North – Shanghai Hongqiao	07:00 – 19:00	12 hr 00 min	¥478.5
Note: There are 3 more bullet trains from Shenzhen North to Shanghai Hongqiao (08:45 – 20:57; 09:55 – 22:12; 10:45 – 22:58), and 2 regular trains from Shenzhen to Shanghai South daily (13:09 – 07:58; 15:46 – 10:20).				
Z98/Z95	Shijiazhuang North – Shanghai	22:35 – 09:35	11 hr 00 min	seat/sleeper: ¥156.5/¥288.5
Note: There are 5 more regular trains from Shijiazhuang (or Shijiazhuang North) to Shanghai daily.				
D294/D291	Zhengzhou – Shanghai Hongqiao	09:00 – 15:37	6 hr 37 min	¥236.5
Note: There are 22 bullet trains from Zhengzhou to Shanghai Hongqiao daily.				
Z98/Z95	Taiyuan – Shanghai	19:45 – 09:35	13 hr 50 min	seat/sleeper: ¥180.5/¥331.5
Note: There are 3 more regular trains from Taiyuan to Shanghai daily (16:58 – 15:06; 22:15 – 13:19; 21:24 – 15:51).				
G578/G575	Changsha South – Shanghai Hongqiao	13:12 – 20:11	6 hr 59 min	¥468.5
Note: There are 4 more bullet trains from Changsha to Shanghai Hongqiao daily.				
D308/D305	Xi'an North – Shanghai	21:01 – 07:48	10 hr 47 min	¥338
Note: There are 13 more regular trains from Xi'an to Shanghai daily taking from 14.5 to 22 hours.				
D3096/D3093	Hankou Wuhan – Shanghai Hongqiao	08:07 – 13:58	5 hr 51 min	¥258
Note: There are 22 bullet trains from Wuhan (or Hankou Wuhan, or Wuchang Wuhan) to Shanghai Hongqiao daily.				
G1202/G1203	Harbin West – Shanghai Hongqiao	08:19 – 21:26	13 hr 07 min	¥898
G1226/G1227	Shenyang North – Shanghai Hongqiao	07:50 – 17:59	10 hr 09 min	¥759
Note: There are 8 more bullet trains from Shenyang North to Shanghai Hongqiao daily.				
G1251/G1254	Dalian North – Shanghai Hongqiao	08:25 – 19:08	10 hr 43 min	¥787
G1212/G1213	Changchun – Shanghai Hongqiao	08:47 – 20:18	11 hr 31 min	¥827.5
Note: There is 1 more bullet trains from Changchun West to Shanghai Hongqiao (09:46 – 21:26), and 4 more regular trains from Changchun to Shanghai or Shanghai South daily.				

Top Attractions

pg 55

Lujiazui Financial District

pg 59

Shanghai Science &
Technology Museum

pg 62

The Bund

pg 68

People's Square

pg 71

Nanjing Road

pg 76

Yu Garden & Old Town

pg 80

French Concession

pg 84

Xintiandi

pg 85

Tianzifang

pg 87

Longhua Temple

pg 95

Qibao Ancient Town

pg 99

Ancient Yi Garden

Lujiazui Financial District

Chinese name: 陆家嘴金融区 (Lùjiāzuǐ Jīnróngqū)
Transport: Take subway Line 2 to Lujiazui Station (陆家
嘴 站) right in the heart of the financial district. Ferries are
also available from the Bund.

Lujiazui in the Pudong District is the urban grove where Shanghai's tallest buildings have sprouted up from the mud of the Huangpu River almost overnight, creating a wonderland of futuristic urban scenery. Actually, if someone had shown Westerners a picture of today's Lujiazui in 1990, they would probably have assumed it was an image from a science-fiction blockbuster. If the Bund is a romantic symbol of Shanghai's commercial past, Lujiazui is the opulent embodiment of China's financial future. Welcome to the nerve center of the world's emergent economic superpower!

History

The history of the Lujiazui Financial District is rather short. Centuries ago, it was nothing but a sleepy fishing village with hardly any inhabitants. During the days of Mao, the area was home to a little more than low-lying homes, warehouses and some simple factories. However, after Deng Xiaoping's economic reforms, Lujiazui blasted into the sky. In the early 1990s, the Shanghai municipal government purposefully promoted Lujiazui as a new financial area, mainly because of its proximity to the Bund.

During the last few decades, Lujiazui has undergone a radical metamorphosis. It is now home to several skyscrapers of enormous height. The iconic Oriental Pearl Tower is located in Lujiazui, as is the massive Shanghai Tower, which (upon it's completion in late 2014) will be the second tallest building in the world.

Today, the gigantic skyscrapers just aren't financial giants, but also tourist sites that define the city. Many have viewing platforms at truly stupendous heights, and there are even cafes, restaurants, shopping plazas, exhibits and bars nestled inside of them.

Layout

The symbolism of Pudong's Lujiazui is very strong, with old Shanghai on one side of the river (i.e the Bund) and the gleaming new on the other (i.e. Lujiazui). However, Lujiazui is not large – it only

occupies a total area of just over 31 sq km (12 sq mi). You can easily visit all of these structures within in an hour.

Famous Buildings

The Oriental Pearl TV Tower

Chinese name: 东方明珠塔 (Dōngfāng Míngzhū Tǎ)
Admission: ¥160
Hours: 9:00-21:30
Phone: 5879 1888
Website: www.orientalpearltower.com/en
Address: 1 Century Ave, Pudong New Area (浦东新区浦东世纪大道 1 号)

This unique structure is probably the most iconic symbol of downtown Shanghai. It is composed of eleven separate spheres of varying size supported by massive columns. Including the antenna, this monument to China's resurgence has a height of 468 m (1,535 ft), and was the tallest building in China from 1994 until 2007.

Fifteen observation decks can be visited in the Oriental Pearl. The tallest one is the Space Module at over 350 m (1,148 ft). A high-end shopping mall is in the tower, along with various restaurants. One of the restaurants revolves, much like the restaurant at the top of Seattle's Space Needle (only at a much more impressive height), and the Oriental Pearl offers unmatched views of Shanghai on clear days. Also in the basement of the tower is the....

Shanghai History & Development Exhibition

Chinese name: 上海城市历史发展陈列馆 (Shànghǎi Chéngshì Lìshǐ Fāzhǎn Chénlièguan)
Admission: ¥35
Hours: 9:00-23:00
Phone: 5239 2222

This museum focuses on the history of the city from its opening to foreign trade in the 1840s to the communist takeover in 1949. It is currently hosted on a temporary basis in the exhibition room of the Oriental Pearl Tower. The museum contains many interesting artifacts and photographs from Shanghai's past.

Jinmao Tower

Chinese name: 金茂大厦 (Jīnmào Dàshà)
Admission: ¥120
Hours: 8:30-21:30
Phone: 5047 0088
Address: 88 Century Ave (世纪大道 88 号)

In 2006, the "Golden Prosperity Building" edged out the Oriental Pearl as China's tallest building, standing at a height of 420.5 m (1,380 ft). The design is distinctively postmodern, incorporating elements of traditional Western skyscrapers with Oriental forms – specifically the shape of China's classical tiered pagodas. It is also supremely

Chinese name: 上 海 环 球 金 融 中 心 (Shànghǎi Huánqiú Jīnróng Zhōngxīn)
Admission: ¥120
Hours: 8:00 – 23:30 (last entry at 23:00)
Website: swfc-shanghai.com
Address: 100 Century Ave (世纪大道 100 号)

lucky. Eight is the most auspicious number in Chinese culture, and the Golden Prosperity Building has 88 floors and sits at 88 Century Avenue. Even the building's exterior is divided into layered octagons. Most of the building's space is rented out to offices, but it also features a large food court in the basement and a viewing tower near the top.

This tower's anchor tenant is the five-star, 555-room Shanghai Grand Hyatt hotel, which occupies floors 53 to 87. It is one of the highest hotels in the world, second in Shanghai only to its sister property, the Shanghai Park Hyatt, occupying the 79th to 93rd floors of the adjacent Shanghai World Financial Center.

A ticket to the observation deck on the 88th floor costs ¥120, however, there is not much to do there except observe. We highly advise you go to Cloud 9, the bar on the 87th floor instead, where you can enjoy the same view while sipping a beverage of choice at leisure. The bar is a very upscale venue and therefore pricey, but ¥120 will get you a drink or two, and your time and money will be better spent. Also, stop by the lobby at the 56th floor to see the atrium; the view is no less stunning from below. A collection of restaurants, including The Grill, the Italian Cucina, the Japanese Kobachi and the Patio Lounge, are located on this floor.

The architectural one-upsmanship of Pudong continued in 2008 with the completion of the Shanghai World Financial Center. At 494.3 m (1,621.7 ft), it is (at the time of writing) the tallest completed building in Shanghai. The exterior of the building is less traditional than the Oriental Pearl or Jinmao Tower, but it is nevertheless quite impressive. It was designed by Kohn Pedersen Fox, one of the most famous architectural firms in the world, and the viewing deck has a unique transparent "sky walk" that is not for the faint of heart.

You may think that the World Financial Center looks like a gigantic bottle opener. If so, you're not the only one – for many others agree with you – though this was not the original plan for the building. The original blueprints had the rectangular gap at the top planned as a perfect circle, but some nationalists in the government pointed out that it looked awfully similar to the Japanese flag. Having anything close to a symbol of Japan, China's main rival, in the center of Shanghai, the city the Japanese invaded and occupied just a mere six decades ago,

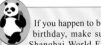

If you happen to be in Shanghai on your birthday, make sure to stop by at the Shanghai World Financial Center with your passport; you can go to all the decks free of charge.

was deemed unacceptable. In the end, the architects changed the hole at the top to its current shape, which no one can deny looks exactly like a bottle opener.

Soon, however, it will no longer be the tallest in the city. Competition continues with the...

Shanghai Tower (Shànghǎi Zhōngxīn; 上海中心)

Due to be finished at the end of 2014, the Shanghai Tower will be the tallest building in Shanghai and the second tallest building in the world upon completion. At 632 m (2,073 ft), it is only dwarfed by the Burj Khalifa in the United Arab Emirates, which soars at a massive 829.8 m (2,722 ft). By the time you read this it might be open, so take a stroll by to check out the progress. Even if it's not finished, it's still a mesmerizing sight.

Riverside Promenade

The Riverside Promenade is directly to the west of the Pearl Oriental TV Tower at the curb of the Lujiazui peninsula. While many

visitors on the other side of the Huangpu are busy snapping their cameras at the behemoths towering the skies above, many forget that the old buildings of the Bund and the rest of Shanghai make for an amazing shot as well. Take a walk along this pleasant riverside park to do just that, or use this oasis of tranquility in the middle of bustling Pudong to catch your breath alongside the stressed-out business crowds out on their lunch/cigarette breaks.

Cautions

The Lujiazui Financial District is clean and orderly. The main risks come from dizziness at observation platforms. Also, this may go without saying, but do not attempt any base-jumping from the top of the buildings; a foreign visitor lost his life in an attempt in 2004.

Furthermore, the new trend of "building climbing" has become popular. In February of 2014, two Russians snuck into the incomplete Shanghai Tower and climed to the very top. They video-recorded the whole thing, and we must say that it's absolutely incredible! Check out this site to see it all:

v.baidu.com/kan/XzZa/Xzi6?fr=v.hao123. com/search.

The embarrassed Shanghai municipal government reportedly beefed up security so that no one else would attempt this extremely dangerous stunt. A few days later, however, two Chinese guys were still able to sneak in and scale the massive building, prompting the government to once again proclaim that this incident will not happen again under their watch. Hmmm...

Shanghai Science & Technology Museum

Chinese name: 上海科技馆 (Shànghǎi Kējìguǎn)
Admission: ¥60
Hours: 9:00- 17:15
Phone: 6854 2000
Website: www.sstm.org.cn (English)
Address: 2000 Century Ave, Pudong (浦东新区世纪大道 2000 号)
Transport: Subway - Line 2, Shanghai Science & Technology Museum Station, Exit 4

Edward Teller, the father of the Hydrogen bomb, once proclaimed that "the science of today is the technology of tomorrow." And so it seems fitting that any trip to Shanghai, once penned as "The City of Tomorrow," should allow for a visit to Shanghai's Science and Technology Museum. Family-friendly and with lots of activities (and buttons) made for the hordes of excited children, there is no shortage of things to see and do here. Although its collection of cinemas and abundance of 3D and 4D movies have earned it a reputation for being the largest educational science cinema in Asia, be warned, there is a lack of English movies and, overall, the museum is definitely more aimed at entertaining and educating the Chinese market than it is to satiating information seeking foreigners.

Layout

Located in Shanghai's Pudong area and neighboring the vast expanse of Century Park, this museum is best tackled by first visiting the information desk located to the right of the entrance and grabbing an English tourist map. There will be a suggested route on the back, with three to choose from depending on what you hope to get out of your visit. Following a route is strongly advised as the museum is huge.

3D Printer in action

Particular highlights of the museum are its interactive exhibitions, including a demonstration on the conversion of energy via gigantic silver balls, a life sized board game to get lost in and a piano-playing robot with whom you can sing a song. There's even a 3D printer in action: we had the pleasure of seeing a tea cup get "printed" into being (it took a while). Arachnophobes beware: there is an entire exhibition dedicated to spiders.

059

The museum is spread over three floors. Those fascinated with traveling amongst the stars will love the third floor, which houses models of various space shuttles and rockets in the **Space Navigation Exhibition**. Take a full health and fitness test in the **Human and Health Exhibition,** or check out the more cerebral of human achievements in the **Light of Exploration Exhibition**, which delves into Einstein's Theory of Relativity and Thomas Hunt Morgan's Fruit Fly experiment.

The second floor is where you will find the **World of Robots**, which puts on demonstrations of the wonders of artificial intelligence. Pit your wits against a robot in a game of Go Bang; the aim of the game is to get five of your colored stones in a row, vertically, horizontally or diagonally. You can also try your chances and see how you fare against a robot in an archery competition, or see a robot take on a Rubik's cube muddled up by an unsuspecting member of the public. We have our money on the robot.

On the first floor there is a whole section called the **Spectrum of Life** which depicts natural scenery from Yunnan Province, complete with artificial greenery and a stone forest in which you can get lost. The **Light of Wisdom Exhibition** on this floor is a fixture that's ubiquitous in many science and technology museums around the world, although the sheer size of this one makes it stand out, as it has hundreds of interactive science stations and as many plasma globes as you could possibly want to get your hands on.

All in all, the museum is fun and worth a visit if you're looking for an activity to keep the kids occupied, but it's not a Top Attraction on its own. However, if you throw in some other attractions to visit in the surrounding area, it turns this site into something worthwhile.

Nearby Attractions

Century Park

Chinese name: 世纪公园 (Shìjì Gōngyuán)
Admission: ¥10
Address: 1001 Jinxiu Rd, Pudong (浦东新区锦绣路 1001 号)

Known as the Central Park of Shanghai, Century Park is where you can rent bikes and boat around the many beautiful waterways. They also hold the annual International Music Fireworks Festival, which happens over three days during September and October.

AP Plaza

Chinese name: 亚太盛汇休闲购物广场 (Yàtài Shènghuì Xiūxián Gòuwù Guǎngchǎng)
Address: 2000 Century Ave, near Yingchun Rd (世纪大道 2000 号 , 近迎春路)

This underground market is the largest of its kind in Pudong. It's found underneath the Science and Technology Museum, and there is an entrance inside the metro station. Here you can find shoes, luggage, clothes and fake designer gear, as well as a tailor market that custom makes dresses, suits, and anything else that tickles your fancy. It's perfect for stocking up on knick knacks or gifts.

Oriental Art Center

Chinese name: 上海东方艺术中心 (Shànghǎi Dōngfāng Yìshù Zhōngxīn)
Address: 425 Dingxiang Rd, near Century Ave (浦东新区丁香路 425 号)

Man vs machine in Chinese chess

This international concert hall was designed by Frenchman Paul Andreu, who is also responsible for designing Shanghai's futuristic Pudong Airport. The Oriental Art Center is representative of a blossoming five petal flower. Constructed of metal, wood and glass, each petal contains a different space: an entrance hall, concert hall, opera hall, performance hall, and gallery exhibition space.

Long Museum

Chinese name: 龙美术馆 (Lóng Měishùguǎn)
Admission: ¥50
Hours: 9:30-17:00 (last admission 16:00)
Website: www.thelongmuseum.org/en
Address: 210, Lane 2255, Luoshan Rd, near Huamu Rd, Pudong (罗山路 2255 弄 210 号，近花木路)

Just a short taxi ride or walk away from the Science & Technology Museum, the Long Museum is worth a visit if you're in the area. This private art museum houses the art collection of tycoon Liú Yìqiān (刘益谦), and it's currently the largest private art gallery in all of China. So much more than just a billionaire's show and tell, the museum's mission to educate visitors on China's illustrious artistic history and its place in the contemporary art market has turned this wonderful place into a testament to 1,000 years of Chinese art.

There are some clunkers on the first floor contemporary exhibit, but most of the paintings evoke the unaffected exuberance of a young and energetic art community. On the basement floor there are grade school students' own renditions of the material, which can either make you say "aw that's so cute" o "did I really come here for this?"

The second floor contains the obligatory socialist realist paintings, but they've obviously been selected by an uncommonly discerning curator. All of them are more artistically interesting than the simple triumphalism they overtly express, and one poster of Chairman Mao is pretty interesting in what it openly proclaims: "Representing the Chinese people, I express resolute support for the righteous struggle of American black people!"

The top floor is given over to traditional art and ceramics and tops everything off with three pieces of true treasure: a pair of stunning lacquer standing screens, an imperial throne – all from the Qing Dynasty – and some of the most beautiful pieces of Chinese furniture you'll see in Shanghai. The art on display will doubtlessly change and hopefully grow, but it's a good bet that the intelligence and energy of this museum won't fade. For art lovers this is an absolute must see.

The Maglev Train (pg 147)

Chinese Traditional Medicine Museum (pg 110)

Gallery of Antique Music Boxes (pg 111)

The Bund

Chinese name: 外滩 (Wài Tān)
Admission: FREE
Hours: 24 hours
Location: On the west bank of the Huangpu River, directly across from the skyscrapers in the Pudong Financial District. Nanjing Rd intersects the Bund near the north end, and Zhongshan Rd (中山路) is the main drag on the Bund running between the historic buildings and the waterfront area.
Transport:
Subway – Lines 2 & 10 go to Nanjing East Rd Station (南京东路站); the Bund is a ten-minute walk to the east. If coming from Pudong (or if you just want some great views) take the Huangpu River ferry for ¥2.
Bus – 33, 37, 55, 65, 123, 135, 305, 307, 576, 910, 912 or 928

You are essentially required to visit the Bund at least once during your Shanghai trip. The iconic views on the shores of the Huangpu River leave deep and lasting impressions of Shanghai's colonial past along with the spectacular economic ascent of Shanghai's present. Get ready for tons of tourists, a taste of history and urban splendor on par with the world's greatest cities.

A well-known Western investor based in Hong Kong once warned his clients "Don't visit the Bund on your first day in China." Why? Because he thought it would give first-time visitors an unrealistic impression of China's level of development. Whether you plan to visit the Bund on your first day in Shanghai or not, remember that while the Bund certainly is in China, China is not the Bund. Nevertheless, this stretch of land offers perhaps the best view of China's ongoing efforts to transform from a broken land of fallen imperial glory into the center of the global economy.

History

In 1842 the British Empire defeated China's Qing Dynasty in the First Opium War. China's rulers were then forced to sign the Treaty of Nanking, granting the British control of Hong Kong and forcing China to open five ports to British trade. Shanghai was among those five ports, and the British quickly set up shop on the west banks of the Huangpu River, just to the north of the old walled city of Shanghai.

This area was called the Bund (a Persian term meaning embarkment or levvee) and it was coined by the Sassoon's: a family of Iraqi Jews that had moved to Shanghai in order to reap tremendous profits in international trade. Ambitious merchants from France, the United States, Russia and Japan soon joined the Sassoons and other British citizens and subjects.

These foreign businesspeople soon established the Shanghai International Settlement, which included much of what is the center of modern Shanghai – including the Bund and Nanjing Road. Although it was technically Chinese land, foreigners were allowed to conduct their own affairs in the zone and even had their own Municipal Council, fire brigade, court houses and police force.

In the early 20th century, the Bund was the center of finance and trade in China. Grand hotels, banks and trading houses were built upon the banks of the Huangpu, while swanky clubs and cinemas soon followed. Many of these striking structures, which combine Western architectural elements with Chinese influences, can still be found in the area.

At first the British and Americans dominated the International Settlement, but by the 1920s both groups were well outnumbered by the Japanese. Once a victim of unequal treaties at the hands of Western powers themselves, the Japanese government used its growing industrial and military might to dominate China. When Japan began a full-scale invasion of China in 1937, the Bund and its surroundings were full of Chinese refugees. Soon running battles were being fought between Chinese guerrillas and Japanese occupation forces on the outskirts of the area, and after the attack on Pearl Harbor, Japanese forces invaded the International Settlement.

The Bund stagnated during the Mao era, but with the recent opening of China's economy to the outside world, the Bund has arisen from the ashes of neglect and mismanagement – much like China itself. It once again serves as a symbol of the opportunities China presents to the world, this time with the Chinese firmly in charge of it.

Layout

Located on the west bank of the Huangpu River, the Bund is essentially the apex of modern Shanghai. The main drag of the Bund stretches for almost 3 km (1 mi). The tallest buildings in Shanghai and the Oriental Pearl Tower are directly across the river in Pudong.

Towards the north side of the Bund is **Huangpu Park** (Huángpǔ Gōngyuán; 黄浦

公园). This is Shanghai's oldest and smallest municipal park, established by the forces of the Shanghai Foreign Settlement who didn't allow Chinese people to enter. Bruce Lee famously kicked down a "No dogs or Chinese allowed" sign outside the entrance in his classic *Fists of Fury*. Now a huge statue of Mao Zedong can be found in Huangpu Park, along with **The Bund Historical Museum** (Wàitān Lìshǐ Ji'niàn'guǎn; 外 滩 历史纪念馆 ; admission: FREE; phone: 5308 8987; hours: 9:00-16:30, closed Sat & Sun). Huangpu Park is also where Suzhou Creek empties into the Huangpu River. Cross Waibaidu Bridge to get to the Astor House and Broadway Mansions hotel (pg 172), and explore the eerie, old-fashioned streets of the **North Bund** neighborhood.

On a lovely note, Huangpu Park also has the **Valentine Wall**, a long wall full of multicolored flowers, which displays different geometric designs and is a favorite place for couples to go on romantic strolls and take pictures with either the flowers or Pudong in the background.

At the end of Nanjing Road on the Bund is **Chen Yi Square** (Chényì Guǎngchǎng; 陈毅广 场), on which stands the statue of Chen Yi, the first mayor of Shanghai in New China. The statue is cast with bronze and stands at 5.5 m (18 ft) on top of a 3.5 m (11.5 ft) pedestal of polished red granite.

From south to north, the main buildings on the Bund are:

Asia Building (Yàxìyà Dàlóu; 亚细亚大楼)

Right at the southern end of the Bund, this structure was originally known as the McBain Building and it once housed Royal Dutch Shell's Asiatic Petroleum Division. Some say that at night the mournful howls of early 20th century Chinese oil riggers can still be heard from its confines.

Address: 1 Zhongshan East Rd

The Shanghai Club (Shànghǎi Zǒnghui Dàlóu; 上海总会大楼)

This building was erected in 1910 as the home for the most exclusive men's club in the Foreign Settlement. It was once the site of the world's longest bar and the world's most despicable expats. As was traditional, membership was restricted to white males "of a certain class." Nowadays it operates as a luxury hotel and class restrictions are enforced by economics rather than British guns and discrimination.

Address: 2 Zhongshan East Rd

Asia Building · The Shanghai Club · The Union Building · The Nissin Building · China Merchants Bank Building · The Great Northern Telegraph Company Building

The Union Building (Yǒulì Dàlóu; 有利大楼)

Once home to insurance companies, this building was completed in 1916 in the neo-Renaissance style. The old Union Building currently houses a luxury shopping center run by a Singaporean company.

Address: 3 Zhongshan East Rd

The Nissin Building (Rìqīng Dàlóu; 日清大楼)

A Japanese shipping company built this structure in 1925. It is now an upscale restaurant with an excellent view from the terrace.

Address: 5 Zhongshan East Rd

China Merchants Bank Building (Zhōngguó Tōngshāng Yínháng Dàlóu; 中国通商银行大楼)

This building housed the first Chinese-owned bank in China and it's currently home to a Dolce & Gabbana flagship store. This is one of the oldest standing structures on the Bund, having been completed in 1887.

Address: 6 Zhongshan East Rd

The Great Northern Telegraph Company Building (Dàběi Diànbào Gōngsī Dàlóu; 大北电报公司大楼)

Built in 1907 as the site of the first telephone switch in Shanghai in 1882, now it houses The Bangkok Bank.

Address: 7 Zhongshan East Rd

The China Merchants Steam Navigation Company Building (Lúnchuán Zhāoshāng Zǒngjú Dàlóu; 轮船招商总局大楼)

Built in 1901, this is the Bund's remaining example of neo-Classical external-corridor architecture hailing from the late Victorian era.

Address: 9 Zhongshan East Rd

The Pudong Development Bank Building (Pǔdōng Fāzhǎn Yínháng Dàlóu; 浦东发展银行大楼)

When this grand structure was completed in 1923, it was the second tallest bank building in the world. Formerly the headquarters of the Shanghai and Hong Kong Development Bank (HSBC), its original owners lost a bid to reclaim the structure in 1996. It was once famously (and very arrogantly) referred to as "the most luxurious building between the Suez Canal and the Bering Strait." Such arrogance was not entirely unfounded – it is a magnificent neo-classical structure. Make sure to view the mosaic ceiling murals from the main lobby.

The China Merchants Steam Navigation Company Building The Pudong Development Bank Building Shanghai Customs House The Bank of Communications Building The Russo-Chinese Bank Building The Bank of Taiwan Building The North China Daily News Building The Chartered Bank Building Palace Hotel The Yokohama Specie Bank Building The Yangtsze Insurance Association Building Jardine Matheson Building

Address: 12 Zhongshan East Rd

Shanghai Customs House (Hǎiguān Dàlóu; 海关大楼)

Perhaps the most iconic building on the Bund, the Customs House features a miniature version of London's Big Ben. It was built on the site of a previous Chinese customs house, and unlike many of the Bund's classical structures, it still serves its original purpose.

Address: 13 Zhongshan East Rd

The Bank of Communications Building (Jiāotōng Yínháng Dàlóu; 交通银行大楼)

The last building to be built on the Bund in 1948, it now houses the Shanghai Council of Trade Unions.

Address: 14 Zhongshan East Rd

The Russo-Chinese Bank Building (Huá'é Dàoshèng Yínháng Dàlóu; 华俄道胜银行大楼)

Now the Shanghai Foreign Exchange Trade Center, this building was finished in 1901.

Address: 15 Zhongshan East Rd

The Bank of Taiwan Building (Táiwān Yínháng Dàlóu; 台湾银行大楼)

Constructed in 1924, it now houses the China Merchants Bank.

Address: 16 Zhongshan East Rd

The North China Daily News Building (Zìlín Xībào Dàlóu; 字林西报大楼)

Built in 1921, it housed the at the time North China Daily News, the most influential English language newspaper in Shanghai. Today, it's where AIA Insurance calls home.

Address: 17 Zhongshan East Rd

The Chartered Bank Building (Màijiālì Yínháng Dàlóu; 麦加利银行大楼)

The Shanghai headquarters of the Standard Chartered Bank moved here upon the building's 1923 completion. Today you'll find designer shops and a creative exhibition space.

Address: 18 Zhongshan East Rd

Palace Hotel (Huìzhōng Fàndiàn; 汇中饭店)

Today it forms part of the Peace Hotel and is one of the nicest lodgings on the Bund.

Address: 19 Zhongshan East Rd

Sassoon House (Shāxùn Dàshà; 沙逊大厦)

Along with the Cathay Hotel, this building was built by Sir Victor Sassoon and the top floor was the residence of Victor Sassoon. At ten stories, it is the tallest building on the Bund. Just like the heady times of the 1930s, this building is still famous for hosting jazz performances. Today, it forms the other part of the Peace Hotel.

Address: 20 Zhongshan East Rd

The Bank of China Building (Zhōngguó Yínháng Dàlóu; 中国银行大楼)

This is perhaps the only building on the Bund whose name hasn't changed. It was originally planned to be taller, but Victor Sassoon insisted no other building in the area should be taller than his.

Address: 23 Zhongshan East Rd

The Yokohama Specie Bank Building (Zhèngjīn Yínháng Dàlóu; 正金银行大楼)

Built in 1924, the Yokohama Specie Bank Building is now the Industry and Commerce Bank of China building.

Address: 24 Zhongshan East Rd

The Yangtsze Insurance Association Building (Yángzǐ Dàlóu; 扬子大楼)

This 1916 building is now the Shanghai branch of the Agricultural Bank of China.

Address: 26 Zhongshan East Rd

Jardine Matheson Building (Yíhé Yángháng Dàlóu; 怡和洋行大楼)

Built in 1920, it housed the then-powerful Jardine Matheson company. Today it is now known as the House of Roosevelt, which houses the Rolex Flagship Store, the largest wine cellar in China, three restaurants and a private club.

Address: 27 Zhongshan East Rd

The Banque de l'Indochine Building (Dōngfāng Huìlǐ Yínháng Dàlóu; 东方汇理银行大楼)

Currently the Everbright Bank of China Shanghai branch, this structure was built in 1914 and once housed the French bank, Banque de l'Indochine.

Address: 29 Zhongshan East Rd

British Consulate General (Yīngguó Zǒng Lǐngshìguǎn; 英国总领事馆)

Once the Consulate-General of the United Kingdom, the building has been renovated and in 2010 re-opened as 1 Waitanyuan (Wàitānyuán Yīhào; 外滩源壹号), a private dining facility for the government. Part of the site also houses the Peninsula Hotel.

Address: 33 Zhongshan East Rd

Other Attractions

The Bund Sightseeing Tunnel

Chinese name: 外滩观光隧道 (Wàitān Guānguāng Suìdào)
Admission: ¥50 (one way); ¥70 (round trip)
Hours: 8:00–22:30 (May-Oct); 8:00–22:00 (Nov-Apr)
Location: There are two entrances: one at 300 Zhongshan East 1st Rd, Puxi (中山东一路 300 号); the other is across the water at 2789 Binjiang Ave, Pudong (滨江大道 2789 号) near the massive Oriental Pearl TV Tower.
Transport: Subway – Line 2, get off at Lujiazui Station (陆家嘴站) in Pudong side

Do you remember the scene in *Willy Wonka and the Chocolate Factory* (the 1971 original) in which an enigmatic Mr Wonka takes a group of unsuspecting children on a psychedelic ride into a tunnel full of strange and confusing visions? Did you watch that and think to yourself "Gee, that looks like fun"? If so, The Bund Sightseeing Tunnel is the perfect Shanghai attraction for you.

Running under the Huangpu River between the Bund and Shanghai's tallest buildings in Pudong, the Bund Sightseeing Tunnel was originally envisioned as a moving pedestrian walkway. Instead, automated electric cars were imported from France and a local Chinese company designed the multimedia effects, which are somewhat reminiscent of a particularly nasty acid trip.

Zhang Bin, the sales director of the Bund

Sightseeing Tunnel, explains the presentation thusly: "The story is about going from space into the core of the Earth and out again. We couldn't show the dirty Huangpu, which has no fish, so we went for something bigger and better. It's the only tunnel like it in the world."

To be fair, the Bund Sightseeing Tunnel certainly is unique. Where else can one see multicolored lights and wacky arm-flailing inflatable characters while listening to strange disembodied voices under a Chinese river in the comfort of a French-made electric vehicle? There are also carnival games at the entrance and a series of bizarre and overpriced souvenirs.

The compartments of the sightseeing trains are completely transparent, allowing for a 360 degree view. For all its tackiness, this is one of the top ten most popular tourist attractions in Shanghai; over two million people have traveled through the Bund Sightseeing Tunnel since its opening in 2000. (Of course, this popularity could be due to its location between the two most famous places in the city.) It is simultaneously a monument to the kitschy side of Chinese tourism and the creativity of (presumably) corrupt city planners.

The Bund Sightseeing Tunnel is also a reliable alternative to taking the ferry across the Huangpu River for those prone to seasickness – so long as you're not also prone to motion sickness. The total length of the tunnel is 646 m (2,122 ft) and the ride takes about five minutes.

Fuzhou Road

Right off the Bund in between Hankou Road and Guangdong Road, this little alley has the largest concentration of stores in all of Shanghai. They consist mostly of small art, music, DVD and book stores, so if you're looking to re-stash your reading list, this is the perfect place to do it. Take a look in **Shanghai Book City**, and also keep an eye out for **Shanghai Classics Bookstore**, **Chinese Science and Technology Bookstore** and the **Beijing Opera Theatre**.

Huangpu River Cruises

The best way to capture the true essence of the Bund is to see it from the water; this way you'll simultaneously catch a view of glamorous Pudong as well. It's one of the most enjoyable and relaxing ways to get the most out of Shanghai, so we highly recommend booking a tour.

There are several boat companies that you can use. Our favorite is **Shanghai Huangpu River Cruise Company** (address: 219 Zhongshan East 2nd Rd; phone: 6374 4461,

6374 0091; website: www.pjrivercruise.com). They have a full afternoon cruise from 14:00-17:00, along with a three-hour morning cruise during the summer. Prices run from ¥50-¥100, depending on seating, and some of the more expensive tickets also come with snacks and beverages. If you're not willing to invest three hours of your time, try one of the shorter, one-hour-long cruises (¥25-¥35) or their hour-long nighttime cruise from the Bund to the Yangpu Bridge (¥35-¥70).

Make sure to check their website for up-to-date prices, tour packages, and departure times since they change depending on the season. You can either book tickets with them directly or through your hotel or hostel. If you don't fancy what Shanghai Huangpu River Cruise Company has to offer, there are plenty of other liners that you can choose from, so ask your hotel or hostel to see if they have any recommendations. However, we must add that they are basically all the same, differing only in where they depart from and end at.

Rockbund Art Museum (pg 114)

Cautions

Like all the places heavily trafficked by foreign visitors in Shanghai, the Bund has its share of tricksters. Don't fall for the infamous Tea or Art House Scams wherein travelers are approached by locals and taken to exorbitantly priced tea houses or art galleries. See page 294 for more on scams. Also beware of pickpockets; they're known to target unsuspecting foreigners here.

People's Square

Chinese name: 人民广场 (Rénmín Guǎngchǎng)
Address: Smack-dab in the middle of Shanghai's Puxi District (浦西), Nanjing Rd marks the northern boundary, Huangpi North Rd (黄陂北路) is to the west and Xizang Middle Rd (西藏中路) is to the east. People's Square is bisected by People's Avenue (人民大道).
Transport: Subway – Lines 1, 2 & 8 all stop at People's Square Station (人民广场站)

People's Square is the urban heart of Shanghai, the spoke in the wheel of one of humanity's most dynamic cities. Not only is People's Square worth a visit in and of itself, it is also home to many of Shanghai's most famous cultural sites. The Shanghai Museum, the MOCA, the Shanghai Urban Planning Exhibition Hall and People's Park are all located within or near People's Square.

This broad open space is surrounded by some of the most unique and cutting-edge architecture in the world. People's Square has an overabundance of photographic treasures, and visitors will surely gaze with wonder at the futuristic buildings. Despite its supremely central urban location, People's Square has many quiet and peaceful areas as well.

Some of Shanghai's tallest and most distinct buildings line People's Square. Be sure to look out for **Tomorrow Square** (Míngtiān Guǎngchǎng; 明天广场) to the west and the

285 m- (934 ft)-tall tower which is home to a **Marriot Hotel** (Wànháo Jiǔdiàn; 万豪酒店 ; address: 399 Nanjing West Rd; phone: 5359 4969) and some of Shanghai's most expensive apartments. The top of the building is a distinctive inverted "V."

Also of note is the **Shimao International Plaza** (Shìmào Guójì Guǎngchǎng; 世茂国际广场) just northeast of People's Square. This building is home to a high-end hotel – **Le Royal Méridien Shanghai** (Shànghǎi Shìmào Huángjiā Àiměi Jiǔdiàn; 上海世茂皇家艾美酒店 ; address: 789 Nanjing East Rd; phone: 3318 9999). It also has clubs and shopping. The Shimao International Plaza is topped by twin spires, giving it the appearance of an oversized cartoon robot.

There is an underground shopping mall here that's known as **"Fakes Market"** by the expat community. While the shops are perhaps nothing special, there is a mock-up of a Shanghai street from the 1930s that is worth a visit. Use subway Exit 10 to reach Fakes Market.

History

During Shanghai's colonial days, the area that is now People's Square was located within the International Settlement. This flat piece of dry earth – a valuable commodity in soggy Shanghai – was the site of the racecourse for the Shanghai Race Club. After the victory of the People's Liberation Army in 1949, gambling was banned and the huge

open grounds were converted into a public square. Once a place for play, it is now the political and spiritual heart of Shanghai: the municipal government is run from a large building in the center of People's Square. The racecourse's clubhouse was also put to new use when it served as the Shanghai Art Museum, but it was moved in 2012 to China's World Expo Pavilion (see pg 115).

Layout

People's Square is roughly 1 km (less than 1 mi) long and half a kilometer wide. Nanjing Road is the northern border, Xizang Middle Road is to the east and is bisected by People's Avenue. People's Park occupies the northern half of the square, while the grounds of the Shanghai Museum are to the south. The Shanghai municipal government, the Shanghai Urban Planning Exhibition Center and the Grand Theatre are all in the middle of People's Square.

Attractions

Shanghai Museum

Chinese name: 上海博物馆 (Shànghǎi Bówùguǎn)
Admission: FREE
Hours: 9:00-17:00 (last admission at 16:00); closed Mon
Website: www.shanghaimuseum.net/en

The Shanghai Museum showcases historical Chinese art through 11 permanent exhibitions covering everything from ancient Chinese bronze, jade and ceramics to seals, calligraphy and more. You'll also find a special display showing the traditional costumes of all of China's 55 officially recognized ethnic minorities, as well as an excellent collection of coins that traveled the Silk Road from as far afield as India, Persia, Arabia and Rome. This is perhaps the best museum in Shanghai for those interested in Chinese history, and that's well represented by the shape of the building itself, which resembles a *ding* (鼎) – an ancient Chinese ritual cooking vessel. Historical artifacts from other countries come in on a rotating schedule. Check their website for info.

People's Park (Rénmín Gōngyuán; 人民公园)

This pleasant and well-maintained park occupies most of People's Square. There are numerous pathways, dozens of species of local and foreign flora, a pond and a funfair within the park. The people of Shanghai are generally a thirsty crowd who love a good opportunity to spend money, so many trendy cafes can be found within People's Park as well. It's famous both domestically and internationally for the **Shanghai Marriage Market** (every weekend from noon to 17:00), a special area in the park where marriage advertisements are carefully written and posted by hopeful relatives of prospective brides and grooms.

Shanghai Urban Planning Exhibition Hall

Chinese name: 上海城市规划展示馆 (Shànghǎi Chéngshì Guīhuà Zhǎnshì Guǎn)
Admission: ¥30
Hours: 9:00-17:00 (last admission at 16:00); closed Mon
Website: www.supec.org/english/english_page.htm

You might think that a museum in Mainland China's richest city could afford better English translations on their website: "Get to know Shanghai begins from here!" Nevertheless, this small museum, located

right in the middle of People's Square near the municipal buildings is well worth a visit. The highlight of this six-story museum is a huge-scale model of the entire city of Shanghai. Here visitors can partially live out any Godzilla fantasies (but no touching, and certainly no smashing!). The Shanghai Urban Planning Exhibition Center also has many images from Shanghai's past and plans for the future. Be careful though, the future can be painful – one of our authors discovered that his apartment will no longer exist in the not-so-distant future.

Shanghai Grand Theater

Chinese name: 上海大剧院 (Shànghǎi Dàjùyuàn)
Admission: ¥ 50
Hours: 9:00-11:00
Phone: 021 6386 8686
Website: www.shgtheatre.com (in Chinese)

Just to the west of the municipal headquarters lies the Shanghai Grand Theatre. This elegant structure houses three separate performance venues – a lyrics theater, a drama theater, and a studio theater. "Grand" in this case means "good" instead of "big," and these venues are surprisingly intimate, with the largest (the lyrics theater) having only 1,800 seats. However, all the stages are equipped with high-technology mechanical, audio and visual systems. The building is open to the public in the morning and special performances can be seen in the evenings.

Shanghai Museum of Contemporary Modern Art (MOCA)

Chinese name: 上海当代艺术馆 (Shànghǎi Dāngdài Yishùguǎn)
Admission: ¥50 regular admission; ¥25 for children under 1.3 m, seniors over 70, students with valid ID and the disabled.
Hours: The hours constantly change, depending on the exhibit, so check the website for specific opening hours. Usually they're open from 10:00-18:00 (Sun-Thu) and 9:00-19:00 (Fri, Sat and national holidays).
Website: www.mocashanghai.org

Located in People's Park, the MOCA is the city's finest gallery dedicated to modern art. It's a little bizarre and all of the exhibits are over the top, similar to other museums of its kind around the world, but it is definitely interesting, especially for those who are into the new art scene. Check their website to see what special exhibit they're hosting when you're in town; they're always bringing something fresh.

Madame Tussauds Shanghai (pg 106)

Cautions

The normal warning about Art and Tea Scams apply to People's Park (see pg 294 for Scams). There are often deaf beggars who hand out cards in English and Chinese asking you to buy their plastic key chains. Fake monks also try to get "donations" from visitors. If someone tries to put something in your hand, don't accept it.

Nanjing Road

Chinese name: 南京路 (Nánjīng Lù)
Admission: FREE (but you can spend lots of money if you want to!)
Hours: 24 hours
Location: Near the center of town in Puxi (浦西), Nanjing East Rd starts at the Bund in the east and goes west to People's Square. Nanjing West Rd runs from People's Square to the Jing'an District. The total length of both sections of Nanjing Rd is about 6 km (3.5 mi).
Transport: Subway – Line 2 has the very convenient Nanjing East Rd (南京东路站) and Nanjing West Rd (南京西路站) Stations. A small wheeled trolley runs along Nanjing East Rd for ¥5.

Welcome to shoppers' paradise – the veritable Heart of Darkness for modern China's consumer culture. This is the most famous, the busiest, and the most iconic pedestrian shopping street in China. Nanjing Road links East and West both geographically and metaphorically; Chinese tourists flock to the local outlets of famous foreign brands while Western tourists marvel at ingenious wares manufactured in the East.

It has been said, "You have not been to Shanghai unless you have been to Nanjing Road." Even if shopping is not your cup of tea, a walk down Nanjing Road is almost obligatory for all visitors to Shanghai. Besides access to nearly every type of good you could ever want – and many you didn't even know existed – Nanjing Road offers excellent opportunities for people watching and general contemplation of the human condition.

With the exception of a wheeled electrical trolley, Nanjing Road is strictly a pedestrian street. Even at its most crowded, this strip of concentrated commercial crassness is very convenient for walking. Most shops are in business from 10:00 to 22:00, though many of the nearby cafes, bars and restaurants are open until much later. Although shopping options are somewhat more limited at night, the street lights up in the evening in a spectacular urban array of color and motion.

History

Nanjing Road was originally named "Park Lane," the most important West-East thoroughfare in the International Settlement. It has been known as Nanjing Road (once romanized as Nanking Road) since 1862, but in Chinese it was simply "Big Street" (Dà Mǎlù; 大马路).

It has long hosted various tailors, jewelers, and dry goods stores, and it once even had a casino. By the early 20th century, this prime stretch of commercial real estate was home to at least eight different department stores.

During the Japanese invasion, Nanjing Road was the scene of a deadly tragedy. A Chinese plane accidentally dropped a bomb on the road, partially destroying two department stores and killing over 600 people.

Beginning in the year 2000, Nanjing Road was designated as a pedestrian-only shopping street. This decision was a very effective strategy for urban planning; since its implementation, Nanjing Road has drawn increasing numbers of shoppers, tourists, and famous brands. Over one million people visit the stretch of road every day!

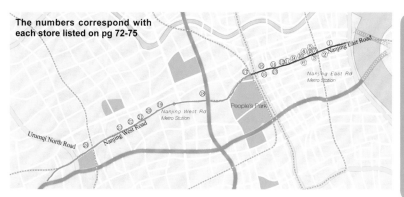

The numbers correspond with each store listed on pg 72-75

The Chinese name of the pedestrian street (Nánjīnglù Bùxíngjiē; 南京路步行街) is inscribed by Shanghai's former Party Secretary and General Secretary of the CCP – Jiang Zemin (江泽民)

Layout

Nanjing East Road runs from the Bund on the bank of the Huangpu River to People's Square. Nanjing West Road begins at People's Square and continues to Wulumuqi North Road (乌鲁木齐北路). Most malls are concentrated near the eastern side. Numerous shops and restaurants can also be found on **Jiujiang Road** (九江路), which is just to the south of Nanjing East Road and runs parallel to the famous shopping artery.

Famous stores on Nanjing East Road, from east to west, include:

1. Shanghai Sports Goods General Shop (Shànghǎi Tǐyù Yòngpǐn Zǒngdiàn; 上海体育用品总店)

This is the largest sporting goods store in Shanghai. You can buy everything from wristbands to inflatable kayaks. It is decidedly upmarket.

Address: 160 Nanjing East Rd
Phone: 6321 4789

2. Shanghai Laojiefu Department Store (Shànghǎi Lǎojiéfú Shāngshà; 上海老介福商厦)

The oldest department store on the strip, Laojiefu has been in operation since 1860. It specializes in high-quality fabrics, including wool and silk.

Address: 257 Nanjing East Rd

3. Hongyi Plaza (Hóngyī Guójì Guǎngchǎng; 宏伊国际广场)

Hongyi Plaza was designed by the Kaili Sen Architects. There are some very popular brands here, such as Ebase, Esprit, Bacca Bocca, Vero Moda, etc. There are many large international retail flagship stores here too, such as Lee, Adidas and Puma. In Hongyi Plaza, you can also enjoy various Chinese and Western cuisines, including Shanghainese, Sichuan, seafood, Korean BBQ, ice cream and much more. There are also some very popular snacks, such as small *xiaolongbao*, *baozi*, fried plain buns, bean paste cakes, dumplings and wontons.

Address: 299 Nanjing East Rd
Phone: 6352 5333
Hours: 10:00-22:00

4. Hengdali Clocks & Watches Co (Hēngdálì Zhōngbiǎo Gōngsī; 亨达利钟表公司)

Located in one of the trendiest buildings on Nanjing Road, this watchmaker is the biggest in China and amongst the oldest. It now offers many famous high-end foreign brands.

Address: 1/F, Hualian Commercial Bldg, 340 Nanjing East Rd
Phone: 6323 5678

5. Caitongde Pharmacy (Càitóngdé Táng; 蔡同德堂)

The façade of the building is built in the traditional Shanghainese style and inside one can find an overwhelming variety of traditional Chinese medicine. Check out the "medicinal liquor" with snakes and seahorses preserved within, and *mahuang* (麻黄) – a Chinese grass that contains the stimulant ephedrine.

Address: 450 Nanjing East Rd
Phone: 6322 1160

6. Landmark Department Store (Shànghǎi Zhìdì Guǎngchǎng; 上海置地广场)

Landmark Department Store has ten air-conditioned floors of clothing, toys, handicrafts, cosmetics and accessories.

Address: 409-459 Nanjing East Rd
Phone: 6350 0225

7. Shaowansheng Foodstuffs Company (Shào Wànshēng; 邵万生)

This is the best place on Nanjing Road to buy bizarre packaged food. It features local specialties such as pickled chicken feet, snails and crab, as well as dried fruits and vegetables palatable for the Western tongue.

Address: 414 Nanjing East Rd
Phone: 6322 4443

8. Laofengxiang Jewellers (Lǎofèngxiáng Yínlóu; 老凤祥银楼)

This is the flagship store of one of the oldest jewelers in Shanghai. Make sure to check out the intricate dragon-phoenix style rings.

Address: 432 Nanjing East Rd
Phone: 6351 6299

9. Wuliangcai Optical (Wúliàngcái Yǎnjing Gōngsī; 吴良材眼镜公司)

Wuliangcai Optical features high-end glasses with optometry services and English-speaking staff. Don't worry if you can't see it – there are two other branches on Nanjing Road.

Address: 2/F, 456 Nanjing East Rd
Phone: 6350 0538

10. Zhangxiaoquan Knives & Scissors Store (Zhāngxiǎoquán Dāojiǎn; 上海张小泉刀剪)

Zhangxiaoquan is a famous, time-honored Chinese brand that was first established in Hangzhou during the Qing Dynasty (1644-1912). It offers various quality knives and scissors for different uses.

Address: 490 Nanjing East Rd
Phone: 6322 3858

11. Shanghai Souvenirs Shopping Center (Shànghǎi Lǚyóupǐn Shāngshà; 上海旅游品商厦)

Don't let the name fool you – you won't find cheap plastic knickknacks here. Instead, this mall specializes in precious stones and wooden handicrafts.

Address: 558 Nanjing East Rd
Phone: 6322 5409

12. Silk King (Zhēnsī Dàwáng; 真丝大王)

This commercial building is named Silk King because of the various excellent silk products it provides. You can buy exquisite silk clothing or cloths here.

Address: 588 Nanjing East Rd

13. Baodaxiang Children's Shopping Center (Bǎodàxiáng Qīngshàonián Értóng Gòuwù Zhōngxīn; 宝大祥青少年儿童购物中心)

Abandon hope all ye who enter! This mall is specifically targeted towards children and the adults who enable them.

Address: 685 Nanjing East Rd
Phone: 6322 5122

14. Shanghai Number One Food Store (Shànghǎishì Dìyī Shípǐn Shāngdiàn; 上海市第一食品商店)

Brave the crowds here to check out the amazing variety of dried mushrooms, ginseng and sea cucumbers, as well as more tempting snacks like sunflower seeds, nuts, dried fruit and tea. If you plan to go food shopping or you are just hungry for nibbles, this store is a good choice.

Address: 720 Nanjing East Rd
Phone: 6322 2777
Website: www.firstfood-cn.com (in Chinese)

15. Bailian Shimao International Plaza (Bǎilián Shìmào Guójì Guǎngchǎng; 百联

世茂国际广场）

Eight floors of high-end shops, cafes, and restaurants can be found at Balian Shimao International Plaza. FYI: the restrooms within are particularly pleasant.

Address: 819 Nanjing East Rd
Phone: 3313 4718

16. Shanghai Number One Department Store (Shànghǎishì Dìyī Bǎihuò Shāngdiàn; 上海市第一百货商店)

Rounding off Nanjing East Road is this eight-story monument to socialism with Chinese characteristics.

Address: 830 Nanjing East Rd
Phone: 6322 3344

Famous stores on Nanjing West Road, from east to west, include:

17. New World City (Xīnshìjiè Chéng; 新世界城)

Most of this massive shopping complex is underground. Besides the usual array of stores, Shanghai New World also features dining options and restaurants.

Address: 2-88 Nanjing West Rd

18. Taobao Market (Táobǎo Chéng; 淘宝城)

This is the true Chinese masterpiece on Nanjing Road. Tourists can find expensive watches and brand-name clothing in shopping malls in nearly every city on the face of the earth, but only the Taobao Market has three floors of fake brand-name electronics, clothes, and accessories. Make sure to really bargain hard – you should never pay more than a third of what you would pay for the real thing. Shop owners here are particularly egregious: they often quote initial prices of more than five times what they are willing to accept. As always with bargaining, think of the maximum price you are willing to pay before you begin the haggling process. Ignore shop owners' pleas of "I have to make a living" – it's a trap

to make you pay. If all else fails, walk away.

Address: 1-3/F, Nanzheng Tower, 580 Nanjing West Rd

19. TAG Heuer

For the largest TAG Heuer in China, look no further.

Address: 990-992 Nanjing West Rd
Phone: 6218 9195

20. Westgate Mall (Méilóngzhèn Guǎngchǎng; 梅龙镇广场)

The first twelve floors of this massive commercial building are dedicated to shopping. The 12th to 37th floors of the main building are for office use. Many famous multinational corporations have their Chinese headquarters here.

Address: 1038 Nanjing West Rd
Phone: 6218 7878

21. CITIC Square (Zhōngxìn Tàifù Guǎngchǎng; 中信泰富广场)

Restaurants, bookstores, and an exhibition hall coexist here with a plethora of brightly lit shops.

Address: 1168 Nanjing West Rd
Phone: 6218 0180

22. Plaza 66 (Hénglóng Guǎngchǎng; 恒隆广场)

Plaza 66 boasts the best collection of luxuries from numerous top world brands. Want to see the latest fashion? You do not need to fly to New York, Milan, Paris or London; Plaza 66 will show you the latest masterpieces from world-class designers such as Christian Dior, Chanel, Prada, Hermes, Louis Vuitton, Fendi, Cartier, Celine, Bvlgari, Loewe, Lagerfeld, Hugo Boss, Escada, Versace, Lanvin, Piaget and more. There are many fashion release

074

conferences and shows held in the atrium of Plaza 66.

Address: 1266 Nanjing West Rd

23. Shanghai Centre (Shànghǎi Shāngchéng; 上海商城)

Also known as the Portman, this is a comprehensive public service center offers a shopping mall, an exhibition hall, a theater, apartments, offices, the Portman Ritz-Carlton Hotel, restaurants, clubs and other personal service establishments. The shopping mall with three floors has a number of top grade stores selling men's clothing, women's clothing, jewelry and imported food. It also has many luxury fashion retailers such as Salvatore Ferragamo, Gucci, Marc Jacobs, Chopard, Paul & Shark and Stefano Ricci.

Address: 1376 Nanjing West Rd
Website: www.shanghaicentre.com

24. Jiuguang Department Store (Jiǔguāng Bǎihuò; 久光百货)

At the west end of Nanjing Road lies the Jiuguang (Nine Bright) department store. It is home to the first Tiffany's in Shanghai and the largest Burberry store in all the Orient. There is also a beauty salon on the ninth floor.

Address: 1618 Nanjing West Rd
Phone: 3217 4838

Other Nanjing West Road Attractions

Bubbling Well Road Apartments

If you exit Nanjing West Road Metro Station and head west for a few paces, take your first left and walk down the Bubbling Well Road Apartments (Jìng'ān Biéshù; 静安别墅). Here, you'll spot a kind of typical Shanghai apartment design style known as *longtang* (弄堂) or *lilong* (里弄). Similar to the hutongs of Beijing and the shikumen of Shanghai, these small alleyways are traced with old, worn-down, cracking, red-brick apartment complexes. Their rustic appearance is an attraction all in themselves, and you might want to hurry up and see them before they get bulldozed or repolished into the next Xintiandi.

If you keep heading south on this road past the *longtang* architecture, you'll eventually hit the former residence of Mao Zedong (pg 126).

Jing'an Temple (pg 134)

Madame Tussauds Shanghai (pg 106)

Cautions

Be wary of Chinese who approach you to "practice English" – the Tea Scam and Art Scam (see pg 294) are alive and well on Nanjing Road. Also be wary of pickpockets. Occasionally, some dealers will try to sell hashish to Western tourists on Nanjing Road, but just remember that marijuana and hashish are very illegal here and the consequences are dire; purchase at your own risk! Stay well hydrated on hot summer days and make sure to wear comfortable shoes.

Yu Garden & Old Town

Chinese name: 豫园 (Yùyuán)
Admission: ¥40 (Apr-Jun, Sep-Nov); ¥30 (July-Aug, Dec-Mar)
Hours: 8:30-17:00 (last admission at 16:40)
Website: www.yugarden.com.cn (in Chinese)
Address: 132 Anren St, near Fuyou Rd (安仁街132号, 近福佑路)
Transport: **Subway** – Line 10, get off at Yuyuan Station, Exit 1; walk east on Fuyou Rd for one block

By whatever mysterious process these things are decided, Yu Garden is one of the most popular and widely cited tourist attractions in Shanghai. This has produced a few effects. First, the entire surrounding area for a block or more has been turned into an enormous souvenir market that can often be a little seedy (though that's not necessarily a bad thing if you're looking for an interesting experience). Second, the sheer amount of Chinese and foreign tourists constantly flooding the place makes for a hectic, not entirely pleasant atmosphere. Third, the garden itself is the best traditional Chinese garden in Shanghai, which isn't exactly great praise considering that Suzhou (pg 235) on the other hand, has peaceful and grand gardens to spare. However, if you haven't seen a traditional Chinese garden before, it's definitely worth the experience, and to be fair, there are a few very photo-friendly spots found only in the garden. The other attraction is the City Gods Temple, which is decidedly not the best temple in Shanghai to see, though for ¥10 it's worth a look, seeing as you're already here.

Before You Go

Prepare your wallet for the variety of souvenirs and trinkets for sale at the souvenir market, and be ready for some fierce bargaining. Shore up your vigilance to defend against the many aggressive touts (and possibly scammers).

History

Yu Garden was constructed by a wealthy government official for his father in the 1500s. Gardens were a preferred method of displaying wealth, especially in southern China, and this display was so grand that it would eventually bankrupt its creator. It passed through numerous hands thereafter, and underwent its share of destructions and alterations. Most recently, the garden was damaged by the Japanese army during the war and later repaired in 1961. As to what it was really like during its prime, one can only wonder. The gardens of the rich were meant to be the setting of endless parties and pleasures for the owner and his guests, and all we have now to evoke that time is the much altered and comparatively empty grounds of the present. But a walk through the gardens is enough time to imagine them in their wonders, and the splendors they contained were great enough to squander a man's fortune.

City temples house the local gods that protect a city, and most cities in ancient China had them. These local gods were often deceased men who had achieved distinction in their lives and so were honored with divinity by the state, a completely natural custom for a society that also practiced ancestral worship. The Shanghai temple was converted to a site for state-sponsored veneration in the Ming Dynasty and was dedicated to two famous government officials of antiquity. In the Qing Dynasty, a third was added: a general who had defended Shanghai in the First Opium War and attained deification for his sacrifices.

Layout

The great strength of Yu Garden is that it seems to possess almost every element a traditional Chinese garden could possibly contain. There are numerous pagodas, bridges across small ponds, promontories on top of sculpted rocks (called rockeries for what it's worth), elegant rooms with antique furniture, an artificial cave and carefully curated plant life. These are common enough in any traditional garden, but this one has two aces up its sleeve in the form of wall roofs that rise up intermittently to become roaring dragon heads (as awesome as it sounds) and a five-ton hunk of porous yellow jade that was apparently scavenged from a sunken ship on its way to the imperial palace.

What the garden lacks is any sense of serenity or expanse due to the fact that all of this is unfortunately crammed into a small space that's made even smaller by the hordes of people constantly walking through it. This problem is exacerbated by the layout, which seems intentionally designed to move people through the garden on a single track, as if the whole thing is an amusement park ride. There's also surprisingly little greenery since most of the ground is covered in stone and concrete to facilitate the heavy traffic. Needless to say, these features are not common in other traditional gardens and they stunt the experience here. Nevertheless, Yu Garden is an enjoyable introduction to this particular aspect of Chinese culture and chock full of photo-ops. And those dragons are indeed pretty cool.

At the entrance of Yu Garden is the **Mid-Lake Pavilion Tea House** (hours: 8:30-21:30; ¥25 and up for tea), perhaps the most famous teahouse in all of Shanghai. It's a beautiful – no, wait – gorgeous place that used to be part of the garden itself; the ideal setting to take off your shoes and sip a cup of China's favorite and catch a break from your long day of sightseeing.

City Gods Temple

Chinese name: 城隍庙 (Chéng Huáng Miào)
Admission: ¥10
Hours: 8:30-16:00

Located near the exit of the garden is the City Gods Temple (which is also small and usually contains too many people). The temple has a hall of golden statues of the three city gods as well as a few other deities for good measure. It'll be interesting for anyone who hasn't seen a Chinese temple before, but there are far better temples to visit in Shanghai

(Jing'an Temple, Jade Buddha Temple and Longhua Temple come to mind). Those who don't particularly care to pray for protection to Shanghai's minor deities might find this temple skippable. The front courtyard is visible from the ticket gate, and there isn't much beyond it, so take a look and judge for yourself whether it's worth venturing in.

Chenxiangge Nunnery

Chinese name: 沉香阁 (Chénxiāng Gé)
Admission: ¥10
Hours: 7:00-17:00
Address: 29 Chenxiangge Rd (沉香阁路 29 号)

Believe it or not, this is an actual nunnery, not just some tourist trap with actresses dressed in coffee brown robes chanting the lyrics to prayers they don't believe in. Showing off the more cultural side of the city, the Chenxiangge Nunnery is a lovely temple to explore. Check out the **Hall of Heavenly Kings**, the **Great Treasure Hall** (where you can witness prayer sessions from the monks), and **Guanyin Tower** (¥2) for a replica effigy of a male-looking Guanyin godess (this ancient religious transgender sometimes looks like a female and other times it resembles a male).

Yu Garden Bazaar

The souvenir market surrounds these two attractions and, to be frank, the experience is not for everyone. It's all a little cheap and a little grimy, and the crowds are exhausting, but it's all in good fun, and there are a few shops with eccentric offerings (though mostly the usual suspects: jade, silk, jewelry, funny T-shirts, figurines... you know the drill).

Are you paying too much? Even if you bargain, which you should, the answer is undoubtedly yes, because this is a tourist spot and prices are higher even for Chinese tourists. But the only real rule of bargaining is that you should decide what price you're willing to pay and walk away if you don't get it. The seller will either lower the price or not, but there are many other shops selling the same thing, so it doesn't matter. When you've got what you want, don't worry about whether you could have gotten it cheaper. If you were willing to pay the price in the first place, then it's a good deal regardless of what other people pay, and that's all that matters.

There's a similarly simple rule to avoid annoying touts and scammers who frequent this area. Don't talk to or even acknowledge anyone who accosts you in a tourist market.

Easy, right?

The many food establishments are mostly overpriced and usually not that good. One small shop called **Nanxiang Bun** (pg 180) is famous for its *xiaolongbao*, Shanghai's culinary pride and joy, but there's always a line.

Old Town

The area to the east, west and south of Yu Garden is considered Old Town. So after spending time with the flocks of tourists at one of Shanghai's most famous tourist attractions and paying homage to the City Gods Temple, get lost in the winding alleys of Old Town to check out some fusty old houses and architecture that, unlike the rest of Shanghai, hasn't been renovated much or at all since the heydays of the 1920s and '30s. Also be sure make your way to some of our other recommended attractions in Old Town listed below.

Dongjiadu Cathedral

Chinese name: 董家渡天主堂 (Dǒngjiādù Tiānzhǔtáng)
Admission: FREE
Address: 185 Dongjiadu Rd (董家渡路 185 号)
Transport: Take bus 55, 65, 305, 324, 576, 581, 736, 801 or 868, get off at Zhongshan South Rd & Dongjiadu Rd Stop (中山南路董家渡路站). Walk south along Zhongshan South Rd for about 100 m (328 ft), and turn right into Dongjiadu Rd. Continue walking for about 100 m (328 ft). The cathedral is on your right side.

Formerly known as the St Francis Xavier Church, this mid-19th century white-washed cathedral is the oldest in Shanghai. Built by Spanish Jesuits, the architecture is gorgeous and there are oil paintings of the Virgin Mary and baby Jesus inside.

Cool Docks

Chinese name: 时尚老码头 (Shíshàng Lǎo Mǎtóu)
Address: 479 Zhongshan South Rd (中山南路 479 号)
Website: www.thecooldocks.com
Transport: **Subway** – Line 9, Xiananmen (小南门) Station, Exit 2, walk east along Wangjiamatou Rd (王家码头路) for about 400 m (1,312 ft), then turn left into Zhongshan South Rd, continue walking for about 300 m (984 ft) and the Cool Docks is on your right

Considered to be the next Xintiandi, the up-and-coming Cool Docks is, as the name suggests, a cool place to hang out. Like its cousin Xintiandi, this area is dominated by red-brick shikumen houses and courtyards, and numerous little cafes, boutique hotels and bars are sprouting up all along the river bank. It's becoming quite the trend-setter these days, and it seems that more and more locals and expats are flocking here each year. Right now it's worth a glance, but we'd imagine that it'll become a Top Attraction within five years. Before and after pics, anyone?

Sunny Beach

Chinese name: 老码头阳光沙滩 (Lǎomǎtóu Yángguāng Shātān)
Admission: ¥50
Hours: 10:00-22:00
Phone: 133 1167 3735
Address: Zhongshan South Rd (中山南路)
Transport: Just north of Cool Docks

Believe it or not, yes, there is a beach in Shanghai. Now, we're not saying that the city is becoming the next Rio by any means, and we don't recommend jumping in the river for a dip, but there are volleyball nets, beach chairs and a wonderful view of Pudong on this man-made sand strip. Come along on a non-polluted day for an alternative experience.

Fazangjiang Temple

Chinese name: 法藏讲寺 (Fǎzàng Jiǎngsì)
Admission: ¥5
Hours: 7:30-16:00
Address: 271 Ji'an Rd (吉安路 271 号)
Transport: **Subway** – Lines 8 or 10, Laoximen (老 西 门) Station, Exit 4., walk west along Fuxing Middle Rd (复兴中路) for about 180 m (590 ft), then turn left into Ji'an Rd, continue walking for about 60 m (197 ft) and the temple is on your left

This is a small and simple temple complex hidden on the back streets of Old Town. There's a statue of Sakyamuni, gilded *luohans*, and even a cool statue of the Buddhist god of the underworld, Dizang Wang. It's not the best attraction of Old Town, but if you're in the neighborhood and have a few *kuai* to spare, why the hell not?

Confucian Temple (pg 101)

Xiaotaoyuan Mosque (pg 139)

French Concession

Chinese name: 上海法租界 (Shànghǎi Fǎzūjiè)
Admission: FREE
Recommended time for visit: 3-4 hours
Address: Huaihai Middle Rd (淮海中路)
Transport:
Subway – Line 10, Shanghai Library Station (上海图书馆站). Line 1, Hengshan Rd Station (衡山路站), Changshu Rd Station (常熟路站), Shaanxi South Rd Station (陕西南路站), or Huangpi South Rd Station (黄陂南路站)

The tree-lined streets of the former French Concession are most responsible for giving Shanghai's central areas their pleasing sense of urbanity and warmth. It can be said that much of what's unique about Shanghai (in comparison with other Chinese cities) can be found in this area, which comprises much of the city proper from the southwest of People's Square to Xujiahui. The best way to sample its essence is to walk along its central avenue, Huaihai Middle Road, making occasional detours to the north and south to view some of the architectural highlights. Huaihai itself is a shopping street with more character and almost as much variety as Nanjing Road. On the west end and to the north lies Fuxing Park, whose French and Chinese aesthetics present the perfect starting point for an exploration of the many historical buildings in the surrounding area. To Huaihai's north runs Changle Road, which features its own collection of small shops, a cluster of hotels and a theater, all built in the art deco style.

Before You Go

This chapter focuses on five streets in order to best encapsulate the French Concession experience. There will be a lot of walking if you want to see everything, and you also might want to use the Parisian sample itinerary on page 278 for starters. One good way to see most of it would be to walk up Huaihai Road, then go to Fuxing Park in the southeast. After exploring that area a bit, go back up to Changle Road (north of Huaihai) to see the old hotels. Every street in this area has its own charms and surprises, so feel free to explore. If you really enjoy the French Concession experience, you could plan one day to walk up Huaihai and then down Changle, ending at Hengshan Road for drinks, and save the southern portion and Fuxing Park for another day. That area is the best place in Shanghai for a leisurely stroll, and you can end your time there walking south to either Yongkang Road or Tianzifang.

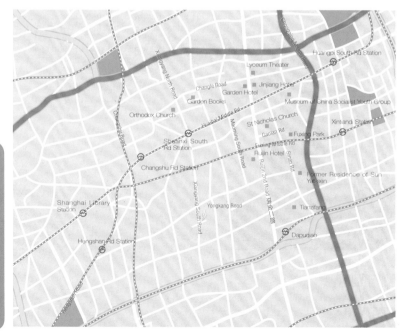

History

Although most Shanghailanders – the name for foreigners who made their home in Shanghai – eventually settled in the foreign concessions along the north side of the Huangpu River, the French decided to keep their large concession separate. The main artery, now Huaihai Middle Road, was called Avenue Joffre and it contained the shopping district. Platane trees were brought from Europe to shade its pedestrians, and now the tree is used widely in urban areas all over China. Later on, after the Russian Revolution, the Concession received an influx of refugees fleeing the country, which explains the two Eastern Orthodox churches to be found in the area.

Use of the term "French Concession" can actually be a touchy subject for the local government. Although even guidebooks created by the government use the term sometimes, there have been a few instances in the recent past when businesses have received fines for using the name in their advertisements. They say that the use of this term purportedly glorifies China's colonial past, a testament to the so-called "Century of Humiliation."

Layout

Huaihai Middle Road

Your journey east on Huaihai can begin at a few different places. You can start at the Shanghai Library Metro Station and see Shanghai's massive library; or you can cut one kilometer off your walk and start at Changshu Road Station, where the shops begin in earnest; or you can start at Huangpi South Road Station, where Huaihai really begins to earn its title as Shanghai's coolest shopping street. Whichever one you choose, the shopping will get steadily more upscale and transition from street-side shops to malls with luxury brands as you go east, eventually climaxing at Shaanxi South Road with a collection of department stores that give Nanjing Road a run for its money.

Also along the road are a few historical sites, including a little alley that contains a free museum in honor of the **China Socialist Youth Group** (Zhōngguó Shèhuìzhǔyì Qīngniántuán Zhōngyāng Jīguān Jiùzhǐ Jì'niànguǎn; 中国社会主义青年团中央机关旧址纪念馆; address: 1-6, Lane 567, Huaihai Middle Rd; 卢湾区淮海中路567弄1-6号; phone: 5382 3370), many of whose members became leading intellectuals of the time. The museum is really just a glorified wall of pictures, but

it's located in a cluster of shikumen houses that are worth the detour to see.

There's nothing to see beyond the Xizang South Road intersection. The rest of the attractions detailed below can all be reached from Huaihai Road.

Fuxing Road

Just east of Chengdu South Road is a little street called Yandang Road that branches off to the south of Huaihai; it's distinguishable by its palm trees. At the end of this street is the entrance to **Fuxing Park** (pg 119), the "Frenchest" place in the whole French Concession. The park begins with a fountain and a tree-lined walkway that could be mistaken for the pedestrian boulevards of Paris. The park is brimming with character and an absolute must for anyone who wants to fully experience the French Concession.

Leaving through the western exit of Fuxing Park will lead you to the intersection of Sinan Road and Gaolan Road. Cross the intersection and walk a little west on Gaolan Road to see the **St Nicholas Russian Orthodox Church** (Shèng Nígǔlāsī Jiàotáng; 圣尼古拉斯教堂; 16 Gaolan Rd; pg 140), which now houses a café. Walk south on Sinan Road towards Fuxing Road and the **Former Residence of Sun Yat-sen** (pg 128) will be to your left. Turn left on Fuxing Road – which runs parallel to Huaihai – and your options multiply.

Walking west, you'll meet Ruijin 2nd Road, and if you turn south you'll encounter the expansive gardens of the **Ruijin Hotel** (Ruìjīn Bīn'guǎn; 瑞金宾馆; address: 118 Ruijin 2nd Rd; phone: 6472 5222) after two blocks. If you continue on for 800 m (2,624 ft) more you'll come to **Tianzifang** (pg 84).

If you go west down on Fuxing Road from Fuxing Park, you will hit Xiangyang South Road, and if you turn south there, one block away are the cafes and fantastic bars of **Yongkang Road** (pg 199). This entire area is densely foliated and dotted with stores, cafes and fruit stands, so you can't go wrong no matter which way you go.

Nanchang Road

Right above Fuxing Park to the north runs Nanchang Road. This is a good little street for window shopping on a nice Sunday afternoon, and they have plenty of men's and women's attire, shoes and accessories. There are also a few places to browse for antiques, too. If you keep walking to the east along Nanchang Road and cross Chongqing South Road, the street turns into Xingye Road, and two blocks later you'll hit **Xintiandi** (pg 84).

Changle Road

Changle Road runs parallel to Huaihai just to the north. The entire street, starting at the intersection of Chongqing Middle Road north of Huaihai, contains the exact same type of

St Nicholas Russian Orthodox Church

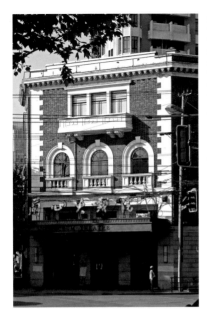

Changle Rd; phone: 5404 8728; website: www.gardenbooks.cn), which sells a wide variety of English-language books. You could also take Xiangyang North Road back down to Huaihai Road, that features another **Orthodox church**, now boarded up. In any event, after all this walking, you can sit for a drink in one of the bars on **Hengshan Road**, starting south of the intersection just to the west of Changshu Road Station (it's actually called Baoqing Road at this point but soon becomes Hengshan Road).

Xinle Road

This small street of just a few blocks is directly south of Changle Road. It doesn't have all the big designer name brands that Changle or Huaihai has, but if you're looking for something a little more down to earth, Xinle is a nice option.

Other Attractions

Propaganda Poster Art Center (pg 108)

Public Security Museum (pg 107)

Former Residences of Zhou Enlai, Sun Yat-sen & Song Qingling (pg 127-129)

See next page for Xintiandi & Tianzifang (both in the French Concession)

small boutiques that Huaihai has without the department stores of Huaihai's eastern end. If you're coming from Fuxing Road, any street going north will get you here, although a good choice would be **Maoming South Road**. The intersection between this street and Changle Road is ground zero for elegant old architecture, and along Maoming South Road there are plenty of stores to get custom made *qipao* (traditional Chinese dresses) for the ladies and tailored suits for men.

To the southeast of the intersection is a large estate containing the **Jinjiang Hotel** (Jǐnjiāng Fàndiàn; 锦 江 饭 店 ; address: 59 Maoming South Rd; phone: 3218 9888), which has two art deco-inspired buildings on the premises. To the southwest is the **Garden Hotel** (Huāyuán Fàndiàn; 花园饭店 ; address: 58 Maoming South Rd; phone: 6415 1111; website: www.gardenhotelshanghai.com), which retains its original opulent interior. Take a look around the lobbies of all these buildings; they don't disappoint. On the northeast corner is the **Lyceum Theater** (Lánxīn Dàxiyuàn; 兰 心 大 戏 院 ; address: 57 Maoming South Rd; phone: 6217 8530), still open 80 years after its construction. Just north from the Lyceum is another large example of colonial era architecture.

Changle Road can be followed all the way to Changshu Road, where you should look out for **Garden Books** (address: 325

Xintiandi & Tianzifang

Xintiandi

Chinese name: 新天地 (Xīntiāndi)
Admission: FREE
Hours: 24 hours
Recommended time for visit: 2 hours
Address: Begins on the northeast block of Madang Rd (马当路) and Zizhong Rd (自忠路) intersection
Website: www.shanghaixintiandi.com/xintiandi/en
Transport: Subway – Line 10, Xintiandi Station, Exit 6; walk north on Madang Lu for one block

Xintiandi is a two-block development predominantly made up of restaurants, shops, galleries and a large mall. Unlike most of central Shanghai, this is a car-free zone. Xintiandi's fame comes mainly from the fact that all this is housed in replica two-story houses of the Shanghai shikumen style. There are more authentic ways to experience this unique local architecture, but there are few places in Shanghai with such a pleasant atmosphere in which to eat al fresco – all of the restaurants have ample outdoor seating. Also, this area is easily accessible for the foreign visitors to Shanghai. The businesses and restaurants are all very upscale, and

most of the food is international. The only free attraction in this area is a small park (Tàipíngqiáo Gōngyuán; 太平桥公园) to the east side, which is mostly occupied by a large pond. It's meant to be a centerpiece for the still developing district, but it's cut off from the shops of Xintiandi by a wall and a road, and its north side is a construction zone for yet unfinished luxury high-rises.

Before You Go

Prepare accordingly if you plan to eat outside. The district is definitely upscale, and prices are commensurate with what you'd encounter back home at a place of similar quality.

History

The shikumen is well represented here, but this guide's article on Tianzifang (next page) gives an in-depth treatment of shikumen architecture and its importance in Shanghai's history. What's notable about Xintiandi's particularly ornamented interpretation of the style is that it's received a surprising amount of attention, both with China and internationally, considering the fact that it's basically just a themed commercial district. Articles have been written about the place in the *New York Times* and *The New Yorker*, and Shanghai citizens have developed a distinct fondness for it, while developers all over China now use Xintiandi as a byword for the sensibility they want for their architecture. What seems to spur this interest is the sense that Xintiandi is the poster child for a new direction in Chinese culture. The country's citizens have become more secure in their basic needs and are now starting to feel the absence of cultural ties to their history, which were first severed violently during the more hysterical early years of communism and have received often-inadequate reparation from the country's recent development. Though obviously maintaining a commercial mindset, Xintiandi represents an effort to regain that heritage.

Attractions & Eating

Xintiandi is one of the more renowned eating districts in Shanghai, so all the restaurants are at the top of their game. However, one is particularly famous for its excellent version of *xiaolongbao* – small pork soup dumplings that are a local delicacy. Strangely enough, the restaurant, called **Din Tai Fung** (Dǐng Tài Fēng; 鼎泰丰; pg 187), is actually a Taiwanese chain that specializes in all manner of dumplings, but

that shouldn't stop you if you want the best and you're willing to pay more for it than other restaurants charge. The soup in these dumplings is always boiling hot, so first poke a hole in one, or let it soak in the vinegar sauce, before slurping out the juice and eating the rest. There are also many other kinds of international dining options – everything from tapas to sushi and steaks.

Within Xintiandi is the **Museum of the First National Congress of the Communist Party of China** (pg 104). Just to the southwest of Xintiandi is....

Tianzifang

Chinese name: 田子坊 (Tiánzifáng)
Admission: FREE
Recommended time for visit: 1 hour
Address: Northeast block from Taikang Rd (泰康路) and Ruijin 1st Rd (瑞金一路) intersection.
Website: www.tianzifang.cn (in Chinese)
Transport: Subway – Line 9, Dapuqiao Station (打浦桥站), Exit 1; Tianzifang is right across Taikang Rd

There's no place in Shanghai with more scrappy charm and energy than Tianzifang. The place is a block-sized warren of small alleyways and old, one-story buildings packed to excess with bars, shops, cafes, and ice cream parlors – each one small and full of character. Just navigating your way through the always-packed alleys is an adventure, since one of Tianzifang's distinct characteristics is its organic layout, which makes for a maze of unexpected passageways. Overhead, electric wires mingle with shop signs and hanging knick-knacks, while the old brick buildings imbue the area with the feel of traditional Shanghai, unlike other more modern developments in the city that hit you over the head with their old architecture allusions. What really gives the place its vigor is the sense that all these small businesses are constantly striving to make themselves heard amidst the chaos, and so these shops put much care into being as unique and fun as their tiny nooks allow. It's competition at its best and not to be missed.

Before You Go

Tianzifang is always crowded and perpetually in motion. Prepare to have your personal bubble invaded.

History

The brick buildings of Tianzifang are some of the last remaining examples of Shanghai's unique shikumen style of architecture. The shikumen style took the materials and construction techniques of Western architecture, particularly English terraced houses, and used them to create housing designs with the courtyard layout that was common in the region. Living spaces were small and closely packed, in keeping with the modest means of the residents as well as their comfort with communal living. The inner courtyards were surrounded by high stone walls, which became very useful as protection from the social chaos of the era.

The name itself can be translated roughly as "stone gates," which were also a common feature. Shikumen architecture developed from the latter half of the 19th century onward, and by the 20th century the majority of residents in Shanghai were living in shikumen. As Shanghai modernized and grew wealthy, most of these houses were demolished in favor of high-rise apartments. However, the style has recently benefited from a growing desire to preserve cultural heritage. The newly developed Xintiandi is a prime example of the city's attempts to revive its historical character with shikumen, but Tianzifang is the real thing.

Where To Go

Foreign food is plentiful in Tianzifang, as are weird drink shops and themed bars. Quality is as varied as the offerings, and businesses are constantly closing as quickly as new ones move in. The best advice is to find a place with a good view, so look for any bar or eatery with a second floor or balcony. (sitting above the street is more relaxing and provides a nice look on the melee below). Another plan of attack is just to explore at your leisure, which really is the most fun part of Tianzifang anyway. There's a surprising amount of hidden charms just waiting to be discovered!

Longhua Temple & Xujiahui

Chinese name: 龙华寺 (Lónghúa Sì)
Admission: ¥10
Hours: 7:00-16:30
Phone: 6456 6085
Address: 2853 Longhua Rd, Xuhui District (徐汇区龙华路 2853 号)
Transport: Subway – Line 11 to Longhua Station (Exit 2)

In Shanghai's southwestern district of Xujiahui is a Buddhist temple that dates back to 242 CE, the oldest temple in Shanghai. Its history is steeped in legend and bloodied by the horrors of war and civil unrest. Despite its dramatic past, today it stands as a place of worship dedicated to the Maitreya Buddha and the Longhua Pagoda. Though the pagoda is closed to the public, this beautiful and faithful testament to the Song Dynasty architectural style can still be observed from outside.

The Longhua Pagoda is the most famous of Shanghai's historic 16 pagodas; one could say it's achieved A-list status, having made an appearance in Steven Spielberg's *Empire of the Sun* (1987). Its brick base and core dates back to 977 CE during the Northern Song Dynasty. The temple was rebuilt that same year following its destruction at the end of the Tang Dynasty, and the current grounds last underwent major renovation in 1954. The layout of the temple follows the "Sangharama Five-Hall Style," which is typical of the Buddhist *Chán* (aka Zen) sect of the Song Dynasty.

Layout

The five main halls include the **Maitreya Hall** (Mílè Diàn; 弥勒殿), which houses the statues of the Maitreya Buddha and another Buddha known as "Budai," whose name translates as "Cloth Bag." Budai was known to carry all his worldly possessions in a cloth bag, but he is more affectionately known as the laughing Buddha. Buddha means "enlightened one" and Budai was originally a *Chán* monk who lived in the Liang Dynasty and was a native of Fenghua. His image serves as a reminder of the nature of contentment. An anecdote that precedes his reputation as a humorous good natured man is told in a tale of when a monk asks him, "What is the meaning of Zen?" Budai drops his cloth bag in response, but the monk ventures to ask further, "How does one achieve Zen?" Budai responds by picking up his bag and continuing his journey.

The Heavenly King Hall (Tiānwáng Diàn; 天王殿) houses four large statues of the Heavenly Kings: King of the North (Duōwén Tiānwáng; 多闻天王), who is associated with Wealth; King of the East (Chíguó Tiānwáng; 持国天王), protector of the Nation; King of the South (Zēngzhǎng Tiānwáng; 增长天王), god of prosperity; and King of the West (Guǎngmù Tiānwáng; 广目天王), who sees all.

The Grand Hall of the Great Sage, or Mahavira Hall (Dàxióng Bǎodiàn; 大雄宝殿) features the Gautama Buddha, whose teachings provide the foundation for Buddhism. He is depicted with two of his disciples, while the front section of this hall contains 20 disciples of Buddhism and the back area is graced by 16 arhats (people who have achieved nirvana) and a statue of Guanyin (Guānyīn Púsà; 观音菩萨; the goddess of mercy). The other two halls of this temple complex are the **Abbots Hall** (Fāngzhàng Lóu; 方丈楼), which is used for formal meetings and lectures, and the **Three Sages Hall** (Sānshèng Diàn; 三圣殿), which houses the Amitābha Buddha, known for longevity; Avalokiteśvara, who embodies compassion; and Mahāsthāmaprāpta, who is associated with wisdom.

If at the end of your temple wanderings you've worked up an appetite, you can head to the nearby cafeteria to try some vegetarian noodles for ¥10; the vegetarian duck, chicken, and ham are also tasty. The cafeteria is located towards the back of the complex.

Longhua Temple is a firmly embedded fixture in Shanghainese culture. Every year, the temple holds a New Year's Evening ceremony, ringing in the lunar New Year with 108 tolls of the bronze bell that was cast in 1382. Lónghuá Sì roughly translates as the Lustre of The Dragon Temple, making a reference to an old legend of a dragon that once came to the site. The legend is honored at the **Longhua Temple Fair**, which has been held annually since the Ming Dynasty and takes place on the third day of the lunar calendar's third month (around mid-April). It is said that dragons visit the area to grant people wishes.

If you are visiting in the spring it is also worth checking out the Peach Blossoms, which are in bloom at **Longhua Park** (Lónghuá Gōngyuán; 龙华公园) located next to the temple. The park was once a part of the temple's vast garden grounds but now it serves as a memorial park of the Longhua Martyrs.

Xujiahui Attractions

After touring the Longhua Temple and Park, there are some other interesting sights in the small district of Xujiahui. Since it's a bit far from the city center, if you make it all the way out here we highly recommend that you at least check a few of the following out to make the trip complete.

Longhua Martyr's Memorial Cemetery

Chinese name: 龙华烈士陵园 (Lónghuá Lièshì Língyuán)
Admission: ¥2 park entrance, ¥5 mausoleum entrance
Address: 180 Longhua West Rd (龙华西路 180 号)

Located directly next door to the Longhua Temple complex, this place is more a memorial park than a cemetery one might expect in the occidental sense. Interesting sculptures adorn manicured lawns and the pyramid-like structure you'll see here is the Memorial Hall, which you can visit if you want to learn more about China's recent political history. The park commemorates those killed during the Japanese occupation when the site was turned into an internment camp for POWs.

Shanghai Botanical Gardens

Chinese name: 上海植物园 (Shànghǎi Zhíwùyuán)
Admission: ¥15 park entrance, or ¥40 all-inclusive entrance to park, gardens and conservatory
Hours: 7:00-17:00
Phone: 5436 3369
Website: www.shbg.org (in Chinese)
Address: 1111 Longwu Rd (龙吴路 1111 号)
Transport: Subway – Line 3, Shilong Rd Station (石龙路站), walk south along Dongquan Rd (东泉路), the number 4 Gate of the garden
If you depart from Longhua Temple, you can take bus 56, 178, 720, 733, 820, 824, 932 or 956 to get to the garden. A taxi ride costs about ¥18.

If visiting the Longhua Temple in the morning, you may want to hop in a taxi and head to the Botanical Gardens for an afternoon jaunt.

Shanghai Botanical Gardens is the biggest municipal botanical garden in China. It has a large collection of thousands of plants, including some rare species, over an area of 82 hectares (202 acres). Luckily, quality was not sacrificed for quantity, and the gardens here are a welcome oasis from the noise and grime of downtown Shanghai, showcasing some superb Chinese garden culture. After decades of construction, it has become a comprehensive base combining plant research, production, tourism and science, and has won many accolades from international flower shows.

Perhaps the most unique area is the **Penjing Garden** (Pénjǐng Yuán; 盆景园). Here, visitors can see the Chinese equivalent of Japan's bonsai. Like bonsai, the art of *penjing* focuses on creating perfect miniature specimens of normal tree species. However, the Chinese art differs from its Japanese cousin in some subtle yet important ways. First, *penjing* offers a wider variety – virtually any species of tree can be cultivated in the *penjing* style. *Penjing* also tends to be more free flowing and "wild" than bonsai. Additionally, there is a greater emphasis on displaying art on the plant's container, wherein the pot and the tree are combined into a splendid harmony. Curious visitors can learn more about *penjing* in the attached museum.

The Shanghai Botanical Gardens also has a notable **Magnolia Garden** (Mùlán Yuán; 木兰园) featuring 40 different species. For a more classical oriental experience, check out the **Bamboo Garden** (Zhú Yuán; 竹园), which contains over a hundred varieties of the world's largest grass (yes, bamboo is technically a grass, not a tree).

Of course, spring is the most popular season in which to visit the garden as blooming azaleas, peonies and roses compete for the attention of the garden's many visitors. The garden is less crowded during Shanghai's hot and humid summers, but it still offers many unique and quiet shaded areas. Fall brings striking changes to the garden's deciduous trees. Even Shanghai's misty cold winters can attract visitors who seek refuge from the cold and the smog in the garden's greenhouses.

There are many paths through the garden, and those who are inclined to do so can spend hours exploring the scenery. If you want privacy, try to visit during the weekdays.

Bibliotheca Zi-Ka-Wei

Chinese name: 徐家汇藏书楼 (Xújiāhuì Cángshūlóu)
Admission: FREE
Hours: 9:00-17:00 (Mon-Sat); closed Sun
Phone: 6487 4096
Address: 80 Caoxi North Rd (曹溪北路 80 号)
Transport:
Subway – Line 1, Xujiahui Station (徐家汇站), Exit 7, the library is just across the street (on the west side of Caoxi North Rd)

Here's something you probably thought you wouldn't see in the Orient. In 1847, Jesuit missionaries set up this extensive library with 560,000 volumes in Latin, Greek and many other languages. Apart from an endless selection of books and scrolls, the building itself is an eye-pleaser.

They are only open on Saturday afternoons with a tour guide (English available), and they only take ten guests at a time, so make sure you book ahead, especially during peak season. Note that the tours are only 15 minutes, but many travelers who are interested in these types of exhibits still give it two thumbs up.

St Ignatius Cathedral

Chinese name: 徐家汇天主教堂 (Xújiāhuì Tiānzhǔ Jiàotáng)
Admission: FREE
Hours: 13:00-16:30 (Sat & Sun). Mass is held on Sun at 6:00, 7:30, 10:00 & 18:00; at 7:00 on weekdays; at 18:00 on Sat; and at 18:00 on the first Fri of each month.
Phone: 6438 2595
Address: 158 Puxi Rd (蒲西路 158 号)
Transport:
Subway – Line 1, Xujiahui Station (徐家汇站), Exit 3, walk about 20 m (65 ft) west

Another one of the astonishing landmarks the Jesuits left behind, this gothic twin-towered cathedral, built in 1904, has plenty of creepy looking gargoyles to keep you on your toes. A lot of the sculptures, stained glass and art were destroyed during the Cultural Revolution (go figure), but the replicas today are just as striking as the originals (or at least that's what they told us, there's no way of really knowing). Mass is still held; check the vital info for times.

Across the street from the cathedral is the former **St Ignatius Convent**. These days it functions as a tasty onsite restaurant, so stop in for lunch.

Tousewe Museum

Chinese name: 土山湾博物馆 (Tǔshānwān Bówùguǎn)
Admission: ¥10

Hours: 9:00-16:30 (Tue-Sun); closed Mon
Address: 55-1 Puhuitang Rd (蒲汇塘路 55-1 号)
Transport: Subway – Line 1, Xujiahui Station (徐家汇站), Exit 1, walk south along Caoxi North Rd (漕溪北路) about 300 m (984 ft), turn right into Puhuitang Rd, continue walking for about 100 m (328 ft); the museum is on your right side

Another Jesuit establishment built in 1864, this interesting museum is dedicated to the arts, crafts and works of the former Tousewe Orphanage, which used to stand on this very site. The Jesuits took Chinese orphans under their wings and gave them a Western education, and most of the items you see on display are religious trinkets and wood crafts – a specialty hand made by the orphans.

Other Jesuit Attractions

As you may have already noticed, Xujiahui is where the Jesuits set up shop back in the day. Apart from the bibliotheca, cathedral and museum, the area is riddled with more architecture and other hidden treasures. Some more Jesuit-themed places of interest include the **Xuhui Public School**, originally built in 1850 and located on the south end of Hongqiao Road; the **Xujiahui Observatory**, which is part of the Shanghai Meterological Bureau and just south of the St Ignatius Cathedral; and the **Major Seminary** situated along Nandan East Road.

Longhua Fashion & Gift Market

Chinese name: 龙华服饰礼品市场 (Lónghuá Fúshi Lǐpǐn Shìchǎng)
Address: 2465 Longhua Rd (徐汇区龙华路 2465 号)
Transport: Walk north from Longhua Temple along Longhua Rd (龙华路) for about 1 km (less than 1 mi), the market will be on your left; otherwise, take subway Line 11, Longhua Station, then walk north along Longhua Rd (龙华路) for about 1.2 km (less than 1 mi)

The Longhua Fashion and Gift Market sells much of the same gear you'll find in many of the other tourist markets of Shanghai, though it will be easier to get a good deal because it's a less touristy market. It's spread over three floors with hundreds of shops, so try your chances at grabbing a bargain.

Duolun Road Cultural Street

Chinese name: 多伦路文化名人街 (Duōlúnlù Wénhuà Míngrénjiē)
Address: Begins at intersection of Sichuan North Rd (四川北路)
Transport: Subway – Line 3, Dongbaoxing Rd Station, Exit 1, walk southwest on Hailun West Rd, turn at first intersection onto Donghengbang Rd, which becomes Duolun Culture St after 200 m (656 ft)

The golden era of this lane peaked during the 1920s and '30s when droves of Shanghai's intellectuals began moving in, and the area eventually became a nest of China's greatest 20th century writers. Some prominent members of the Association of Left-Wing Writers like Dīng Líng (丁玲) and Qú Qiūbái (瞿秋白) lived on Duolun Street, and other prestigious authors like Guō Mòruò (郭沫若), Máo Dùn (茅盾), Lǔ Xùn (鲁迅) and Yè Shèngtáo (叶圣陶) are also known to have spent years here. Today, Duolun Road Cultural Street is bursting at the seams with history, culture, old-timey shikumen architecture and, of course, shopping.

After walking by the second jewelry store and seeing more shops ahead, you might begin to wonder whether this "cultural street" is just an excuse to create another shopping district with historical flair, as is the case with the more famous Xintiandi. However, that's not entirely true. A small row of stone-carved images representing the famous literary figures of the past century and several statues of spectacled Chinese scholars somewhat elevate the situation. One of the first Christian churches of Shanghai deserves more than a passing glance due to its unique blending of the basic Christian church layout and the aesthetic flourishes of traditional

Chinese temples. Also located on Duolun Street is the erstwhile lair of the **League of Left-Wing Writers**, founded in 1930. It's highly recommended for anyone interested in literature and/or China's socialist past, since these literary stars had enormous influence on the country's political consciousness. In fact, Lu Xun – one of the founders of the Association of Left-Wing Writers – was one of Chairman Mao's favorite writers. Lu's work later became required school reading.

Shanghai Duolun Museum of Modern Art

Chinese name: 上海多伦现代美术馆 (Shànghǎi Duōlún Xiàndài Měishùguǎn)
Phone: 6587 0448
Address: 27 Duolun Rd

It should be no surprise that the Shanghai Museum of Modern Art decided to set up shop on Duolun Road since it was once the main area for revolutionary thinkers, intellectuals and artists. With the

establishment of the Duolun Museum of Modern Art, the road is seeing a revival in the traditions of the past and is contributing to the production of a lasting cultural atmosphere for generations to come. With an open mind, progressive strategy and liberal attitude, the museum aims to both play an important role in the future of Chinese contemporary art and make an impact on the international art community.

The Shanghai Duolun Museum of Modern Art is a multi-purpose, nonprofit institution of culture, academia and art, providing services to the development of Chinese art and a platform for the international exchange of contemporary movements. What this means for practical purposes is that it is the first professional museum in the country that seeks to establish art exchanges with foreign countries. They also boast the five major functions of exhibition, research, education, collection and communication, so definitely check out this unique place while strolling along the intellectual lanes of Duolun Culture Street.

Old Film Café

Chinese name: 老电影咖啡馆 (Lǎodiànyǐng Kāfēiguǎn)
Phone: 5696 4763
Address: 123 Duolun Rd

This historic relic on old Duolun doesn't have much in terms of food, but its charisma and coffee are what set it apart. The classic shikumen house honors Shanghai's silver screen by showcasing black and white films from the '20s and '30s, so pop in for a caffeine fix then catch a flick to end your day on Duolun.

Lu Xun Park & Memorial Hall

Chinese name: 鲁迅公园 (Lǔxùn Gōngyuán); 鲁迅纪念馆 (Lǔxùn Jì'niàn'guǎn)
Admission: FREE
Hours: 6:00-18:00 for the park; 9:00-16:00 for memorial hall
Recommended time for visit: 1 hour
Address: 2288 Sichuan North Rd (四川北路 2288 号)
Transport: Subway – Lines 3 & 8, Hongkou Football Stadium Station (虹口足球场站), Exit 1 or 2

Originally known as Hongkou Park (exclusively reserved for foreigners from 1905-1928), it was eventually named after one of the country's best 20th century writers: Lu Xun (1881-1936). Lu is known as the "father of modern Chinese literature" for developing a modern style of Chinese writing in the common vernacular. He also translated many foreign novels into Chinese, and criticized historic thinkers such as Confucius and superstitions in Chinese culture. Though Lu was never officially a member of the CCP, he did show sympathy for socialism and became the head of the League of Left-Wing Writers in Shanghai in the 1930s.

The park itself is small yet elegantly groomed and a nice place to get inspired to write your own poems or travel journal entries. On the eastern side of the park is a memorial hall dedicated to this famous writer. Here visitors can see all things of Lu, including photographs, first editions, letters, poems, a few wax figurines (in case you didn't get enough at Madam Tussauds) and bizarre personal belongings like his "death mask." Also here is a bookstore where you can purchase some of his greatest works; keep an eye out for his best known piece, *The True Story of Ah Q*. On the north end of the park lies Lu's tomb and final resting place, and there is even an inscription written by Mao to honor one of his favorite writers.

If you walk ten minutes east of the park, you can take a tour of Lu Xun's former residence. It's a beautiful, three-story house where he lived out his final years, and it's still embellished as it was back then with its original furnishings and personal items, most notably his favorite writing brush.

Lu Xun (1881-1936)

Lu Xun was a man obsessed with curing his country. In his early years, he took the mission literally and decided to become a doctor. Believing traditional Chinese medicine to be a scam and a superstition that had hastened the death of his ill father, Lu Xun began the then rare process of obtaining a Western education, which put him in contact with Western science, literature and philosophy. This eventually lead him to study in Japan, where he would have finished his studies if it weren't for an epiphany he experienced when looking at slides his teacher brought showing attrocities from the Russo-Japanese War. The pictures showed Japanese soldiers seconds away from shooting a supposed Chinese spy, but what horrified him was that the crowd of Chinese that surrounded the spectacle looked on with complete indifference, or even passive interest, in their own countryman's death. Lu Xun would later write that this picture convinced him that Chinese society suffered most pressingly from a spiritual sickness that he would try his best to document and cure by returning to China to become a writer.

His first work of lasting fame was a short story "A Madman's Diary," published in 1918, some years after the establishment of the Republic of China. The story is an allegory of the viciousness of Chinese society, wherein a man slowly realizes the people in his village and even his family are cannibals. He followed this with perhaps his best known work *The True Story of Ah Q*, a novella that satirized the many faults Lu Xun saw in his country's character. In 1927, he moved to Shanghai, where he would live for the rest of his life, and continued to write essays and short stories. He also founded, with encouragement from the Communist Party, the League of Left-Wing Writers, but he would later renounce his membership when he felt the group had become enthralled in leftist doctrine, which valued art only insofar as it promoted leftist politics (you won't find this piece of information anywhere on Duolun Street, where the League was located). In truth, Lu Xun was disappointed with both sides of the Chinese political spectrum. He believed the Nationalist government to be a failure, but was uncomfortable with much of communist thought. He eventually grew to believe China's problems were beyond the help of politics and probably had something more to do with ineradicable defects of human nature – like Dickens' diagnosis of his own country.

Lu Xun died with a rather dim view of his own efforts to correct these defects, but Mao Zedong was one person who disagreed. He believed Lu Xun to be the greatest writer of modern China, and his writings have been a part of the curriculum for Chinese students ever since, under the perspective that Lu Xun's works were a critique of feudal society before the communists changed everything "for the better." He remains by far the most famous writer of modern China, and many of his most famous books are available in English translation.

Qibao Ancient Town

Chinese name: 七宝古镇 (Qībǎo Gǔzhèn)
Admission: There is no fee to wander the old street but a ¥30 ticket gains you access to the Pawn House, Cotton Textile Mill, Shadow Play Museum, Memorial Hall of Zhang Chongren, Old Trades House, Zhou's Miniature Model Museum and Cricket House
Transport:
Subway – Line 9, Qibao Station, Exit 2, take right and follow the signs
Bus – 87, 91, 92, 513, 735, 748 or 803, get off at Qibao Stop

Qibao Ancient Town has a history that dates back over 1,000 years. Originally built in the Northern Song Dynasty (960-1126), Qibao flourished as a trade town during the Ming (1368-1644) and Qing Dynasties (1644-1912). Located in the heart of Shanghai's Minhang District, it is easily accessed from Shanghai's city center and can be a worthwhile day trip. While the area (and much of Shanghai) is undergoing massive development, there seems to be a theme that follows history. Already faced with two large shopping malls when leaving the Qibao Metro Station and a promenade of shops that line the streets leading up to the Old Town, the ancient town was in the process of adding another shopping plaza at the time of writing.

Trade is clearly the backbone of this area, so if you do fancy a shopping trip, then maybe consider using this as your one-stop shop.

As the face of modernity further encroaches upon the now crumbling ancient buildings, the streets are busy with an atmospheric buzz that gives you a real sense of how things might have been in the glory days of this township and its legendary history.

Qibao means "seven treasures" and refers to seven sacred items that local folktales have long said could be found here. These items were a Ming Dynasty iron Buddha, a golden-script Lotus Sutra written by an imperial concubine in the 10th century, a one 1,000-year-old Chinese catalpa tree said to be magical, a gold cockerel, a pair of jade chopsticks, a jade axe, and a bronze bell that is said to have mysteriously materialized from thin air during the Ming Dynasty. The bell and the script are the only two relics that can be accounted for today.

We suggest starting on Qingnian Road (Qīngnián Lù; 青年路), where the decorated *páilóu* (牌楼) archway marks the beginning of the ancient district. In this courtyard stands the Bell Tower, and here you can also find one of the original seven treasures. Inside the tower is a ticket desk where you should ask for a tourist map along with your ticket. You can pay ¥10 to climb the stairs of the tower and ring the bell, or ¥30 for access to seven sites and a museum in the old town. Whichever ticket option you go for, it's worth climbing the Bell Tower to give it a ring; a local saying goes, "Ring the bell once, your cares and worries will disappear; ring the bell twice, you will be blessed; ring the bell three times, all will be blessed."

Layout

If you follow the path to the left as you leave the Bell Tower, you'll find yourself on Beida Street (Běi Dàjiē; 北大街), a place where public safety announcements blare from loudspeakers and common sense calls you to follow the direction of the crowd. If visiting this place on a weekend, be warned: Beida Street will be packed. The next stop (according to your tourist ticket) will be the **Cotton Textile Mill** (Miánzhī Fāng; 棉织坊), and even if its wax-work figurines aren't your thing, you can escape the crowds by grabbing one of the many snacks along the way and taking a moment to chill out. Cotton was a huge commodity here during the Ming Dynasty, and thanks to Qibao's fortuitous geography, which joins the two rivers of the Huangpu and Wusong, the ease of transporting goods gave rise to the financial success of the area. Two other museums included in your tourist ticket, the **Pawn House** (Dàngpù; 当铺) and the **Old Trades House** (Lǎo Hángdang; 老行当), also go into this in detail. Take these sights with a grain of salt and expect mildly interesting antiquities amongst cheesy wax-work models.

Art lovers may be appeased by three other locations that are included in the tourist ticket deal. **The Shadow Graph Museum** (Píyǐngxì Guǎn; 皮影戏馆) is dedicated to Shadow Puppetry. Shadow Play (Píyǐngxì; 皮影戏) is an important folk art that can be traced back to the Western Han Dynasty some 2,000 years ago. It was made a popular art form in Shanghai through Máo Gēngyú (毛耕渔), a native of Qibao Town. His Shadow Play troupe made Shadow Play a fashionable pastime among the Shanghainese, so much so that during his 30 year career he coined a name for himself: the "Originator of Shanghai Shadow Play." In 1907, his troupe performed in a town rife with plague, which Mao contracted, and the great puppeteer died on stage in an almost-too-perfect quasi martyrdom. As a testament to his life's work, this museum is adorned with colorful effigies'

created out of sheepskin, which was used to make puppets. If you're lucky you might be treated to a *kuǐlěixì* puppet show.

The next stop along the way is the **Memorial Hall of Zhang Chongren** (Zhāng Chōngrén Jì'niàn'guǎn; 张充仁纪念馆). Zhang, a famous artist and sculptor, was another one of Qibao's creative natives, and in his memorial you'll find some of the artist's paintings and bronze sculptures. A bronze bust of Hergé, the Belgian cartoonist famous for creating the *Adventures of Tintin,* can be found here as well. Hergé was a dear friend of Zhang Chongren and based his character "Chang Chong-Chen" of *Tintin's Adventure: The Blue Lotus*, on Zhang.

The memorial house charts the life of Zhang from his modest beginnings, through several wars, and on to great notoriety. First reduced to a humble street sweeper during the difficult early times of his life, he eventually rose to become Head of the Shanghai Fine Arts Academy. Later he settled down to teach in Paris, where he spent his final days. After the museum and before venturing further down the south side of the hall, you can head to the nearby wharf and for ¥10 be ferried about the waterways of Qibao.

To the south, artistic offerings come in the form of miniature models at **Zhou's Miniature Museum** (Zhōushì Wēidiāoguǎn; 周氏微雕馆), which houses the life's work of award winning artist and Guinness World Record holder, Zhōu Chángxíng (周长形) and his daughter Zhōu Lìjú (周丽菊). Changxing was a master of miniature models, and his daughter followed in his footsteps. The amazing collection is awe-inspiring in its intricate detail and you shouldn't feel guilty for indulging your inner Gulliver.

Next door to the Miniature Museum is the **Calligraphy Art Gallery** (Shūfǎ Yìshùguǎn; 书法艺术馆). Unfortunately this is not included in your tourist ticket, but for ¥10 you can have the pleasure of viewing the artistry of master Chinese calligraphy.

Across the road from the gallery is the **Cricket House** (Xīshuài Cǎotáng; 蟋蟀草堂). Here, the beauty of ceremonial cricket fighting is showcased, and if you're interested in the entomological art of war, you'll probably be chirping over their large collection of dead crickets and cricket paraphernalia. The stone frieze in the backyard of this house depicts a tale of how the legendary fighting cricket's native to the area came to be: A shipment destined for Emperor Qianlong of the Qing Dynasty contained some of the finest cricket specimens in the empire, but they escaped when the horse hauling them slipped and lost its load in the fields of Qibao. During Mid-Autumn Festival and Spring Festival, you can see daily cricket performances and get a feel for this ancient pastime.

Attractions

Qibao Temple & Pagoda

Chinese name: 七宝教寺 (Qībǎo Jiāosi) ; 七宝塔 (Qībǎo Tǎ)
Admission: ¥5
Address: 1205 Xinzhen Rd (新镇路 1205 号)

Rising above the old houses in the not-so-far-off distance, a pagoda of epic proportions may spark your curiosity. Part of the renowned Qibao Temple, this pagoda and it's surrounding complex are one of Qibao Ancient Town's most beautiful sights, and temple promoters will assure visitors that the name of the town actually originated here. The

temple you see today was rebuilt in 2002 in the architectural styles of the Han (206 BCE – 220 CE) and Tang (618-907) Dynasties. Climb the seven-story pagoda for a bird's eye view of the area, and don't forget to visit the garden on the side of the temple, which boasts a large iron bell, plenty of chirping birds, and an all around peaceful scene.

Qibao Catholic Church

Chinese name: 七宝天主教堂 (Qībǎo Tiānzhǔ Jiāotáng)
Admission: FREE
Address: 50 South St (七宝镇南街 50 号)

It may be a little tricky to find, but if you keep your eyes out for a statue of the Virgin Mary, she will point you in the right direction to this handsome Catholic church. First opened in 1866, it underwent a revitalizing facelift and paintjob in 2010, and today its welcoming white- and yellow-painted walls make for a picturesque view.

Food & Drink

Art and waxwork figurines aside, there is a reason for the packed streets in Qibao: good food. Locals and tourists alike come to enjoy the culinary delights of Qibao, which are bountiful and varied in their offering. Spanish *churros* with chocolate sauce, hush puppies and pig trotters can all be found along these streets, not to mention the opportunity to see traditional Chinese sweets hand-made before your very eyes. Colorful glutinous rice cakes are available on every corner as well. Most snacks on their own cost ¥2-3 each, so bust out that pocket change and try to sample each one. We highly suggest the *tāngtuán* (汤团) balls of glutinous pockets filled with meat or sweet fillings. Our favorites are pork and sesame; the latter is perfect for satisfying your sweet tooth.

If the smell of stinky tofu – which is in abundance here – isn't doing it for you, try snacking on some deep fried crab or roasted quail's eggs. *Xiaolongbao* fans may notice the queues outside the famous Shanghainese dumpling place **Longpao Xiefen Dumplings** (Lóngpáo Xièfěn Xiǎolóngguǎn; 龙袍蟹粉小笼馆 ; address: 43 South St – 南大街43号) next to the north side of the bridge – the crab roe dumplings here are definitely worth a try. To wash it all down, head to the **Qibao Distillery** (Qībǎo Jiǔfāng; 七宝酒坊 ; address: 2/F, 21 South St – 南大街21号乙2楼 ; hours: 10:30-21:00). It's free to enter this workshop specializing in *baijiu*, and you can saddle up to their a bar for a taste of China's national liquor.

Nearby Attractions

Qibao indeed has something for everyone: history buffs can feed off of its rich cultural history, art fans can feast on felicitous offerings, and foodies can gorge to their hearts content. It's even possible to satisfy the metaphysical self with some soul searching on the holy grounds of Qibao Temple (so long as the crowds don't ruin the mood) or worship the god of coin with some retail therapy. Whatever floats your boat (literally, they have boat rides here, too), you can likely find something to fill the water in Qibao. Because Qibao is fairly far from town and just a little inconvenient to get to, you may want to check out some of these other attractions that are just a few kilometers north of Qibao. Taking a taxi to any one of the following sites is not only the quickest and most convenient way to travel; it's also extremely cheap since they're all in close.

Dino Beach (pg 155)

Yingxing Indoor Skiing (pg 155)

Shanghai Zoo (pg 154)

Ancient Yi Garden

Chinese Name: 古猗园 (Gǔyī Yuán)
Admission: ¥12
Hours: 8:30 – 16:30
Address: 218 Huyi Highway, Nanxiang (南翔镇沪宜路 218号)
Website: www.guyigarden.com (English available)
Transport: Subway – Line 11, Nanxiang Station, Exit 2, take a left onto Zhongjia Rd, walk straight and cross over Zhennan Rd, continue to walk straight up Minzhu East St and take a left onto Guyiyuan Rd where you'll find the north entrance

Nestled away in Nanxiang, a suburb of Shanghai, is an escape from the hectic hustle and bustle of city life. The Ancient Yi (or Guyi) Garden, parts of which date back to the Ming Dynasty era, are more peaceful and cheaper to enjoy than other major tourist sites like Yu Garden.

Inspired by two epic poems from the oldest collection of Chinese poetry, the "Book of Songs," the garden was originally named "Yi" Garden, which here means "the beautiful sight of bamboo bushes." 200 years after it was built, it was renamed Guyi Garden during the Qing Dynasty, whith *gu* adding the meaning of "ancient." It certainly has lived up to its name, and nearly 500 years later, the garden has grown, expanded, and been quartered into themed divisions.

Layout

The oldest of the four quarters, the original "Yi" garden is dotted with pavilions whose wonderful architecture is typical of the Ming Dynasty era and are characterized by small tiles and upturned hollow roof ridges. Look out for the **Angle Missing Pavilion**, built in 1933. When Japan invaded China in September of 1931, the Japanese army conquered three northeastern provinces. The people of Nanxiang town showed solidarity with their nation by building this monument as a representation of their anger, constructing the pavilion with the northeastern corner missing and the remaining corners in the form of raised fists. The people named it the Bu Que Pavilion, which means "to restore the missing part."

Nearby is the **Five Old Men Peak** (Wǔlǎo Fēng; 五老峰), a set of five rockeries that looks like old men singing and playing musical instruments. Also worth visiting is the **Tranquil Pavilion** (Yōushǎng Tíng; 幽赏 亭), where it was once tradition for ancient scholars to spend quiet evenings amongst osmanthus trees during the Moon Festival. As so, osmanthus trees were planted next to the Tranquil Pavilion during the Qing

Dynasty. Should you happen to visit the garden in late autumn, you'll be lucky to see and smell the fragrant flowers of the osmanthus trees in bloom.

As you move on from the Yi quarter, the next area will be the **Crane in Stream Pond** (Qūxī Hèyǐng; 曲溪鹤影). Pay a visit to the Floating Cloud Pavilion (Xiángyún Gé; 翔云阁), which is located at the top of the steps of Turtle Hill (Guī Shān; 龟山). Here, you'll have a wonderful view of the garden in its entirety. In the Floating Cloud Pavilion there is a stone monument with the character *shòu* (寿 ; longevity) inscribed into it. The monument is upheld by a tortoise-like animal known as a *bìxì* (赑屃), a legendary animal that is thought to bring good fortune. Another pavilion to visit is the **Crane Longevity Pavilion** (Hèshòu Xuān; 鹤寿轩), which sits with crane-decorated eaves overlooking a fine lotus pond (the small tower in the middle was built in 1222 by a Buddhist disciple).

The next section of the garden is the **Moonlit Bamboo Park** (Yōuhuáng Yānyuè; 幽篁烟月); this extension was completed in 1988 and boasts a vast collection of over 80 different types of bamboo. Its pavilions merge into a bamboo forest that provides secluded spots for tranquil moments. Here you'll find the very Chinglish and aptly named **Stone Enjoy House** (Wánshí Zhāi; 玩石斋), which showcases oddly shaped stones donated from the private collection of Mr Hu Zhaokang, the former Chairman of Hong Kong Rico Hero Ltd. Stone collecting is an ancient tradition

practiced by Chinese scholars, whereby they collected and appreciated rocks according to their color, shape, markings and surface. While visiting this quarter of the garden, you can hire a boat for ¥25 to cruise around a small section of the lake.

If by this point you are in need of a rest, the **Residence with Bamboo** (Búkě Wúzhújū; 不可无竹居) offers some respite through its display of classical Chinese furniture. Built upon a lake and with a semi-open design, it's a wonderful place to kick back and enjoy the bamboo views. So important is bamboo in the traditional lives of local Chinese, the famous poet Su Dongpo once wrote, "People can eat no meat, but cannot reside without bamboo. No meat only makes a person lean, but no bamboo will make a person vulgar."

The fourth quarter of the garden is the **Flower Fragrance Park** (Huāxiāng Xiānyuàn; 花香仙苑), where you'll find the beautiful Nine Zigzag Bridge (Jiǔqǔ Qiáo; 九曲桥). It's said that the bridge was zig-zagged in order to confuse any evil spirits attempting to cross. This particular bridge spans Mandarin Duck Lake (Yuānyāng Hú; 鸳鸯湖), and as you pass over the bridge (hopefully without confusion) you should keep an eye out for these ducks and their eye-catching plumage.

South of the duck pond is the **Fragrance Veranda** (Qǔxiāng Láng; 曲香廊). In the garden of this building, osmanthus, plum trees, orchids and chrysanthemum have been planted amidst bamboo to provide a fragrance for all seasons. Peonies planted almost a century ago can be found here and if you come during spring, you'll be able to catch their impressive bloom, which can reach the size of a large bowl. The Flower Fragrance Park here also has a children's playground, and the **Nanxiang Wall** (Nánxiáng Bì; 南翔壁) is also crane-crazy and covered by the white birds.

If you've worked up some munchies after gallivanting across the garden grounds, you may wish to visit the **Guyi Teahouse** (Gǔyīyuán Cháshì; 古猗园茶室), situated on Mandarin Duck Lake. Here you can enjoy servings of Nanxiang's famous soup dumplings (xiǎolóngbāo; 小笼包) and tea for around ¥30 per head. On hot days, we recommend a refreshing flower tea.

There are plenty of places to explore in lovely Yi Garden, so jump right in and meander at your leisure. The calming rockeries, gurgling waterways, wonderful art and enchanting architecture create a superbly dreamy scenario evocative of the China of old. So if you're hurting for some quiet time – maybe even a little romance – and something to take you back through time, notch Guyi Garden into the top of your "Shanghai to-do" list.

Nanxiang District

It may only take you a couple of hours to walk around the Guyi Garden, and after that, what will you do? Consider making a full daytrip of your visit to this area by visiting the nearby old town of Nanxiang, – formerly known as Cuoxi (槎溪) – a quaint water town thankfully bereft of tourist hordes. Hire a boat to navigate the town's waterways, or wander down the charming cobbledstone streets in search of Chinese culinary delights. Nanxiang is actually famous for being the birthplace of the Shanghainese soup-dumpling delicacy *xioalongbao*. Also within

walking distance is one of Shanghai's largest temples, **Liuyun Temple** (Liúyún Chánsì; 留云禅寺), and the **Nanxiang Twin Towers** (Shuāng Tǎ; 双塔).

Jiading District

Nanxiang is the gateway to the Jiading District of northwestern Shanghai. Just a 20-minute drive away from Shanghai's International Hongqiao Airport, this is where the annual Chinese Grand Prix is held, and car lovers as well as history buffs can all find something to get revved up about.

Confucian Temple of Jiading

Chinese Name: 嘉定孔庙 (Jiādìng Kǒngmiào)
Admission: ¥20
Address: 183 South St, Jiading Town (嘉定南大街183号)

Built 800 years ago, this is one of the best preserved Confucian temples in China. This temple is the reason why Jiading is known as a "place of education."

Wuxing Temple

Chinese Name: 吴兴寺 (Wúxìng Sì)

Admission: ¥5
Address: 5428 Huiyi Highway, Waigang Town (沪宜公路
5428 号)

Located beside the Yantie River (盐铁河), this colorful temple was built over 1,000 years ago and has only recently been reopened to the public and worshippers.

Fahua Pagoda

Chinese Name: 法华塔 (Fǎhuá Tǎ)
Admission: ¥5
Address: 349 South St, Jiading District (嘉定区南大街349号)

This towering structure has had the misfortune of collapsing multiple times throughout history, but its faithful reconstructions and restorations still make it an impressive monument. It is the iconic symbol of Jiading.

Auto Expo Park

Chinese Name: 汽车博览公园 (Qìchē Bólǎn Gōngyuán)
Admission: FREE
Address: 7001 Boyuan Rd, Anting Town (嘉定区安亭博园路
7001 号)

This slice of modernity is for lovers of all things automobile. You'll find an impressive array of cars interwoven with a well-kept lakeside grounds.

Anting Old Street

Chinese Name: 安亭古街 (Āntíng Gǔjiē)
Admission: FREE
Address: Xinyuan Rd & Changji Rd Crossing, Anting Town (安亭镇新源路和昌吉路路口附近)

Located near the Auto Expo Park, this street is a mix of old and new and offers a flavor of the charms of Ming and Qing Dynasty architectural styles. Ancient structures such as the authentic Ming Dynasty **Yansi Bridge** (Yánsì Qiáo; 严 泗 桥) can be appreciated alongside the imposing, newly constructed, nine-story **Yong'an Pagoda** (Yǒng'ān Tǎ; 永 安 塔). There is also a reconstruction of the ancient **Bodhi Temple** (Pútí Sì; 菩提寺) of the Three Kingdoms Period, as well as old-style streets full of shopping, food and teahouses.

Wellington Koo Exhibition (pg 133)

Other Attractions

Museums

There is no shortage of museums in this town – you can bet on that – but even if you were already expecting them in a world-class city like Shanghai, the diversity here will still blow you away. Of course, you have the traditional exhibits that display Chinese/Shanghainese history and what not, but most of those have already been showcased in Top Attractions. To mix things up and step out of the norm, visit some of the more alternative museums we have listed in this section to experience the other side of Shanghai.

Museum of the First National Congress of the Chinese Communist Party

Chinese name: 中共一大会址 (Zhōnggòng Yīdà Huìzhǐ)
Admission: FREE
Hours: 9:00–17:00 (last admission at 16:00)
Phone: 5383 2171
Website: www.zgyd1921.com (in Chinese)
Address: 374 Huangpi South Rd (黄陂南路 374 号)
Transport: Subway – Line 1, Huangpi South Rd Station (黄陂南路站), Exit 2
Bus 146 and City Sightseeing bus Line 1 also service this attraction

This museum stands at the scene of one of the most pivotal moments in Chinese history. In 1921, 13 delegates held the first National Congress of the Chinese Communist Party, representing the party's 50 members. A young Mao Zedong was in attendance, representing the communists of Hunan Province. Since that meeting, the Communist Party of China has grown somewhat – it now has over 70 million members, making it by far the world's largest political party.

The museum is broken up into three main sections, detailing the formation of the Party, the revolutionary history of China and the history of the Party in Shanghai. Particularly interesting are displays concerning the Shanghai Massacre of 1927, when the rival Nationalist Party (KMT) killed hundreds of communists, breaking an alliance between the two. This event sparked a civil war that left millions dead, and eventually led to the current division between Mainland China and Taiwan. Of course, the museum has a rather strong bias in favor of the CCP.

The highlight for most visitors is the small room where the First Congress of the CCP was held. Photographs are strictly forbidden in this well-guarded inner sanctum. The main museum displays are upstairs and there is also a wax-figure display showing a beaming Mao Zedong making a speech to the other 12 delegates.

The Museum of the First National Congress of the Chinese Communist Party is located in a pleasant tree-lined neighborhood. Many structures in the area, including the museum itself, are built in the traditional shikumen style, which blends Chinese and Western architectural elements. In fact, the **Shikumen Wulixiang Open House Museum** (Shíkùmén Wūlǐxiāng Bówùguǎn; 石库门屋里厢博物馆) is just up the road (address: 25, Lane 181, Taicang Rd; 太仓路 181 弄 25 号 ; hours: 11:00-22:30).

For every Shanghai resident, the word *Wulixiang* warms the heart. Over 70% of the local Shanghai residents were born and raised in shikumen houses, but they are now fast

disappearing. The Shikumen Wulixiang Open House Museum, however, offers a chance to cherish the memories of old Shanghai.

Built in 1920s, the museum building features eight exhibition rooms: the master bedroom, the sitting room, the study, the elderly people's room, the son's room, the daughter's room, the kitchen and the *tíngzijiān* (亭子间 ; see orange box below). All of the museum's exhibits, furniture, kitchen utensils, clothes and books are authentic and donated by local Shanghainese.

This museum is worth a visit due to its historic location, and the neighborhood itself is relatively quiet and pleasant. The museum is of particular interest to history buffs, or those seeking the flavor of Shanghai's golden years. Also, remember that the museum is free and air conditioned. Bonus!

Tingzijian

Shikumen houses were normally occupied by one family. However, the owners usually rented out a small room for extra income. Located between staircases, usually with the kitchen underneath, *tingzijian*, literally meaning "pavilion" or "kiosk room," were initially intended for storage. But with the rapidly growing urban population, more and more families started renting them out to cash-strapped newcomers. Typically facing north, tiny *tingzijian* were cold in the winter and hot in the summer and lacked privacy and comfort, but they still allowed fairly decent and inexpensive living in the city. In the 1920s and 1930s, a lot of intellectuals and artists came to Shanghai to escape social and political unrest in other parts of the country, and many of them were single and broke, leading plenty to settle in *tingzijian*. Thus rooms soon acquired a certain romantic air as many of the most famous writers of the time, such as Lǔ Xùn (鲁迅), Cài Yuánpéi (蔡元培), Guō Mòruò (郭沫若), Máo Dùn (茅盾), Bā Jīn (巴金), Dīng Líng (丁玲) and Fēng Zǐkǎi (丰子恺), spent time living in the *tingzijian*. Many of their works reflected life in the *tingzijian* and shikumen, and were hence dubbed "Tingzijian Literature."

Madame Tussauds Shanghai

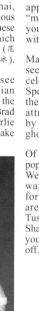

Chinese name: 上海杜莎夫人蜡像馆 (Shànghǎi Dùshā Fūrén Làxiàngguǎn)
Admission: ¥150 for adults, ¥110 for students (with ID), ¥90 for children under 1.3 m and senior citizens (65+ with ID)
Hours: 10:00-22:00 (last admission at 21:00)
Phone: 6358 7878
Website: www.madametussauds.com/Shanghai/en
Address: 10/F, New World Bldg, 2-68 Nanjing West Rd, near Xizang Middle Rd (黄浦区南京西路 2-68 号新世界城 10 楼, 近西藏中路)
Transport: Subway – Lines 1, 2 & 8, People's Square Station (人民广场站), Exit 7
Bus – 18, 20, 37, 46, 167, 518, 537, 930 and 952

Shanghai is a huge international metropolis, and as such it is home to many celebrities. However, most foreign visitors to Shanghai are not very familiar with Chinese celebrities (with the exceptions of Jackie Chan and Yao Ming), and few of them know who to look out for when checking out Shanghai's swanky clubs or elegant restaurants.

Luckily, there is a solution to this problem. Just head to Madam Tussauds Shanghai, the local branch of the world's most famous wax museum, for a crash course on Chinese superstars. Here you can check out which faces to look out for, such as Fan Bingbing (范冰冰), Sun Li (孙俪) and Li Bingbing (李冰冰).

Don't worry, if the opportunity to see realistic wax sculptures of these Asian luminaries does not excite you, there are the staple Western icons as well, including Brad Pitt, Bill Clinton, Tom Cruise and Charlie Chaplin. Albert Einstein and Bill Gates make

appearances as well. If you buy a special "magic combo" ticket (¥310 for two adults), you can take a photo up close and personal with the wax figure of your choosing.

Madam Tussauds is divided into different sections for the various categories of wax celebrities and includes Music, Hollywood, Sports and Shanghai Glamor. Additionally, there is the "Scream Hall," a haunted-house attraction that is rumored to be haunted by Charlie Chaplin's confused and angry ghost.

Of course, there is the cheaper option – very popular with the hordes of tourists on Nanjing West Road – to just take a picture with the wax figure of Jackie Chan at the entrance for free. However, seeing as wax figures are naturally very heat sensitive, Madam Tussauds is pleasantly air-conditioned during Shanghai's intense and humid summer days; you might as well just pop in anyway to cool off.

Public Security Museum

Chinese name: 上海公安博物馆 (Shànghǎi Gōng'ān Bówùguǎn)
Admission: FREE
Hours: 9:00-16:30 (Mon-Sat)
Recommended time for visit: 1 hour
Address: 2/F-4/F, 518 Ruijin South Rd (瑞金南路518号)
Transport:
Subway – Line 4, Luban Rd Station (鲁班路站), Exit 3, walk west on Quxi Rd (瞿溪路) for 450 m (1,476 ft), turn right on Ruijin South Rd and continue for 80 m (262 ft), the museum is on left

The Public Security Museum takes the mandate of all Chinese historical museums by showing a lot of stuff, then pushes it up a notch, carries it past excess, and lands in glory. It starts on the second floor with an innocent enough explanaation of the history of policing in Shanghai. The original force was a joint venture of the colonial powers that used a surprising amount of Indian Sikhs to fill the ranks, but by the time the communists were firmly in power, the police were all-Chinese and the various objects they accrued were apparently beginning to be stored for later exhibitions.

First comes documentation of efforts to stamp out "vile social evils left over from the old society," including a Nationalist Party assassin that killed hundreds of people. Then come scale models of buildings that represent every police station in the city, plus the Public Security College (and its dormitory) and the Shanghai Stadium for good measure. Along the way the most annoying song ever made plays over and over in a corner, sung by a little girl who lays it on entirely too thick and which translates to: "I found money on the street and gave it to a policeman; he patted me on the head and I said 'Goodbye uncle!'" Don't worry, there's more.

The third floor starts in a room with exhibits of famous serious killers complete with grisly crime scene photos that visitors with small children should avoid. It continues on to display not one but two cool old motorcycles, the embalmed poisoned fish made by another dastardly criminal, a room of shrines to great policeman of the past, a model of a three-story gallows (hanging room, corpse inspection room, carry-out-coffin room) used to execute Japanese war criminals by the Americans, and what appear to be some of the first printers ever invented. Both firefighters and traffic cops get their own themed room also.

Now for the fourth floor: Guns. The golden pistol of Sun Yat-sen, destroyer of the last dynasty, is one of the most beautiful firearms you will ever see. Actually, it's reason enough to visit the museum. But there's also an entire room of various guns arranged according to country of origin. Are there guns disguised as switchblades? Yes. Disguised as canes? Of course. Pens? What do you think? At the end, naturally, there's an ornate ceremonial sword.

Propaganda Poster Art Center

Chinese name: 宣传画年画艺术中心 (Xuānchuánhuà Niánhuà Yìshù Zhōngxīn)
Admission: ¥20
Hours: 10:00-17:00
Phone: 6211 1845; 139 0184 1246
Recommended time for visit: half an hour
Website: www.shanghaipropagandaart.com
Address: Basement, Bldg B, President Mansion, 868 Huashan Rd, near Zhenning Rd (华山路868号B幢，近镇宁路)
Transport:
Subway – Line 11, Jiangsu Rd Station (江苏路站), Exit 6, walk south along Jiangsu Rd, past Yan'an Elevated Rd, turn left into Hushan Rd, walk straight for about 50 m (164 ft), you'll find an apartment complex on the left side; enter at the main gate. The parking lot security guards will point you in the right direction with a little card with a simple map. You can take the elevator one floor down to the basement level at Bldg 4.

Slogans such as "Liberate Taiwan," "Workers of the World Unite," "Defend Korea Against US Aggression" and "Follow the Virtues of Chairman Mao" are just some of the many themes you'll run across in this fascinating museum dedicated to the propaganda of China's red days. There are over 3,000 original – we repeat "original," not copies like the ones you'll find being sold on Nanjing Road – posters from the 1950s-'70s that were used to promote socialist ideology, nationalism and, perhaps more importantly, Mao's personality cult.

The exhibit is divided into two rooms: first is a showroom with all the socialist-realist art from the days of Mao, and the second is the shop that sells replicas and copies so you can have your very own Cultural Revolution in your living room. Though it's not the biggest or fanciest gallery in Shanghai, original prints like the ones showcased here are very rare these days, so for those interested in Cold War history, you definitely want to save time for this one when strolling the French Concession. It would also be a good idea to call in advance since they periodically close without warning.

Shanghai Jewish Refugees Museum

Chinese name: 上海犹太难民纪念馆 (Shànghǎi Yóutài Nànmín Jì'niàn'guǎn)
Admission: ¥50
Hours: 9:00–17:00 (last entry 16:30)
Phone: 6512 6669
Website: www.shanghaijews.org.cn
Address: 62 Changyang Rd, Hongkou District (虹口区长阳路 62 号)
Transport: Subway – Line 12, Tilanqiao (提篮桥) Station, Exit 2, walk east 130 m (426 ft)

China saw more than its fair share of hardship before and during the Second World War. Tens of millions of Chinese died during the Japanese invasion from 1937 to 1945, but despite the incredible devastation and suffering, China was a major destination for inbound refugees.

Over twenty thousand European Jews found refuge from Nazi persecution in the cosmopolitan city of Shanghai. While many countries closed their doors to desperate Jewish refugees, China allowed entrance without visas. Even though thousands of Jews came into Shanghai in the 1930s and early '40s, there were already small communities of Russian and Middle Eastern Jews living in the city.

After the Japanese occupation of the city in 1937, the Jews were forced by the "Proclamation Concerning Restriction of Residence and Business of Stateless Refugees" to live in Hongkou. At that time Hongkou was among the poorest and most crowded areas in all of Shanghai. Although conditions were tough, they survived with the cooperation and goodwill of their Chinese neighbors.

Most of the Shanghai Jews moved to other countries after the Allied victory. However, they did not forget the kindness showed to them by the Chinese people. After the establishment of diplomatic relations between China and Israel in 1992, Yitzhak Rabin, the former Israeli Prime Minister, visited Shanghai and said: "To the people of Shanghai for the unique humanitarian act of saving thousands of Jews during the Second World War, thanks in the name of the government of Israel."

The museum itself is located on the former site of the Ohel Moshe Synagogue, built by Russian Jews in 1907. It has since undergone renovation funded by the Shanghai municipal government. The exhibits themselves provide colorful details into the daily life of the Shanghai Jews, as well as information about the notable former residents of the area, including film producer Mike Medavoy and US Secretary of the Treasury Werner Michael Blumenthal.

Other Attractions

Animation Museum

Chinese name: 上海漫画博物馆 (Shànghǎi Mànhuà Bówùguǎn)
Admission: ¥30
Hours: 10:00-17:00; closed Mon
Recommended time for visit: 1 hour
Address: 69 Zhangjiang Rd, near Zuchongzhi Rd (张江路69号,祖冲之路)
Website: www.sh-moca.com (in Chinese)
Transport:
Subway – Line 2, Guanglan Rd Station (广兰路站), Exit 5, walk west along Zuchongzhi Rd for about 150 m (492 ft), then turn right into Zhangjiang Rd, continue walking for about 100 m (328 ft), the musuem is on the right

From the tiny carousel and paddle boat pool outside the front door, one might assume this museum is strictly a matter of kiddie attractions with not much in the way of culture. Thankfully, both are provided, and in portions that should leave everyone satisfied. Play things are to be found in the main hall, while the exhibits themselves start off with the history of cartoons in China. Political cartoons gradually became popular in the late Qing Dynasty and eventually whole magazines were devoted to *mànhuà* (漫画), the Chinese name for cartoons and comics. One of the more striking publications, Shanghai Manhua, is featured in a display of its magazine covers that even today seem electric with the combined charge of politics and modern art.

A section on Chinese animated films is no less visually arresting. Small screens broadcast vibrantly-colored cartoons that sometimes evoke the artistry of early Disney movies with a unique Chinese flavor; one in particular looks like a moving world set in a traditional Chinese painting. The third section begins with a homage to game consoles (an odd choice given that all game consoles were technically banned in China at one point) and moves into an appreciation of American animated films and comic books. Full-sized plastic Marvel characters will entrance a certain age set, while the museum still finds space for a small exhibit on the delicate art of Chinese shadow puppetry at the end of the gallery.

Chinese Traditional Medicine Museum

Chinese name: 上海中医药博物馆 (Shànghǎi Zhōngyīyào Bówùguǎn)
Admission: ¥15
Hours: 9:00-16:00; closed Mon
Recommended time for visit: 1 hour
Address: 1200 Cailun Rd, near Jinke Rd, inside Chinese Traditional Medicine University (蔡伦路1200号,近金科路,上海中医药大学内)
Transport:
Subway – Line 2, Zhangjiang High-Tech Park Station (张江高科站), Exit 3, walk west on Zuchongzhi Rd (祖冲之路), turn left at first intersection onto Jinke Rd, continue for 1 km (less than 1 mi) and turn right into University, then turn left at first intersection on campus and follow it as it veers right to the circular building

Traditional Chinese Medicine (TCM) is one of the few aspects of China's ancient culture that the communists approved of during a time when sometimes violent modernization destroyed many other customs. In fact, the government has decided to support and promote it as not only an important expression of Chinese culture, but also a great contribution to the world of medical science. This in part explains the enormous college devoted to the practice (whether it's a science is not exactly a settled question outside of China) wherein this museum makes its home. The best way to experience it is to walk along through the gracefully designed exhibits wondering what TCM is all about... consider these Chinglish descriptions: "a special part of elephant," "ivory-carving models of diagnosing gynecology disease," "tooth fumigator," "Acupuncture Technique Parameter Analyzer."

The last one is part of a particularly baffling collection of modern technological instruments used by TCM experts, but most of the items here are as old, odd and beautiful as their unexplained titles suggest. The top floor contains various frogs and pearls, horns and minerals, plants and animal skins, that constitute the ingredients for traditional medicine. Don't forget to use the touch screens on the bottom floor, which play small movies with English subtitles about great figures in TCM. The movies help to explain a little more about the theory behind the practice.

Gallery of Antique Music Boxes

Chinese name: 上海八音盒珍品陈列馆 (Shànghǎi Bāyīnhé Zhēnpǐn Chénlièguǎn)
Admission: ¥50
Hours: 10:00-18:00
Recommended time for visit: 30 minutes
Address: 425 Dingxiang Rd, near Yingchun Rd (丁香路 425号, 近迎春路)
Transport: Subway – Line 2, Science and Technology Museum Station (上海科技馆站), Exit 1, go west to Dingxiang Rd, walk north on Dingxiang Rd a bit, the gallery is on the left in the Oriental Art Center (上海东方艺术中心)

Originally the personal collection of a Japanese businessman, this set of mechanical toys has more than enough vacant doll eyes and creepy monkeys to fuel a hundred nightmares. Fortunately, most of the assorted music boxes, automatons and mechanical clocks are jokey and charming. Make sure you're given a guided tour. Though the whole thing is in Chinese, the tour guide will offer demonstrations of many of the music boxes and reveal a few music boxes that don't seem to be so at first glance. The tour ends with a theatrical performance by some of the more intricate automatons on a small stage. The most amazing specimens are a pair of automatons that draw incredibly detailed sketches on demand; the oldest specimen is a small musical toy from 1796; the strangest specimen is a title for which competition is too close to call. Go and see if you can decide for yourself.

Glass Museum

Chinese name: 上海玻璃博物馆 (Shànghǎi Bōlí Bówùguǎn)
Admission: ¥20
Hours: 9:30-17:00, last admission at 16:30; closed Mon
Recommended time for visit: 1 hour
Website: en.shmog.org
Phone: 6618 1970
Address: 685 Changjiang West Rd, near Jiangyang South Rd (长江西路685号, 近江杨南路)
Transport:
Subway – Line 1, Tonghe Xincun Station (通河新村站), Exit 1, walk east on Changjiang West Rd for about 1,200 m (3,937), the museum is on the left

Improbably placed amidst factories and car dealerships in an obscure suburb of the city, the Shanghai Glass Museum puts on a surprisingly professional show. It all starts with a genuinely interesting history of glass crafting and continues through a few more equally engaging exhibits. All are supported with uniformly beautiful artifacts, and all contain interactive activities for the kids. The secret to the whole experience is that glass is inherently alluring, no matter what century it's from or what form it takes, and the museum takes full advantage of this fact on the excellently designed second floor, which backgrounds gorgeous glass art pieces and a Tang Dynasty glass bead exhibit in a field of black with soft futuristic lighting.

What really warrants the long journey to the museum is the wealth of activities and performances, which include glass blowing, DIY sand blasting, and a creative workshop for kids. All come at different times and with different prices, so be sure to check the website for the most appropriate time to catch it all.

Other Attractions

Matchbox & Brand Museum

Chinese name: 上海商标火花收藏馆 (Shànghǎi Shāngbiāo Huǒhuā Shōucángguǎn)
Admission: FREE
Hours: 9:00-11:30, 12:30-4:45
Recommended time for visit: half an hour
Phone: 6223 7998
Address: 251 Daduhe Rd, near Changning Rd (大渡河路251号, 近长宁路)
Transport: Subway – Line 2, Loushanguan Rd Station (娄山关路站), Exit 4, walk west on Tianshan Rd (天山路), turn right at the first intersection onto Gubei Rd (古北路), continue for 800 m (2,624 ft) and cross bridge; head to the building with the enormous mural, it's visible from the bridge to the right

The highlight of this museum is the building itself, whose entire south face is given over to a mural depicting an old matchbox design of a majestic dragon and clouds. In case you still don't get it, the museum also has massive matchsticks used as support for the overhang. Inside, the first floor is an exhibit of early Shanghai brands that combine Chinese themes with a vibrant period flair. To fill space, there are also international beer brands, which causes one to wonder whether The Labatt Blue Light logo will ever receive as respectful a treatment as it does here. The second floor, gained by an unmarked stairway behind a door, portends the third floor exhibition of matchboxes with a history of fire that begins with a plastic caveman pathetically rubbing sticks together, continues through a genuinely interesting display of old flints, and eventually ends, as all Chinese museums must, with the space program (strangely enough, the 2008 Olympics do not make an appearance).

The third floor brings matchbox covers by the thousands: Spanish matchbox covers of bullfighters, American matchbox covers of sports teams, Russian matchbox covers of iron-jawed peasants sternly looking toward a future of international communism. And then come the Chinese, organized by province and theme, featuring a preponderance of pagodas, pandas and stylized Chinese script. There are some real beauties if you're willing to look for them, or you can just take it all in at once and spend the rest of your time wondering at the will of the obsessive fanatic who conceived and manifested this shrine to the mundane.

National Anthem Memorial

Chinese name: 国歌纪念广场 (Guógē Jìniàn Guǎngchǎng)
Admission: FREE
Hours: 9:00-11:30 & 14:00-16:00 (Mon-Sat)
Recommended time for visit: half an hour
Address: 151 Jingzhou Rd (荆州路151号)
Transport:
Subway – Line 4, Dalian Rd Station (大连路站), Exit 2, walk southeast on Dalian Rd, memorial park is on the left

Now here is a perfect little slice of the Chinese history museum experience. A little nationalistic, a little corny (OK, a lot of both) and in its own way, completely endearing. The dominating statue at the center of the memorial park sets the tone. An expressive sweep of massive stone is fronted by a triumphant hand grasping... a bugle. The small museum nearby houses various photographs and mostly Chinese texts explaining the history of the anthem, whose English name is "March of the Volunteers." It was taken from the 1935 Shanghai film *Children of Troubled Times*, and the first floor accordingly displays many artifacts of that era's old Shanghai style.

Look for the name of Paul Robeson on the second floor. A brilliant actor of the Harlem Renaissance, Soviet sympathizer, and one-time singer of the Chinese national anthem, the man's exceptionally accomplished life deserves at least an internet search and also a bit of reflection on how history conspires to have his face pop up halfway across the world in a sleepy Shanghai museum. Also on this floor are listening stations to hear every country's national anthem and a "360 degree" movie that manages to bring up space exploration and the 2008 Olympics in a five-minute paean to that most perky of military marches to which this museum is dedicated.

Railway Museum

Chinese name: 上海铁路博物馆 (Shànghǎi Tiělù Bówùguǎn)
Admission: ¥10
Hours: 9:00-11:30, 14:00-16:00; closed Mon
Recommended time for visit: half an hour
Address: 200 Tianmu East Rd (天目东路200号)
Website: www.museum.shrail.com
Transport:
Subway – Lines 3 or 4, Baoshan Rd Station (宝山路站), Exit 1, walk south on Baoshan Rd, turn right at first intersection onto Tianmu East Rd, continue for 300 m (984 ft)

The construction of China's railways is one of the more interesting chapters in the country's history. Most were originally built basically as commercial endeavors by colonialist entrepreneurs who needed to ship goods from the interior and went about laying tracks whether the decaying Qing Dynasty permitted it or not. When the Chinese government did finally get in the game, it initially allowed the provinces to construct their own railways and then promptly decided to seize them and sell them to foreign banks for quick cash, thereby helping to incite the revolution that would depose China's last emperor. But since most of the text in this museum is Chinese, non-Chinese speaking visitors will have to content themselves with some of the museum's more visual pleasures.

Highlights, such as they are, include two big train engines in the front courtyard, a computer game that inexplicably challenges the player to dock a ship in various tide conditions, and some genuinely fascinating and beautiful photographs showing a turn-of-the-century China gradually acclimating to advancing in technology. Especially interesting are photographs of Chinese train stations, past and present. First built by Europeans on a scale that wouldn't be out of place in an English hamlet, almost every city of any size in China now requires hulking steel and glass behemoths to accommodate by far the largest number of train passengers in the world.

Museum of the Chinese Imperial Examination System

Chinese name: 中国科举博物馆 (Zhōngguó Kējǔ Bówùguǎn)
Admission: ¥20
Hours: 8:00-16:00
Recommended time for visit: 1 hour
Address: 183 Sout St, near Tacheng Rd (南大街183号, 近塔城路)
Transport:
Subway & Bus: Subway – Line 11, North Jiading Station (嘉定北站), Exit 1, go to the bus stop outside the subway station and take bus 9 or 13 to Tacheng Rd & Chengzhong Rd (塔城路城中路) Stop, then walk northwest on Chengzhong Rd, turn right at first intersection onto Tacheng Rd, continue to first intersection at South St and turn right, continue 100 m (328 ft)

The Imperial Examination was a defining aspect of Chinese civilization from its first systematized implementation in 605 CE to the last dynasty in 1905. Success in the exams was required for official posts, and the early lives of virtually all young men of the aristocracy were consumed by study of the Confucian classics in pursuit of that goal, which often required taking the exams multiple times over many years. The museum devoted to this system begins with a testament to Chinese record keeping: The exact numbers of people who successfully attained high degrees in the exam are listed from the Tang Dynasty onward, as is the number of individuals who attained the highest grade in each exam – 611 in the exam's 1,300 years of history.

The exhibits are handsomely designed, and English text is provided for most descriptions. Actual exam papers are displayed, as well as such interesting artifacts as the note of a desperate aristocrat who pleaded with the emperor to give him a degree after already failing the exams three times (answer: no) and giant tablets explaining the exam rules sitting on the backs of stone turtles.

The museum resides in the small and lovely **Jiading Confucian Temple** (Kǒng Miào; 孔庙) – possessed of unexpectedly grand trees and three grand bridges at its entrance – which itself resides to the left of the entrance to **Huilongtan Park** (Huílóngtán Gōngyuán; 汇龙潭公园). Huilongtan is a normal Chinese park save for the almost jungly amount of trees and the presence of bumper cars, a carousel and other miniature carnival attractions for the kids.

Art Galleries

You could spend a week or more touring all of Shanghai's art galleries, and we have listed some of the best in Top Attractions. But for many true aficionados deeply submerged in the world of art, the art galleries listed in Top Attractions may be a bit too mainstream. Even though the ones we have listed here aren't "off the beaten path" since...well, they're mentioned in a guidebook, they are still underrated and lesser-known than the city's big shots. That's not to say they're of any less quality, however; it is here that you can find some hidden gems, and you won't have to worry about the flocks of tourists smudging your camera lens along the way.

Rockbund Art Museum

Chinese name: 上海外滩美术馆 (Shànghǎi Wàitān Měishùguǎn)
Admission: ¥15
Hours: 10:00-18:00 (Tue-Sun); closed Mon
Phone: 3310 9985
Recommended time for visit: 1 hour
Website: www.rockbundartmuseum.org
Address: 20 Huqiu Rd (虎丘路 20 号)
Transport:
Subway – Lines 2 or 10, Nanjing East Rd Station (南京东路站), Exit 6, walk north along Henan Middle Rd (河南中路), turn right into Beijing East Rd (北京东路), past Jiangxi Middle Rd (江西中路) and Sichuan Middle Rd (四川中路), turn left onto Huqiu Rd

This private collection tucked right behind the Bund and just south of Suzhou Creek is housed in the former Royal Asiatic Society Building that was erected in 1933. The museum has a focus on contemporary Chinese art, but they showcase new exhibits from foreign artists throughout the year, so make sure to check out their website to see what's going on during your visit.

Established in 2010 as part of a new project by the Rockefeller Group to rejuvenate the north Bund neighborhood, the museum is considered one of the city's premier modern art museums, and there are many cool cafes, art houses and shops popping up in this trendy district. Some of the neighborhood's highlights include the British Consulate, Huqiu Road for architecture and the Capital Theater, and Yuanmingyuan Road for upscale shopping.

China Art Museum

Chinese name: 中华艺术宫 (Zhōnghuá Yìshù Gōng)
Admission: FREE (¥20 for special exhibits)
Hours: 9:00–17:00 (last admission at 16:00); closed Mon
Phone: 400 921 9021
Website: www.artmuseumonline.org (in Chinese)
Recommended time for visit: 1-2 hours
Address: 205 Shangnan Rd, Pudong (浦东新区上南路 205号)
Transport: Subway – Line 8, China Art Museum Station (中华艺术宫站), Exit 2.

The China Art Museum – located in the former China Pavilion (Zhōngguó Guójiā Guǎn; 中国国家馆) of the Shanghai 2010 World Expo – is the scene of many superlatives. With a floor space of 166,000 sq m (1,790,000 sq ft), it is the largest art museum in Asia. It is also located at the tallest structure of the world's most-visited World Expo. Critics might point out that it was also the most expensive structure ever built for the World Expo, with a price tag of over US$330 million (or ¥2 billion, that's 100 million bottles of Qingdao beer!). However, unlike many grand municipal projects built for international events, the China Pavilion is still being put to good use.

The building itself is very striking. The design was based off a design of a Chinese *ding* vessel, used by the emperor to make offerings to the spirits. In bright lucky Chinese red, the structure also resembles an ancient Chinese crown, and a traditional Chinese garden sits on the top of the inverted pyramid.

As is fitting for Shanghai, traditional elements blend with modern technology. A large solar electric system sits near the traditional courtyard of the rooftop. The building – made to showcase "Chinese wisdom in urban development" incorporates many energy-efficient design elements.

Of course, the Chinese Art Museum has artistic temptations to accompany its architectural wonders. The largest permanent exhibition showcases contemporary Chinese art, from the end of the Qing Dynasty to the present. Paintings, sculptures, and multimedia projects of renowned international artists can often be found in the special exhibition area, which costs another ¥20 to visit.

Amongst the finest paintings in the museum is "Where Spring Returns" (Chūn Guī Héchù; 春归何处) by Wú Guànzhōng (吴冠中). This piece blends elements of impressionism with traditional Chinese motifs. Also of note is "Nanjing Road Shanghao Eight Company" (Nánjīnglùshàng Hǎobālián; 南京路上好八连), which uses a modern take on Socialist Realism to present an image of Shanghai in the early 1900s.

Within a short walking distance of the China Art Museum is the Expo Axis, a strange and futuristic building made of steel glass tunnels and a membraned roof. Also nearby is an indoor stadium and music venue formerly known as the Shanghai World Expo Cultural Center. This venue is now called – in a rather fitting tribute to socialism with Chinese characteristics – the Mercedes-Benz Arena. The site of classical Chinese music performances during the World Expo has since hosted Usher and Jennifer Lopez.

Other Attractions

Moganshan Road & M50 Creative Park

Chinese name: 莫干山路 (Mògànshān Lù) ; M50 创意园 (M Wǔlíng Chuàngyìyuán)
Recommended time for visit: 1-2 hours
Address: Moganshan Rd, near Aomen Rd （莫干山路，近澳门路）
Website: www.m50.cn (in Chinese)
Transport:
Subway – Line 1, Shanghai Railway Station, Exit 5, walk west on Tianmu West Rd（天目西路）for 800 m (2,624 ft), right after crossing bridge turn right on West Suzhou Rd（西苏州路）, which after 250 m (820 ft) becomes Moganshan Rd

Located at the beginning of Moganshan Road, M50 has undergone the usual life cycle of art spaces in a city, from low rent derelict building to a growing artist colony gradually gaining recognition, and finally to a place where a Porsche or two wouldn't be out of place. Over 100 art galleries inhabit this former factory, and the fun is in the fact that every gallery you step into offers another chance to snicker at pretension, admire imitations of old masters, be befuddled by weirdness, watch a painter as she creates a new work, be helplessly taken with kitsch, or even find a thing of true beauty. Of course, there are also gift shops for those of us who don't have a few thousand to spare.

There are over 120 studios and galleries in M50, but some of the best are **ShanghART** (Xiānggénà Huàláng; 香格纳画廊 ;phone: 6359 3923; www.shanghartgallery.com), **Island6** (Liù Dǎo; 六 岛 ; www.island6.org) and **EastLink Gallery**(Dōngláng Yishù; 东廊艺术 ; phone: 6276 9932; address: 5/F, Bldg 6, 50 Moganshan Lu). Some of Shanghai's best artists, like Zhou Tiehai and Xu Zhen, also work here. Further up the road, Moganshan has one more surprise. On the left is what seems to be the backside of a building specializing in wholesale furniture. To the right is an empty lot where the fallow grass grows high. And in this rather unimpressive setting, a wall separating the field from the street carries a ribbon of brilliant graffiti stretching hundreds of meters and wrapping around the wall to meet Suzhou Creek. It is a perfect scene: a forgotten road in the middle of the city, revivified by color.

Power Station of Art

Chinese name: 上海当代艺术博物馆 (Shànghǎi Dāngdài Yìshù Bówùguǎn)
Admission: FREE (special exhibitions require fee)
Hours: 9:00-17:00 (last admission at 16:00); closed Sun
Recommended time for visit: 1 hour
Address: 200 Huayuangang Rd, near Miaojiang Rd (花园港路200号, 近苗江路)
Website: www.powerstationofart.org/en
Transport:
Subway – Lines 4 or 8, Xizang South Rd Station (西藏南路站), Exit 2, walk northeast on Zhongshan South Rd for 375 m (1,230 ft), turn right on Nanchezhan Rd which becomes Huayuangang Rd and continue for 600 m (1,968 ft)

Power Station of Art seems like a slightly off Chinglish phrase until, far before reaching the museum, an enormous smokestack becomes visible, confirming that this is indeed a retrofitted power station. Close inspection of the smokestack reveals a neon thermometer shooting up the side, confirming this is also a repository for modern art. The fantastic structures made for the Shanghai Expo form a ghost town of rusting husks around the museum, confirming the surrealism of the whole situation and constituting something to see in and of themselves.

There is a slight problem with the non-power plant aspect of the building, which is to say the art: There isn't a lot of it. The power plant is absolutely massive, and the entry area alone could fit a few houses. In all this, however, one can find about three to four exhibitions and no real permanent collection to speak of. About two thirds of the museum's gallery space is closed to the public. Fundamentally, it suffers the same problem as its giant art museum sibling, The Art Palace, on the other side of the river. It was built to house an Expo collection far larger than it now commands, and its directors don't seem to have the capability, or desire, to turn it into a museum fitting of its size. Still, art can be seen in any city. Where else are you going to experience a humongous power station with a thermometer on the side of it presiding over the decaying corpse of an amusement park while the placid Huangpu River floats by? Go see it.

Chinese name: 上海工艺美术博物馆 (Shànghǎi Gōngyì Měishù Bówùguǎn)
Admission: ¥8
Hours: 9:00-17:00
Recommended time for visit: 1 hour
Address: 79 Fenyang Rd, near Fuxing Rd (汾阳路 79 号，近复兴路)
Website: www.shgmb.com (in Chinese)
Transport:
Subway – Line 1, Changshu Rd Station (常熟路站), Exit 4, walk west on Huaihai Middle Rd (淮海中路) for 50 m (164 ft), turn left onto Baoqing Rd (宝庆路) and continue for 350 m (1,148 ft), the road becomes Hengshan Rd (衡山路), turn left onto Taojiang Rd (桃江路) and continue for 150 m (492 ft), keep to the left at the fork and the street becomes Fenyang Rd, continue for 250 m (820 ft)

It's not always clear which parts of the Arts and Crafts Museum are for education and which are for commerce. The uncharitable tourist might wonder why he or she should pay even ¥8 to visit a site that is inundated with so many gift shops (complete with English signs and currency exchange), but the museum has more than a few worthy charms up its sleeve, and the shops give way to displays by the second floor. The whole affair resides in a completely white mansion built in 1905 by a French businessman, and though much of the splendor has obviously been lost in the restoration, it's still a fun building to walk through while looking at the embroidery, ivory carvings and other pieces of decorative art that the museum displays (unexpected bonus: the mansion also contains the original toilet, bidet and shower, which looks like a torture device).

Almost all of the items on display were made in the later 20th century and, accordingly, many evince the particular spirit of those times. One ivory sculpture that shows two children playing with model airplanes is titled "We Love Science." Another carving, made of wood and titled "Giving a Good Beat" shows children aggressively straddling what seems to be a battering ram, some holding guns, with a sign overhead that says "Taiwan must be liberated" in Chinese. The biggest draw of the museum is the chance to watch local craftspeople at work. Each room on the top floor features a different trade: jade carvers, painters, embroiderers, even dough sculptors.

Commerce is never far behind, however. How else to explain the presence of a three foot reproduction of a Princess Diana photo realized through the ancient art of Chinese embroidery?

Parks

There are parks scattered all across Shanghai, and you'll never be too far from one in case you need a quick break or, if you really want to go tribal and act like the locals, take a nap on a bench. Even though you can find parks coupled with other attractions – and it's certainly hard to beat Yu Garden and Ancient Yi Garden – these four alternatives that we have listed here are unique in their own manner and perfect for a splendid day outside. (Just make sure to check the pollution readings beforehand.)

Fuxing Park

Chinese name: 复兴公园 (Fùxìng Gōngyuán)
Admission: FREE
Hours: 6:00-18:00
Recommended time for visit: 1 hour
Address: 2 Gaolan Rd (皋兰路 2 号)
Transport: **Subway** – Line 10, Xintiandi Station, Exit 6, walk west for about 80 m (262 ft)

Located in the heart of the French Concession, this strikingly elegant garden was originally designed by the French in 1909 and was then called Gu's Park. Later, the Japanese named it Daxing Park, but once China regained control of the city, the municipal government changed the name to Fuxing Park.

The 10 hectare landscape is quintessentially French in layout, architecture and design, and is shadowed with streams, a lake, swathes of fragrant flowers and quaint European pavilions. The park also contains a yellow and turquoise Chinese pagoda complex that presides over a lily pond and looks as if it were designed by a Western architect in the '60s.

A stroll through the park during the early hours of daybreak is the best time to experience lovely Fuxing. Locals flock to practice tai chi and do their morning exercise routines, and an hour or two later the winding lanes fill up with others playing cards, Chinese chess and *mahjong*, while others stroke the *erhu*, chat about the "good ole days" over a smoke, and hang out to enjoy the ambiance. In the evening, many older ladies use the park as a place to show off their line dancing skills; feel free to join them if you think you can hang!

Zuibaichi Park

Chinese name: 醉白池公园 (Zuìbáichí Gōngyuán)
Admission: ¥12
Hours: 9:00-16:00
Recommended time for visit: 1 hour
Address: 64 Renmin South Rd, near Songhui Rd (人民南路64号, 近松汇路)
Transport:
Subway – Line 9, Zuibaichi Station, Exit 3

There's nary a city in all of China that doesn't have a traditional garden or two, but Zuibaichi sets itself apart with the quality of its design and the abundance of its offerings. It perfectly illustrates the purpose of winding paths and dense trees in Chinese gardens, which is to create a steady flow of small discoveries and intimate spaces. Walking aimlessly along the stone paths of Zuibaichi, you may encounter a shaded tea room with a shrine in the back, or pass through a gate in a wall to suddenly find yourself in a garden of bonsai trees. Further on, a collection of small furnished rooms are artfully placed around lily ponds and bridged channels, and a walled enclosure yields a fountain in a pool or a subtle arrangement of sculpted rocks and foliage. The park also seems to be a favorite of the retired, so surprises may include happening upon an ongoing game of cards in one of the pavilions or a grandpa frozen awkwardly into one of the stances of his tai chi routine.

Sheshan National Holiday Resort

Chinese name: 佘山国家旅游度假区 (Shéshān Guójiā Lǚyóu Dùjiàqū)
Admission: Most areas are FREE, ¥10 for entrance to the nearby Tianmashan Park (Tiānmǎshān Gōngyuán; 天马山公园)
Phone: 5765 3324
Website: www.sheshantravel.com (English available)
Address: 18 Linyin Rd, Sheshan Town (林荫路 18 号)
Transportation: **Subway** – Line 9 has a stop at Sheshan Station (佘 山 站). Bicycles are available for rent in the area.

At about 100 m (328 ft) tall, Sheshan is one of the higher hills within the Shanghai city limits and is known for its natural beauty, great views and historical sights. While Sheshan can get crowded – especially during the weekends – it offers a convenient retreat away from Shanghai's concrete jungle. Sheshan is particularly interesting for those seeking the spiritual side of the ultra-materialistic city of Shanghai.

In order to avoid the crowds, take one of the quieter paths up the hill. Perhaps the best of these paths goes through a (relatively) quiet bamboo forest. Be on the lookout for wildlife, especially the many colorful birds that inhabit the woodlands.

On the peak of Sheshan sits **Our Lady of Sheshan Catholic Church**. This place of worship is the largest Catholic basilica in China, offering a unique glimpse into Shanghai's colonial past all while providing an excellent example of neo-gothic architecture. Perhaps due to the political rift between China's Catholic Patriotic Association and the Vatican, services are still held in Latin. The church is also an active pilgrimage site for Chinese Catholics, especially in the spring.

A Jesuit observatory is also on the top of the hill. It functions as a sort of museum, featuring both modern and classical equipment used to study the stars. It also has a detailed replica of a Han Dynasty device used to measure the intensity of earthquakes.

Heaven Horse Mountain (Tiānmǎ Shān; 天马 山) is also worth a visit. At the top is the more than 900-year-old **Huzhu Pagoda** (Hùzhū Tǎ; 护 珠 塔), leaning to one side at a 6.87-degree incline – a more pronounced lean than the famous Leaning Tower of Pisa. The unlucky pagoda was not only erected on an architecturally unsuitable site (with some of its foundation lying on mud), it was also damaged by peasants searching for gold during the tough times of the 1800s.

Besides these spiritual and historical areas you find the typical exemplars of modern mass consumerism. Numerous overpriced tea and coffee shops dot the slopes of the mountain. For those so inclined, Sheshan has everything from billiards and fishing to bungee jumping. Of course, the main draw is the view. On clear days, one can see far into the urban majesty of Shanghai.

Other Attractions

121

Yuehu Sculpture Park

Chinese name: 月湖雕塑公园 (Yuèhú Diāosù Gōngyuán)
Admission: ¥120
Hours: 9:00-17:00
Recommended time for visit: 1 hour
Address: 1158 Linyin New Rd, near Shebei Highway (松江区林荫新路 1158 号，近余北公路)
Website: www.shanghai-sculpture-park.com.cn
Transport:
Subway & Bus: Subway – Line 9, Sheshan Station, Exit 2, go to the bus station outside of the subway station, take bus 92 to Shebei Highway (余北公路), walk down Shebei Rd, which branches off to the east from the main road at bus station, continue a short while and enter the parking lot filled with sculptures

The Yuehu Sculpture Park's largest annoyances, the fee and the distant location, are also two of its best assets. They ensure that there's never a crowd on the expansive grounds and thereby provide one of the hardest luxuries to come by in Shanghai: solitude, in this case accompanied by harp music that plays softly throughout the entire park and lends the place a dreamy atmosphere. The sculptures themselves are sometimes delightfully odd, but for the most part not worth mentioning; whoever selected them has a questionable affection for shiny spinning metal objects. Likewise, there's nothing to say about the museum either, which offers more of the same. What the park does have is a real beach and ample lawn space (it really is very large), making it the perfect place for a picnic with friends, a quiet read, or a pick up game of ball. Just don't let the mood go from dreamy to creepy when you see the rusted human sculptures paralyzed in various states of play on the beach's surface. This sculputre park is relatively close to the aforementioned Sheshan National Holiday Resort. Consider combining the two for a day's outing since they're both far from downtown.

Ancient Water Towns

The surrounding water villages of Shanghai have often been compared to Venice. Definitely reserve a few days to explore these ancient water towns; they're truly magnificent works of 3D art, combining winding streams with gondola cruises, excellent cuisine from the dynastic heydays, and charming traditional architecture that inspired an entire culture. Some of the best water towns are found on the outskirts of Shanghai (see Side Trips on pg 234), and Qibao has already been mentioned in Top Attractions, but there are several that are a little bit closer in case you just don't have enough time to venture too far from the city's raving nightlife.

Fengjing Ancient Water Town

Chinese name: 枫泾古镇 (Fēngjīng Gǔzhèn)
Admission: ¥50 for access to the ancient town, ¥30 for entrance into the Peasant's Painting Village (Nóngmín Huàcūn; 农民画村)
Hours: 8:00-16:30 (closes at 17:00 from May-Sep)
Phone: 5735 5555
Address: 39 Xinfeng Rd, Fengjing Town (金山区枫泾镇 新枫路39号)
Transport:
Subway & Bus: Take Subway Line 1 to Jinjiang Park Station (锦江乐园站) and walk south for 20 m (65 ft) to the New Southwest Bus Station (新西南汽车站). Take the Fengmei Line (枫梅线) directly to Fengjing. The bus journey should take about 45 minutes.

Fengjing Ancient Water Town is a relatively unspoiled historic area roughly one hour to the southwest of downtown Shanghai. The town is renowned for its ancient buildings and bridges, the oldest of which was built around the same time the town came into existence over 750 years ago (during the Yuan Dynasty). Worthwhile for those with a hankering for ancient homes and temples, the town is also particularly attractive for visitors interested in the arts.

A distinctive folk art known as **Jinshan Peasant Painting** (Jīnshān Nóngmín Huà; 金山农民画) originates in Fengjing. In 1972, professional painter Wú Tóngzhāng (吴 彤 章) came to the village and cooperated with local women to create an entirely new form of visual art. Wu taught the local women – who were already skilled in embroidery – how to use paper canvas as a cloth and specially designed paint brushes as needles. This created a unique style that combines embroidery with painting and they use this special medium to create colorful images

from their daily lives. Fengjing is also famous for its high quality woodwork and lantern making.

Fengjing is considerably smaller than Zhujiajiao (see next pg), the another famous aquatic ancient town to the south of Shanghai. Also, unlike Zhujiajiao, tickets are required for entrance into the main historic area of Fengjing. While these conditions may sound like disadvantages, they can actually work out to a visitor's benefit. An entrance fee keeps the proverbial barbarians at the gate, so Fengjing tends to be much less crowded and commercialized. Its smaller area also makes Fengjing Ancient Town easier to digest than Zhujiajiao.

Fengjing provides a pleasant mix of authentic historic feeling and accessibility to foreign and domestic visitors. Local residents make a point of being friendly and fair to their guests – after all, a good local reputation is in their best business interest. Along with art, history, and relative tranquility, Fengjing has great food at generally reasonable prices. Steamed dumplings and *zongzi* (rice and pork mashed together and served in bamboo leaves) are the local specialties.

Zhujiajiao Ancient Town

Chinese name: 朱家角古镇 (Zhūjiājiǎo Gǔzhèn)
Admission: Free (some sites within the town require entrance tickets). ¥80 buys a "cruise boat trip" and admission to nine scenic spots. A three hour-tour with an English-speaking tour guide costs ¥120.
Location: Roughly one hour south of downtown Shanghai
Transport: Buses leave from People's Square every half hour during the day. Look for the buses at the intersection of Pu'an Rd (普安路) and Jinling Rd (金陵路) that say Huzhu Express Line (沪朱高速快线)

This is the perfect daytrip for those seeking historic ambiance and great photo opportunities. Zhujiajiao has many legitimate old buildings crisscrossed by canals that are still used for transportation. While the town has a history of over 1,500 years, most of the old buildings and bridges still standing today were built during the Ming and Qing Dynasties.

Zhujiajiao once prospered from textiles and rice. Transportation was made easier by the construction of the Grand Canal – a massive, man-made ancient Chinese waterway that linked southern China with the north. Successful local residents built exquisite dwellings with walled courtyards, distinctive bridges and unique temples. Amongst the old buildings, the most striking are the **Qing Dynasty Post Office** (Dàqīng Yóujú; 大清邮局), the **Yuanjin Meditation Room** (Yuánjīn Chányuàn; 圆津禅院) and the **Tongtianhe Medicine Shop** (Tóngtiānhé Yàohào; 童天和药号); entrance to these areas requires the purchase of a ticket. **Moon View Pavilion** (Wàngyuè Lóu; 望月楼) is the tallest classical building in Zhujiajiao and offers the most spectacular views. It is located on Xijing Street (西井街) in the northern part of the town.

Of course, as with any well-known historical site in China, the local economy is now completely dominated by tourism; there are throngs of visitors during the weekends. What's more, the area has experienced a large degree of commercialization, especially as China's domestic tourism industry has blossomed. Visit Zhujiajiao while you can – large shopping centers are being built within the old city, and more and more historic buildings are undergoing renovation.

That's not to say one can't find a quiet corner within the old town. Numerous gardens, temples and cafes provide comfortable opportunities for relaxation. Just be aware of scammers in temples – if any old Chinese person tries to give you anything in Zhujiajiao, never take it. Numerous fake Buddhist monks prey on foreign and Chinese tourists alike, asking for "donations" in exchange for mass-produced trinkets. Ignore them.

There is a bright side to Zhujiajiao's commercialization, however. Hundreds of street vendors sell a tantalizing variety of local snacks, including lotus root soup, salty soy beans, and deep-fried tofu. There are also many touristy souvenirs.

Zhujiajiao is, of course, most famous for its waterways and bridges. There are many old stone bridges, the oldest of which were built well over 500 years ago. A small trip in a local gondola is quite enjoyable.

Jinze Water Town

Chinese name: 金泽水乡 (Jīnzé Shuǐxiāng)
Recommended time for visit: 1-2 hours
Transport:
Subway & Bus: Subway – Line 1, Huangpi South Rd Station (黄陂南路站), Exit 2, walk northeast on Huaihai Middle Rd for 300 m (984 ft), turn left onto Pu'an Rd, continue for 200 m (656 ft) to the bus station, take Huzhu Gaosu Kuaixian (沪朱高速快线) to Zhujiajiao Bus Station (朱家角汽车站), walk west on Xiangningbang Rd for a few meters to the bus stop, take Qingjin Xian (青金线) to Jinze Water Town

Jinze is what Zhujiajiao was before a direct tourist line from Shanghai was created and a hundred trendy coffee shops bloomed. It's about 30 minutes away from its larger cousin and an interesting comparison for those who want to see a water town in its original state. Along the canals are the houses, gardens and laundry lines of the local residents; the only amenities a tourist can use are the public toilets. The waterways are interspersed among the more modern parts of town. Right at the bus stop is a road that forms a T-section with the highway, and the best way to experience the old town is to find and start walking down a canal north or south of this road directly east of the highway.

Besides the idiosyncratic architecture and the greenery lining the banks and floating on the water, the most beautiful features of the town are the seven or so bridges that connect the roads at various points along the canals.

Each bridge is unique in design, but the most striking is a bridge in a 19th century scroll painting whose complex construction method was only recently rediscovered by a Chinese engineer. He used the ancient method to build a replica bridge in Jinze with the help of *NOVA*, an American TV science program. It's the closest thing the town has to a proper tourist attraction.

As mentioned, Jinze is only half an hour away from Zhujiajiao. To make the most out of your day (and avoid the confusing maze of directions needed to get here), hire a taxi from Zhujiajiao.

Former Residences

Everyone from China's far left (Mao Zedong) to its staunch right (Wellington Koo), and everyone in between (Sun Yat-sen), has spent significant amounts of time in Shanghai. For a look back into the history of some of China's most revolutionary thinkers, politicians and businessmen, check out some of the former residences of Shanghai. See Duolun Culture Street on pg 91 for additional ancient residences.

Former Residence of Mao Zedong

Chinese name: 毛泽东故居 (Máozédōng Gùjū)
Admission: FREE
Hours: 9:00-11:00 and 13:00-16:00; closed Mon
Recommended time for visit: 1 hour
Address: 7, Lane 583, Weihai Rd (威海路 583 弄 7 号)
Transport: Subway – Line 2, Nanjing West Rd Station, Exit 4, walk south for about 50 m (164 ft)

Mao Zedong – Marxists revolutionary, father of modern China and one of the most influential people in the country's long history – lived in this small humble dwelling in 1924. Though a native of Hunan Province, Mao is said to have visited Shanghai over 50 times in his lifespan, and it was at this address that he spent the most time in Shanghai. The house is fashioned in

Shanghai's quintessential shikumen façade of the 1920s and '30s, and there is a large stone entrance gate, dark green brick floors and walls, and poems written by Mao scattered throughout the compound (Mao was an avid writer, essayist and poet).

The exterior is a work of art and gives one the true feeling of old timey Shanghai, but the inside is a little more kitsch, with wax figurines of the Great Helmsman, his wife Yang Kaihui and other family members. The residence is furbished with desks, chairs, tables and other items from the Qing era (the actual furniture Mao used), and there are numerous photos, exhibits and even displays of his favorite cigars.

Chinese name: 周恩来故居 (Zhōu'ēnlái Gùjū)
Admission: FREE
Hours: 9:00-11:00 and 13:00-16:00
Phone: 6473 0420
Recommended time for visit: 1 hour
Address: 73 Sinan Rd (思南路 73 号)
Transport:
Subway – Lines 10 & 13, Xintiandi Station, Exit 2, walk west along Fuxing Rd for about 200 m (656 ft), turn left at Sinan Rd, then continue walking about 20 m (65 ft), the residence is on your left side

As Karl Marx once said, "All animals are created equal, but some animals are more equal than others." Upon seeing this former cadre's stylish crib, you'll definitely see why. Zhou Enlai's (1898-1976) home is a gorgeous three-story French-designed mansion with an extravagant garden. In the back, Zhou's sleek black Buick is still parked in the garage, and a statue of the politician stands mightily amidst the beautiful grounds.

The house originally served as the Communist Party's Shanghai office before the Revolution, and it is where Zhou stayed when he visited Shanghai. Zhou's room is on the first floor (you can still see some of his personal belongings and bed), newspapers were printed on the second floor, and there was a dormitory on the third floor for visiting comrades. The compound outside is tranquil and relaxing for the weary-eyed visitor, and there are numerous

photos and exhibits throughout the place that detail Zhou's life and the history of the CCP.

Zhou Enlai was a keen politician, military strategist and diplomat (he masterminded the first meeting between US president Richard Nixon and Mao Zedong in the early '70s). He was also the first Foreign Minister of the PRC and Vice Chairman of the Communist Party, and he held the all important post of Premier of the PRC from 1949 until his death in 1976 (coincidentally, the same year Mao Zedong passed away). His legacy as one of the fathers of modern China is one of the most revered in the country.

Chinese name: 孙中山故居 (Sūnzhōngshān Gùjū)
Admission: ¥20
Hours: 9:00-16:00
Phone: 6437 2954
Address: 7 Xiangshan Rd (香山路 7 号)
Transport: Subway – Line 6, Xintiandi (新 天 地) Station, Exit 6, walk west for about 10 minutes, it's next to Fuxing Park (复兴公园)

This pleasant Western-style house was the home of Sun Yat-sen from 1918 to his death in 1925. Sun is revered in Mainland China as "the forerunner of the democratic revolution," and visitors from Taiwan also flock to the building to honor the man they consider to be "The Father of the Nation." Sun's ideals and activism helped to topple China's last dynasty and usher in the modern period of Chinese history.

The Former Residence of Sun Yat-sen was purpose-built for Mr Sun with donations from ethnic Chinese living in Canada. The building has now been turned into an institution that blurs the line between museum and shrine. Many of the furnishings and utensils used by Mr Sun have been lovingly preserved.

Sun Yat-sen was a political thinker and revolutionary who struggled against the Qing Empire to establish the Republic of China. He was also co-founder of the Kuomingtang (KMT) Nationalist Party. After a brief stint as the first President of China, Sun's government fell into factional infighting, and the situation in China became very chaotic. Sun made an alliance with the Communist Party of China in order to combat the warlords who had seized power over much of the country, and Sun's alliance with the Communists and his cooperation with the Soviet Union are very much stressed in the museum housed in his former Shanghai residence.

The usually somber Former Residence of Sun Yat-sen becomes very lively twice a year. On December 12 his birth is celebrated, and on March 12 his passing is remembered. Tens of thousands of emotional visitors stream into the site on these days and leave flowers at Sun's statue.

This historical site is located in a quiet and pleasant neighborhood. Fuxing Park, adjacent to the residence, is a great example of a typical Shanghai park without the hordes of tourists. Retired people dance, practice tai chi, and play games in the park, while children fly kites or ride the park's many small rides. There are also numerous green spaces and well-shaded quiet pathways.

Song Qingling Memorial Residence

Chinese name: 宋庆龄故居 (Sòngqìnglíng Gùjū)
Admission: ¥20
Hours: 9:00-16:30
Phone: 6437 6268
Website: www.shSong-chingling.com (in Chinese)
Address: 1843 Huaihai Middle Rd (淮海中路 1843 号)
Transport: Subway – Line 10, Jiaotong University (交通大学), Exit 1, walk east along Huaihai Middle Rd for 20 m (65 ft)

Song Qingling (also known as Song Ching-ling) was one of Shanghai's most influential natives. She was the wife of President Sun Yat-sen and an important political figure in her own right. After her husband's death, Song remained very active politically. She fled to Moscow following Chiang Kai-shek's betrayal of his former Communist allies, and during the Chinese Civil War and the Japanese invasion, Song lobbied internationally on behalf of the Communist Party of China.

The Song Qingling Memorial Residence is located in the former French Concession and the elegant building and its adjoining grounds cover over 4,300 sq m (46,285 sq ft). The property once belonged to a Greek shipping tycoon, but after the establishment of the People's Republic of China in 1949, Song donated her previous residence (the one before this site) to serve as a memorial to her late husband, and the new government gave her this stately residence as compensation.

Dozens of important Chinese and international leaders – from Mao Zedong to Indonesia's Sukarno – visited Song at her new home. Although she spent most of her final years in Beijing, the local government helped to maintain her residence, even through the chaotic times of the Cultural Revolution.

Today, the grounds are so comfortable and well maintained that one could be forgiven for thinking Song Qingling still resides in the building. Many of Song's favorite art pieces decorate the residence. Her office upstairs looks practical and comfortable, and her bed is lovingly made each morning.

The museum offers particularly excellent English translations. Over 15,000 of Song's original belongings, various awards (including a "Stalin Peace Prize") and written works can be found in her residence. There is also a limo gifted by Joseph Stalin. Song's dedication to her country, and her sophistication, still shine through this memorial many years after her death.

```
                    Charlie Song ──┬── Ni Kwei-tseng
         ┌──────────┬──────────────┼──────────────┬──────────────┐
   Ailing Song ─ H H Kung   Qingling Song ─ Sun Yat-sen   T V (Tse-Ven) Song   Meiling Song ─ Chiang Kai-shek
```

(Left) Oil painting of the three Song sisters.

(Above) A family potrait of the Songs: from left to right on the bottom row: Meiling, Ni Kwei-tseng and Ailing. Pictured above is Chiang Kai-shek (second to the left on the top row)

It was to the dismay of her father, Charlie Song (Sòng Yàorú; 宋耀如), that Qingling (Sòng Qìnglíng; 宋庆龄) married his close friend Sun Yat-sen (Sūn Zhōngshān; 孙中山), who was 30 years her elder. One of the most prominent and politically influential families in the history of modern China, the Song family included three daughters and three sons (but Tse-Ven is the only well-known one) raised under the wealth of father Charlie, who became a rich businessman after obtaining a Methodist education in the United States. Qingling's sisters, Ailing (Sòng Ǎilíng; 宋霭龄) and Meiling (Sòng Měilíng; 宋美龄), are known to the Chinese to have loved money and power, but only Qingling truly loved China. She was the only Song to live in China after 1949, and it is said that she used her wealth to donate trucks, ambulances and uniforms to the military in Shanghai during the devastating Sino-Japanese War of 1937.

Beyond Qingling and Sun Yat-sen, the political arms of the Songs ran deep. Ailing – said to be the first Chinese girl to own a bicycle – married H H Kung (Kǒng Xiángxī; 孔祥熙), a wealthy descendant of Confucius, head of the Bank of China, and later the finance minister of the Republic of China. Meiling likewise married Chiang Kai-shek (Jiǎng Jièshí; 蒋介石), the head of the Kuomintang (Nationalist Party of China) and later president of the Republic of China. She fled with Chiang to Taiwan when the Nationalists were overrun by Mao's Communists.

Charlie's cherished son, T V (Tse-Ven) Song (Sòng Zǐwén; 宋子文), captured his share of the spotlight as well. Educated in economics at Harvard University, T V worked briefly at the International Banking Corporation in New York before returning to China to become one of the most prolific Chinese men of the 20th century. Under the Nationalist government of brothers-in-law Chiang Kai-shek and Sun Yat-sen, T V served in a succession of financial offices – where he successfully balanced the budget as Finance Minister – before becoming unsettled by Chiang's appeasement of the Japanese during the war. During his frank and unyielding negotiations with Joseph Stalin, T V cited his connections to American military might to extract from Stalin recognition of the Republic of China as the legitimate government of China and made an oral treaty to end Soviet occupation of Chinese Manchuria. The wealthiest Chinese man of his generation, he retreated to New York when the Nationalists were driven from China, where he lived until his death at 79.

Former Residence of Chen Yun

Chinese name: 陈云故居 (Chényún Gùjū)
Admission: FREE
Hours: 9:00-16:00; closed Mon
Recommended time for visit: 1 hour
Phone: 5925 7178
Address: 3516 Zhufeng Rd, Liantang Town, Qingpu District (青浦区练塘镇朱枫公路 3516 号)
Transport: Take Huqing Line (沪青专线) or Huqingying Line (沪青盈专线) to Qingpu (青浦) Bus Station, then change to Qingzheng (青蒸) Line, Qingfeng (青枫) Line or Qingshi (青石) Line to Liantang (练塘)

Chen Yun (1905-1995) was a revolutionary, politician and Marxist. Along with Mao Zedong, Zhou Enlai, Liu Shaoqi and others, Chen was one of the major leaders during the Communists' battle against the Nationalists during the Chinese Civil War. For this reason, he later became known as one of the great Eight Elders of the CCP. Throughout his role as a politician in the Party, Chen held the prestigious positions of Chairman of the CCP Central Advisory Commission, Vice Premier of the PRC, and Vice Chairman of the Communist Party. Despite his Marxist upbringings, Chen became critical of Maoism in his later years, and was an opponent of the Great Leap Forward campaign.

During the post-Mao years, Chen, along with Deng Xiaoping, masterminded China's new open economic policy. In fact, his "bird cage" economic theory – where the bird represents the free market and is allowed to fly around freely, and the cage is the control and regulations of the central government – that he proposed during the 1950s became the backbone of Chinese economics in the 1980s.

Chen's legacy is viewed positively and negatively from both sides of the political spectrum, but at the core he was considered a man of morality who never succumbed to corruption.

Today, the Former Residence of Chen Yun and the Qingpu Revolutionary History Memorial Hall is a museum dedicated to Chen's life, the history of the Chinese Revolution and the people of the Qingpu District (who were said to be passionate Marxists). The quaint and simple two-story timber house is built in the classic Jiangnan (i.e. South Yangtze River bank) style and is located outside of the city center, making it an educational and peaceful getaway from chaotic Shanghai.

Former Residence of Cai Yuanpei

Chinese name: 蔡元培故居 (Càiyuánpéi Gùjū)
Admission: FREE
Hours: 9:00-11:00 and 13:00-16:30; closed Mon
Phone: 6248 4996
Recommended time for visit: 1 hour
Address: 16, Lane 303, Huashan Rd (静安区华山路 303 弄 16 号)
Transport: Subway – Lines 2 & 7, Jing'an Temple Station, Exit 9, walk west along Yan'an Middle Rd, turn left at Huashan Rd, continue walking about 30 m (98 ft), the residence will be on your left

Cai Yuanpei (1868-1940) was a Chinese intellect and Esperantist, and was the President of Peking University and founder of the Academia Sinica. He was a reformer in the sense that he evaluated Chinese culture with a synthesis of Western ideas, and he is credited with assembling key figures in the nationalistic New Culture and May Fourth Movements that stood up for Chinese culture against foreign imperialism.

In 1937, just three years before his death, Cai moved into this large and spacious Western-style house, and it was from here that he wrote letters protesting against fervent Japanese aggression. In the back sits a garden and greenhouse with various species of flora, and the inside is decorated with late 19th century/early 20th century pictures of Cai and his family. In the eastern room, Cai's writings, books, letters furniture and other décor are on display.

Unfortunately, Cai did not live in this residence for long, and after the Japanese took over Shanghai he and his wife moved to Hong Kong in 1940, where he died of illness shortly thereafter. His last words were: "Save the country with science, and save the nation with aesthetic education."

Exhibition Hall of the Life of Wellington Koo

Chinese name: 顾维钧生平陈列室 (Gùwéijūn Shēngpíng Chénlièshì)
Admission: FREE
Hours: 8:00-16:00
Recommended time for visit: half an hour
Address: 349 South St, near Zhangma Rd (南大街349号, 近张马路)
Transport:
Subway & Bus: Subway – Line 11, North Jiading Station (嘉定北站), Exit 1. Go to bus stop outside the subway station and take bus 9 or 13 to Tacheng Rd & Chengzhong Rd (塔城路城中路) Stop, walk northwest on Chengzhong Rd, turn right at first intersection onto Tacheng Rd, continue to first intersection at South St and turn left. Continue 275 m (902 ft) and it becomes a pedestrian street, and the gate to the Exhibition Hall is right before small bridge. The Exhibition Hall is up a flight of stairs in the courtyard behind the gate.

Wellington Koo (1888-1985) was born in Shanghai, but his family had roots in Jiading, which is reason enough to have a room tucked away on the second floor of a historical courtyard dedicated to his remarkable life. He was a member of a particularly tragic generation in Chinese history, a group of amazingly talented and ambitious young people who were born at the end of a dynasty and in the middle of turmoil at every level of society. Determined to bring modernity and prosperity back to the homeland, many went abroad to study and came back with great knowledge and energy only to vainly struggle against China's continued descent into penury and chaos through successive wars and occupations.

Wellington played his part by studying international politics at Columbia and returning with a PhD to serve as the representative of China in almost all of the country's watershed diplomatic events: He fought unsuccessfully against the cynical transfer of Shandong from German to Japanese hands at the Paris Peace Conference, he represented China in the signing of the charter of the League of Nations, and he later accompanied a diplomatic mission of that body to Japanese-controlled Manchuria, which caused the League to denounce Japan's imperialism and thereby underline the institution's complete impotency. Scattered throughout the photos that show a glamorous diplomatic life are touching effects of the man's personal life: a ceramic pig, a toilet kit, a picture of him in his 70s hula hooping, and others. Absent is any mention that, as former Foreign Minister

of the Nationalist Government, Koo would later reside in the US and work to maintain the alliance between that country and the Republic of China (aka Taiwan).

Other Attractions

133

Temples

Just because this is Shanghai – the country's most international, metropolitan and progressive city – doesn't mean its ancient religious heritage is nonexistent. Churches, synagogues, mosques, and Buddhist, Taoist and Confucius temples, are scattered throughout the metropolis. In this section you'll see some of the best of what Shanghai has to offer from the spiritual side of town.

Jing'an Temple

Chinese name: 静安寺 (Jìng'ān Sì)
Admission: ¥30
Hours: 7:30-17.00
Recommended time for visit: 45 minutes
Address: 1686 Nanjing West Rd, near Huashan Rd (南京路 1686 号 , 近华山路)
Transport: Subway – Jing'an Temple Station, Line 2 or 7, Exit 1

The golden roofed Jing'an Temple is located in the middle of Shanghai's downtown, hidden among the hectic roads and high end shopping boutiques affiliated with Nanjing Road. Known in English as the Temple of Peace and Tranquility, it guarantees a moment of calm from the hustle and bustle of Shanghai, despite the imposing skyscrapers that seem to cheekily peek over its gold roof. It all makes for an interesting juxtaposition of Shanghai's rapid development and rich cultural history.

The original temple was built in 247 CE, but during the Cultural Revolution it was converted into a plastics factory and then reverted back into a temple in 1983. The temple has been carefully renovated according to its original state, with Song Dynasty-style woodwork and opulent white marble walls, but there is something about it that doesn't quite live up to its 1,766 year old history. Its most recently dated refurbishments and shops built into the outer façade have earned it a reputation among locals and expats as a "Disney World-style Temple," but make no mistake – this is still very much a place of worship and on the weekends you're more likely to see it busy with worshipers burning incense than camera-toting tourists.

If you fancy paying less than a third of the ¥30 entrance fee, head to Exit 1 of the subway station, where there is a ticket window designated for Chinese visitors and Chinese speaking *laowai*. Chances are there will be a rather long queue, but you could test out your Chinese and try your hand at snatching a bargain ticket. For lazy travelers, there is a tourist ticket counter located at the gates to the temple. As you enter, you'll find a booth where you can purchase incense for a ¥2 minimum donation. You can also try throwing a couple of coins into the authentic **Ming Dynasty Hongwu Bell** (Hóngwǔ

Dàzhōng; 洪武大钟); the higher up you throw the coin, the bigger the blessing.

Some of the temple's most noteworthy sights include the largest seated jade Buddha in China, located in the **Jade Buddha Hall**. Across the courtyard you'll find **Guanyin Hall**, which has a five-ton statue of the bodhisattva Guanyin, the goddess of compassion, carved entirely out of camphor wood. At the back of the complex is the **Abbott's house**, offering a glimpse into the workings of a Shanghainese Buddhist community, but large parts are closed off to the public. And though the site closes at 17:00, it is particularly lovely to photograph it at night from the elevated ring road that neighbors the temple.

Jade Buddha Temple

Chinese name: 玉佛寺 (Yùfó Sì)
Admission: ¥20, extra ¥10 to see the jade Buddhas
Hours: 8:00-16:30
Recommended time for visit: 1 hour
Website: www.yufotemple.com (in Chinese)
Address: 170 Anyuan Rd, near Jiangning Rd (安 远 路 170 号，近江宁路)
Transport: Subway – Line 7, Changshou Rd (长寿路) Station, Exit 5, walk south on Changde Rd (常德路) for 200 m (656 ft), turn left onto Anyuan Rd and continue for 600 m (1,968 ft), temple will be on the left

As the name suggests, the Jade Buddha Temple is notable for its two jade statues of the Buddha. The statues aren't spectacular, but they are unique, and the rest of the temple is full of similarly beautiful objects. However, the beauty can be more than a little tarnished by the overt commercialism that pervades this popular tourist site.

China seems to be more comfortable with a close relationship between religion and commerce than many Western cultures, but the Jade Buddha Temple is a bit excessive, even for China. One shrine is flanked by two different shops with matching drink refrigerators placed on either side of a Buddhist statue.

Another has a booth selling stone seals and an English sign right next to it saying "We will carve your name in two minutes." Add to this the inconvenience of the location, and the result is perhaps the least recommendable of Shanghai's famous attractions. Still, the temple is very popular with local Chinese, so there's a good chance of seeing a Buddhist ritual being performed during your visit. There's also a café and tea room at the north end.

In the twilight years of the Qing Dynasty, a Buddhist abbot made a pilgrimage to a string of holy sites that ended in Burma. There, he met a wealthy Chinese businessman who donated five jade statues for him to bring to temples in China. Two found their way to Shanghai and would eventually be installed in the present Jade Buddha Temple in 1928. These religious statues of such fame were not harmed in the Cultural Revolution because of the fact that the abbot of those times was careful to make many public displays of fealty towards Mao and communist ideology.

On the ground level there are two very pretty white Buddha statues that are NOT the jade Buddhas (they're marble). For the real ones, you need to go to the second floor of the main hall and pay a fee. One of the central halls contains a striking wood carving towards the back that takes up an entire wall and depicts a world of Buddhist saints surrounding a large statue of Guanyin, the Buddhist goddess of mercy. There is also a tea room outside the temple on the north side, as well as a man selling vibrant plastic lotus flowers for your garden pond.

Outside the temple (and indeed most temples in the country), the sign above the ticket window has an indication of the peculiar accord that Chinese Buddhism and Chinese communism have come to. There's an entire list of "superstitious activities" that are forbidden, including burning paper money for dead ancestors, telling fortunes and attempting to cure people of physical ailments using ancient breathing techniques called *qigong*.

During the Cultural Revolution, many ancient customs – and all religions – were labeled "superstitious," but modern China has seen much growth in religious belief, though of course, only under the ever-watchful eye of the Communist Party.

Note: It's always a good idea to bring your camera to places like these, but photos of the actual jade Buddhas are strictly prohibited.

Confucian Temple

Chinese name: 上海文庙 (Shànghǎi Wénmiào)
Admission: ¥10
Hours: 9:00-16:30
Recommended time for visit: 1 hour
Address: 215 Wenmiao Rd, Huangpu District (黄埔区文庙路 215 号)
Website: www.confuciantemple.com (in Chinese)
Transport:
Subway – Lines 8 or 10, Laoximen (老 西 门) Station, walk south down Xizang South Rd (西藏南路), turn left on Fangxie Rd (方斜路), continue for about 400 m (1,312 ft), the street becomes Wenmiao Rd and the temple will be on the left

Surrounded by small stationery stores hawking cell phone covers, and other trinkets to middle schoolers, the Shanghai Confucian temple offers a surprisingly peaceful tour of Chinese literary history. The temple was completed in 1292 during the Yuan Dynasty, and served as a place to worship Confucius and study the Confucian classics, which undergirded much of ancient Chinese thought and culture. The temple underwent many relocations and a few destructions, but was finally rebuilt and reopened to the public in 1999 on Confucius' 2,550th birthday.

The grounds and buildings are arranged along two straight paths, one for worship and the other for study. The former, which begins at the ticket gate, is flanked by small halls devoted to oddly beautiful root carvings that range from one to 500 years old. Made from gnarled roots that grew in bizarre and suggestive ways, these sculptures have had subtle details carved into their surfaces to form things such as "phoenix facing the sun," "gold dragon driving on the clouds," and "Arabic man's head." At the end of this first path is the main hall of worship for Confucius. The hall contains a statue of the philosopher made of camphor and painted in gold with ceremonial drums and bells placed on each side. At the entrance to the hall are racks to hang prayers to Confucius written on yellow cards, which have overflowed onto the surrounding trees.

The second path, which in older times was reserved for scholars who had passed the imperial examinations and sits to the west of the first, starts with a small Chinese garden complete with a koi pond and a hexagonal pagoda, the oldest structure in the temple, and a shrine to Kuixing, the god of study and

literature. Further along the path is the Ming Lun Hall, which was originally used for lectures but briefly housed a militant group called the Small Sword Society that fought against the Qing Dynasty in support of the Christian Taiping Rebellion. At the end of the path resides **Zun Jing Hall**, a library that is one of the most interesting buildings in the temple. Take the time to read all the titles on display. There are thoughts on statecraft from an emperor, "Notes and Comments on Philial Piety," instructions for the processing of herbal medicines, and numerous other books that collectively indicate the pervasiveness and variety of philosophy and scholarship in ancient Chinese society.

On Sundays at 14:00 the temple holds a well-attended book fair, while throughout the week a large and chaotic book market on Xuegong Road (学 宫 路), along the west side of the temple, sells books by the boxload (Chinese language only). Also on this road is the popular and – considering it shares a building with the Confucian temple – cheekily named restaurant, Kongyiji. The word comes from one of China's most famous modern short stories and is the name of a character who wastes his life trying and failing to pass the imperial exams, so he would never be allowed to study in the temple.

Songjiang Mosque

Songjiang is a small town south of Shanghai that seems to be making a concerted effort to turn itself into a historically-themed tourist spot for a pleasant day away from the city. The most unique attraction is the Songjiang mosque, which was first constructed in the 1300s when Mongolians ruled China – making it one of the oldest Muslim buildings in the country.

It still serves as a place of worship so that means the prayer hall is off-limits to non-Muslims, but the rest of the mosque is well worth a visit for the architecture, which combines the Chinese traditional style with a few Arabic touches. A cypress tree hundreds of years old still grows in the gardens and gravestones are marked in both Chinese characters and Arabic script.

Xiaotaoyuan Mosque

The "Little Peach Park" mosque sits at the end of a small street and is housed in a slim building as charming as the name. Built in 1917 to accommodate Shanghai's Muslim population, the mosque is still a functioning place of prayer and a community center. This means wandering tourists shouldn't go too far in exploring the building, but no one will object to visitors taking a look at the main courtyard, from which one can view the intricate tile floors and dignified architecture of the site. The aesthetics here are a mix of European and Islamic styles not commonly seen in Shanghai, and are well worth the detour should the bustle of surrounding Huangpu District become too great.

Chinese name: 圣尼古拉斯教堂 (Shèng Nígǔlāsī Jiàotáng)
Admission: Free
Recommended time for a visit: 20 minutes
Address: 16 Gaolan Rd (皋兰路 16 号)
Transport: A 10-minute walk down Gaolan Rd, directly to the west of Fuxing Park

Shanghai received a large number of Russians between WWI and WWII: the years after the Russian Revolution when Stalin's reign of terror began heating up. Many of these Russians were whites or anti-communists, and were fleeing persecution from the Bolshevik Party. They fled to Shanghai seeking a better life, but they quickly discovered that conditions in their new land were anything but ideal, and many were forced to take unfavorable jobs. In one particular example, it's estimated that in 1935 about one in five Russian women living in Shanghai between the ages of 16 and 45 were prostitutes.

Despite the hard times, many immigrants sought spiritual refuge. The most popular of the Russian Orthodox churches constructed was St Nicholas. Created in the French Concession in 1932, this classical structure with traditional Russian designs (onion domes, Byzantine crosses) was consecrated in 1937 in honor of St Nicholas. For several years, it allowed the devoted to practice their religion freely, something they couldn't do back in the Soviet Union, but after the Chinese Revolution in 1949 and Shanghai's swing to the left, the Russian and Eastern European immigrants packed up just as they had decades earlier and moved to other countries.

During the communist years of China, the church was immediately closed and converted into a warehouse. The building has been a protected structure since 1994, but the municipal government just recently allowed religious services to take place.

Chongming County

Everyone's image of Shanghai probably falls along the lines of a big city metropolis with futuristic steel buildings and highways clogged with traffic. However, this is only a part of what the city has to offer. Chongming County (Chóngmíng Xiàn; 崇明县) is the only county of the Shanghai Municipality. It encompasses three islands wedged between Shanghai and Jiangsu in the mouth of the Yangtze that emerged around 1,400 years ago due to a change in sea levels, but the largest of the trio is called Chongming Island. In fact it's the largest island in greater China after Taiwan and Hainan. The most populated city on Chongming Island is Chengqiao, home to Nanmen Port, but the majority of the county is swampy uninhabited marshland. For a retreat into nature away from big city life, Chongming offers many outdoor getaways that aren't recognized in many guidebooks.

On another note, Chongming is essentially where Pudong was 20 years ago: a wet bog with a few villages and wild animals (and we all know where Pudong is today). Eventually, Pudong, like Puxi, will run out of room, and Shanghai will have to expand into uncharted territory. Could Chongming become the next Pudong? It's hard to say, but two new bridges and a new tunnel have just opened and connected the island with Shanghai and Jiangsu Province, meaning the seeds of development may have already been planted. Perhaps our grandchildren will travel to Shanghai one day and look at the enormous new and modern buildings sprouting up on Chongming, while viewing the then out-of-date structures of Pudong as old and historic relics, much in the way visitors today view the structures of the Bund. So, even if you're not the nature type, it still might be cool to check out Chongming before the development boom strikes; future generations might appreciate the comparison pictures one day.

Dongtan Wetland Park

Chinese name: 东滩湿地公园 (Dōngtān Shīdì Gōngyuán)
Admission: ¥70
Hours: 9:00-17:00
Phone: 3936 7000
Website: www.dongtanshidi.com
Recommended time for visit: half a day
Address: Dongwang Lu, Dongtan, next to a windmill (崇明东滩东旺路，风车旁)
Transport: Bus – Chenqian Line (陈前线), get off at Lixincun (立新村) Stop, then take a taxi, it's only 5 km (3 mi) away

Created in 2003, the Dongtan Wetlands, located at the far eastern tip of Chongming Island, is Mainland China's only wetland park that borders a migratory bird sanctuary. The 24 sq km (9 sq mi) national park is graced with rolling streams, lush greenery and crisp skies, but the reason most visitors venture out here is for the spectacular bird watching. During the fall months, various species of birds from Asia, Europe and the Americas flock to Dongtan. Despite the beauty of this natural phenomenon, it's still very low key; this is a good thing since it won't be bursting with obnoxious tour groups. If you're unlucky enough not to be in the greater Shanghai area during the fall migratory season, Dongtan is still a pleasant place to spend a chill day outside.

www.pandaguides.com

Dongping National Forest Park

Chinese name: 东平国家森林公园 (Dōngpíng Guójiā Sēnlín Gōngyuán)

Admission: ¥70

Hours: 8:30-16:30; closes at 17:00 on weekends and holidays

Recommended time for visit: 2-3 hours

Phone: 5933 8266

Website: www.dpslpark.com (in Chinese)

Address: 2288 Beiyan Highway (北沿公路 2288 号原东平林场)

Transport: Bus – Shenchong Line (申 崇 线) at North District Bus Station and Nandong Line (南东专线) and Nanjiang Line (南江专线) at Chongming South Gate Bus Station can reach Dongping National Forest Park. Line 5 of Shanghai Tourism Line can bring visitors to the park.

Dongping is an artificial forest newly planted for your enjoyment, but it gives rise to a strange phenomenon. The trees are all young, straight, evenly spaced and tall, with branches and leaves only on the very top, while the ground below has almost no tall plants. The result is a bright green canopy above and a brilliant plane below, created by light that falls uninterrupted from high leaves to ground-hugging plants. The middle is a glowing space that softly bathes the trees' slender trunks and many of the park's more eclectic features: various baffling sculptures, a 1950s fighter jet, and some unused buildings of strange design.

The overriding feeling of the forest is that of a regular Chinese park, except much, much larger and with bigger trees. Paved paths and numerous attractions that one might find at a county fair work together to expunge any real sense of being in the wild. The zip-line and the go-karts are probably the best of these attractions, though the park also manages to cram in paint ball, bumper cars, obstacle courses, a mini-roller coaster, and more. Despite this, the grounds are large enough that in many spaces, including the camping area, one can feel entirely surrounded by nature – tame and manicured to be sure, but relaxing. Regarding the size, you would do well to rent a bike from the front gate, lest you be forced to travel to the various parts of the forest and park using the only other means of vehicular transportation: choo-choo train people movers.

Qianwei Ecological Village

Chinese name: 前卫生态村 (Qiánwèi Shēngtài Cūn)
Admission: ¥60
Hours: 8:00-17:00
Phone: 5964 9170
Recommended time for visit: 2 hours
Address: Linfeng Gong Lu, near Beiyan Gong Lu (近林风公路 , 近北沿公路)
Transport: Take bus Shenchong 3rd Line (申 崇 三 线) at Wenshui Rd (汶 水 路) in Puxi or bus Shenchong 6th Line (申崇六线) at Jufeng Rd (巨峰路) in Pudong, get off at Chongming Nanmen Matou (崇明南门码头), then transfer to Nandong Line (南东专线), get off at Qianwei Shengtaicun (前卫生态村) Stop

Who said eco-tourism isn't alive in China? Visit the Qianwei Ecological Village and you'll be eating those words, vegan style. Originally built in 1969 on reed beds, the town is dedicated to clean energy and runs on solar, wind, geothermal and other green sources of energy. Visitors to Qianwei can enjoy many outdoor activities, such as horseback riding, fruit picking, fishing and/or taking a peaceful walk through the fragrant vanilla garden, which houses various species of flora. If Chongming becomes the future of Shanghai, let's all hope they learn a lesson from Qianwei's clean and renewable energy example.

Yingdong Fishing Village

Chinese name: 瀛东村 (Yíngdōng Cūn)
Admission: ¥20
Hours: 7:00-17:00
Phone: 5493 6276
Recommended time for visit: 1-2 hours
Address: Beichen Highway, near Yu'an Rd (北陈公路 , 近裕安路)
Transport: **Bus** – Chenbai Line (陈 白 线), get off at Yingdongcun (瀛东村) Stop

Yingdong is the best place to meet the first rays of the morning sun in all of Shanghai. But if you're not going to make it up early to watch the magnificent fluorescent sunrise over the vast Pacific, consider coming for what this "fishing" village is known for. A wooden boardwalk crisscrosses the land, and you can either bring your own fishing rod or rent supplies here for a reasonable fee.

While they don't guarantee that you'll catch any fish, we're near certain you will since the waters below are filled with them. After you get your hard-earned meal, bring it to one of the locals in town and they'll cook it up for you using traditional family recipes.

Xisha Wetland Park

Chinese name: 西沙湿地 (Xīshā Shīdì)
Admission: FREE
Hours: 8:00-16:00
Recommended time for visit: 1-2 hours
Phone: 5935 3151
Address: Baohu Rd (堡 湖 路), 500 m (1,640 ft) to the west of Mingzhu Lake Park (明珠湖公园)
Transport: Bus – From Ximen Bus Station (西门汽车站), take Nanjian Line (南建专线) to Xinjianshuizha (新建水闸) Stop. The park is to the south.

Some might feel a bit out of place during their Chongming travels while walking amidst the go-karts and paintball games of Dongping Forest. For those who want a purer experience in nature, Xisha Wetlands Park is worth the trip to Chongming's far west coast. (Note: Dongtan Wetlands Park on the exact opposite side of the island is more convenient to get to but also has a fee, more visitors, and is simply not as beautiful.) Wooden walkways are frequently required to traverse across the waves of grass, which at some angles stretch all the way to the horizon. Besides the feeling of unlimited space, an

uncommon enough pleasure anywhere in the Shanghai Municipality, the park also provides the opportunity to catch crabs, which are plentiful in certain areas.

Venders sell the bamboo poles and bait needed to accomplish the task, but you'll have to figure out how to cook them on your own. A suggestion: take the crabs to a small restaurant and pantomime your desire to eat them but sorrowful inability to cook them. The restaurant owner can usually be persuaded to do it for you at a reasonable price. As for actually eating them: find a Chinese person to show you how. The method for getting meat from a steamed crab is too complex to explain in these pages, but the taste is worth it.

Shou'an Temple & Jin'ao Hill Park

Chinese name: 寿安寺 (Shòu'ān Sì); 金鳌山 (Jīn'áo Shān)
Admission: ¥10 for the temple; ¥5 for the park
Hours: 7:00-16:00
Recommended time for visit: 1 hour
Website: www.shouansi.com.cn (in Chinese)
Address: Aoshan Rd, near Jiangfan Rd, Chengqiao Town, Chongming County (鳌山路, 江帆路)
Transport: Bus – Take Shenchong Line (申崇专线) to Chongming Ximen Bus Station (崇明西门汽车站), then walk east on Nanmen Rd (which becomes Aoshan Rd) for 2.5 km (1.6 mi)

Located in the south of Jin'ao Hill, 2.5 km (1.5 mi) to the east of Chongming downtown, the Shou'an Temple is a rather roomy operation and fully stocked with all the golden statues and incense burners one could expect in a Chinese temple. If there's one difference between this and all the other temples you see in Shanghai, it's that this one's seclusion ensures that most of the visitors are actually here to pray. The **Mahavira Hall** of Shou'an Temple is 22 m (72 ft) tall and it's the highest one in

Shanghai. A **reclining Buddha** that has a weight of 13 tons and a length of 6 m (20 ft) is placed in the west wing-room (also the highest jade Buddha in Shanghai). Respectfully take a peek at the ritual if you haven't seen it before, or have only seen it in a more commercialized temple setting. Like many Buddhist temples, this one also serves vegetarian food.

In Jin'ao Hill Park, whose entrance is directly to the left of the temple, a tiny cave path has been dug through the mountain; at one point it forks, only to have both prongs end up at the same exit later. The whole thing snakes around the temple, and the hill is actually a mound 5 m (15 ft) tall and "generously" topped with a small purple tower.

Chongming Museum & Yingzhou Park

Chinese name: 崇明博物馆 (Chóngmíng Bówùguǎn)
瀛洲公园 (Yíngzhōu Gōngyuán)
Admission: FREE
Hours: Museum: Tue-Sun, 8:30-11:00, 14:00-17:00
Park: 5:30-17:00
Recommended time for visit: 1 hour
Address: Aoshan Rd, near Dongmen Rd (鳌山路 , 近东门路). The museum is on the northeast corner and the park is on the southeast corner.
Transport: Bus – Take Shenchong Line (申崇专线) to Chongming Ximen Bus Station (崇明西门汽车站), then walk east on Nanmen Rd (which becomes Aoshan Rd) for 850 m (2,788 ft), the museum is to the left and the park is to the right

The Chongming Museum is really just the Chongming Confucian Temple with exhibits. The temple grounds are par for the course, but well maintained and possess some particularly ornate roof designs. The exhibits are few, but a display of models of ancient ships is a small treat. Yingzhou Park on the other side of the road offers a bit more in the way of oddness. The park itself is nice enough, and anyone with a desire to foot paddle through the water only need to follow the signs to the "yacht pier." But on the way it's hard not to notice the brown color of all

those features. That's because this park gets its water directly from the surrounding mouth of the Yangtze River, a viewing of which is provided on the southern side of the area. One look will sufficiently educate anyone as to why beach-going isn't a common past time in Shanghai. The dominant themes are cranes, construction and mud.

Other Notable Attractions

This section outlines an eclectic mix of some of Shanghai's coolest and weirdest attractions: think zoos and marine creatures, mass entertainment complexes of roller coasters, artificial beaches and indoor ski resorts, and quirky districts made to imitate Western life and culture. Scroll through the list to see if any of the following call your attention... we bet one or two might just be right up your alley.

The Shanghai Maglev Train

Chinese name: 上海磁悬浮列车 (Shànghǎi Cíxuánfú Lièchē)
Fare: ¥50 (one way, ¥40 with air ticket); ¥80 (round trip with the return air ticket valid for seven days)
Hours: 6:45-21:40 to Longyang Rd Station
7:02-21:42 to Airport Station
Phone: 2890 7777
Website: www.smtdc.com/en
Location: There are only two stations: One at Shanghai Pudong International Airport (浦东机场) and the other 30 km (19 mi) away at Longyang Rd Subway Station (龙阳路地铁站) in Pudong
Transport: There are dozens of daily flights to Pudong Airport. Subway Lines 2 & 7, and bus 975 and 978 service the Longyan Rd Metro Station.

The Shanghai Maglev Train (SMT) is an excellent introduction to the city's ultra-modern side. It is also a convenient and practical method of transportation from Shanghai to the city's main airport. Even if you don't need to go to Pudong Airport, it is an interesting and fun ride for those interested in technology and train travel.

Trains leave every 15 to 20 minutes, and the entire journey takes about seven minutes. Make sure to charge your camera before boarding – you can take an impressive video of Shanghai zipping past at speeds of up to 431 km (268 mi) per hour.

Real transportation buffs (or those with some time to kill) can even check out the small **Shanghai Maglev Museum** on the first floor of the Longyang Road Metro Station.

The SMT is the world's first high-speed, commercial Maglev train. German high-technology firms Siemens and ThyssenKrupp built the trains, while a local partner laid down the tracks. The trains can quickly reach incredibly high speeds because it does not actually create friction on the tracks. Instead it uses the power of magnetism to levitate the entire machine off the track (thus "Maglev"). For this reason, when you take a ride on the Maglev, there's no heavy metal clashing below because you're actually not even touching the rail line; it's a smooth, quiet and quick glide. Work on the line began in 2001, and it was completed in 2004. Construction is currently underway to extend the line to Shanghai Hongqiao International Airport.

Riding the Shanghai Maglev is significantly less dangerous than taking a shower in the morning. However, there have been local concerns about electromagnetic radiation, and there was a small electronic fire in 2006. Your main concern will be keeping close tabs on your belongings, especially if you have many bags and are sleep deprived after a long flight. Furthermore, the Maglev Station at Pudong Airport is located between Terminal One and Terminal Two on the walkway. Don't trust anyone who tells you the Maglev is broken along the way – they have an economic interest in tricking you into their taxis. After disembarking at the Longyang Road Station, an escalator to your right goes to Subway Line 2.

Shanghai Happy Valley

Chinese name: 上海欢乐谷 (Shànghǎi Huānlègǔ)
Hours: 10:00–17:00 (weekdays); 9:30–17:30 (weekends)
Admission: ¥200 (¥100 for children between 1.2-1.3 m (3.9-4.2 ft), free for children under 1.2 m).
Phone: 3355 2222
Website: sh.happyvalley.cn (in Chinese)
Address: 888 Linhu Rd, Songjiang District (松江区林湖路888号)
Transport: Shanghai Happy Valley is about 40 km (25 mi) to the west of the main downtown areas. Take Subway Line 9 to Sheshan Station (佘山站), across the overpass there is a free shuttle bus to Happy Valley.

Happy Valley is Shanghai's most famous and highest-quality amusement park. Unfortunately, it is also the most popular. It is to be avoided at all costs on the weekends and near important Chinese holidays, when visitors can wait in line for over an hour to ride the various roller coasters and other standard amusement park rides. However, a trip in the middle of the week can be a fun and rewarding experience. Happy Valley offers a pleasant/cheesy contrast to the well-heeled, ultra modern, super slick and, at times, overly self-conscious city of Shanghai.

There are seven different areas in the park, each with a unique theme. These areas are called Sunshine Beach (Yángguāng Gǎng; 阳 光 港), Typhoon Bay (Jùfēng Wān; 飓 风 湾), Shanghai Beach (Shànghǎi Tān; 上海滩), Shangri-la Woods (Xiānggélìlā; 香 格 里 拉), Gold Mine Town (Jīnkuàng Zhèn; 金 矿 镇), Ant Kingdom (Mǎyǐ Wángguó; 蚂蚁王国) and Happy Times (Huānlè Shíguāng; 欢乐时光). Despite the nautical theme of some of these areas, they are actually dozens and dozens of miles away from the ocean.

There are some surprisingly good roller coasters in the park. The largest and most famous is called **Fireball**, and it can satisfy most thrill-seekers without totally alienating more cautious visitors. Luckily, Chinese internet reports indicate that no deaths have occurred at Shanghai Happy Valley (although there are rumors of one person being paralyzed).

Besides roller coasters, there are also bumper cars, a Ferris wheel, a merry-go-round, bungee-jumping and other amusement park staples. What's more, the park features several elaborate performances involving dozens of costumed dancers. Almost all of the park's decorations are delightfully tasteless, but they make up for it with free wifi throughout the entire complex. Horses are (somewhat incongruously) available for rides at ¥20 per lap.

Shanghai Happy Valley is most attractive to Chinese tourists visiting the city from far-flung provinces, and as such it can sometimes suffer from a relative lack of… what the Chinese call *sùzhì* (素 质), which translates roughly as "quality." The rides themselves are fine, but the grounds become progressively more trash-strewn throughout the course of the day, and foreign visitors will most definitely attract a lot of attention. Intrepid visitors can turn this into an advantage – try to charge anyone taking your picture ¥10, and your visit to Happy Valley might pay for itself.

Foreigner Street

Chinese name: 老外街 (Lǎowài Jiē)
Recommended time for visit: 1 hour
Address: starting at intersection of Hongmei Rd (虹梅路)
Transport:
Subway – Line10, Longxi Rd (龙溪路), Exit 2, walk west on Hongqiao Rd (虹桥路) and turn right at the first intersection onto Hongmei Rd (虹梅路), continue for 575 m (1,886 ft), Laowai Jie is on the left.

Although sometimes misinterpreted as derogatory, *laowai* is really just a neutral Mandarin colloquialism for foreigners, like "foreign guy." In accordance with the meaning, Laowai Street offers up a roster of foreign restaurants that at the time of writing included Iranian, Indian, Belgian, French, Thai and Mexican. That's not to mention the tapas, the Canadian food (whatever that is), and the many, many bars. But what really sets this walking street apart is the urbane and serene atmosphere far away from street noise; you can actually hear the trees swaying under glasses clinking. Gubei, the district in which the street resides, is home to a large established expat community, and the preponderance of families among the diners makes for an unusual and pleasant combination of sensibilities: international and homey.

Thames Town

Chinese name: 泰晤士小镇 (Tàiwùshì Xiǎozhèn)
Admission: FREE
Recommended time for visit: 1 hour
Address: Front gate at intersection of Wencheng Rd and Yuhua Rd (文诚路, 近玉华路)
Transport: Line 9, Songjiang Xincheng Station, Exit 3, walk west along Sixian Rd (思贤路) for about 1,500 m (4,921 ft)

Thames Town was originally conceived as a replica English hamlet that could house 10,000 of Shanghai's growing middle class residents at a construction cost of over US$800 million. Fortunately for tourists with a taste for brash on a grand scale, barely anyone moved in, and the hamlet now feels like an abandoned movie set. Apartment buildings with flourishes of Anglo-cliché surround the main attraction: shops and restaurants in the town center that copy various architectural styling of old England with a level of subtlety comparable to Disneyland. The real treat is the small cathedral that sports stained-glass windows, religious paintings and the clean, vacant quality of a pointless prop. The town has become a popular destination for wedding photos, so expect to see as many as ten (no exaggeration) couples at any one time roaming about the old town square in full formal dress trying to find the perfect angle.

Thames Town reaches the apex of tackiness in those few variations on the theme of England whose laziness is so complete that the shallow references from which they derive remain momentarily mysterious. The security guards for the subdivision walk around in disheveled red-orange uniforms that may take one a long while to realize are simply incredibly unsuccessful imitations of those worn by guards at Buckingham Palace. And near the marina, the town pays homage to that most esteemed of English figures with the sculpture of a messy haired boy riding his broomstick (Harry Potter).

You can spend a whole day walking around the township, sipping coffee, relaxing on the grass or flying kites in the park. But, if you are in a hurry and just want a quick look at Thames Town, you can also take a London-style red tram car for a ride for just ¥10. If you want to experience a piece of England here in Shanghai, Thames Town, with all its quirky charm, fills you with the best.

Shanghai Ocean Aquarium

Chinese name: 上海海洋水族馆 (Shànghǎi Hǎiyáng Shuǐzúguǎn)
Admission: ¥160 for adult; ¥110 for child
Hours: 9:00-18:00; last admission at 17:30. The closing time is extended to 21:00 during summer vacation (Jul-Aug), National Day Golden Week (the first week of Oct), and Spring Festival.
Phone: 5877 9988
Address: 1388 Lujiazui Ring Rd (浦东新区陆家嘴环路 1388号)
Website: www.sh-soa.com/en
Transport: Subway – Line 2, Lujiazui Station, Exit 1, take a right out of the station and walk 200 m (646 ft)

Situated in the financial district of Lujiazui, the Shanghai Ocean Aquarium (SOA) is worth checking out if searching for a family-friendly activity or if you're a lover of all things aquatic.

Built in 2001, SOA boasts the largest underwater viewing tunnel in the world at 155 m (509 ft). You start off on the third floor and work your way through the building to the basement. This will only take you a couple of hours, so you might want to couple your visit with one to the Oriental Pearl Tower and Jinmao Tower. The aquarium is divided into nine different sections, the first being the China Zone, which is the only Aquarium in the world to have a section devoted to China's Aquatic life. Look out for the Chinese giant salamander in this section. Its call sounds like a crying baby, something that has earned it the name Wah-Wah Fish (WáWá Yú; 娃娃鱼).

Carrying on this theme of freshwater ecology, the next four sections look at the freshwater fish from around the planet. The second exhibition focuses on South America, specifically the types of fish found in the longest river in the world, the Amazon. Next you'll move on to the Australia exhibition. This one explores the unique species of fresh water fish found only in the region. The Africa zone looks at the types of fish found in the continent's rich river resources, from the Nile to the Congo, and the Southeast Asia zone looks at the fish species found in the Mekong River Delta, which is home to over 1,200 species.

Further sections include the Cold Water zone, which has an underwater observation tunnel for spotted seals, and in the Polar Zone you can find adorable penguins. Check out the feeding times below in case you want to see the animals get their grub on.

Exhibition	Morning	Afternoon
Spotted Seal (Coldwater Zone)	9:45-9:55	14:15-14:25
Penguin (Antarctic Zone)	10:00-10:15	14:30-14:45
The Open Ocean (Deep Ocean Zone)	10:30-10:45	15:00-15:15
Schooling Seas (Deep Ocean Zone)	10:50-11:00	15:20-15:30
Shark Cove (Deep Ocean Zone)	10:50-11:10	15:20-15:40

A dish that dates back to the Ming Dynasty, shark fin soup was eaten by emperors and served to courtiers as a symbol of wealth and power. Nowadays, it's part of the Big Four Dishes – abalone (bàoyú; 鲍鱼), sea cucumber (hǎishēn; 海参), shark fin (yúchì; 鱼翅) and fish maw (yúdǔ; 鱼肚) – that are served at banquets and weddings. These dishes are said to represent health and prosperity and are served on special occasions.

It was once said in China that "a bride marrying into a family without shark fin soup on the table is married into a poor family." The delicacy has long been a symbol of "face and respect," with most wealthy families regularly partaking in its consumption in order to show their economic status, and with China's economic boom and a burgeoning middle class, the last decade has seen the demand and consumption of shark fin soup rise significantly.

Recently, however, the sustainability of this process is being called into question as shark populations are dropping drastically. Plus, it's a common practice for fisherman to catch the shark, saw off its fin while it's alive, then throw it back into the ocean to die a painful death. It may be tempting to try this dish, but remember: less demand will lessen the need for supply and effectively drive down the poaching of this protected species. And with a bowl of shark fin soup fetching price of over ¥1,800 (US$300), it will be better for your wallet (and the sharks) to steer clear.

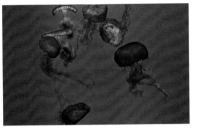

Perhaps the best display in the Sea and Shore section is the jellyfish area, highlighted by its well-implemented lighting that illuminates the hidden majesty of these delicate creatures. It's very cool, a little trippy, and in many ways incredibly relaxing. Many people find themselves spending hours here peacefully swaying with the jellyfish without even realizing it.

Then you'll move into the Deep Ocean zone, a place where a long underwater tunnel provides an up close and personal view of sharks and other aquatic predators. One of the big conservation drives of SOA is actually to raise awareness of the incredibly wasteful practice of shark finning, and in 2009 the SOA launched the Save Our Sharks Exhibition, which you can find here.

The end of the underwater tunnel marks the conclusion of your visit to Shanghai's most popular aquarium; you will have journeyed through five continents and seen a vast array of over 450 different species of aquatic animals. SOA's mission to provide an informative and fun environment for its visitors, coupled with interactive games for children and an abundance of information in both Chinese and English, makes it a great journey for all visitors, children and adults alike.

Shanghai Wild Animal Park

Chinese name: 上海野生动物园 (Shànghǎi Yěshēng Dòngwùyuán)
Admission: ¥130
Hours: 8:00–17:00 (Mar-Nov), 8:00–16:30 (Dec-Feb) (Please note: last tickets are sold an hour before closing)
Phone: 6118 0000
Website: www.shwzoo.com (in Chinese)
Address: The Shanghai Wild Animal Park is about 35 km (22 mi) east of the city center in Pudong District, not far from the Pudong Airport. The address is 178 Nanliu Highway (浦东新区南六公路178号).
Transport: Subway – Line 2, Zhangjiang Hi-Tech Park Station (张江高科站), Exit 5, find the Zhangnan Line (张南专线) bus. The bus ride from the subway to the park takes about 40 minutes. Taxis are also an option (about ¥100), just make sure they hit the meter.

Conditions at the Shanghai Wild Animal Park are much better than at most zoos in Asia. The animals live in generally spacious and humane habitats, and the grounds of the Wild Animal Park itself are quite pleasant, especially if the weather is agreeable. You're advised to visit during the week, when foot traffic is at a minimum.

Some locals and long-term expats do, however, have a major complaint about the Shanghai Wild Animal Park. The consensus is that it has gotten too tame in recent years. In the good old days (circa 2010), visitors could buy live chickens to feed to the resident lions and tigers, while buses – without any extra security barriers – took visitors into the enclosures of wild beasts. It was a great opportunity to get pictures of lions with nothing separating the photographer from the animal but a few millimeters of glass in a bus window.

Nowadays, there are extra security measures on vehicles that embark upon the "Safari" (¥30). However, there are still plenty of opportunities to get up close and personal with some of the animals. Elephants, camels, and horses are available for rides (for an additional fee). Smaller beasts can be fed with specially-sold foodstuffs. Food for humans is somewhat lacking, though, and what is available at the park tends to be overpriced. Bringing some hardy snacks (or even a full picnic meal) from the outside is highly recommended.

There is a good variety of wild beast at the park, including chimpanzees, zebras, bears and flamingos. There is also a special exhibit for China's pride – the one animal off the menu in the entire country – pandas. Chinese tourists are particularly keen to get pictures of this animal and there is also a special incubator section with adorable infants.

Visitors are invited to check out live performances throughout the day. From 8:30 to 9:30 is the Animal Welcoming Performance just inside the main gate. At 11:00 is the Show of Lions and Tigers at the Animal Training Ground. Sea Lion shows can be seen at 10:00 and 15:15 at Sea Lion Hall. At 14:15 there is horse and dog racing at the Dog Racing Circuit (unfortunately no formal gambling is available for this race, but you might be able to place a handshake bet with a fellow visitor).

The park is worth visiting for the entire day. The grounds are spacious, but quite walkable. Most visitors shouldn't need to splurge on the ¥30 all-day cart ticket.

Shanghai Zoo

Chinese name: 上海动物园 (Shànghǎi Dòngwùyuán)
Admission: ¥40
Hours: 6:30-17:00
Recommended time for visit: 1 hour
Phone: 6268 7775
Website: www.shanghaizoo.cn (in Chinese)
Address: 2381 Hongqiao Rd (虹桥路 2381 号)
Transport: Subway – Line 10, Shanghai Zoo Station, Exit 1 or 2

The zoo often gets swept under the rug when compared to the aquarium and Wild Animal Park, but it's fairly cool in its own right and shouldn't be skipped if you're fond of exotic animals. Home to more than 6,000 species, including 600 that are indigenous to China, the zoo even boasts some local endangered species, including the giant panda, the golden snub-nosed monkey, and the South China tigers. Other typical zoo animals like kangaroos, gorillas, elephants and giraffes can be spotted around as well, while Swan Lake in the center of it all is a soothing natural getaway for pelicans, geese and, as the name suggests, swans.

Apart from animal life, the Shanghai zoo boasts a massive 10,000 sq m (107,639 sq ft) eco-friendly garden full of plants. There are over 100,000 trees and over 600 species scattered throughout the grounds.

The zoo is the perfect place for families with small children, and management does a great job of mixing leisure, amusement and education, providing a fun outing for people of all ages. There are also numerous restaurants and rest areas that are never far from reach. Of course, prices are drastically inflated, so consider bringing a few of your own snacks if you're on a tight budget.

Dino Beach

Chinese name: 热带风暴 (Rèdài Fēngbào)
Admission: Mon, Tue & Thu ¥120; Wed & Fri ¥120-150; Sat & Sun ¥120-200
Hours: 9:00-22:00 (Jun 22-Jun 30); 9:00-24:00 (Jul 1-Aug 25); 9:00-22:00 (Aug 26-Sep 8)
Phone: 6478 3333
Recommended time for visit: half a day.
Website: www.64783333.com
Address: 78 Xinzhen Rd (新镇路 78 号)
Transport:
Subway & Bus: Subway Line 1, Xinzhuang Station (莘庄站), then take buses 763 or 173, get off at Xinzhen Rd & Gudai Rd (新镇路顾戴路) Stop

If you need another attraction for your little emperor, or you just feel like having some very innocent fun, this outdoor water park can cheese its way into the heart of your inner child. Waterslides, tubing, wave pools and an artificial beach are just some of the highlights this hangout offers.

Surprisingly, it's fairly well organized and managed, and it definitely surpasses the lackluster stereotype other Chinese water parks have. That being said, it must be mentioned that this place becomes like a shark pool feeding frenzy on the weekend as seemingly every Chinese kid from the greater Shanghai area under the age of ten flocks here to cool off from the suffocating summer heat (who blames them?). Come on the weekdays when it's a little less hectic, but still don't expect too much breathing room.

For the record, there is a bit of a "dino" theme here, but for the most part it's just a water park; forget the giant green T-rex at the entrance and don't be expecting Jurassic Park.

Yinqixing Indoor Skiing

Chinese name: 银七星室内滑雪场
   (Yínqīxīng Shìnèi Huáxuěchǎng)
Admission: Adults per hour: ¥98 (Mon–Thu); ¥118 (Fri & Sat). Children per hour: ¥80 (Mon–Thu); ¥100 (Fri & Sat)
Hours: 9:30-22:30 (Mon–Thu); 9:30-1:00 (Fri & Sat); closed Sun
Phone: 6478 8666
Website: www.yinqixing.com
Address: 1835 Qixing Rd, Xinzhuang (莘庄七星路 1835 号)
Transport: Free shuttle bus at North Square of Xinzhuang Station of subway Line 1 every 30 minutes from 9:00 to 21:00; or take bus 91, 92, 803 or 953; get off at Gudai Rd (顾戴路) Stop

If bumming around at Dino Beach isn't your preferred way to beat the sweltering summer heat of Shanghai, your alternative is to shred up the slopes at Yinqixing. Actually, there's really very little shredding to be done here as this gigantic icebox caters more to the novice skier, but if you're dying to get a little snow time during the middle of July, this is really your only option. Yiqinxing actually might be better for the snowboarders instead. The snowboard park isn't on par with Sochi, but the pipes and jumps are adequate. It also seems that the indoor park is doing quite well since management is improving facilities year after year, especially in the aforementioned snowboard park. By the time you read this, there could be some new upgrades.

The Paramount

Chinese name: 百乐门 (Bǎilèmén)
Admission: Tea Time dancing, ¥40; Ballroom Champagne dancing, ¥100; Standard Social dancing, ¥258
Hours: Tea Time dancing, 14:00-16:30; Ballroom Champagne dancing, 16:40-20:00; Standard Social dancing, 20:20-00:30
Recommended time for visit: 1 hour
Address: 218 Yuyuan Rd, near Huashan Rd (愚园路 218 号，近华山路)
Transport: Subway – Line 2, Jing'an Temple Station (静安寺站), Exit 1, at intersection walk 100 m (328 ft) north on Huashan Rd

The art deco architecture of The Paramount seems to be transported directly from an LA noir film of the 1940s (though it was actually built in 1933) and a look at the entrance room quickly grounds the building in its actual history with a wall of pictures featuring old Shanghai starlets. Once the height of sophisticated night life in the city, this dance hall has suffered its share of indignities in the turbulence of later 20th century China, but in the new millennium, it has been renewed and restored to its original purpose. Even those who don't count dancing among their hobbies can get a drink and watch the mostly older local crowd waltz around the ornate ballroom. Afternoon dancing is usually more lightly attended; partners are available for a price.

Acrobatic Shows

Acrobatics has a long history in China, stretching for hundreds of years from when their popularity spread throughout the country via the Silk Road. Feats such as human pyramids and contortionist acts excited ancient audiences for centuries, but eventually the art faded nearly to the point of disappearance. After the communists took over, they deemed acrobatics as an "acceptable" art form of the proletariat, and the performance art began a major revival throughout the country. Today, there are numerous acrobatics shows to choose from in vibrant Shanghai, but in our opinion by far the best and most exciting is the ERA Intersection of Time.

ERA Intersection of Time (Shíkōng Zhīlǚ; 时空之旅)

The ERA Intersection of Time is quite unique in the sense that it, like the city of Shanghai itself, combines elements of its traditional past and gleaming future into one, spectacular stage. A mix between a Broadway musical and a Chinese acrobatic show using state of the art technologies in lights, sounds, visual displays, special effects and a water screen, ERA's performance transforms this one-of-a-kind venue into a vibrant, mind-blowing event. Tracing China's history from early man to contemporary boom times, dynasty through dynasty (while using acrobatic

moves used during those dynasties), the 100-minute show is a real blockbuster. Check out the website **www.era-shanghai.com/era/en/** for more information on the awesome show, and be sure to click the ERA trailer to catch a quick preview of all the incredible action found here.

Venue: Shanghai Circus World (see below)
Time: 19:30-21:00

Shanghai Acrobatic Troupe (Shànghǎi Zájìtuán; 上海杂技团 *)*

This internationally-renowned acrobatics team focuses more on the moves rather than the flair and high tech whammies that ERA throws at you. Nose balancing, juggling, hoop diving and all the other usual suspects will be seen, but you should also be ready for some exciting surprises.

Venue: Huxi Theatre (see list for details)
Time: 19:30-21:00

Other acrobatics and non-acrobatic shows, like magic and circus performances, can be viewed at the following venues. Check their websites for pricing, seating and other info.

Shanghai Center Theater (Shànghǎi Shāngchéng Jùyuàn; 上海商城剧院 *)*

Address: 3/F, 1376 Nanjing West Rd (静安区南京西路 1376 号 3 楼)
Phone: 6279 8663
Website: www.shanghaiacrobaticshow.com/shanghai-center-theater.htm

Shanghai Huxi Theater (Shànghǎi Hùxī Dàjùyuàn; 上海沪西大剧院 *)*

Address: 205 Wuning Rd (武宁路 205 号)
Phone: 6652 6822
Website: www.shanghaiacrobaticshow.com/shanghai-huxi-theatre.htm

Shanghai Circus World (Shànghǎi Mǎxì Chéng; 上海马戏城 *)*

Address: 2266 Gonghe New Rd (闸北区共和新路 2266 号)
Phone: 5665 6622
Website: www.shanghaiacrobaticshow.com/shanghai-circus-world.htm

Shanghai Baiyulan Theatre (Báiyùlán Jùchǎng; 白玉兰剧场 *)*

Address: 308 Chongqing South Rd (重庆南路 308 号)
Phone: 6322 1208
Website: www.shanghaiacrobaticshow.com/baiyulan-theater.htm

Shanghai Cloud Theater (Shànghǎi Yúnfēng Jùyuàn; 上海云峰剧院 *)*

Address: 1700 Beijing West Rd (静安区北京西路 1700 号)
Phone: 5353 0746
Website: www.shanghaiacrobaticshow.com

Other Attractions

157

Sleeping

Shanghai might be the city that never sleeps, but occasionally you are going to have to pull yourself away from the action and get some shut-eye. You could go local and just nod off anywhere the urge catches you – at a reception desk, reclining on a scooter, or on a stack of recycled cardboard – but being able to stretch out for a solid 40 winks is the best way to get the most out of the following day.

If you decide that you do want the luxury hotel experience, well, you're in luck. Shanghai is home to dozens of ultra-chic name brand and boutique hotels and a ton of five-star, internationally renowned, world-class landmarks. And while they might put a bit of a pinch on a backpacker's budget, the rates are usually incredibly affordable when you consider what you'd pay back home. So maybe slum it in a grungy hostel for a while and then splurge on your last night with the luxury treatment (just don't go too "rock star" and throw any TVs out the window).

On the other end of the spectrum, at the cheapest hostels in town, you probably won't be able to push the price any lower than it already is. But everywhere else, a 10%-50% discount is easily obtainable, either by asking at the front desk or by doing your research online (we particularly like **www.agoda.com**) are offering. But if you cannot find any deals on the web, don't worry, we have you covered. Just look for the blue ribbons to see which hotels and hostels are Panda Partners and receive discounts by showing them this guidebook.

Where to stay?

Like every other major megalopolis on the planet, Shanghai is carved up into distinct neighborhoods. There are 17 districts

Hotel Tips

Whether you book directly with the hotel or through a third-party site, make sure you have confirmation in writing when you arrive to check in.

Ask your hotel concierge to fill out the Emergency Card (see pg 43). Better safe than sorry, and it'll help you from getting lost.

English is generally spoken much better at youth hostels than at mid-range or pricier hotels.

Most hostels and hotels can help you with ticketing – train tickets, plane tickets, tickets to local shows and performances – for a small commission.

The recommendations listed are not comprehensive – if you want to explore further options in Shanghai, hit the internet. Two websites that are excellent for hostels in particular are: **www.hostels.com** and **www.hostelworld.com**.

and one county that make up the Pearl of the Orient, and each one has its own unique style and flavor, so you should try to check out as many as you can while in town to get the true Shanghai experience. Though visiting each neighborhood is easy breezy, packing and unpacking at different accommodations throughout the city may not be so convenient or fun, so it's best to pick a neighborhood that matches your attitude, leaving your days free to explore elsewhere.

Listed below are the most popular neighborhoods to stay in for your Shanghai vacation, so before you start flipping through the endless list of hotels and hostels, take a look here first to see which one has your name written on it.

Recommended for the business traveler or the luxury addict. 15 years ago, the area to the east of the Huangpu River (known as Pudong) was nothing more than flooded rice paddies and rickety farm houses. Almost overnight, the area transformed into one of the world's most spectacular (and most recognizable) skylines. Home to the city's new financial district and a few of the world's tallest buildings, Pudong is not for the budget conscious. The only downside is that you're cut off from the rest of Shanghai: you'll have to cross a bridge, drive through a tunnel, or take the metro to get to the city center.

The Bund & City Center

Recommended for the tourist, backpacker and sightseer of all budget ranges. On the western flanks of the Huangpu River rests the Huangpu District. Before Pudong eclipsed Shanghai's shining Bund, this area was the money shot for Shanghai's wealth and this was where the majority of the foreigners (minus the French, but we'll get to them in a second) set up their autonomous concessions more than a century ago. Today, along the Bund promenade, there are various structures left over from the days of 19th and 20th century colonialism, and the area is spiked with history, art galleries, trendy cafes, and lots of sightseeing. Further to the east is the city center with People's Square and Park at the apex, and just like the Bund there's plenty to do, eat, drink and see from this central neighborhood.

Jing'an & Nanjing Road

Recommended for the shopaholic urbanite of all shapes, sizes and bank numbers. Jing'an is the smallest district of the city, but its central location makes it a fine neighborhood for those looking to explore diverse parts of the city and/or the shopper. The Jing'an District is known primarily for Nanjing East Road, the shopping Mecca of Shanghai. There are a gazillion malls and shops selling everything from top-of-the-line European brand names to knock-off four-striped "Abidas." There is also a ton of eating options: you can find every fast food chain available, international selections and, of course, traditional Shanghai and Chinese cuisine.

French Concession

Recommended for the jet-setting trend maker with money to blow who'd rather be sipping a coffee on the Champs Elysees. While the rest of the world's colonial powers set up shop in the Bund, the French (go figure) separated themselves and established their concession here in the area of town fittingly known as the French Concession. A little upscale in nature and dotted with Parisian fountain-gushing parks, tree lined boulevards, rod iron balconies and petite cafes, the French Concession is the ideal neighborhood for the traveler wanting to enjoy a peaceful abode of eating, drinking and shopping, or those who need a dose of Western culture after spending a bit too much time in the Orient.

Express Hotels

There are a few out there, but most of Shanghai's lodging comes in the form of two-star hotels that have many branches across China. These are still fairly affordable by Western standards (all fall within our "mid-range" category), but they will not offer the same attention to detail that you might expect from a "real" hotel (stain-free carpets, uniform lighting, windows, etc). However, are you really here to experience a hotel room? Most people will be happy with a clean bed and a door that locks, as they will be spending a minial time cooped up in the room.

Check out some of these company websites below for good express hotel options.

Ctrip (Xiéchéng; 携程)

Phone: 400 619 9999
Website: www.english.ctrip.com

Elong (Yilóng; 艺龙)

Phone: 400 617 1717
Website: www.elong.net

Green Tree Inn (Gélínháotài Kuàijié Jiǔdiàn; 格林豪泰快捷酒店)
Phone: 400 699 8998
Website: www.998.com/eng

Home Inn (Rújiā Kuàijié Jiǔdiàn; 如家快捷酒店)
Phone:400 820 3333
Website: www.homeinns.com
(English option top right corner)

Hanting Express (Hàntíng Kuàijié Jiǔdiàn; 汉庭快捷酒店)
Phone: 400 812 1121
Website: ir.htinns.com

Pod Inn (Bùdīng Kuàijié Jiǔdiàn; 布丁快捷酒店)
Phone:400 880 2802
Website: en.podinns.com

7 Days Inn (Qītiān Kuàijié Jiǔdiàn 七天快捷酒店)
Phone: 400 874 0087
Website: en.7daysinn.cn (in Chinese)

Pudong

Budget

Bee Home International Youth Hostel (Bīnjiā Guóji Qīngnián Lǚshè; 宾家国际青年旅舍)

One of the best (and the only) budget hostels in business oriented Pudong, it's a newcomer to Shanghai's blossoming hostel scene, and it's conveniently located close to Line 2 of the metro and within walking distance of the Jinmao Tower, Oriental Pearl TV Tower, Shanghai World Financial Center and the Shanghai Tower. There are over 40 private rooms and 40 dormitory beds, and it's equipped with clean, modern facilities.

Address: 210, Lane 490, Dongchang Rd (东昌路 490 弄 210 号 . 东园二村)
Phone: 5887 9801

Captain International Youth Hostel (Lǎochuánzhǎng Qīngnián Lǚshè; 老船长国际青年旅舍)

Not to be confused with the Captain on the other side of the Huangpu, this one is in the thick of things tucked among the soaring skyscrapers of Pudong. This establishment is brand-spanking new, and you'll definitely notice it with the sleek interior, modern furnishings, spotless white bedding and shiny windows. The dorms are clean as a whistle (though some complain that the communal dorm toilets need an extra scrub down), and the singles and doubles look as if they belong in a hotel. The style differs slightly from its Puxi cousin, but you'll still find all the fishing and boating utensils that customers love for some odd reason. The only big difference between the two is that this one lacks the brilliant view of Pudong that made the original Captain so famous.

Address: 527 Laoshan Rd, near Zhangyang Rd (浦东新区崂山路 527 号)
Phone: 5836 5966

Mid-range

Pudong Hotel (Pǔdōng Dàjiǔdiàn; 浦东大酒店)

Situated near great restaurants and shopping in the heart of Pudong, this comfortable hotel does the trick for business, family and independent travelers. The free breakfast buffet gets rave reviews for its Chinese and intercontinental selections, and as always you can never go wrong with a heated pool.

The only complaint is that none of the staff seemed to have aced high school English, but they can still communicate with the basics. Rooms start at ¥322.

Address: 1888 Pudong South Rd (浦东南路1888号)
Phone: 6875 8800
Website: www.pudong-hotel.com (in Chinese)

Holiday Inn Pudong Hotel (Pǔdōng Jiàrì Jiǔdiàn; 浦东假日酒店)

Holiday Inns may give you the impression of the quintessential middle-of-the-road joint, but they (like so many other Western companies moving to China) changed their business model and upped the ante on this side of the Pacific. The Holiday Inn in Pudong is perhaps one of the nicest branches in all of Mainland China: they have a glamorous pool, helpful staff, clean habitations, a generous breakfast, great restaurants with Chinese and Western dishes and a very relaxing lobby bar. Though some travelers had complaints in the past, it seems that they're improving the smallest details year after year to turn this location into a very good, mid-range hotel. Rooms start at ¥440.

Address: 899 Dongfang Rd (浦东东方路899号)
Phone: 5830 6666

Splurge

Pudong Shangri-la (Pǔdōng Xiānggélǐlā Dàjiǔdiàn; 浦东香格里拉大酒店)

The twin-tower five-star Shangri-la sets the bar for luxury Pudong hotels. It may go without saying that the modern bathrooms and outstanding rooms with a view of the river and Bund are almost as good as they get, but our favorite aspect of this branch is their dining, particularly the buffet that constantly changes its selection between traditional and international flavors (when we were there they had an Arab theme with hummus, flat breads, falafel, etc). Rooms start at ¥1,100.

Address: 33 Fucheng Rd, Pudong (富成路33号)
Phone: 6882 8888

Jumeirah (Zhuóměiyà Xīmǎlāyǎ Jiǔdiàn; 卓美亚喜玛拉雅酒店)

If money isn't an issue, and opulence with a hint of snobbery is what you demand, the Jumeirah is calling your name. While many of Shanghai's top luxury cornerstones are Westernized with an ultra-modern setting, this one sticks to its roots and follows the principles of *feng shui* religiously. Some of the artwork and antiques should belong in the Louvre, while the classical pavilion is mesmerizing. The rooms have also been fitted with enough pillows and state of the art electronics to keep you satisfied for weeks on end. Of course, there is a gym, spa, pool (with underwater music) and top notch dining. Rooms start at ¥1,048.

Address: 1108 Meihua Rd (浦东新区梅花路1108号)
Phone: 3858 0888
Email: JHSinfo@jumeirah.com

Ritz-Carlton Shanghai Pudong (Shànghǎi Pǔdōng Lìsīkǎ'ěrdùn Jiǔdiàn; 上海浦东丽思卡尔顿酒店)

This branch is considered one of the finest hotels in Pudong (and that's saying a lot given the stiff competition in this neighborhood). You name it, the Ritz excels in it: service, dining, fitness center, spa, comfort, location, view, whatever; but our personal favorites were the spacious bathrooms with freestanding bathtubs! As a rule of thumb, you can never go wrong with any Ritz-Carlton in the world. Rooms start at ¥1,500.

Address: Shanghai IFC, 8 Century Ave,

Lujiazui, Pudong (世纪大道 8 号上海国金中心)
Phone: 2020 1888

Park Hyatt Shanghai (Shànghǎi Bǎiyuè Jiǔdiàn; 上海柏悦酒店)

PANDA PICK

With a name most people are familiar with, you can expect a certain quality of service and style in all aspects of this hotel, but there are a few features here that go above and beyond – way, way above! Located in the Shanghai World Financial center, one of the world's fastest elevators will whisk you up 80 stories to check in. As the highest hotel in the world, they also boast the highest bar in the world, with a huge outdoor patio that makes you feel like you could reach out and touch the Oriental Pearl TV Tower. The restaurant, the bar, the hotel – they're not cheap, but they can give you a taste of luxury if you haven't depleted your budget by the end of your trip. Rooms start at ¥2,120.

Address: 79-93/F, Shanghai World Financial Center, 100 Century Ave, near Dongtai Rd, Pudong (浦东新区世纪大道 100 号)
Phone: 6888 1234
Website: www.shanghai.park.hyatt.com

The Bund & City Center

Budget

Captain Youth Hostel (Lǎochuánzhǎng Qīngnián Lǔshè; 老船长青年旅舍)

PANDA PICK

Long regarded as the best hostel in Shanghai. If you want to spend time in Shanghai's tourist district, then it is tough to beat the Captain for its location. Standing just off the Bund, it is in walking distance to Nanjing East Road, People's Square and the Bund Sightseeing Tunnel to take you on a trippy voyage to Pudong. Plus, its bar has one of the city's best patios for a view of Pudong.

Address: 37 Fuzhou Rd, near Sichuan Middle Rd (福州路 37 号)
Phone: 6323 5053
Website: www.captainhostelshanghai.com

Mingtown Hiker Youth Hostel (Shànghǎi Lǔxíngzhě Guójì Qīngnián Lǔshè; 上海旅行者国际青年旅舍)

Mingtown Hiker is a good budget hostel with four- to six-person dorms and a few upscale singles and doubles. The English speaking staff is amicable and extremely helpful, and its location just a short reach from the Bund is excellent. The pool table surrounded by the bar is a fun place to kick back and meet fellow travelers.

Address: 450 Jiangxi Middle Rd (江西中路 450 号)
Phone: 6329 7889

Mingtown Etour Youth Hostel (Shànghǎi Xīnyìtú Guójì Qīngnián Lǔshè; 上海新易途国际青年旅舍)

¥5 OFF

This hostel centrally located near People's

Square has a nice outdoor patio where all the backpackers like to hangout and exchange tales of China travel experiences (both good and bad), and many of the rooms surprisingly have old-fashioned, antique furniture from Shanghai's glory days.

Address: 55 Jiangyin Rd (江阴路 55 号)
Phone: 6327 7766

Phoenix (Lǎoshān Kèzhàn; 老陕客栈)

> One FREE coffee, tea or beer

If you want to save some cash but need a break from the world of hostels, Phoenix (also called Laoshan Hostel) has dorms, doubles and singles for your convenience. It has seen better days, but it still stands up to acceptable standards. The beautiful rooftop bar, dumpling restaurant and supreme location next to People's Square keep it as a top choice in the budget category.

Address: 17 Yunnan South Rd, near Yan'an East Rd (云南南路 17 号, 近延安东路)
Phone: 6328 8680

Blue Mountain Hostel (Lánshān Qīngnián Lǚshè; 蓝山青年旅舍)

Travelers love this pleasant and tidy hostel with an extremely friendly staff. It's a bit out of the way, but the separated girls and boys dorm rooms make privacy issues a non factor. Their prime real estate just a short walk from Nanjing East Road and 15 minutes to the Bund is ideal, and there are plenty of shops, restaurants and attractions within striking distance. Blue Mountain always attracts a

good, diverse crowd of backpackers and travelers, making it a fun place to pass your Shanghai excursion.

Address: 6/F, 350 Shanxi South Rd (山西南路 350 号 6 楼)
Phone: 3366 1561
Website: www.bmhostel.com

Mid-range

24K International Hotel (Èrshísìkài Guójì Liánsuǒ Jiǔdiàn ; 24k 国际连锁酒店)

24K is actually a smaller chain with a few decent locations around People's Square and Nanjing East Road. Unfortunately no one mentioned the "international" part to their web designer or reception staff, so it's a little tricky to navigate unless you speak some Mandarin. The rooms are nice enough, though, to classify it into your standard level business traveler's hotel. Rooms start at ¥130.

Address: 555 Fuzhou Rd (福州路 555 号)
Phone: 5150 3588
Toll free: 400 888 6119
Website: www.24khotels.com (English available)

Marvel Hotel (Shànghǎi Shāngyuè Qīngniánhuì Dàjiǔdiàn; 上海商悦青年会大酒店)

One of the more expensive, mid-range options in Puxi, you get what you pay for as Marvel offers a historic yet classy vibe, central location next to People's Square, a refurbished interior with modern appliances, and cozy bedding. In our humble opinion, this one is great bang for buck. Rooms start at ¥498.

Address: 123 Xizang South Rd (西藏南路123号)
Phone: 3305 9999
Website: www.marvel-hotel.com

Pacific Hotel (Jīnmén Dàjiǔdiàn; 金门大酒店)

Located inside a clock-tower building that was originally built in 1926, the interior has been re-done with marble floors, attractive paintings, burgundy carpets and wooden furniture. Request a room facing People's Park, they have the best view and are a little more spacious. Rooms start at ¥368.

Address: 108 Nanjing West Rd (南京西路108号)
Phone: 6327 6226; 5352 9898
Website: www.pacifichotelshanghai.cn

Splurge

The Peninsula (Shànghǎi Bàndǎo Jiǔdiàn; 上海半岛酒店)

This place is a wonderful five-star luxury hotel on the northern side of the Bund. Many of the rooms have an outstanding view of the Huangpu River, while others face the Bund promenade. As with all other Peninsula chains across the world, your room will be fitted with fine luxuries along with astute service and a classy vibe. The lobby bar is also tremendous. Rooms start at ¥798.

Address: 32 Zhongshan East 1st Rd (中山东一路32号)
Phone: 2327 2888

Waldorf Astoria (Huá'ěrdàofū Jiǔdiàn; 华尔道夫酒店)

On the Bund at the former Shanghai Club (est 1910) is where the renowned Waldorf Astoria opened one of the city's newest ultra-modern hotels in 2010. The 20 premium suites are located in the original Shanghai Club, and some have an phenomenal view of Pudong, while the remaining rooms are located behind in a contemporary tower. All the rooms are equipped with the latest technology, and the TVs in the mirrors prove it. Rooms start at ¥1,510.

Address: 2 Zhongshan East 1st Rd (中山东一路2号)
Phone: 6322 9988
Website: www.waldorfastoriashanghai.com (English available)

Fairmont Peace Hotel (Hépíng Fàndiàn; 和平饭店)

To relive the heydays of 1930s Shanghai, this hotel located in the former Cathay (at one time one of the nicest hotels in all of Asia) right on the Bund has been renovated and was reopened in 2010. The modern refurbishing effort and newly equipped luxuries are a nice touch and skillfully avoid taking away from this iconic building's early 20th century charm. Rooms start at ¥1,130.

Address: 20 Nanjing East Rd (南京路20号)
Phone: 6321 6888

Hotel Indigo (Yīngdígé Jiǔdiàn; 英迪格酒店)

This trend setting hotel in the Old Town mixes the old with the new in style. Some of the quirky yet intriguing eye-catchers are the Indigo's bird cage seats, metallic walls, multicolored chandeliers, tree branches and a lobby that looks like a space capsule. The rooms stick with the interior design schema, making you feel like you're stuck in a Dali painting. Oh yeah, and they've added an infinity pool for good measure. It certainly is bizarre, but that doesn't mean its quality is hindered. Rooms start at ¥1,208.

Address: 585 Zhongshan East 2nd Rd (中山东二路585号)
Phone: 3302 9999
Website: www.shanghai.hotelindigo.com

Jing'an & Nanjing Road

Budget

Le Tour Traveler's Rest Youth Hostel (Lètú Guójì Qīngnián Lǚshè; 乐途国际青年旅舍)

10% OFF

In the heart of Jing'an you'll find this Hostelling International associate. The place is bright and attracts a crowd of international and local tourists. Lots of bars and restaurants surround you, so you'll never be hungry or thirsty here. Its location deep in a winding lane means you won't hear too much noise as you're trying to sleep off that hangover.

Address: 36, Lane 319, Jiaozhou Rd, near Wuding Rd (胶州路319弄36号)
Phone: 6267 1912
Website: www.letourshanghai.com
Email: tr@letourshanghai.com

Mingtown Nanjing Road Youth Hostel (Míngtáng Nánjīnglù Qīngnián Lǚshè; 明堂南京路青年旅舍)

Another hostel just a block north of the Nanjing East Road pedestrian street and a few blocks from the Bund, Mingtown is set in a bit of an industrial supply neighborhood, but it's still very close to the metro and tons of good little restaurants.

Address: 258 Tianjin Rd, near Shanxi South Rd (天津路258号)
Phone: 6322 0939

Mid-range

Holiday Inn Downtown (Shànghǎi Guǎngchǎng Chángchéng Jiàri Jiǔdiàn 上海广场长城假日酒店)

This four-star Holiday Inn is conveniently placed right next to the train station (it's a bit further from Nanjing Road). Cleanliness, friendliness and good management characterize this branch, but other than that the main reason travelers stay here is to catch an early morning train. Rooms start at ¥371.

Address: 585 Hengfeng Rd, Zhabei (闸北区恒丰路585号)
Phone: 6016 7777

Jinjiang Inn (Jǐnjiāng Zhīxīng Jiǔdiàn; 锦江之星酒店)

Jingjiang ia a national chain found all over the country. Their formula is simplicity, comfort and low prices; it's a solid option.

Location One (Rooms start at ¥199)

Address: 400 Xikang Rd, near Wuding Rd, Jiang'an (静安区西康路400号)
Phone: 5213 8811

Location Two (Rooms start at ¥119)

Address: 339 Jiaozhou Rd, Jiang'an (静安区胶州路339号)
Phone: 6253 5577

Splurge

JIA (Shànghǎi Jiā Jiǔdiàn; 上海家酒店)

JIA is an uber-designed boutique hotel aimed at business travelers. They describe their rooms as "quietly theatrical," but all you need to know is that they are super chic and super clean. All the rooms also have a little kitchenette, and while you might not be doing much cooking, it's nice to have a fridge and microwave for those leftovers. Also, in case you're missing out on the sociability of the hostel dorm room, JIA offers free wine events in the lobby every evening for their guests. They also have the usual wifi and even a "technogym" in case you are feeling sluggish during your stay in China's nightlife capital. Rooms start at ¥799.

Address: 931 Nanjing West Rd, near Taixing Rd (南京西路931号)
Phone: 6217 9000
Website: www.jiashanghai.com

Portman Ritz-Carlton (波特曼丽思卡尔顿酒店)

It's the Ritz-Carlton, a name that is synonymous with class and style, but in addition to that, its stellar location on Nanjing West Road is key. In the same building is the Shanghai Center, which shows daily performances of one of Shanghai's circus/acrobatic groups (pg 157). There's also a foreign specialty grocery in the basement, top notch independent restaurants throughout

the complex and a deluxe pool within the hotel. It's about two blocks from Jing'an Temple, and directly across the street from the beautiful Soviet-era behemoth now used as the Shanghai Exhibition Center. The squash and tennis courts and gym may be a perk if you need to break a sweat. Rooms start at ¥889.

Address: 1376 Nanjing West Rd, near Xikang Rd (静安区南京西路 1376 号)
Phone: 6279 8888

URBN (Yǎyuè Jiǔdiàn; 雅悦酒店)

So you want to treat yourself but not at the expense of Mother Earth? Or maybe you like luxury, but not all the wannabe glamorbots that come with it? Then check out URBN, a boutique hotel tucked off a bustling street that's just a five minute walk to Jing'an Temple. Most of the hotel's construction materials were reclaimed from older buildings and structures in China that had been slated for demolition. The hotel also strives to be carbon neutral, allowing you to enjoy its interesting style, great location and lush accommodation without destroying the planet. The hotel is home to Downstairs, a great restaurant from Chef David Laris, who has several other successful joints around the city. Rooms start at ¥1,500.

Address: 183 Jiaozhou Rd, near Beijing West Rd (静安区胶州路 183 号)
Phone: 5153 4600
Website: www.urbnhotels.com
Email: reservation@urbnhotels.com

The Puli (Púli Jiǔdiàn; 璞丽酒店)

One of the many Shanghai hotels that places heavy emphasis on modernity and futuristic designs, The Puli clearly intends to follow this trend with radiant colors, metal furniture

and plenty of geeky gizmos scattered throughout the massive 26-story building. However the flowers, Chinese artwork, and mahogany furniture cut back on the place looking like Deep Space Nine. Book ahead to receive discounts. Rooms start at ¥1,628.

Address: 1 Changde Rd (静安区常德路 1 号)
Phone: 3203 9999
Website: www.thepuli.com
Email: information@thepuli.com

French Concession

Budget

Blue Mountain Youth Hostel (Lánshān Guójì Qīngnián Lǚshè; 蓝山国际青年旅舍)

> First night ¥5 OFF dorm bed, ¥10 OFF room

At the time of writing, this was the only hostel in the French Concession. You've seen places like this before; think standard hostel with a washing machine, fully equipped kitchenette, movie screenings, female dormitories, bar and pool table. This simple yet quaint hostel is a bit out of the way, but luckily it's close to the metro station. Panda Partner discount here cannot be combined with YHA card discount.

Address: 2/F, Bldg 1, Lane 1072, Quxi Rd (瞿溪路 1072 弄 1 号甲二楼)
Phone: 63043938
Website: www.bmhostel.com
Email: expo@bmhostel.com

Mid-range

Yan'an Hotel (Yán'ān Fàndiàn; 延安饭店)

Built in the 1960s, Ya'an did a major overhaul in 2006. It's not as glamorous as the Four Seasons, but it is a step up from the two-star offerings like Hanting and the like. It is also on the south side of Yan'an Road; one block might not seem like much, but you will feel a lot closer to the hotspots on Huaiha Road or Fumin Road than you would if you were on Nanjing Road. The hotel has its own large restaurant, but just outside the door you'll find plenty of local and international options that will fit every price range. Rooms start at ¥346.

Address: 1111 Yan'an Middle Rd, near Huashan Rd (延安中路1111号)
Phone: 6133 1188
Website: www.yananhotel.com

Magnolia B&B (Xiǎomùlán Lǚguǎn; 小木兰旅馆)

This is a quaint five-room bed and breakfast located in a 1927 concession-style home. With a perfect mix between of the old and the new and an art deco interior design, this is one of our favorite lodges in the city. Rooms start at ¥650.

Address: 36 Yangqing Rd (徐汇区延庆路36号)
Phone: 138 1794 0848
Website: www.magnoliabnbshanghai.com
Email: magnoliabnbshanghai@gmail.com

Quinet B&B (Wǔchóngzòu Lǚdiàn; 五重奏旅店)

An adorable B&B in the French Concession that has a classic 1930s Shanghai feel, Quinet finds the perfect balance between the glitzy days of Shanghai's colonial past and a twist of modernity of the city's vibrant future: the porcelain bathtubs are phenomenal, and the big-screen satellite TVs are a good addition for added comfort. Rooms start at ¥788.

Address: 808 Changle Rd (长乐路808号)
Phone: 6249 9088
Website: www.quintet-shanghai.com

Kevin's Old House (Kǎiwén Zhījiā; 凯文之家)

10% OFF

In the building of a 1927 old concession cottage, this splendid lodge has been remolded to meet the demands of 21st century travelers. The artwork, wooden furniture, and antiques give it a gracious touch of elegance, and the prices are hard to beat. Book ahead, there are only six rooms. Rooms start at ¥500.

Address: 4, Lane 946, Changle Rd (徐汇区长乐路946弄4号)
Phone: 6248 6800; 135 6413 8740
Website: www.kevinsoldhouse.com
Email: postmaster@kevinsoldhouse.com

Splurge

Andaz (Āndáshì Jiǔdiàn; 安达仕酒店)

One of the nicest hotels in the French Concession with an outstanding location close to Xintiandi, Andaz (the Hindi word for "personal style") sets itself apart from the old-money establishments on the Bund by offering a slick, Japanese-designed layout with flat screens, marble bathrooms and funky lighting. Rooms start at ¥1,016.

Address: 88 Songshan Rd (嵩山路 88 号)
Phone: 2310 1234

Ruijin Hotel (Ruìjīn Bīn'guǎn; 瑞金宾馆)

Its four building complex circling a fabulous, European garden in the French Concession makes this upscale, non-pretentious hotel a nice option. Building 1 is the oldest and most classic of the bunch: it was built in 1919 and was the former mansion of a wealthy expat. Check the website for discounts. Rooms start at ¥1,340.

Address: 118 Ruijin 2nd Rd (瑞金二路 118 号)
Phone: 6472 5222

88 Xintiandi (Bābā Xīntiāndì; 88 新天地)

This splendid boutique hotel has more than 50 modern rooms, but they maintain a classical Chinese vibe with red lanterns, antique wooden cabinets and Oriental carpets. There is a small health club with a view of the park and city, and guests here can use the pool next door at the Langham Xintiandi hotel. If upscale eating, shopping and drinking are to dominate your Shanghai vacation, 88 is a fine choice since it's one of the best places to stay in trendy Xintiandi. Rooms start at ¥1,218.

Address: 380 Huangpi South Rd (黄陂南路 380 号)
Phone: 5383 8833
Website: shanghai.88xintiandi.com

Le Sun Chine (Shēn Gōngguǎn; 绅公馆)

This boutique hotel (built in 1932 and the former mansion of Dr Sun Yat-sen) underwent a major face-lift recently to modernize the scene (the pool and steam bath are some of the great additions), but the antiques, cultural relics, art and Chinese wooden furnishing have been preserved to keep the mansion's antique charm. There are only 17 rooms, so book in advanced to reserve yours. It's a bit hard to find so you may want to take a taxi the first time you come. Rooms start at ¥1,030.

Address: 6, Lane 1220, Huashan Rd, Changning (长宁区华山路 1220 弄 6 号)
Phone: 5256 9977
Website: www.lesunchine.com

Suzhou Creek & Other Options

If you're looking for something a little more peaceful outside the loud overcrowd city, there are several options across the price board in the northern, southern and western parts of town.

Budget

City Central International Hostel (Wànlǐlù Guójì Qīngnián Jiǔdiàn; 万里路国际青年酒店)

¥5 OFF bed, 10 OFF room, or beer/coffe coupons

Besides the fact that it is not really in the city center, this is a solid choice for a hostel. Perhaps due to its just-outside-of-downtown location, you can expect a pretty social crowd that makes their own fun, as evidenced by the hostel's official beer pong nights.

Address: 50, Lane 300, Wuning Rd, near Kaixuan North Rd (普陀区武宁路300弄50号)
Phone: 5290 5577
Website: www.hostelshanghai.cn
Email: shanghaiwanlilu@gmail.com

Naza International Youth Hostel (Nàzhái Guójì Qīngnián Lǚshè; 那宅国际青年旅舍)

This is a quaint and quiet hostel located in Hongkou that features an outdoor courtyard, communal space with a pool table and a bar. Naza can be as sociable or as introverted as you wish. You can rent the dorms or singles for a long term stay at a discounted price.

Address: 318 Baoding Rd, Hongkou (虹口区保定路318号)
Phone: 6541 7062

Koala Garden House (Kǎolā Huāyuán Lǚshè; 考拉花园旅舍)

Check out this fluffy, cute, flowery hostel if you're more into Hello Kitty than GI Joe. The prices are always low and the lobby is a great place to have a quiet drink and meet other travelers, but it is a tad bit out of the way. Two of the rooms have a private balcony.

Address: 240 Duolun Rd, Hongkou (虹口区多伦路240号)
Phone: 5671 1038

Rock & Wood International Hostel (Lǎomù Guójì Qīngnián Lǚshè; 老木国际青年旅舍)

10% OFF or one FREE drink at lobby bar

Rock & Wood is outside of downtown but only five minutes from the metro and pretty close to hot bars and clubs like Dada (pg 201) and LOgO (pg 201). A nice touch here is that it is managed by a Westerner, so communication shouldn't be quite so exhausting.

Address: 278, Lane 615, Zhaohua Rd, near Zhongdeqiao Rd (长宁区昭化路615弄278号)
Phone: 3360 2361
Website: www.rockwood.hostel.com

Shanghai Soho International Youth Hostel (Sūzhōuhépàn Guójì Qīngnián Lǚshè; 苏州河畔国际青年旅舍)

Built in a former warehouse nestled on the banks of Suzhou Creek, this hostel is quite far from downtown, though just a five-minute walk from Xinzha Road Metro Station. The advantage here is the hostel's tranquil neighborhood in a serene environment, making it the perfect place for anyone needing an abode of peace and quiet away from chaotic downtown Shanghai.

Address: 1307 South Suzhou Rd, near Chengdu North Rd (黄浦区南苏州路 1307 号)
Phone: 5888 8817

Mid-range

Junye Mini Hotel (Jūnyè Jīngpǐn Jiǔdiàn; 君叶精品酒店)

15% OFF

Junye is a fine business hotel located on the historic tree-lined Xinhua Road in the western part of the city. The silky beds, rainforest showers and a fridge are great additions for the long-term traveler.

Address: 643 Xinhua Rd (新华路 643 号)
Phone: 5258 2000

Hotel Carolina (Méikǎ Shāngwù Jiǔdiàn; 美卡商务酒店)

Hotel Carolina is owned by a group of businesspeople from the US states of South Carolina, North Carolina, and Georgia. The owners understand foreigners' needs and make you feel that Hotel Carolina is your home away from home.

Address: 1728 Yishan Rd (宜山路 1728 号)
Phone: 3462 7111
Email: sales@hotelcarolina.com.cn

Marriott Hotel Hongqiao (Wànháo Hóngqiáo Dàjiǔdiàn; 万豪虹桥大酒店)

Recommended for those who'd rather stay in Hongqiao. The tennis courts, pool and bar are of better quality than the rooms, but it's a decent choice that won't bankrupt you. Rooms start at ¥460.

Address: 2270 Hongqiao Rd (虹桥路 2270 号)
Phone: 6237 6000
Website: www.marriott-hongqiao.com

Xijiao State Guesthouse (Xījiāo Bīn'guǎn; 西郊宾馆)

Xijiao claims to be the largest garden hotel in Shanghai, and the spacious landscape filled with exotic trees arround a lake seem to back up its words. In fact, Chairman Mao and Queen Elizabeth have even stayed here before. Unfortunately, hotels with this much green space aren't centrally located. Rooms start at ¥566.

Address: 1921 Hongqiao Rd (虹桥路 1921 号)
Phone: 6219 8800

Splurge

The Waterhouse at South Bund (Shànghǎi Shuǐshè Jiǔdiàn; 上海水舍酒店)

Located in the South Bund, Waterhouse was a warehouse in the 1930s. This stylish, modern and conveniently located lodge has an outstanding rooftop bar, and some rooms even have terraces (which is quite rare in Shanghai). The only problem is that it's not close to the main promenade of the Bund, but it is pleasantly surrounded by the charisma of Old Town. Rooms start at ¥982.

Address: 1-3 Maojiayuan Rd, Huangpu (毛家园路 1-3 号)
Phone: 6080 2988
Website: www.waterhouseshanghai.com

Astor House (Pǔjiāng Fàndiàn; 浦江饭店)

Laced with wood paneling that creaks every time you step, this dinosaur of an establishment is older than your great grandpa and may feel haunted at first, but in reality it has a nice old-world charm that can't be found in many hotels these days. Discounts are generous (check the website) and the location is superb: about 500 m (1,640 ft) north of the Bund, right on the banks of peaceful Suzhou Creek. Rooms start at ¥688.

Address: 15 Huangpu Rd (黄浦路 15 号)
Phone: 6324 6388
Website: www.astorhousehotel.com
Email: sales@astorhousehotel.com

Broadway Mansions (Shànghǎi Dàshà; 上海大厦)

Located right next to the Astor House, this elegant European building (built in 1934 by a British merchant) is one of the most luxurious buildings along Suzhou Creek. The spa, business center, modern workout facilities, exquisite restaurant and splendid view of the Bund and Pudong without the flocks of tourists is unbeatable. It's fit for business, recreational and family travel. Rooms start at ¥489. See Astor House map.

Address: 20 North Suzhou Rd (北苏州路 20 号)
Phone: 6324 6260
Website: www.broadwaymansions.com

Chai Living Residence (Càn Kèzhàn; 灿客栈)

10% OFF

This is the ideal option for those staying in Shanghai for weeks or even months who prefer a homey apartment rather than a commercialized hotel. These luxury living quarters will make you feel right at home with giant TVs, a fully equipped kitchen and comfortable furniture. The daily maid service here is the only thing you may not get at your original home. Rooms start at ¥800.

Address: 400 North Suzhou Rd (北苏州路 400 号)
Phone: 6306 8936
Website: www.chailiving.com

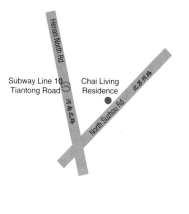

Eating

Eating in China

China has been perfecting the art of gastronomy for thousands of years and boasts a culinary culture that has been greatly influenced by foreign invaders, ethnic minorities and even the emperor's own palate. This makes it quite difficult to classify what Chinese food is due to its diversity and the sheer amount of distinct culinary styles. In fact, if you travel extensively around China, one of the first things you'll notice is the change in food culture, ingredients and preparation from one town to another.

When considering "Chinese food," many Westerners may think of things like fortune cookies, chop suey and General Tso's Chicken – all of which are not actually authentic Chinese dishes. The Chinese food found in Western countries is mostly influenced by the southern school of Chinese cooking since the area around Guangdong is where the majority of Chinese immigrants came from, but their original recipes were greatly modified to meet Western tastes. That means you shouldn't expect to find too many of your favorites from home here. However, there are a few mainstream Chinese dishes – sweet and sour pork, kung pao chicken, spring rolls, fried rice, dumplings, won ton soup, Peking Duck and stir-fried noodles – that you may recognize.

The Chinese love nothing more than a good meal, so it should be no surprise that one of the greatest pleasures in traveling around China is eating. And with hundreds, if not thousands, of types of diverse meals, there's always something new to try. But before plunging in head first, check out **www. sugarednspiced.com**, a wonderful Shanghai food blog, for more about the local eating culture. We also highly recommend you read the 15 very important tips on the next page to keep from "losing face" at a Chinese restaurant.

Eating

173

Panda Restaurant Tips

1. Chinese restaurants will not have forks and knifes, only chopsticks. If you don't know how to use the two flimsy twigs, then you better start learning (see How to Use Chopsticks on pg 197). For soup, some establishments may provide an oriental style spoon; if not, drink it straight from the bowl.

2. Don't expect any English to be spoken by the staff or written on the menu. The good news is that picture menus are quite common.

3. If you ask for napkins, you'll most likely get a roll of toilet paper or some tissues.

4. You probably won't see ice cubes here, and if you want a cold beer or drink, you must specify that you want it cold (bīng de; 冰的) or else it'll come at room temperature.

5. When nature calls and you need to use the bathroom, be prepared to squat, and don't expect it to be up to the Western standards of cleanliness.

6. When you sit down at your table, the waiter will hover over you like a vulture, waiting for you to make a decision. Don't feel pressured, and just take your time, because this is normal. If you absolutely need some space say, "I'll call you" (Wǒ huì jiào nǐ; 我会叫你).

7. Although no smoking signs are everywhere, and it's technically illegal to smoke indoors here, hardly anyone abides. If you want to smoke, light up. If not, you must unfortunately hold your breath.

8. No one tips unless you're at a very fancy restaurant or hotel. When you try to leave money on the table, your attendants will chase you down the road to return your cash. When you try paying extra as a tip, they will think you don't know how to count.

9. If you don't eat meat, try telling the waiter, "I'm a vegetarian" (Wǒ chī sù de; 我吃素的). That being said, they'll still probably throw some bits of bacon fat into your veggie dish just because the concept of vegetarianism hasn't caught on yet, despite centuries of Buddhist and Taoist influence. Meat was a luxury during the Cultural Revolution, so many Chinese today still don't understand why some people refuse to eat it.

10. When Chinese people go out to eat, it's common for one person to order all the food. Several dishes are ordered and shared by all, with everyone picking food from the various platters presented. Usually the host (the one who ordered) will pay. It's OK to split the bill with your friends, but if a Chinese friend or host insists on paying, let them.

11. There are hardly any table manners in China, so forget what mom told you and put your elbows on the table, spit chicken bones out on the floor and even let out a belch if you fancy. No one will raise an eyebrow.

12. Desserts aren't common in China. Locals prefer to eat a little bit of fruit after dinner instead of a chocolate mousse cake.

13. The drinking culture is very different in China. If you order a bottle of beer, it will come with some small glasses, which you should fill for everyone. Cheers by saying "dry glass" (gànbēi; 干杯) and take a healthy drink. The glass is often drained in one shot, but not always. If you're really adventurous, consider forgoing the beer and trying *báijiǔ* (白酒), which is 120 proof distilled Chinese liquor with a paint-thinner aroma. Drink at your own risk.

14. If you're sitting down and a complete stranger comes to sit at your table to eat, don't be scared. This is a country of 1.4 billion people and seats are limited.

15. Last but not least, try to be as open minded as possible. There's a vast cultural difference between the East and West, so if you thought you ordered something correctly by pointing at pictures, there's still a chance that you will get something completely different. Roll with the punches, laugh it off and put it in the "good stories to tell people back home" box.

By now you know that Chinese food goes far beyond day-old orange chunks of pork and pineapple with egg-fried rice. Not only have Chinese chefs been honing and perfecting their recipes for thousands of years, they've been doing it in one of the largest countries in the world — giving them a choice of diverse ingredients from the tropics to the tundras, along with influences from Korea to Kazakhstan.

Geographically speaking, China spans a huge region, from just south of the Arctic to just north of the Equator, and from the Pacific Ocean to Pakistan. This multitude of climates and ecosystems gives rise to an incredibly diverse diet, far too broad to just be considered "Chinese food." Each region and section of the country is home to their own distinct cuisine, something the local residents will be especially proud of. In some parts of the country you'll taste dishes you'd swear were Thai. Other places will serve your Middle Eastern-like favorites. You'll find food that resembles Japanese, and yes, you'll even find stereotypical classics like egg-fried rice. It's all here.

The Shanghai Way

So what can you expect out of quintessential Shanghai cuisine? Very sweet, pretty oily, with some soy sauce and vinegar thrown in for good measure. This isn't necessarily a bad thing. There are many Shanghainese dishes that have become worldwide favorites. But overall, this is the basic mentality in food preparation in Shanghai.

That means that even when you are eating other regional cuisines – say Sichuan or Hunan – the dishes are likely to be prepared in a Shanghai style, unless the chef is fresh from his home province. It's sort of like how Texas changed the taco. Tex-Mex might be different than true Mexican, but it doesn't mean it's not tasty.

One challenge for restaurants here has always been the supply of fresh quality ingredients. Remember that every day more than 20 million people must be fed, so that means a lot of rice, meat and vegetables have to be distributed through the city. It is a logistical nightmare, one that starts every morning before dawn when the first vegetable suppliers set up their stalls.

There are farms all around Shanghai, including many in business-oriented Pudong, that supply the city with these fresh greens and meats. Pig farmers in fact play a double role in the system, supplying restaurants and grocers with pork, and removing waste food scraps. Late at night you might happen to see a man on a bicycle with a disgusting, greasy barrel strapped on either side of it. This is a pig farmer, and he goes to restaurants and gets your leftovers and any other scrap food, peels, pits and skins to dump in these buckets and take back to his farm to feed his pigs.

In addition to pork, which is synonymous with meat in China, seafood plays an important part in the Shanghai culinary landscape. As the city is coastal and straddles the Huangpu River, it means that dinners have plenty of both saltwater and freshwater seafood.

One other thing to note about Shanghai cuisine is that, thanks to the city's popularity, there is a wide variety of tastes available. It's not just foreigners who come to Shanghai; this metropolis is a tourist destination for people all across China. More than just a few chefs have dreamed of leaving their small towns in distant provinces and heading to the bright lights of Shanghai to open up shop. That means you can find a huge variety of Chinese and international cuisines throughout this great city.

The glitz and commercialism of Shanghai have also led it to be incredibly prosperous for many businesses, including restaurants. Many of the venues on our list have become so successful that they have spawned dozens of sequels and spinoffs in a very short time. Some of these are cookie-cutter in design, with identical layouts and menus. Others have only kept the name and the underlying philosophy of the original establishment, leaving each outlet to create their own mood and trademark dishes.

Shanghai Specialties

Shanghai cuisine, also known as Hu cuisine, is not one of China's Eight Great Culinary Traditions, but it's still damn good. Nevertheless, the city has never really relied on its ancient past, opting to focus on the future instead. So, while Shanghai's kitchen may not be in the top eight of China's palate, the megalopolis has climbed its way to perhaps being one of the top eight most international cities in the world. This notion has consequentially popularized Shanghai food not only throughout China, but also the world, all while the city goes through what some would call a "foodie revival" to gain more credibility for Shanghai's tasty snacks.

Shanghai cuisine is greatly influenced by nearby Jiangsu Province, Zhejiang Province and the region of Huaiyang (which is classified as one of China's Great Eight). There are a few characteristics that define traditional Shanghainese cuisine: 1. The use of alcohol for cooking 2. Lots of sugar, even for non desserts 3. Salted and cured meats 4. Soy sauce and Chinese black vinegar 5. Fresh seafood preferably caught from the rivers and coastline around Shanghai.

The great city of Shanghai has also popularized a few famous cooking preparation methods that can now be found all over the streets and villages of China, as well as Chinatowns in places like NYC and London. Red cooking (hóngshāo, 红烧) is the process of using soy sauce, sugar and fermented bean paste to slow roast meats, creating a reddish color and a succulent, juicy taste. Another popular Shanghai dish is sweet and sour pork ribs. The region's obsession with sweet meats, sour vinegar and soy sauce created this one, but we guarantee that it tastes better here than at your local Chinese hole-in-the-wall back home.

Here are some of the classic Shanghai dishes you are sure to run into:

Shanghai Hairy Crab (Shànghǎi Máoxiè; 上海毛蟹)

While it sounds more like the punch-line to a dirty joke than a gourmet dish, hairy crab is incredibly popular here. Every autumn, restaurants across the city participate in the Hairy Crab Festival, retooling their menus to include every iteration of the crab and its roe. The true gourmands will claim that only crabs caught in Yangcheng Lake (Yángchéng Hú, 阳澄湖) will do, but you'll have to let your own taste buds (or perhaps your wallet, since the Yangcheng Lake crabs are steep) decide. If you go for hairy crab, be sure to find a primer on how to eat one; it is quite an elaborate process.

Lion's Head Meatball (Shīzi Tóu; 狮子头)

Fear not, you won't be eating the king of the jungle. This is just good old fashioned pork, and Lion's Head refers to the sheer size of the meatball. As opposed to a bite-sized wonton, these babies are about the size of your fist (or bigger) and are either served steamed in a soup or braised in soy sauce till they're a dark reddish brown.

Shanghai Fried Noodles (Shànghǎi Chǎomiàn; 上海炒面)

This is neither angel-hair pasta nor a broad fettuccini noodle. Instead, you get a fairly thick shoelace-of-a-noodle wok-fried with small pieces of meat and vegetables, all lovingly smothered in the Shanghai concoction of soy sauce, sugar and oil. Not the healthiest way to get your carbs, but it is delicious.

Steamed Buns (Xiǎolóngbāo; 小笼包)

These tiny dumplings usually come eight to a serving, and they are pulled directly out of the steamer tray into your dish. Inside the cone of steamed dough is a little bit of pork and a lot of juiciness. They are often served with red vinegar, which helps cut what could otherwise be an extremely greasy little snack. A word of caution on these: don't bite directly into them unless you want a jet of pork broth to come flying out. A good tactic is to first nibble a hole in the top and slurp some juice out to relieve the pressure inside and save your clothes from a greasy stain.

Fried Steamed Bun (Shēngjiān Mántóu; 生煎馒头)

Similar to the *xiaolongbao*, these dumplings are pan fried in oil long enough for the bottoms to be crispy and golden. Inside, the pork has been mixed with a bit of broth and some gelatin so that you get a dumpling that is gooey and juicy on the inside. Use the same caution as noted above when eating these; the fatty soup inside could be scalding and can easily squirt in any direction, burning friends and ruining clothes. Again, it's not the healthiest snack, but people have made it a breakfast staple here for over a hundred years.

Tea Eggs (Cháyè Dàn; 茶叶蛋)

While Tea Eggs technically did not originate in Shanghai, they are everywhere here, even in places where you don't want them. Imagine stumbling into a 24-hour convenience store in search of your favorite hangover cure, only to be greeted with vaporous clouds from a bubbling vat of black fluid filled with hard boiled eggs. These are Tea Eggs, and those steaming vats seem to adorn every counter in every tiny shop across the city.

Stinky Tofu (Chòu Dòufu; 臭豆腐)

This is not a joke, it's the literal translation of this dish that is (thankfully) usually prepared outdoors. There will be times when you are walking down the streets in Shanghai and you will suddenly catch a whiff of a putrid, sour stench in the air. You might be surprised to discover that the stench is food, the highly praised Stinky Tofu. This is tofu that has been marinated in a brine of fermented milk, vegetables and meat, sometimes for months. Hungry yet? If so, join the queue and try it for yourself; the locals can't get enough of this stuff!

Crawfish (Xiǎolóngxiā; 小龙虾)

This is the food that Shanghainese go crazy for in the summer; the scorching temperature is just not bearable without these. Buckets of crawfish are tossed with chili and chased down with a frosty Tsingtao (the only thing missing is the Zydeco). Don't be scared to sit eye-to-eye with locals as you challenge them to a crawfish de-shelling battle on their own turf.

Four Heavenly Kings (Sìdà Jīn'gāng; 四大金刚)

No, we didn't get this one mixed up from our Temple section. Instead, the Four Heavenly Kings refers to a big breakfast done the Shanghai way: *dàbǐng* (大饼; Shanghainese pancake); *yóutiáo* (油条; a long fried stick of dough); *cìfàntuán* (糍饭团: a sticky rice ball); and a giant glass of hot or cold soy milk (dòujiāng; 豆浆).

Red Braised Pork (Hóngshāo Ròu; 红烧肉)

Love *hongshao rou*? You have that in common with Chairman Mao and 90% of people ever to try this dish of soy sauce-braised pork belly. The amount of *hongshao rou* cooked each night in home kitchens and restaurants in Shanghai is surely epic. Our favorite version is the signature *hongshao rou* from Xiao Nan Guo (pg 181), which comes in a rather sweet soy glaze and has just the right fat to meat ratio.

Street Food

No visit to any Asian city would be complete without a snack or a full-course al fresco meal with the locals. Shanghai's street food selection is delicious, but it lacks the dynamic variety that other cities can claim. Here you won't find fried cockroaches or dog meat kebabs (although a recent scandal caught some vendors selling rat and ferret in place of pork or lamb), but you will find a wide variety of kebabs and fried rice and noodles, as well as wonton soup in the winter.

Growing attempts to gentrify Shanghai and to license and legalize appropriate vendors has meant that many one-time hotspots have been abandoned, shut down by the city's security forces. Vendors that do brave the street corners do so very tentatively after 22:00, and with extremely portable gear; they're ready to cycle away at a moment's notice should the city authorities suddenly appear.

Most street food experiences don't require a whole lot of Mandarin. However there is one phrase that is bound to come up again and again:

Do you want it spicy or not? (*Làjiāo, yào bùyào?* 辣椒, 要不要?)

To which you can reply:

Yes, spicy. (Yào; 要 .)
No, not spicy. (Bú yào ; 不要 .)
Just a little bit. (Yī diǎndiǎn; 一点点 .)

You can usually find a few vendors flanking a popular nightclub or bar street, preparing late night snacks for a drunken and appreciative crowd. Here's what they'll most often be hawking:

Note: The following three are the most standard semi-stationary street foods you'll come across. If they've got their territory well defended – or if all the right "connections" have been made – they'll even have a little dining area. This will often consist of furniture that looks like it comes from a daycare tea party room. Take care when sitting on these tiny plastic chairs – if it doesn't look like it'll hold your weight, it won't.

Kebabs (Kǎochuàn; 烤串)

Often (but not always) run by Chinese of Uighur descent, the kebab guys are the city's most ubiquitous form of street food. Maybe it has something to do with their simple set-up: a narrow metal trough of coals, a few spice jars and a cooler packed with a huge selection of kebabs.

Kebabs include various parts of chickens, beef, lamb and fish, the basic muscle meat, as well as random organs like kidney and heart. For veggies they've got an even bigger selection, ranging from basic potatoes or shitake mushrooms to garlic shoots or chives. Usually you'll make your own selection, then hand them to the grill-man, who will lay them over the fire and slather them with oil and spices before declaring them cooked.

Fried Noodles or Rice (Chǎomiàn; 炒面 / Chǎofàn; 炒饭)

The large surface of these carts will have a spot for a wok and gas burner, and the rest of the space is taken up with various kinds

of noodles and other ingredients. Most of the carts will have about four or five bags of different noodles: broad rice noodles, angel hair and fatter more yellow spaghetti noodles, as well as a big bag of steamed rice. You don't need much Mandarin to get a filling meal here, just point to the noodle or rice that you want and hold up a finger for how many bowls you want. They'll fry it up with some green leafy vegetables (the exact type might change day to day), bean sprouts, salt, pepper, sugar, chilies and of course, a little scoop of MSG. Once again, point to the ingredients you want, and sit back and watch a master at work.

Stir-Fry

Occasionally you'll also see a cart that looks very similar to the noodle cart, but in place of bags of noodles, it'll have cello-wrapped plates of various meat and vegetable combos. If any look good to you, inquire about the price and, if it seems right, he'll fry it up on the spot. It's a little more expensive than the standard fried rice or noodles, but it is a bigger meal with more than just a day's worth of carbs in it.

Roaming Street Food

In addition to the semi-temporary noodle and kebab stations, there are many other carts that drift around the city, popping up in various spots to serve their wares.

Cold Noodles

Look for a large glass display case on the back of a bike and you'll find one of the most popular summer treats. They'll start with a sheet of rice pasta and slice it into broad noodles. Then they mix it with a combination of vinegar, shredded cucumber and the all-important creamy sesame seed sauce. Served to go in a paper bowl, they are perfect for those days when it's so hot you don't want to eat anything with steam coming off of it.

Popcorn

This is something that must be seen (and heard) to believe in China. The vendor will seal some popcorn into a charred earthen jar then slowly crank it over a gas flame. When it's ready, he attaches a huge nylon sleeve to the top of the urn, then pops the top with an explosive BOOM! The popped corn instantly fills up the sleeve, ready to be sugared and spiced to your taste.

Sugarcane Juice

From a distance you might think this guy is hauling around purplish bamboo and an old industrial sewing machine on the back of his bike. A closer inspection will show that it is not a sewing machine but an ingenious and beautiful device for crushing and straining sugarcane into a cloudy golden juice. Be sure to ask for a small cup, as you probably don't want a large cup of pure sugar water.

Nutloaf (Qiēgāo; 切糕)

Many Uighur vendors will cycle across the city with huge slabs of crushed nuts pressed into a loaf. Your best bet here is to first tell him how much you want to pay and let him cut a corresponding size, instead of letting him cut a "suggested serving" and paying an arm and a leg for far more than you could ever eat.

Fruit

Even though fruit stores abound across Shanghai, you can also find plenty of pop-up fruit stands on vacant corners and broad sidewalks. Usually these stands will focus entirely on one kind of fruit, and while watermelon is king here, you can find people that sell seasonal fruits like peaches too. There is also an army of walking salespeople who wander around town with an old-fashioned bamboo yolk across their shoulders hanging with baskets filled to the brim with cherries, lotus, loquats, etc.

Shanghainese Restaurants

Pricing Guide per person (excluding extra cost for drinks):

$ Under ¥50
$$ From ¥50-150
$$$ More than ¥150

$$ Xinjishi Restaurant (Xīnjíshì Jiǔlóu; 新吉士酒楼)

Xinjishi serves up all the traditional Shanghai favorites in a modern environment. It's not the coziest of places, but you'll get a decent meal that won't bankrupt you.

Address: 3-28 Taojiang Rd, near Wulumuqi Rd (桃江路 28-3 号, 乌鲁木齐路)
Phone: 6445 0068

$$ Jesse (Lǎojíshì Shànghǎicài; 老吉士上海菜)

Jesse's cuisine and atmosphere have made it popular enough to create the chain of "New Jesse," as well as the sophisticated family of Constellation cocktail bars (pg 206).

Address: 41 Tianping Rd, near Huaihai Middle Rd (天平路 41 号, 近淮海中路)
Phone: 6282 9260

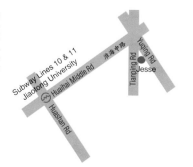

$$ Yuan Yuan (Yuányuàn Jiǔjiā; 圓苑酒家)

Expect all the Shanghai classics in a slightly more upscale environment here. Yuan Yun has numerous locations across town, and they maintain a high standard in food and service at each of them.

Address: 1-2/F, K Wah Center, 108 Xiangyang North Rd, near Huaihai Middle Rd (襄阳北路 108 号嘉华中心会所 1-2 楼 . 近淮海中路)
Phone: 5108 3377

$$ Shanghai Old Station (Shànghǎi Lǎozhàn Cāntīng; 上海老站餐厅)

Like to mix your dinner with some history? Then stop here for a meal in a turn of the century train car that is now stationed at a former French monastery. The atmosphere is kitschy and the food is standard.

Address: 201 Caoxi North Rd, near Zhaojiabang Rd (漕溪北路 201 号 . 近肇嘉浜路)
Phone: 6427 2233

$$ Shanghai Night (Yè Shànghǎi; 夜上海)

A beautiful layout for when you're shopping in Xintiandi and have a sudden hankering for

some Shanghainese treats.

Address: Xintiandi, North Block, 338 Huangpi South Rd, near Taicang Rd (黄陂南路 338 号 . 近太仓路)
Phone: 6311 2323

$ Lan Ting (Lántíng Cāntīng; 兰亭餐厅)

PANDA PICK

If it weren't for the huge crowds queuing up out front, you'd never guess that this grubby hole-in-the-wall would have some of the city's best loved Shanghai cuisine. Be prepared for a wait, and for a price-tag that might not match the décor (or lack thereof).

Address: 107 Songshan Rd, near Taicang Rd (嵩山路 107 号 . 近太仓路)
Phone: 5306 9650

$$ Wáng Bǎo Hé (王宝和)

The unofficial home for one of Shanghai's famous delicacies (the hairy crab), this place is super popular with the locals. The food is tasty, but it might be tough to get a seat when the crabs are in season.

Address: 603 Fuzhou Rd, near Zhejiang Middle Rd (福州路 603 号 . 近浙江中路)
Phone: 6322 3673

$ Nanxiang Bun (Nánxiáng Mántóu Diàn; 南翔馒头店)

PANDA PICK

While there are a few locations around town, the most popular one is probably in Yu Garden. If you're spending a day there be sure to stop in at this institution for some outstanding homemade *xiǎolóngbāo*.

Address: 85 Yuyuan Rd, near Jiuqu Qiao (豫园路 85 号 . 近九曲桥)
Phone: 6355 4206

$ Yang's Fry Dumplings (Xiǎoyáng Shēngjiān; 小杨生煎)

With countless locations all across Shanghai, Yang's owes its success to their mastery of the *shēngjiānbāo*, a scalding hot pan-fried pork dumpling. Most people order their dumplings to go (in a melting Styrofoam tray), but some of the venues do include a small seating area.

Address: 3/F, No. 1 Food Store, 720 Nanjing East Rd, near Guizhou Rd (南京东路 720 号第一食品商店 3 楼 . 近贵州路)

$$$ The Chinoise Story (Jǐnlú; 锦庐)

The story here is classic Shanghainese fare

given a modern twist with new ingredients. Don't expect to order family style here, this upscale establishment serves you your own personal choice.

Address: Jinjiang Hotel, 59 Maoming South Rd, near Changle Rd (茂名南路 59 号锦江宾馆 . 近长乐路)
Phone: 6445 1717
Website: www.jinlu-china.com

$$ Cheng Cheng's Art Salon (Wūlǐxiāng Shífǔ; 屋里香食府)

The name of the game at Cheng's is great food in an artistic setting. In fact, the art is all for sale. Perfect for those with an appetite for well-crafted meals and an eye for design.

Address: 164 Nanchang Rd, near Sinan Rd (南昌路 164 号 . 近思南路)
Phone: 5306 5462

$$$ Xiǎo Nán Guó (小南国)

Xiao Nan Guo is another mega-successful chain. It's not the cheapest place on the list, but the atmosphere is calm and the menu is exhaustive, offering more Shanghainese dishes than others. The *hongshao rou* cooked here is definitely worth a try.

Address: Block A, 565 Zhongshan East 2nd Rd, near Dongmen Rd (中山东二路 565 号 A 栋 . 近东门路)
Phone: 5757 5777

$$ Hóng Ruì Xīng (鴻瑞興)

One FREE cold dish

A great option if you are south of Xujiahui. Hong's second floor has more choices, but if you're just looking for some basic noodle or rice dishes, you might be content on the main floor.

Address: Shanghai East Asia Hotel, in the Shanghai Stadium, 1500 Zhongshan South 2nd Rd, near Yingbin Rd (中山南二路 1500 号，东亚大厦 1–3 楼 . 近迎宾路)
Phone: 6427 5177

$ Wèi Xiāng Zhāi (味香斋)

This place doesn't look appetizing, but the food here most definitely is, especially their famous spicy sesame noodles.

Address: 14 Yandang Rd, near Huaihai Rd (雁荡路 14 号 . 近淮海路)
Phone: 5383 9032

$$ Ruì Fú Yuán (瑞福园)

It's always a good sign when a place is jammed with locals, and that holds true with Rui Fu Yuan. They specialize in Ningbo dishes, making it heaven for fans of freshwater seafood.

Address: 132 Maoming South Rd, near Fuxing Middle Rd (茂名南路 132 号 . 近复兴中路)
Phone: 6445 8999; 6437 4609

$$ Down Home Kitchen (Lǎo Zào Diàn; 老灶店)

The food here is classic Shanghainese set to modern standards, but the vibe resonates with the golden era of old Shanghai. Great for getting a good meal and a feel of the town's history.

Address: Bldg 15, 48 Yuyao Rd, New Factories (余姚路 48 号 . 近海防路和西康路)
Phone: 5213 5277

$ Lín Lóng Fāng (麟笼坊特色小笼包)

A spinoff of the wildly popular Jia Jia Tangbao, this is another great place to stop for your fill of delicious dumplings.

Address: 10 Jianguo East Rd, near Zhaozhou Rd (建国东路 10 号 . 近肇周路)
Phone: 6386 7021

$ Hai Jin Zi (Hǎijīnzī Jiǔjiā; 海金滋酒家)

Another classic standby, this is a superb budget option when you want some authentic Shanghainese.

Address: 240 Jinxian Rd, near Shaanxi South

Rd (进贤路 240 号，近陕西南路)
Phone: 6255 0371

$$ Lynn (Línyí Zhōngcānguǎn; 琳怡中餐馆)

One FREE snack

Offering classy contemporary Shanghainese throughout the week, Lynn is perhaps more famous for its weekend special of ¥88 for all you can eat dim sum. Either way, you can't miss with this one.

Address: 99 Xikang Rd, near Nanjing West Rd (西康路 99 号，近南京西路)
Phone: 6247 0101

$ Jian Guo 328 (Jiànguó Sān'èrbā Xiǎoguǎn; 建国 328 小馆)

328 is a delicious, clean and modern Shanghainese eatery. It's also one of the few places in town where you can enjoy the food without any second-hand smoke.

Address: 328 Jiangguo West Rd, near Xiangyang South Rd (建国西路 328 号，近襄阳南路)
Phone: 6471 3819

$$$ Lè Shēng (乐笙)

10% OFF

Shanghainese flavor given an overhaul by David Laris, one of the city's most successful restauranteurs. You'll pay a lot, but you can be sure of having a fantastic dining experience.

Address: Suite 102, 308 Anfu Rd, near Wukang Rd (安福路 308 号 102 室，近武康路)
Phone: 5406 6011

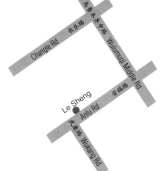

$ Jiajia Bun (Jiājiā Tāngbāo; 佳家汤包)

This joint could barely qualify as a restaurant, yet Jiajia still has a crowd lined up out the door. Don't expect any late nights here; when they sell their last *xiǎolóngbāo* they're done for the day.

Address: 90 Huanghe Rd, near Beijing Rd (黄河路 90 号，近北京路)
Phone: 6327 6878

$ Hóngqílín Lǎozhèn (洪齐林老镇)

An off-the-beaten-track hole-in-the-wall where you can find some of the city's best sweet and salty classics. Hungry visitors should go for the Lion's Head Meatball (Shīzi Tóu) as they are known for being the biggest in town.

Address: 2-727 Anyuan Rd, near Yanping Rd (安远路 727-2 号，近延平路)
Phone: 6232 9012

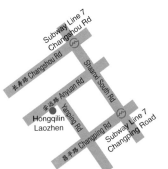

$$$ Club Jinmao (Jīnmào Jūnyuè Dàjiŭdiàn; 金茂君悦大酒店)

As you might expect from its esteemed location, you will get some amazing food with an incredible view of Shanghai, but it will cost you. Great for a big, classy night out.

Address: 86/F, Grand Hyatt, Jinmao Tower, 88 Century Ave, near Lujiazui Ring Rd (世纪大道 88 号 86 楼 . 近陆家嘴环路)
Phone: 5049 1234

$$ Fudede (Fúdédé Hǎipài Rénwén Cāntīng; 福得德海派人文餐厅)

10% OFF (sea food and drinks excluded)

Another nice option for Shanghainese, Fudede offers you all the city's standard favorites. The food is good and will leave you satisfied.

Address: 1/F, District B, 56 Maoming South Rd, near Changle Rd (茂名南路 56 号 B 区 1 楼 . 近长乐路)
Phone: 6218 7988

$$ Spring Restaurant (Chūn Cāntīng; 春餐厅)

A tiny room on the first floor of a private home, Spring has no menu here, so be prepared to speak a little bit of Mandarin or blindly accept what the chef is offering that day (which is probably going to be fresh and good).

Address: 124 Jinxian Rd, near Maoming South Rd (进贤路 124 号 . 茂名南路口)
Phone: 6256 0301

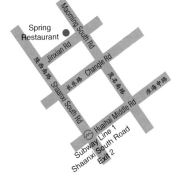

$$ The Grape (Géruìpǔ Jiǔjiā; 格瑞普酒家)

One FREE fried banana

The grape serves good Shanghainese food in a very nice neighborhood. It's was founded in 1987 and is a consistently popular choice for both expats and locals. They cater to foreigners (e.g. they take out the bones in their deep-fried Mandarin fish) and serve kung pao chicken and Peking Duck.

Address: 55 Xinle Rd, near Xiangyang Rd (新乐路 55 号 . 近襄阳路)
Phone: 5404 0486

$ Mom's Noodle (Tàihé Yīnshídiàn Āniáng Miàn; 泰和饮食店阿娘面)

Extremely affordable and delicious, this classic noodle joint has been a favorite of locals for generations now. Prepare to come for a very early dinner or a very long queue.

Address: 36 Sinan Rd, near Nanchang Rd (思南路 36 号 , 近南昌路)

Phone: 5306 6604

$$ 1221 (Yāo'èr'èr'yāo Cān'guǎn; 1221 餐馆)

One FREE dessert (any time); 20% OFF lunch

You'll find all the Shanghai classics at this restaurant. Even if you're not hungry, it's worth stopping in just for their creative tea service.

Address: 1221 Yan'an West Rd, near Panyu Rd (延安西路 1221 号 , 近番禺路)

Phone: 6213 6585

Regional Chinese Cuisine

Hunan

$$ Dripping Cave (Dīshuǐdòng; 滴水洞)

5% OFF

Three locations serve from the same menu of spicy Hunan classics, but the Maoming Road one is better if you're with a big group that needs a private room. If you're just a few people, head for the Dongping Road location, unless you want your dining hot and noisy.

Address: 2/F, 56 Maoming South Rd, near Changle Rd (茂名南路 56 号 2 楼 , 近长乐路口)

Phone: 6253 2689

Location Two

Address: 485 Guyang Rd, near Yaohong Rd (古羊路 485 号 , 近姚虹路)

Phone: 5175 3067

Location Three

Address: 5 Dongping Rd, near Hengshan Rd (东平路 5 号 B 座 , 近衡山路)

Phone: 6415 9448

$$$ Guyi (Gǔyì Xiāngwèinóng; 古意湘味浓)

This slightly upscale place serves Hunan classics in a quiet, softly-lit room. It's good for a date or a chill dinner.

Address: 89 Fumin Rd, near Julu Rd (富民路 89 号 , 近巨鹿路)

Phone: 6249 5628

Hong Kong

$$ Tsui Wah Restaurant (Cuìhuá Cāntīng; 翠华餐厅)

A Hong Kong chain with numerous outlets across the city, Tsui Wah's is always a good choice for a wide selection of tasty choices in a bright modern environment.

Address: 291 Fumin Rd, near Changle Rd (富民路 291 号, 近长乐路)
Phone: 6170 1282

$$ Cha's (Chá Cāntīng; 查餐厅)

In the mood for a classic Hong Kong cafeteria? Cha's proved so popular within months of its opening that, the owners were forced to add a second location. Still, wait times can be excessive for the cheap-ish home of Cantonese comfort foods.

Address: 4-30 Sinan Rd, near Huaihai Middle Rd (思南路 30-4 号, 近淮海中路)
Phone: 6093 2062

Xinjiang

$ Hole-in-the-Wall Uighur Restaurants

These places are found all across the city and the menus are about 95% the same no matter who's running the shop. The prices are low, the food (including fresh hand-pulled noodles) is delicious, and the ambience is almost non-existent. No address necessary – they're easily identifiable by the guys with white Islamic hats hand pulling noodles out in front, large picture menus on the wall, and several children playing out front on the street.

$ Xinjiang Jaaskelainen Expedition (Xīnjiāng Yíníng Yuǎnzhēng Cāntīng; 新疆伊宁远征餐厅)

If you're tired of the hole-in-the-wall Uighur joints and want to try a real restaurant version, then this is the place. They've got a decent picture menu and prices really aren't much higher than the little shops.

Address: 20 Yuyuan Rd, near Wulumuqi North Rd (愚园支路 20 号. 近乌鲁木齐北路)
Phone: 136 1160 3279

$$ Shanghai Xinjiang Gourmet Restaurant (Shànghǎi Xīnjiāng Fēngwèi Fànguǎn; 上海新疆风味饭馆)

One FREE Xinjiang Milk Tea

With distinctive Xinjiang features, the dishes here are authentic and the waiters are all from the motherland. The shashliks, cumin mutton and Dapan chicken are superb.

Address: 280 Yishan Rd, Xuhui District, between Nandan Rd and Puhuitang Rd (宜山路 280 号. 南丹路蒲汇塘路间)
Phone: 6468 9198

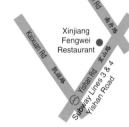

Yunnan

$$ Legend Taste (Diāndào Yúnnán Tèsè Liàolǐ; 滇道云南特色料理)

Modern Yunnan food on Kangding Road with a menu that has a broad range of delights. Prices are reasonable and the atmosphere is subtle and quiet, including a large front patio when weather permits. Try the shrimp fried with tea leaves.

Address: 1025 Kangding Rd, near Wuning Rd (康定路 1025 号. 近武宁路)
Phone: 5228 9961; 186 1602 7049

$$ Southern Barbarian (Nánmánzi Yúnnán Shāokǎoba; 南蛮子云南烧烤吧)

Though it technically serves Yunnan cuisine, this place has fused the ingredients and updated the flavors on a lot of the classics. Try the fried bees just to say you did and then wash them down with an imported beer from their well-stocked fridge.

Address: 2/F, 169 Jinxian Rd, near Maoming South Rd (进贤路 169 号 56 食尚谷 E 区 2 楼，近茂名南路)
Phone: 5157 5510

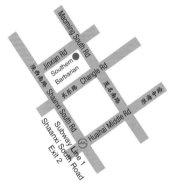

Guangdong

$ Kung Fu Restaurant (Zhēn Gōngfū; 真功夫)

While McDonald's, KFC and Burger King still dominate the fast-food skyline here, Kung Fu is coming in a strong second, with almost 500 locations across China and 24 hour delivery. Cheap, fast and clean noodles and rice dishes are served under the scowling logo of none other than kung fu legend Bruce Lee.

Website: www.zkungfu.com

$$ Grandma's Kitchen (Wūqī Tāngguǎn; 屋企汤馆)

Another place serving Cantonese style comfort food in a restaurant that is short on atmosphere and price. See Crystal Jade map.

Address: Lane 1213, Nanjing West Rd, near Shaanxi North Rd (南京西路 1213 弄，近陕西北路)
Phone: 6279 2929

$$ Crystal Jade (Fěicuì Jiǔjiā; 翡翠酒家)

This quiet but bright restaurant chain from Singapore is delicious and clean Cantonese fare is consistently served here, including many kinds of dim sum.

Address: 7/F, Westgate Mall, 1038 Nanjing West Rd, near Jiangning Rd (南京西路 1038 号梅龙镇广场 7 楼，近江宁路)
Phone: 5228 1133

$ Eason (Bīngbīng Jǔruò; 冰冰茹箬)

This narrow split-level spot serves up delicious Cantonese dishes. Its location on Yongkang Road means it's perfect for that between-rounds energizer meal.

Address: 132 Yongkang Rd, near Xiangyang Rd (永康路 132 号，近襄阳路)
Phone: 6473 5602

Taiwan

$$ Din Tai Fung (Dīngtàifēng; 鼎泰丰)

Din Tai Fung is world famous. This light and

tasty Taiwanese chain has locations across the globe, but the one here is located in upscale Xintiandi. They're known to have the best dumplings and *xiaolongbao* around.

> Address: Unit 11A, 2/F, Bldg 6, Xintiandi, South Block Plaza, Lane 123, Xingye Rd, near Madang (兴业路 123 弄新天地广场南里 6 号楼 2 楼 11A 单元 . 近马当路)
> Phone: 6385 8378

$$ Charmant (Xiǎochéng Gùshì; 小城故事)

Charmant is a tasty and quiet Taiwanese spot that's open late. Be sure to try the beef with Chinese doughnut, followed by a massive peanut smoothie parfait for dessert.

> Address: 1414 Huaihai Middle Rd, corner of Fuxing West Rd (淮海中路 1414 号 . 近复兴西路)
> Phone: 6431 8107

$$ Bellagio (Lùgǎng Xiǎozhèn; 鹿港小镇)

Along the same lines as Charmant, Bellagio is great for dinner or for an after dinner dessert or drink. (Note: There is another restaurant called "Bellagio" near Jing'an Temple that has no affiliation to this one. Avoid it.)

> Address: 68 Taicang Rd, near Songshan Rd (太仓路 68 号 . 近嵩山路)
> Phone: 6386 5701

Macau

$$ Macau Dolar (Àomén Dòuláo; 澳门豆捞)

For hot pot lovers with intimacy issues comes this offering, where each person gets

their own small sized hot pot. They also have a sauce bar, where you can build an elaborate tray of dipping sauces to your taste.

> Address: 817 Yan'an West Rd, near Shaanxi South Rd (延安中路 817 号 . 近陕西南路)
> Phone: 6279 3167

Northwest

$$ Xibei Noodle (Xībèi Xīběicài ; 西贝西北菜)

Xibei Noodle is a little bit outside of downtown, but well worth the journey for its amazing oat noodles. The noodles come in a bamboo steamer and are packed in a honeycomb pattern. It's something you won't forget.

> Address: 5/F, West Wing of Hongxin Plaza, 762 Tianshan Rd, near Gubei Rd (天山路 762 号 5 楼 . 泓鑫广场西区 . 近古北路)
> Phone: 5875 2999

Sichuan

$$ South Beauty (Qiào Jiāngnán; 俏江南)

Known for its classy establishments and modern take on traditional Sichuan dishes, South Beauty is a hugely popular chain of restaurants in China.

> Address: 881 Yan'an Middle Rd, near Tongren Rd, across from the Shanghai Exhibition Center (延安中路 881 号 . 近铜仁路)
> Phone: 6247 5878; 6247 1581

Address: 2/F, 428 Madang Rd, near Hefei Rd（马当路 428 号 2 楼，近合肥路）
Phone: 6373 0288

$$ Spicy Joint (Xīn Xiāng Huì; 辛香汇)

Make reservations here when you are in the mood for some tasty Sichuan food that won't bust your budget. Be sure to balance all that spice with plenty of cheap beer, or feel the pain the following day.

Address: 3/F, K Wah Center, 1028 Huaihai Middle Rd, near Donghu Rd (淮海中路 1028 号 嘉华中心嘉华坊 3 楼，近东湖路)
Phone: 6470 2777

Other

Chinese Vegetarian

$$ Lucky Zen (Jíxiángcǎo Sùshiguǎn; 吉 祥草素食馆)

Lucky is a beautiful vegetarian restaurant in the style of an old Chinese library. It has an extensive, well laid-out English picture menu, so your biggest risk is ordering too much. Be sure to try the fried hibiscus flowers (11:00-21:00, closed on Mondays).

$$ Jujube Tree (Zǎozi Shù; 枣子树)

Jujube is a nice veggie spot that looks like your standard Chinese restaurant. In fact, even the menu looks the same, with dishes like sweet and sour pork. Fear not though, all meat here is "fake meat" made of gluten, soy or nut loaf. Check out their wsebsite **www.jujubetree.com**.

Location One

Address: 258 Fengxian Rd, near Jiangning Rd (奉贤路 258 号，近江宁路)
Phone: 6215 7566; 6215 7557

Location Two

Address: 77 Songshan Rd, near Huaihai Middle Rd（嵩山路 77 号，近淮海中路）
Phone: 6384 8000

Themed

10% OFF (weekdays; July & Aug excluded)

For the 12-year old in all of us comes this novelty chain of poop themed restaurants from Taiwan. Think of every fecal-looking dish you can, served to diners in miniature toilets and bedpans.

Address: 5, Lane 274, Taikang Rd, near Ruijin 2nd Rd, Tianzifang (田子坊泰康路 274 弄 5 号 . 近瑞金二路)
Phone: 5412 2821

Foreign

Middle Eastern

$$ 1001 Nights (Yīqiānyī Yè; 一千一夜)

Shanghai's premiere Middle Eastern restaurant features a good sized picture menu. Try the hummus with pine nuts alongside a fattouche salad. After dinner, enjoy a hookah while you watch the hourly belly dancing number.

Address: 2/F, 4 Hengshan Rd, near Wulumuqi Rd (衡山路 4 号 , 近乌鲁木齐路)
Phone: 6473 1178

$$ Haya's (Hāyà Dìzhōnghǎi Cāntīng; 哈亚地中海餐厅)

An Israeli deli that specializes in the usual Middle Eastern and Mediterranean fare, as well as some of the best fresh-baked bread in town.

Address: 415 Dagu Rd, near Chengdu North Rd (大沽路 415 号 . 近成都北路)
Phone: 6295 9511

$$ Anadolu (Ānàduōlú Cānyǐn; 阿纳多卢餐饮)

This upmarket Turkish restaurant has a decent menu but is pricey considering their lack of atmosphere. If only Turkish will do, then check it out. Otherwise head upstairs to 1001 Nights.

Address: 4-7 Hengshan Rd, near Wulumuqi Rd (衡山路 4-7 号 , 近乌鲁木齐路)
Phone: 5465 0977

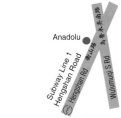

Southeast Asian

$$$ Bali Laguna (Bālí Dǎo; 巴厘岛)

For Indonesian food in a beautiful environment, Bali Laguna cannot be beat. Set in a wooden mansion overlooking the lake in Jing'an Park, the view is amazing both inside and from the candlelit seats outside around the lake.

> Address: 189 Huashan Rd, inside Jing'an Park, near Yan'an Rd (华山路 189 号 . 静安公园内 . 近延安路)
> Phone: 6248 6970

$$ Coconut Paradise (Yēxiāng Tiāntáng; 椰香天堂)

An old, candlelit mansion with a beautiful garden patio that serves some of the best Thai cuisine in the city. Perfect for a meal with that special someone.

> Address: 38 Fumin Rd, near Yan'an Middle Rd (富民路 38 号 . 近延安中路)
> Phone: 6248 1998

Indian

$$ Vedas (Yìnwèishàng Cānyǐn; 印味尚餐饮)

Consistently the top rated Indian restaurant in Shanghai, Vedas offers refined flavors in an intimate environment.

> Address: 3/F, 83 Changshu Rd, near Julu Rd (常熟路 83 号 3 楼 . 近巨鹿路)
> Phone: 6445 8100

$ Ganesha (Kānǎixiāng; 咖乃芗)

These guys might lack Vedas's atmosphere, but the food is tasty and a lot cheaper than most Indian elsewhere.

> Address: 2/F, 458 Jiangsu Rd, near Xuanhua Rd (江苏路 458 号 2 楼 . 近宣化路)
> Phone: 3250 6100

$$ Punjabi (Běnjiébǐ; 本杰比)

This all-you-can-eat (including beer) Indian place is pretty popular, as much for the beer as for the buffet. It's OK if your party is two or three but any larger groups would be better off checking Vedas or Nepali Kitchen.

> Address: 5/F, 627 Huaihai Middle Rd, near Sinan Rd (淮海中路 627 号 5 楼 . 近思南路)
> Phone: 6472 5464

$$ Nepali Kitchen

In a creaky, winding wooden mansion comes this offering of a style you could describe as north Indian. Choose from a Western table-

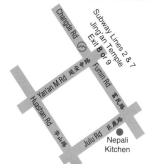

and-chair setup or go for the classic low table, cushion-on-the-floor approach.

Address: 4, Lane 819, Julu Rd, near Fumin Rd (巨鹿路 819 弄 4 号，近富民路)
Phone: 5404 6281

Japanese

$$ *Kiki's*

Even in the back of a shopping mall, this Japanese place gives the impression of a truly intimate restaurant with a wide menu to choose from. They also offer ¥128 all you can eat specials on the weekend!

Address: 2/F, 458 Jiangsu Rd, near Xuanhua Rd (江苏路 458 号 2 楼，近宣化路)
Phone: 3250 5667

$$$ *Gintei (Yíntíng; 银亭)* ¥10 OFF (buffet)

Gintei is one of the better all-you-can-eat Teppanyaki places in the city. For a big group you can book a table around the grill, otherwise smaller tables are available.

Address: 75 Nanhui Rd, near Beijing West Rd (南汇路 75 号，近北京西路)
Phone: 6218 1932

$$ *Ajisen Ramen (Wèiqiān Lāmiàn; 味千拉面)*

A fast food-style Japanese chain that offers Ramen, soups and meal sets in a cool room that has both private booths and communal tables.

Address: 327 Nanjing East Rd (南京东路 327 号)
Phone: 6360 7194

$$ *Gokohai (Yù Xiāng Hǎi; 御香海)*

One of the city's better all-you-can-eat places, this Japanese hot pot restaurant is always packed and loud (unless you have enough in your group for a private room). Here you get your own personal hot pot spiced to your liking and they have a wide selection on the menu. Don't forget to try the beef sashimi.

Address: 1720 Huaihai Middle Rd, near Wuxing Rd (淮海中路 1720 号，近吴兴路)
Phone: 6471 7657

$$$ *Sushi Abuse*

A delicious (but expensive) sushi venue that only serves "sustainable sushi," Sushi Abuse has an open layout and highly designed atmosphere.

Address: 2/F, 98 Yanping Rd, near Xinzha Rd (延平路 98 号 2 楼，近新闸路)
Phone: 5175 9818

Sandwiches, Burgers & Tacos

$$ Cantina Agave

Though the menu looks like it was designed by TGI Fridays, the food at Cantina is not generic. Come by for great tacos, burritos and the usual suspects, along with a wide variety of margaritas.

Address: 291 Fumin Rd, near Changle Rd (富民路 291 号 . 近长乐路)
Phone: 6170 1310

$$ Munchies

See anything significant about their phone number? If you do, that should give you an idea of the type of food here. Tasty, especially when you really just want to stuff your face.

Address: 974 Wuding Rd, near Jiaozhou Rd (武定路 974 号 . 近胶州路)
Phone: 6218 4616; 400 800 8420
Website: www.munchies.cn

$$ New York Steak and Burger

NYSB is a small two-story restaurant in Tianzifang, where the steaks are pricey (but good) and the burgers are some of the best in town. (Note: don't be surprised if you see an extra charge on your bill for the Tianzifang Restoration Fund.)

Address: 22, Lane 155, Jianguo Middle Rd, near Ruijin 2nd Rd, Tianzifang (田子坊建国中路 155 弄 22 号 . 近瑞金二路)
Phone: 6473 6070

$ Sarnies

With by far the city's best deal on sandwiches, Sarnies' three outlets cover a wide swathe of downtown. It's less of a restaurant than a service window; swing by and pick up a menu for delivery.

Address: 101 Nanyang Rd, near Xikang Rd (南阳路 101 号 . 近西康路)
Phone: 6289 2550; 6217 5223

$$ Beef and Liberty (Shàngniú Shèhuì; 尚牛社会)

This high-end burger joint uses imported Australian beef and gourmet ingredients; these guys make some delicious burgers. Check them out on a Monday for their two-for-one burger nights, and if weather permits, be sure

to grab a spot on their huge terrace.

Address: 1/F, Shanghai Centre, 1376 Nanjing West Rd, near Xikang Rd (南京西路 1376 号 . 上海商城 1 楼 . 近西康路)
Phone: 6289 5733
Website: www.beef-liberty.com

$$ Tock's

A new arrival on the Shanghai scene, this Canadian restaurant offers authentic Montreal smoked-meat sandwiches and poutine.

Address: 221 Henan Middle Rd, near Fuzhou Rd (河南中路 221 号 . 近福州路)
Phone: 6346 3735; 152 2113 3516

Meat Lovers

$$$ Morton's Steakhouse (Mò'ěrdùn Niúpáifāng; 莫尔顿牛排坊)

Try this Chicago-based steakhouse in the International Finance Center when you're in need of a big slab of red meat and don't mind paying for quality. Their "Mortini" happy hours are far more affordable and include free Filet Mignon sandwiches as you watch the lights of Pudong come to life.

Address: 4/F, IFC Pudong, 8 Century Ave, near Lujiazui Ring Rd (世纪大道 8 号 国金中心 IFC 商场 4 楼 . 近陆家嘴环路)
Phone: 6075 8888

$$ Latina

For Brazilian *churrasco* with unlimited meats served from a sword to your plate, Latina is a classy choice, perhaps due in part to its location in Xintiandi.

Address: Unit 101-102, Bldg 5, South Block Plaza, Xintiandi, Lane 123, Xingye Rd, near Madang Rd (新天地南里广场 5 号楼 101-102. 兴业路 123 弄 . 近马当路)
Phone: 6320 3566

$$ Brasil Steakhouse (Bāxī Shāokǎowū; 巴屏烧烤屋)

When you need your animal protein, Brasil delivers with an all you can eat special. Waiters serve various meats from swords they carry through the brightly lit restaurant, and there's also a small buffet of side dishes and desserts.

Address: 4 Hengshan Rd, near Gao'an Rd (衡山路 4 号 . 近高安路)
Phone: 6255 9898

Euro Style

$$$ Mr & Mrs Bund

For a fancy night out, you might want to start with dinner here on the luxurious Bund with a view of the Pudong skyline. Think Buddha Bar sounds in a huge open space with some of the best food to be found anywhere. Bring lots of money.

Address: 6/F, Bund 18, 18 Zhongshan East 1st Rd, near Nanjing East Rd (中山东一路18号6楼. 近南京东路)
Phone: 6323 9898

$$$ el Willy (Díyǎjū; 迪雅居)

El Willy's is described as a "happy Spanish restaurant" and you'll definitely notice the pizzazz of the joint after stepping in. Eccentric Willy is not only "da man," but a great and creative chef, constantly changing the seasonal menu with Barcelona-inspired dishes and a cellar stocked with quality, well-priced vinos. The venue itself is housed in a 1920s colonial building in the French Concession, and the bright colors, funky patterns and modernized interior truly make el Willy a… well, for lack of a better term, happy Spanish restaurant!

Address: 5/F, 22 Zhongshan East 2nd Rd, near Xinkaihe Rd (中山东二路22号5楼. 近新开河路)
Hours: Lunch 11:00-14:30 (Mon-Fri), dinner 17:30 (Mon-Sat), and brunch 11:00 15:00 (Sat); closed Sun
Phone: 5404 5757
Website: www.el-willy.com

$$ Element Fresh (Xīn Yuánsù; 新元素)

Although it offers relatively expensive salads, Element is well done and consistent. With several locations around the city and reliable delivery, it is a favorite of many jaded expats.

Address: 1/F, Shanghai Centre, 1376 Nanjing West Rd, near Xikang Rd (南京西路1376号. 上海商城1楼. 近西康路)
Phone: 6279 8682

$$ Pure & Whole

One FREE dessert (over ¥200 & dinner only)

This quiet vegetarian spot doesn't go for the fake-meat menu. Instead they serve balanced dishes with comprehensive nutritional data. Great if you're watching your figure…not as great for watching your budget. See map above.

Address: Suite 104, Shanghai Centre, 1376 Nanjing West Rd, near Xikang Rd (南京西路1376 号. 上海商城104室. 近西康路) (See map above)
Phone: 5175 9822
Website: www.pureandwhole.com

$$ Bon App

Bon App is a nice quiet choice for Western brunch or a dinner of crepes or tartines. The food is delicious and the service is great.

Address: 1116 Wuding Rd, near Yanping Rd (武定路1116号. 近延平路).
Phone: 5265 5365

$$$ El Patio

This Spanish tapas place offers a refined selection of dishes. Expect tasty Sangria and the occasional flamenco performance.

Address: 110 Fenyang Rd, near Fuxing Middle Rd (汾阳路110号. 近复兴中路)
Phone: 6437 5839

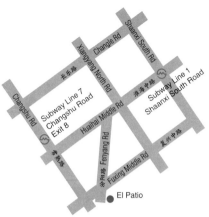

$ Saizeriya (Sàlìyà; 萨莉亚)

This ultra cheap place sells Italian noodles and main courses. The large cafeteria setting and self-serve soft drinks set the tone for the ¥15 lunch set.

Address: B1-555 Nanjing West Rd, near Chengdu North Rd (南京西路 555 号 B1 楼, 近成都北路)
Phone: 6255 3754

$$$ Da Marco (Dàmǎkě; 大马可)

Da Marco is your standard pizza/pasta place, all made with quality ingredients set to a fairly high

Italian standard. Regular winner of "Best Italian" from local expat magazines and websites.

Address: 1/F, Grand Gateway Square, 1 Hongqiao Rd, near Huashan Rd (虹桥路 1 号 . 港汇广场 1651 楼 , 近华山路)
Phone: 6447 7577

Dessert

$ Awfully Chocolate

These guys don't have a huge menu but that hasn't stopped them from becoming super popular with the local crowd. This is strictly a take-out place though, so it's perfect if you need to pick up a birthday cake for a friend.

Address: 174 Xiangyang South Rd, near Fuxing Middle Rd (襄阳南路 174 号 . 近复兴中路)
Phone: 6474 5336

$$ HOF

HOF is a chocolate themed café/cocktail lounge with an emphasis on the finest desserts created by the former pastry Chef of the Four Seasons Hotel. It's not to be missed if you've got a sweet tooth.

Address: 30 Sinan Rd, near Huaihai Middle Rd (思南路 30 号 , 近淮海中路)
Phone: 6093 2058

How to Use Chopsticks

Don't know how to use chopsticks? Then you better learn quickly because you won't find too many forks and knives around here, and we guarantee no one will know how to tie the rubber bands at the end like they do at your local Chinese eatery. Like anything, you won't learn in a day, but while you're here you really have no other choice, so let's get started!

1.

Rest the first stick in between your index finger and middle finger and place the back end on the soft area between your index finger and thumb (pointy end facing the same direction as your fingers). This is your anchor stick and it should not move while eating.

2.

Grasp the second stick with your index finger and thumb tips. This is the stick that moves, and you can position it by simply twisting your thumb and index finger. You can brace it on your middle finger for better control. Make sure both pointy ends are facing the same direction.

3.

To pick up food, place the bite in between the two pointy edges and tighten up using the stick in between your index and thumb tips.

4.

Note that many meals in China will be served with a bowl of rice. It is acceptable to place bites of food on top of the rice, so bring the bowl close to your mouth with your left hand and use your chopsticks to shovel the rice and food into your mouth. Using chopsticks as a shovel is easier and it's perfectly acceptable in Chinese table etiquette.

5.

Another common misconception is that stabbing the food with your chopsticks like a fork is unacceptable. This is perfectly fine and no one will laugh at your amateur skills. Chinese people do this all the time, especially with hard-to-eat foods that are slippery, slimy or simply too large to pick up the old fashioned way.

6.

Last but not least, practice. After a few meals you'll be on your way to chopstick mastery!

Drinking & Nightlife

The "Golden Era" of the 1920s and 30s was when Shanghai, "the Pearl of the Orient," was considered one of the most international cities in the world. Nightclubs and cabarets were packed with foreigners from all around the globe, and the streets were crawling with flappers and gangsters alike. Things took a quiet turn for the next several decades after the Japanese invasion and the communist takeover, but the first decade of the 21st century has seen the ushering in of Shanghai's second Golden Age and an explosion in the diversity of nightlife.

Shanghai is not one of China's most ancient cities, and while there are a few temples and museums to explore, the main activities for many tourists are shopping, dining, drinking and dancing the night away. Fortunately, no matter what kind of partier you are, Shanghai has something for your palate. In fact, one of the hallmarks of the city's scene is that there are always more options as the night progresses; it is incredibly rare to start and end your night in the same venue. Instead, prepare yourself for endless partying, pub-crawling, bar-hopping and clubbing across the city, as cheap and plentiful taxis make it easy to zip your way across the downtown core from the glitz and glamour of the Bund (Wàitān; 外滩) to the gritty underground beats of Xingfu Road.

If the thought of spending so much of your night in a grimy VW taxi doesn't appeal to you, fear not: in recent years a slew of new bar streets and neighborhoods have opened in Shanghai, so when you're ready for the next stop you can just head next door. That being said, here are the best bar streets and neighborhoods in the city:

Yonkang Road, near Xiangyang Road (永康路，近襄阳路)

The newest bar street in Shanghai is Yongkang Road, much to the frustration of local residents. For an entire block between Xiangyang Road and Taiyuan Road you can find countless pubs, wine bars and cafes with the occasional local restaurant seeded in the mix. And while the crowds will swell onto the streets on a busy night, the mood changes drastically by 22:00, when venues are forced to close their doors and windows. At this point residents begin making their noise complaints, which often consist of dumping buckets of water from their balconies onto the partiers below. You can still find a drink here late into the evening, but by 23:00 the party has basically ended and moved on to another destination.

Major Players: Café de Stagiares (pg 200), Sliders (pg 205)

Wuding Road, near Jiaozhou Road (武定路，近胶州路)

Out of the ruins of a run-down Blade Runner-esque electronics market comes another interesting strip of places to wet your whistle. Located just a few blocks from Jing'an Temple, this entire block has seen a major renaissance in the last five years with wine bars, brew pubs and lounges that cater to locals and foreigners alike. An added benefit of hanging out here is that the fun continues just around the corner, where new bars and restaurants are opening up on **Yanping Road** and **Jiaozhou Road** every day.

Major Players: Café de Stagiares II (pg 200), Enoterra (pg 209), Malabar (pg 205)

Yongfu Road, near Fuxing West Road (永福路，近复兴西路)

With jazz music giant JZ Club just around the corner on Fuxing Road, it was only a matter of time before Yongfu Road would become a night owl's dream. But for years the only club on the street was a converted underground bomb shelter known as Blue Ice. This was the club that eventually became the super popular Shelter, and shortly after that other venues popped up like mushrooms. The street now gives you every option from high-end happy hour cocktails to chilled-out mellow lounges to thumping dubstep till dawn.

Major Players: Shelter (pg 211), The Apartment (pg 210), el Coctel (pg 208)

Sinan Mansions on Sinan Road, near Fuxing West Road (思南公馆，思南路，近复兴西路)

Covering two city blocks, Sinan Mansions is a modern collection of bars, restaurants and retail space that has kept the influence of the original winding lanes of a typical Shanghai shikumen. From end to end you can enjoy international cuisine and al fresco drinking at local brew houses, or immerse yourself in the highest caliber cocktail bars. The best time to enjoy it all would be during their annual Beer Fest, held every year at the end of May.

Major Players: Boxing Cat Brewery (pg 202), The Fat Olive (pg 210)

Xintiandi, Taicang Road, near Madang Road (太仓路，新天地里，近马当路)

Similar to Sinan Mansions, Xintiandi is a sprawling pedestrian mall with the illusion of an old Shanghai lane house. Things tend to be a little pricier at these two neighborhoods though, so keep in mind that a backpacker's budget will not last long. For shoppers, diners, and drinkers who can afford it, though, the cobblestoned paths can provide hours of entertainment with eye-catching architecture and endless options for partying.

Major Players: Paulaner Brauhaus (pg 206), CA Club (pg 209)

Huashan Road, near Yan'an Middle Road (华山路，近延安中路)

As Shanghai gets cleaned up and gentrified, many of the seedier bar streets have been shut down or moved off into obscurity. But if this is really what you're looking for you can still find those back-to-back bars where teams of women on the sidewalk try to drag you inside hoping you'll buy overpriced, watered-down drinks, all for the pleasure of their "enthusiastic" conversation.

Major Players: These bars are pretty much all the same: dark, thumping rock and/or last decade's pop-club, and a pool table. Oh, and the girls.

Bars & Pubs

Here it is, our list of Shanghai's best places to knock back some cold ones or sip some fine imported wine. The list is by no means complete, and with a city that has so much construction happening every day, there might even be a few new establishments opening their doors by the time you get to town. Keep in mind that Shanghai's expat population is extremely friendly and open with their favorite party spots. Ask around and you might find a few new gems.

Drink Pricing Guide:

$ Drinks from ¥20
$$ Drinks from ¥40
$$$ Drinks from ¥60

$$ Café des Stagiares   **PANDA PICK**

The crew behind the *trés* successful Café family of pubs is the newest powerhouse on the scene. Founded by a group of alumni from Lausanne, Switzerland, their formula is quite simple: a good selection of quality draft beers, soft lighting, lively music and free peanuts. In 2013 they opened their third location in Shanghai, centrally located on Dagu Road. Expect to find a steady crowd of Europeans and (surprisingly) very little pretentiousness. It's also interesting to note that it is one of the city's only non-smoking establishments, so if you find yourself needing a puff, join the rest outside the front door. Website: **www.cafestagiaires.com**

Location One

Address: 54-56 Yongkang Rd, near Xiangyang Rd (永康路 54−56 号 . 近襄阳路)
Phone: 3425 0210

Location Two

Address: 1085 Wuding Rd, near Jiaozhou Rd (武定路 1085 号 . 近胶州路)
Phone: 5270 6851

Location Three

Address: 386 Dagu Rd, near Chengdu North Rd (大沽路 386 号 . 近成都北路)
Phone: 6312 9302

$ Windows   **PANDA PICK**

With three very different venues, Windows caters to a variety of crowds. Scoreboard is for your die hard sports fans and features a brighter room with rock music, Windows Too is for the hip hop junkies, and Windows Garage is for the clubbers. However, even with all these differences, some things remain the same, including sports on the screen and some of the cheapest food and drinks in Shanghai. Windows is not the classiest night out, and while there is a loyal crowd which will happily stay all night playing pool, darts, foosball and beer pong, it is used by many of the city's premiere partiers as their exclusive pre-drink and/or late night wind down location. Their ¥15 burgers have saved more than one soul from a hangover. Website: **www.windowsbars.com**

Windows Scoreboard

Address: 11/F, 527 Huaihai Middle Rd, near Chengdu Rd (淮海中路 527 号 11 楼 . 近成都路)
Phone: 5382 7757

Windows Too

Address: 2/F, 1618 Nanjing West Rd, near Huashan Rd (南京西路 1618 号久光百货 2 楼 . 近华山路)
Phone: 6288 9007

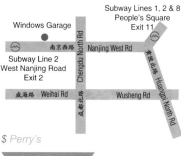

Windows Garage

Address: 702 Nanjing West Rd, near Qinghai Rd (南京西路 702 号 . 近青海路)
Phone: 6218 1360

$ Perry's

One FREE drink

Another new blip on the Shanghai radar, Perry's (now with two locations) has unbelievably usurped Windows' title as the cheapest party spot in town. Your only cheaper option for drinks is your local convenience store. Décor at Perry's is an interactive work in progress, as black Sharpies line the tables waiting for you to scribble your graffiti into the mix. Kick back, tag your name, enjoy a shisha, mingle with your fellow cheapskates, – whatever – just remember that the crowd is surprisingly more sophisticated than the bar's "Free Cigarette Sundays" would have you believe.

Location One

Address: 1139 Kaixuan Rd, near Anshun Rd (凯旋路 1139 号 . 近安顺路)
Phone: 3255 8117

Location Two

Address: 1333 Huaihai Middle Rd, near Baoqing Rd (淮海中路 1333 号 . 近宝庆路)
Phone: 5436 5169

$ LOgO

One of Shanghai's first bars dedicated to truly underground electronica and rock, LOgO was an instant hit with the uber-too-cool-for-school crowd. After years of neighbors complaining about loud drunken foreigners taking the party out to the sidewalk, LOgO moved across town, only to move back to its old neighborhood a couple of years later. The original LOgO was a shadowy, smoky concrete room that reeked of fun and BO. The new one is pretty much the same: a place to see pashmina scarves (even in July), thick framed glasses, ironic moustaches and self-inflicted haircuts...and to hear some of the best music in town. On the same map as Dada.

Address: 298 Xingfu Rd, near Pingwu Rd (幸福路 298 号 . 近平武路)
Phone: 6216 2865

$ Dada

Michael Michael, former DJ and promoter with the Antidote crew, did not forget his roots when he opened up this place devoted to cool tunes and late night beats: Drinks are cheap, cover charge is rare, and the DJ's are fresh. Don't forget to check this place out in its downtime as well, when you can find everything from cult movie nights to arts and design swap meets.

Address: 115 Xingfu Rd, near Fahuazhen Rd (幸福路 115 号 . 近法华镇路)

Phone: 150 0018 2212

Boxing Cat Breweries for a finely crafted, locally-brewed beer. They've got something for every taste and they make new ones seasonally, so you'll always find something new. Website: **www.boxingcatbrewery.com**

Location One

Address: 82 Fuxing West Rd, near Yongfu Rd (复兴西路 82 号 . 近永福路)

Phone: 6431 2091

Location Two

Address: Sinan Mansions, Unit 26A, 519-521 Fuxing Middle Rd, near Sinan Rd (思南公馆 . 复兴中路 519 号 26A. 近思南路)

Phone: 6426 0360

$ Lune

Over in Jing'an the hipster party continues with Lune, an offering from some of the minds behind LOgO. A squishy ride up in the world's tiniest elevator will usher you into a tightly packed cave with cheap drinks, cool people and great musicians and DJs.

Address: 4/F, 218 Xinle Rd, at Donghu Rd (新乐路 218 号 . 东湖路路口)

Phone: 6426 2982

$$ Kaiba

If beer is your passion then look no further than Kaiba. The Belgian owner stocks an astonishing collection of international beer, both bottled and on tap. Prices are not cheap, but that hasn't held many people back. Kaiba

$$ Boxing Cat Brewery (Quánjī Māo; 拳击猫)

PANDA PICK

Maybe you're content sucking on your Tsingtao 40-ounce, and that's cool, but every now and then you might feel a craving for something less watery and bland. When this happens head over to either one of the

now boasts three locations scattered across Shanghai, all of which are fairly chill. It's not a party, but if you want to relax with a quality beer, this is the place. Website: **www.kaiba-beerbar.com**

Kaiba, The Tap Room

Address: 479 Wuding Rd, near Shaanxi North Rd (武定路 479 号 . 近陕西北路)
Phone: 6288 9676

Kaiba, The Belgian Beer Garden

Address: 739 Dingxi Rd, near Yan'an West Rd (定西路 739 号 . 近延安西路)
Phone: 6280 5688

Kaiba Tap House

Address: Taikang Terrace, 2/F, 202, Lane 169, Jianguo Middle Rd, near Ruijin 2nd Rd (建国中路 169 弄 202 号 . 近瑞金二路)
Phone: 6418 2252

$ Captain's Bar (Chuánzhǎng Jiǔba; 船长酒吧)

PANDA PICK

By now you know that the Bund is home to Shanghai's upper crust, the elite crowd of clubbers who dress to impress and like their champagne delivered with road flares lighting the scene. Captain's Hostel is an interesting alternative to this mold, giving you a laid back atmosphere, affordable drinks, and a big patio with a beautiful view of Shanghai's iconic skyline. Great for taking that selfie to post on Facebook and show the world that you really were in Shanghai.

Address: 6/F, Captain's Hostel , 37 Fuzhou Rd, near Sichuan Middle Rd (福州路 37 号 . 近四川中路)
Phone: 6323 7869
Website: www.captainhostelshanghai.com

$ I Love Shanghai (Wǒ'ài Shànghǎi; 我爱上海)

PANDA PICK

Proud holder of the "Dive Bar of the Year" title, ILS is under new management but is still the same old hot spot for trashy good times. The lights are bright, and pool and darts make up a lot of the action, but they are better known for their (in)famous ladies' nights and beer pong tournaments. Feeling some national pride? Then stop by and take an absinthe shot in honor of your country and have it added to the giant tally board behind the bar. ILS is a little tricky to find (it's upstairs of a benign looking Singaporean restaurant). It might also prove difficult to leave.

Address: 3/F, 1788 Xinzha Rd, near Jiaozhou Rd (新闸路 1788 号 3 楼 . 近胶州路)
Phone: 5228 6899

$ C's Bar   One FREE mojito & small gift

One of the city's filthiest, dirtiest and most beloved dive bars, C's is a subterranean mess of smoke and graffiti, a place that reminds everyone of a certain bar they knew back home. Once home to some of the best parties in the city, the Antidote nights (see Dada, pg 201), they still host the occasional DJ night. Those parties are usually packed with everyone who enjoys a good party (go figure) and extremely cheap drinks.

Address: 685 Dingxi Rd, near Yan'an West Rd
(定西路 685 号 , 近延安西路)
Phone: 6294 0547

$$ *Rhumerie Bounty*

A dark, wood-paneled interior will give you the impression that you're in the hole of a French pirate ship, and the drinks they serve only enhance this. You'll be missing out on the Bounty experience if you order from the regular bar menu. Instead, order one or two of their flavored rums (all infused in-house with natural ingredients ranging from ginger to mango). It'll be brought to your table with shot glasses and a bowl of crushed ice. Mix, sip, and let the evening unfold. Website: **www.bountybar.cn**

Location One:

Address: 550 Wuding Rd, near Xikang Rd (武
定路 550 号 , 近西康路)
Phone: 2661 9368

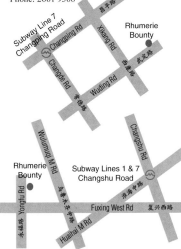

Location Two:

Address: 47 Yongfu Rd, near Fuxing West Rd
(永福路 47 号 , 近复兴西路)
Phone: 137 6451 0616

$$ *Dr Wine & Dr Beer*

Just a block apart from each other on Fumin Road, these two bars offer extremely different vibes. Dr Wine is located in a dark old mansion with a creaky staircase leading to the second floor, while Dr Beer is a sprawling beer hall in a stark, modern concrete space. Check them both out, but remember, "Wine before beer, you're in the clear." …or is that, "beer before wine and you'll be fine…"? Whatever...

Dr Beer

Address: 83 Fumin Rd, near Yan'an Rd (富民路
83 号 . 近延安路)
Phone: 5468 1077

Dr Wine

Address: 177 Fumin Rd, near Julu Rd (富民路
177 号 . 近巨鹿路)
Phone: 5403 5717

$ *Masse Bar & Bistro*

There are lots of options in Shanghai to grab a drink and play a game of pool, but few of them really make a point of it like Masse. Canadian owned and operated, they offer a wide variety of affordable beer, including

Moosehead. Even if you're not into billiards you still might enjoy their large covered patio or their weekly pub quiz. They've also recently started hosting comedy shows, so get down if you're ready to laugh.

Address: 5/F, 219 Jinxian Rd, near Shaanxi South Rd (进贤路 221 号 . 近陕西南路)
Phone: 5212 5971

$$ Shanghai Brewery (Shànghǎi Píjiǔ Gōngfāng; 上海啤酒工坊)

A two story heaven for beer lovers, Shanghai brewery pours their own creations as well as a huge selection of quality imports. For those who aren't completely sure of their beer tastes, the bar also offers a tasting flight of four smaller glasses of your choice of brew. A friendly atmosphere with sports on the TVs helps keep the crowd from getting too snobbish about their beer. Website: **www.shanghaibrewery.com**

Location One

Address: 15 Dongping Rd, near Hengshan Rd (东平路 15 号 . 近衡山路)
Phone: 3461 0717

Location Two

Address: 21C Hongmei Pedestrian St, Lane 3338, Hongmei Rd, near Yan'an West Rd (闵行区虹梅路 3338 弄虹梅路休闲街 21C. 近近延安西路)
Phone: 6406 5919

$$ Sliders PANDA PICK

Hands down Yongkang's best drinking hole, Sliders has a sleek, wooden and clean atmosphere with good music, imported brews, and above average mixed drinks. It's simple, but sometimes, especially in over-the-top Shanghai, less is certainly more. Oh yeah, and in case you were wondering, they do indeed have tasty sliders, and the breakfast special "Yongkang Cure" should be clinically classified as a hangover remedy. Note: business hours are from 16:00-22:00, so use the all day breakfast special as a true drunkard would after 16:00.

Address: 45 Yongkang Rd, near Jiashan Rd (永康路 45 号 . 近嘉善路)
Phone: 6433 0201
Website: www.shanghaisliders.com
Email: sliders@asia.com

$$ Malabar

Spanish owned and operated, this stylish and quaint neighborhood bar reminds you of that place from home where you'd grab a quiet drink with a friend or two and discuss the crisis in Darfur. Even the manager Justin has gone on record saying that it's "not a party bar." However, that doesn't stop them from serving some potent drinks that will have you up and dancing flamenco like a pro. Malabar is perfect for a relaxing drunk night, or for dinner with classic north Spanish specialties (order a plate of the *pulpo*) and pre-gaming. Open from 18:00 until late, closed on Sundays.

Address: 1081 Wuding Rd, near Jiaozhou Rd (静安区武定路 1081 号 . 近胶州路)
Phone: 5237 3085

$$ *Paulaner Brauhaus*

You've seen them or others like them all across China and all over the world, and this one is no exception. It's your cookie-cutter German Brauhaus: steins of brew are served by adorable waitresses in lederhosen, there's enough meat to circle the city of Munich, and it has a lively atmosphere with rocking music. Of course, they have Paulaner beer and the food is slightly above average, but you'll be overpaying for what you get. Still though, it's a fun place with outdoor seating, and you should definitely come during the month of "Oktober" to get drunk and sing songs with the local German expat community. There are a few other locations scattered across town, so check their kitsch website in either German, English or Chinese. Open daily from 11:00 until late.

Address: 19-20, North Block Xintiandi, Lane 181, Taicang Rd, near Madang Rd (太仓路 181 弄新天地北里 19-20 号 . 近马当路)
Phone: 6320 3935
Website: www.bln.com.cn

Cocktail Bars & Lounges

$$$ *Constellation (Jiǔchí Xīngzuò;* 酒池星 座)

PANDA PICK

It says a lot that an expensive cocktail bar can be successful enough to spawn three other outlets, but that should give you an idea of the level of quality beverages served at Constellation and its sister bars. All of the venues serve from a sophisticated menu with the old classics as well as original combinations (try a Smoky Margarita). Each place offers a slightly different vibe (Constellation, for instance, has the feel of an upscale cigar lounge, while Constellation 3 has more of the "1890s London gentleman's club" flavor), but all have great service and great (and strong) drinks.

Location One

Address: 86 Xinle Rd, near Xiangyang North Rd (新乐路 86 号 . 近襄阳北路)
Phone: 5404 0970; 139 1661 8661

Location Two

Address: 31 Yongjia Rd, near Maoming South Rd (永嘉路 31 号 . 近茂名南路)
Phone: 5465 5993

Location Three

Address: 251 Huangpi North Rd, near Jiangyin Rd (黄陂北路 251 号 . 近江阴路)
Phone: 5375 2712

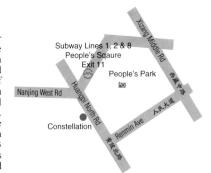

Location Four

Address: 398 Zizhong Rd, near Danshui Rd (自忠路 398 号 . 近淡水路)
Phone: 6333 7009

Location Five – Southern Cross

Address: 1276 Huaihai Middle Rd, near Huating Rd (淮海中路 1276 号 . 近华亭路)
Phone: 5404 7211

$$$ Senator Saloon

An American South-inspired cocktail bar, Senator Saloon has an exhaustive, well-organized menu listing almost any type of spirit you can imagine. And if you can't

imagine it, simply tell the bartender what you're in the mood for and prepare yourself for satisfaction. The drinks are quality, though expensive, but the biggest drawback to Senator is its chain smoking clientele. You have to have faith that the drink is a good one, since you might not be able to taste it over the second hand smoke.

Address: 98 Wuyuan Rd, near Wulumuqi Middle Rd (五原路 98 号 . 近乌鲁木齐中路)
Phone: 5423 1330
Website: www.senatorsaloon.com
Email: senatorsaloon@gmail.com

$$ Mokkos

Once you've had your share of standard cocktails, scoped out the scene and done your posing, head off to Mokkos. This out of the way Japanese bar specializes in cocktails made of *shōchū*, a spirit made from a base of barley or sweet potato. A little bit like Japanese *saké*, or its violent Chinese brother, *báijiǔ*, *shōchū* packs a punch. There's no menu, but the bartenders at Mokkos can delicately mix it into extremely palatable combinations based on your flavor preference. With small, wood-paneled rooms and non-stop reggae music, this is definitely not your typical Japanese cocktail bar.

Address: 1245 Wuding West Rd, near Wanhangdu Rd (武定西路 1245 号 . 近万航渡路)
Phone: 6212 1114

$$ Barbarossa

In the heart of Peoples Park sits what might be Shanghai's most beautiful venue, if only for its setting. Just a stone's throw from the Museum of Contemporary Art, Barbarossa is a Moroccan-inspired restaurant and bar that is surrounded on three sides by a lily covered pond. The view from the rooftop terrace offers you a peek of some of Shanghai's most famous landmarks, while comfortably nestled in nature. Perfect after a visit to the MOCA.

Address: Inside People's Park, 231 Nanjing West Rd, near Huangpi South Rd (南京西路 231 号 . 人民公园内 . 近黄陂南路)

Phone: 6318 0220
Website: www.barbarossa.com.cn

$$ *Monkey Champagne*

Originally just called the Monkey Bar, this is a nice little surprise at the end of a back lane. The atmosphere is classy yet casual and the room is warmly lit, with decent hip hop music filling the silence. Another interesting touch is the secret entrance through the back of the Dakota Steakhouse.

Address: 38 Donghu Rd, near Xinle Rd (东湖路 38 号．近新乐路)
Phone: 6255 6000
Website: www.houseofmonkey.com

$$ *Craft*

Whiskey bars were all the rage a few years ago, and Craft is hoping to be the first major player in the vodka bar trend. In addition to a huge selection of that fine white spirit, they've got several house-infused varieties with flavors ranging from plum to chili pepper. There is no "vodka only" snobbery here though, and the weekends will see the place packed to the rafters while DJs spin electronica.

Address: 2/F, Donghu Hotel South Wing, 7

Donghu Rd, near Xinle Rd (东湖宾馆．东湖路 7 号)
Phone: 139 1798 5763

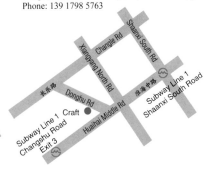

$$$ *el Coctel*

From the mind of "el Willy" restaurant comes this fine cocktail option on Yongfu Road. The Spanish name extends only so far as the tapas and appetizers. The drinks are all of the back-to-the-classics variety, presented in the Japanese style of precision pours and mixing. It's an interesting room to chill in for a while with a (very) well-made beverage.

Address: 2/F, 47 Yongfu Rd, near Fuxing West Rd (永福路 47 号．近复兴西路)
Phone: 6433 6511
Website: www.el-coctel.com

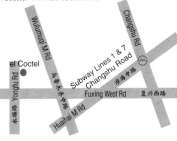

$$$ *New Heights (Xīnshìjiǎo Cāntīng Jiǔláng;* 新视角餐厅酒廊)

While technically a restaurant, New Heights attracts some of the late night crowd, which tends to come around to listen to live jazz-ish music, but most will be found outside on the huge deck, enjoying one of the best views the city has to offer. There's not a ton of dancing to be found, but it is a place where you can expect to rub shoulders with all different kinds of Shanghaiers.

Address: Three on the Bund, 7/F, 17 Guangdong Rd, near Zhongshan East 1st Rd (广东路 17 号．外滩三号 7 楼．近中山东一路)
Phone: 6321 0909

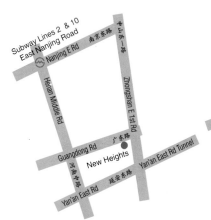

$$$ *People 7 (Yīngqī Rénjiān; 莹七人间)*

This cocktail bar is tough to find (look for the "7" projected on the sidewalk, and a candlelit stairway in front of it) and even tougher to enter. It's not a strict doorman keeping wannabes at bay, it's an electronic code you must crack by inserting your hands into the correct pattern of lights. Of course you can always call ahead for the nightly passcode. If that sounds intriguing then you'll probably enjoy a lot of the other interesting design traits of this quiet, spacious lounge.

> Address: 805 Julu Rd, near Fumin Rd (巨鹿路 805 号 . 近富民路)
> Phone: 5404 0707

$$ *The Chalet*

With its Swiss ski-lodge inspiration, Chalet is a cozy place to spend a few hours, even in the summer. The room is divided into a seating area and a bar area, but they have wisely left it spacious enough to allow for maximum mingling and flirting. It's probably the most low key on this list of lounges, but a good time nonetheless.

> Address: 385 Yongjia Rd, near Taiyuan Rd (永 嘉路 385 号 . 近太原路)
> Phone: 3401 0958

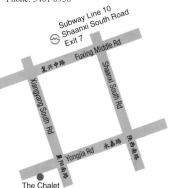

The Chalet

$$$ *CA Club*

This big lounge is where Brown Sugar used to be. It's owned by the fashion company Christian Audigier, which means you'll see plenty of "dark" yet trendy art work related to rock n' roll, skulls and creepy looking flowers. Don't think 16th century dungeon, think more on the lines of a glam Guns N' Roses. The VIP service is out of this world, and it's more of a table and bottle service establishment, so you can bet your last buck it'll be expensive. Furthermore, the place is always packed with China's infamous *fuerdai* (the "second rich" generation who love to spend daddy's money) and other nouveaux riche of China. Dress to impress, and make sure your designer tag is showing.

> Address: Xintiandi, North Block, Lane 181, Taicang Rd, near Huangpi South Rd (太仓路 181 号 . 新天地北里 . 近黄陂南路)
> Phone: 5382 8998

CA Club

$$ *Enoterra*

More along the lines of an upper-ish scale wine bar, this classy French bistro-style establishment has an outstanding wine list with reasonably priced selections. Come any day of the week for brunch featuring delicious French/ Western classics. Open every day from 11:00 to late night, happy hour is from 16:00-20:00.

Address: 343 Jiaozhou Rd, near Wuding Rd, Jing'an District (静安区胶州路 343 号 . 近武定路)
Phone: 6256 5005
Website: www.enoteca.com.cn

$$ The Fat Olive

Another wine bar that gives Enoterra a run for its money, The Fat Olive, as you may have already imagined, is a Greek themed mezze and wine bar. If you don't know what mezze is, it's basically Greek tapas, and trust us – they are as good as they sound. Order a bottle or two of some good imported wine and several appetizer-sized plates of mezze (we recommend any one of their outstanding cheese dishes, Greek salad and paella). Open every day to late night, happy hour buy one get one free is on the weekdays from 16:00-20:00.

Address: 6/F, 98 Shouning Rd, near Xizang South Rd (寿宁路 98 号盛辉酒店公寓 6 楼 . 近西藏南路)
Phone: 6334 3288
Website: www.thefatolive.com

Clubs

$$ The Apartment   PANDA PICK ‹

The first offering from party crew Collective Concepts (see Geisha, pg 211), The Apartment was an instant success with expats and locals alike. It's set in the style of a New York City loft apartment, and the crowd quickly outgrew the original room, allowing the club to take over the neighboring establishment as a secondary dance floor (complete with different music) and the upper floor as a VIP room. That, plus its beautiful top floor terrace and their consistently bumping parties, makes The Apartment one of THE places to see and to be seen in Shanghai.

Address: 3/F, 47 Yongfu Rd, near Fuxing West Rd (永福路 47 号 3 楼 . 近复兴西路)
Phone: 6437 9478
Website: www.theapartment-shanghai.com

$$ No. 88

Step into No. 88 and witness the awakening of a new generation of Chinese partying in their own style. The place is a pastiche of steam punk decorations, VIP booths and tables, spine-numbing bass speakers, and a lighting system to rival NASA. Along with pricey standard drinks, they have a food menu that includes lamb kebabs and bizarrely carved fruit platters. Take a good look, but don't stare too long: the legal standing of some of the clientele is questionable, and

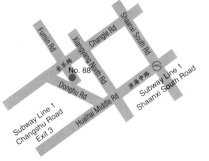

expat beat-downs are not uncommon, both inside the club and on the sidewalk out front. But keep a friendly demeanor and defer to the local crowd, and you should be able to enjoy the experience safely.

Address: 2/F, 291 Fumin Rd, near Donghu Rd (富民路 291 号 2 楼，近东湖路)
Phone: 6136 0288

$$$ M1NT

Shanghai's premiere "members only" club (that's right, you can become a shareholder at M1NT) is perhaps a little more brightly lit than your booming club back home, but that makes it easier to be seen, which is kind of the point here. M1NT is split into two sides, each with their own separate DJ and dance floor, so you can wander back and forth between the huge rooms, watching the beautiful people (or marine life inside the aquarium) from all around the world. Don't forget to stop by the shark tank to take your next FB profile pic. M1NT has started showing an extra dedication to your party life by offering a home alcohol delivery service, with some of the best prices in town.

Address: 24/F, 318 Fuzhou Rd, near Shandong Middle Rd (福州路 318 号 24 楼，近山东中路)
Phone: 6391 3191; 6391 2811
Website: www.m1ntglobal.com

$ The Shelter   **PANDA PICK**

An underground club in the truest sense of the word, Shelter is a converted Cold War-era bomb shelter that is packed every weekend with people who just want to dance their

faces off. They don't often charge a cover, and when they do it's pretty cheap, as are their drinks. The sound system is as good as the DJs they bring in, and they know how to use it to its full potential, but take note that it's not for the claustrophobic.

Address: B/F, 5 Yongfu Rd, near Fuxing West Rd (永复兴路 5 号，近复兴西路)
Email: thesheltershanghai@gmail.com

$$ Geisha (Yún; 芸)

After the success of The Apartment, the team quickly followed it up with Geisha, a two-floor affair near Sinan Mansions. Upstairs is more of a relaxed vibe for people who want to chat or catch their breath on the patio. When you're ready for the excitement, head downstairs for DJs and dancers. Music genres depend on the night, but expect some pop and hip-hop to get the crowd going.

Address: 2/F, 390 Shaanxi South Rd, near Fuxing Middle Rd (陕西南路390 号，近复兴中路)
Phone: 6403 0244
Website: www.thegeisha-shanghai.com

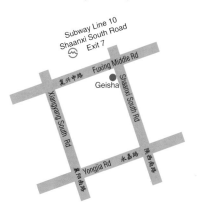

$$ The Flamingo

In a city where there is no closing time for bars, an "after-hours" joint might seem a little redundant. But Shanghai's partiers routinely push it so hard that club owners and staff are finally forced to say, "you don't have to go home, but you can't stay here." The Flamingo is an '80s-style bar a la Miami Vice that caters mostly to the crowds being kicked out of Geisha (which is directly downstairs). It opens early in the evening, but don't expect the party to get going until 2:00, when people start pouring in. In addition to classic '80s tunes and modern dance, the club's entertainment also includes Russian pole dancers…and drunken amateur pole dancers when the Russian girls are otherwise "occupied" in the VIP rooms.

Address: 1/F, 390 Shaanxi South Rd, near Fuxing Middle Rd (陕西南路 390 号 1 楼 . 近复兴中路)
Phone: 3461 9073
Website: www.flamingoshanghai.com

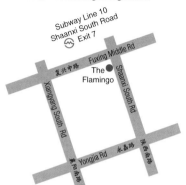

$$ Amber Lounge

Another seemingly unnecessary after-hours club that is still somehow jam packed until daybreak, it's the last stop for most of Shanghai's hardcore partiers before they either roll their way home or sit down to a champagne brunch. Clubbers really have a love-hate relationship with Amber: They love it at the time and then hate it when they finally get out of bed at 19:00 the following evening.

Address: 370 Huashan Rd, near Wulumuqi Rd (华山路 370 号 . 近乌鲁木齐路)
Phone: 6248 8818

$$ Lola

Lola is the envy of all its bar neighbors at Surpass Court, as it seems to have succeeded where the others have floundered. It's a good sized space that's split pretty much 50/50 into lounge-bar and dance floor. The music is house and electro (but a welcome break

from the kind you can sing along with) and is blasted out of a state of the art sound system that lets you feel every throb of the bass without deafening you in the process. Lola is a good party until it's time to hit the after-hours joints.

Address: Bldg 4, 570 Yongjia Rd, near Yueyang Rd (永嘉路 570 号 4 号楼 . 近岳阳路)
Phone: 6074 0015
Email: teasy@eastern-side.com

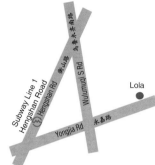

$$$ Bar Rouge

The very image of the Bund party scene, Bar Rouge has had its nose high in the air for longer than almost any club in town. Not everyone likes what they do, but they do it extremely well. Head in most nights of the week to find a club inundated with slick-dressed Euro types and leggy models dancing to well-mixed house and electronica. It is definitely not one of your cheaper options for the night, but check their website (**www.bar-rouge-shanghai.com**) and you might find a password that lets you avoid a cover charge. Once inside, avoid the poseurs and head straight for their famous terrace overlooking the Bund.

Address: Bund 18, 7/F, 18 Zhongshan East 1st Rd, near Nanjing East Rd (中山东一路 18 号 7 楼 . 近南京东路)
Phone: 6339 1199
Website: www.bar-rouge-shanghai.com

$$ 390 Shanghai

This is one of Shanghai's last remaining gay clubs (well, not until 23:00 at least). During the day it's a restaurant and in the evening it's one of the city's up-and-coming live music venues. Its vibe is friendly and its layout is interesting and spacious. Basically, anytime you stop in you can be sure of enjoying a great party no matter what your orientation under the rainbow flag might be.

Address: 390 Panyu Rd, near Fahuazhen Rd (番禺路 390 号 . 法华镇路). Note: some cab drivers will pronounce this as "Fanyu" Rd
Phone: 186 2124 985
Website: www.390shanghai.com

$$ Shanghai Studio

Another re-purposed bomb shelter (see Shelter, pg 211), Shanghai Studio is a colorful underground maze of interlinking rooms with friendly partiers and pumping music. The vibe might be flaming, but it's best not to imagine what would happen if a fire breaks out.

Address: Bldg 4, 1950 Huaihai Middle Rd, near Wukang Rd (淮海中路 1950 弄 4 号楼 . 近武康路)
Phone: 6283 1043
Website: www.shanghai-studio.com

$$ Phebe

With its garish décor (imagine a 1980s karaoke video updated for the digital age) and questionable cocktails, Phebe is a quintessential Chinese club... that caters almost exclusively to foreigners. It might have something to do with their frequent open bar nights or unlimited ladies nights. If you do choose to take part in the festivities, expect tons of fun and madness…and a skull-splitting headache the next day.

Address: 10 Hengshan Rd, near Gao'an Rd (衡山路 10 号 . 近高安路)
Phone: 6555 9998; 6878 4258

$$$ Unico

Unico is one of the latest Bund entrants, and they have definitely raised the bar. They've still got the well-heeled crowd, the mix of pop-electro, Café de Mar sounds and the stellar view of Shanghai's skyline, but they also offer incredibly well made cocktails. If you've only got enough RMB in your budget for one classic Bund bar, make it this one.

Address: Three on the Bund, 2/F, 3 Zhongshan East 1st Rd, near Guangdong Rd (中山东一路 3 号外滩三号 2 楼 . 近广东路)
Phone: 5308 5399

$$ Zapata's

If you've ever ventured into a Carlos and Charley's or Senor Frog's, then you already know the vibe that Zapata's is going for. Don't expect too many drunken frat boys in tank tops and flip flops, though – here they'll be sharply dressed and drenched in cologne. If you're in the mood for a big blast of a night out, then this is the place, where dancing on the bar is not just accepted, it's encouraged. Be on the lookout for their tequila girls, who pour it out for free every hour on the half hour mark…if you can handle drinking it straight from the bottle.

Address: 5 Hengshan Rd, near Dongping Rd (衡山路 5 号 , 近东平路)
Phone: 152 2103 5065; 6433 4104
Website: www.zapatas-shanghai.com

$$ Shiva

PANDA PICK

Founded by local yoga legend Weila Wu, Shiva is the place to hear house music with a touch of world beat in it. It's a smaller club, so the party feels friendly and full at most times of the night. Cocktails are of a similar Southeast Asian theme, along with all the standards. If you like deep bass with a splash of bongos, you'll be in nirvana.

Address: 47 Yongfu Rd, near Fuxing Rd (永福路 47 号 , 近复兴路)
Phone: 6433 5330

Live Music

$ Yùyīntáng (育音堂)

Shanghai nightlife is known more for its DJ scene than its live music, but there is still a strong culture of punk, rock, indie, metal and more if you look for it. The mecca for all these musicians is YYT. Just outside of the real downtown section, YYT has everything you'd expect from a music venue that has provided a stage for pretty much every up and coming band in town. If you want true, original music instead of Philippine cover bands, then YYT will be well worth the extra ¥5 you'll pay in a taxi to get here.

Address: 851 Kaixuan Rd, near Yan'an West Rd (just by Zhongshan Park Metro Station) (凯旋路 851 号 , 近延安西路口)
Phone: 5237 8662

$$ MAO Livehouse

A very nice mid-sized music venue, MAO Livehouse provides music lovers with a huge range of artists and genres, from Nouvelle Vague to Pete Tong and from the Red Hot Chili Peppers to local artists. It's not a place where you'll just happen to show up and catch a show, though, so check their website to see who's playing while you're in town.

Address: 3/F, 308 Chongqing South Rd, near Jianguo Middle Rd (重庆南路 308 号 近建国中路)
Phone: 6445 0086
Website: www.mao-music.com/index/ (in Chinese)

$$$ JZ Club

One of Shanghai's longest running venues, JZ pumps out live jazz and Latin music every night of the week. The place is often full and the crowd is always moving, swing dancing, salsa-ing or simply nodding their head to the beat. They've also got their own music school, in case you want to brush up on your virtuoso skills. Keep an ear out for their annual JZ music festival (**www.jzfestival.com/en/2013/**), held every September on stages all across Shanghai, indoors and out.

Address: 46 Fuxing West Rd, near Yongfu Rd
(复兴西路 46 号 . 近永福路)
Phone: 6431 0269
Website: www.jzclub.cn

None of the Above: Drinking Alternatives

It happens to the toughest of troopers. In a city with endless watering holes and no closing time, you start to tell the days of the week by the bar special. Anyone can get clubbed out in Shanghai, and when that inevitably happens to you, here are a few ways to spend a fun evening out of the club, but not off the bottle.

$$ Your Place

No matter how amazing the clubs are, once you've found your crew of friends, it's tough to beat a house party. There are a couple of new home delivery services that are helping to make those house parties a little more frequent and a little more happening. Cheers-in has a few bar locations around town, but they also offer deluxe beer delivered ice cold to your door, while M1NT has a few bartender packages to supply you with the basic hard stuff. It's all cash-on-delivery, so all you need to do is provide the address.

Cheers-in: www.cheers-in.com
M1NT delivery: www.m1ntcellars.com

$$ Partyworld

If you've never done karaoke in Asia, then gather your friends for a night at Partyworld, one of the few safe and legit karaoke chains in the city. Unlike singing your guts out for the entire bar back home, at a KTV your party rents a private room and orders drinks by the bottle. It can make for an exceptionally fun night, and an affordable one too (as long as your group is big enough to split the costs comfortably). Be sure to have one Chinese reader with you, or just enjoy blindly tapping your way through the endless music library touchscreen. Note: Partyworld has numerous locations across town. **Hǎolèdí** (好乐迪) is another legit KTV chain with a ton of locations, but Partyworld is the most foreigner-friendly.

Pudong Branch (浦东旗舰店)

Address: B1, Shanghai Bay Ordos Building, 1118 Pudong South Rd, facing 1 Yaohan (浦东南路 1118 号上海湾国际大厦 B1 楼 . 第一八佰伴对面).
Phone: 6859 7666

Xuhui Branch (徐汇旗舰店)

Address: 5/F & 6/F, 580 Tianyaoqiao Rd, near Lingling Rd (天钥桥路 580 号 5–6 楼 . 近零陵路)
Phone: 6161 9888

Luwan Branch (卢湾店)

Address: Inside Fuxing Park, 2 Gaolan Rd (皋兰路 2 号复兴公园内)
Phone: 5306 3888

Putuo Branch (普陀店)

Address: 139 Xinhui Rd, near Jade Buddha Temple (新会路 139 号 . 近玉佛寺)
Phone: 5172 1888

Hongkou Branch (虹口店)

Address: 1661 Sichuan North Rd, near East Baoxing Rd (四川北路 1661 号 . 近东宝兴路)
Phone: 5128 8300

$ Big E

Big E is a newly opened indoor amusement park that offers black light mini golf, laser tag, air hockey, pool and foosball, all while letting you get your drink on. Check out their listings for happy hour times or special events, such as All-You-Can-Drink, All-You-Can-Play nights. Pudong might seem like a lot of trouble to get to, but a night out like this could easily be worth your while.

Address: B2/F, World Plaza, 855 Pudong South Rd, near Dongchang Rd (浦东南路 855 号 B2 楼 . 近东昌路)

Phone: 400 030 9992; 131 6268 4861

$ Orden Bowling (Ōudēng Bǎolíngqiúguǎn; 欧登保龄球馆)

There are a few bowling alleys in Shanghai, but only one is a) 24 hours, and b) within walking distance to a variety of clubs and bars. In fact, Orden Bowling Center is in a building that is home to several venues for pre- and post-game drinking. Bowling and beer are both cheap, as are shoe rentals (and yes, they've got big shoes for big Western feet). Bring your own hand sanitizer.

Address: 3/F, 10 Hengshan Rd, near Gao'an Rd (衡山路 10 号欧登大厦 3 楼 . 近高安路)

Phone: 64746666

$$ Stampede Karting

Stampede is probably the best go-karting option the city has. It is a bit of a schlep outside the city center, but for those who think they might've learned a few tricks watching Shanghai's taxi drivers, here's your chance to test them out. There are no breathalyzer tests here, in fact, there's an onsite bar where you can wait for your group's race to begin (more fun than a drunken Mario Kart session). Just take a look at the website and you'll be fueled up and ready to do some drunk driving!

Address: Section C, Basement, 1288 Zhenguang Rd, near Meichuan Rd (真光路 1288 号 C 区地下 室 . 近梅川路)

Phone: 6139 5095; 156 1805 0566

Website: www.stampedekarting.com

$ Convenience Store Bingo

It's important to note that Shanghai does not have any open bottle laws like some other uptight cities. So enjoy that freedom and take to the streets for a night of wandering and people watching. You can make a game of it by choosing a convenience store (All Days, Family Mart, 7-11, Lawsons, etc) before setting out and then stopping for a refill every time you pass that store. There's one on every corner, so you won't be thirsty for long.

Address: Anywhere you want!

Shopping

Shopping and Shanghai go hand in hand. Back in those glory years of the 1920s and '30s you'll hear spoken about so often, it was often said that you could find anything you wanted from anywhere in the world (provided you could pay for it).

Then there came a cooling off period for many years, where stores and shelves were virtually empty. A diverse fashion scene was replaced with a standard uniform for most of the city's residents. Women's hairstyles lost their elaborate flair in favor of simple, short coifs, which were more easily managed and maintained. People still shopped, but the major status symbols were bicycles and radios. In fact, these items were so popular you needed to have a waiting list ticket before you could buy one.

But since China opened up, Shanghai has bounced back in a big way, taking back its status as a world capital of commerce. A survey published by *Hurun* in 2012 stated that there were about 370,000 millionaires living in Shanghai. So imagine a city the size of Florence or New Orleans where every single resident is a millionaire.

Shanghai has a reputation in China as being THE city to seek your fortune, and because of that there are plenty of ways to spend your fortune. Five-star restaurants and hotels are abound all across the city. Maserati, Bentley, Ferrari, Porsche and others all have extremely high profile outlets in the center of downtown. Even when one would probably suffice, Gucci, Prada, Louis Vuitton and other major fashion labels each have numerous outlets across town.

That's all well and good for the millionaires, but what are the average locals (and tourists on a budget) supposed to do? Well, try and keep up with the Joneses (or in this case, the Zhangs) of course.

If you aren't a millionaire, there is no saying you can't look like one. The moment a celebrity appears in a magazine, copycat looks start sprouting up all across the city. True, a trained eye will be able to see those slight distinctions in prints, cuts, patterns and finishes, but for the casual observer Shanghai's streets are packed with fashionistas and fashionistos, and you can be one too.

If you can handle the splurge, then you will gladly find new treasures at any of the big brand name shops or the stores targeting expats, which offer imported goods or bigger sizes. Otherwise, head straight for any of the city's fake markets for the best deal. After all, fashion is a very temporary thing, so why make a big investment in it?

Actually, the term "fake market" is not entirely accurate. There are many levels of fakes when it comes to clothing and many different levels of quality. At any clothing street or fake market, or even in any independent store, here's what you might find:

Factory Seconds / Recalls: These are products that do not lie. If it says A&F or Chanel or Nike, then that is in fact what it is. However, for one reason or another the product was deemed "unsatisfactory" and is now being sold off at a reduced price. Often they haven't passed the factory inspection, but occasionally they'll still get shipped to foreign countries. Sometimes, if a foreign outlet notices a high rate of flaws, they send back the entire shipment, so you might in fact get a perfect item... if you're really lucky. Otherwise, the seams might be twisted or crooked, or the shoes are off balance – maybe only subtly, but something you'll notice in time.

Factory Off-hours: Let's say you have a clothing factory and Diesel asks you to make 100,000 pairs of jeans in a month. Well now that you have the factory set to make that pattern, why not keep the machines running after hours and make twice as many (aside from it being illegal)? That's what a lot of factories end up doing here, so you'll find items with the right cuts and labels. These products look completely genuine and are top notch, but they've usually cut corners on something, like the glue used to hold the sole on your shoe or the thread that stitches the pants together. After a few wearings (maybe less), they'll fall apart.

Straight-up Rip-offs: These are the T-shirts with the misspelled slogans, labels in the wrong color or mismatched logos and designs: who knew that Oakley, Ray-Ban and Prada all made the exact same model of sunglasses? Sure, you might be tempted to pick up a couple of these items for the sheer irony, but if you do, make sure they are cheap, cheap, cheap... which could require you to pay for it with time and haggling.

But if the idea of wandering a market packed with aggressive salespeople and bargaining with all your might gets your blood flowing, you've come to the right place. Though it might be something you enjoy, keep in mind that this can be an exhausting experience, so be sure to pace yourself, stay hydrated and don't lose your patience. Even local Chinese people get tired of it, which is one reason for the extreme popularity of stores like Carrefour and IKEA, where prices are clearly marked and there is no question about what kind of deal you are getting.

As long as you're not dead set on getting the real deal, you can have a lot of fun shopping in Shanghai. Read on for tips on what to buy, where to go, and how to get the best deal.

What Can I Buy in Shanghai?

From traditional Chinese handicrafts to knockoff "Abibas" shoes, there's an insane range of goods on offer in Shanghai's markets and stores. Whether you're a true collector or just looking to score some cool souvenirs and clothes, Shanghai is a great place to be.

The adage "if it seems too good to be true, it is" definitely applies to shopping in Shanghai, and it's not just limited to brand-name clothes. The quality of fakes has become so good that even New York's Metropolitan Museum may have been duped: while they stand behind an exceptionally rare silk scroll they acquired in 2007, some experts have questioned its authenticity. By some estimates, bogus antiques and art constitute as much as 80% of the value of goods for sale in Hong Kong, and most of them originate in Mainland China.

The export of genuine antiques dating before 1911 is not allowed without special government approval, but a special wax seal, usually red, signifies permission and many of these items can be found at government stores. A certificate is also given to allow for legal export, and buying antique porcelain without the seal or proper paperwork can be risky. It could be a fake, or it could be real and obtained by dubious methods, but either way if it does not have the proper documentation, it could be confiscated upon departure from China.

"Watch, bag, shoes...DVD..." This is practically a mantra of Shanghai street shopping, one that you will hear repeated time and time again. The criers usually carry a laminated poster with standard images of Rolex watches and LV purses, and will try to guide you to a particular shop down a series of back alleys. Fashion, fashion, fashion is probably the number one most purchased item here.

Also, because this is China, where most of the world's goods are produced, you can find many tech or household items at a substantially cheaper price than you could back home (although sometimes the same item will be more expensive in China, owing to its "foreign" popularity). Playstations, smart-phones, speakers, you name it – you can find any high-tech gizmo while strolling the shopping lanes of Shanghai. But we've said it once and we'll say it again: beware of forgeries, especially in the electronics department. "iFones" are more common than you'd imagine.

When it comes to clothes and shoes, you may find yourself out of luck if your size is especially large (for shoes, above size 11 for guys and size 9 for ladies). See the chart below to convert your American shoe size to its Chinese equivalent (it's very similar to European sizes). Trying on clothes isn't always done, either, especially if you are the least bit shy. Often the "fitting room" will consist of a sheet held up by the shopkeeper. Of course, no matter how the item ends up fitting you, they will enthusiastically tell you it looks, "*Hěn hǎo! Very good! Cool!*"

Women's shoe sizes

US	5	5.5	6	6.5	7	7.5	8	8.5	9	9.5	10	10.5	12
China	35.5	36	37	37.5	38	39	39.5	40	41	41.5	42	43	44.5

Men's shoe sizes

US	7.5	8	8.5	9	9.5	10	10.5	11	11.5	12	12.5	13	13.5	14
China	-	42	42	43	43.5	44	44.5	45	45.5	46	46.5	47	47.5	48.5

SHOPPING TIPS ▶▶

1 If you're not used to bargaining, you might not know when to do it and when to pay the sticker price. Here's where you should bargain really hard: public markets, souvenir stands, and really anywhere that doesn't have marked prices. In restaurants, shopping centers, grocery stores, 7-11s, etc, prices are fixed.

2 If you don't get excited about bargaining, there's a low-energy strategy that can be equally effective. Act like you're bored, in a hurry or not that interested, and refuse to say a price, no matter how much the seller asks you to. Just walk away after you've worn them down and they'll probably chase after you with an offer.

3 If an item doesn't have a price tag, just know that you're probably going to end up paying more than a Chinese person would. The assumption is that foreigners have more money than locals. If you hate the idea of getting "ripped off" by paying foreigner prices, avoid buying anything that doesn't have a stated price. Another sure sign that you're probably paying too much is that the seller speaks very, very good English. The likeliest reason for this is that they cater exclusively to foreigners and have built up their skill in order to sweet talk more money out of you. It doesn't have to stop you from buying – maybe that pack of postcards is really worth ¥60 to you – but just know you're not getting the best deal.

4 Don't assume something is a good deal just because it's cheaper than it would be in your home country. It might still be marked up significantly from the real value. Also consider quality: is getting a pair of jeans for US$10 really a bargain if they fall apart the first time you wear them?

5 Take a very good look at your products before starting your bargaining. Important features to look at are zippers, seams and glue (if it has spread farther than the spot requires). Also see if the garment hangs straight or twists or kinks to one side or another.

6 If a seller seems annoyed that you're bargaining really hard, don't be deterred. They're not upset with you personally; they're upset that they won't get a huge profit off of you. In fact, more often than not, they will like you more if you bargain hard, but friendly.

7 The great equalizer in the bargaining war is **www.taobao.com**, an online shopping Mecca built by Chinese, for Chinese. Use Google translate to navigate your way around the site and find out what similar products are going for before you hit the market. You know that these are the prices they are trying to get Chinese people to pay, and they include delivery. Anything that you buy at the market should be somewhere close to that price.

How to Bargain

As mentioned, the best strategy for paving your way to a good deal is to arm yourself with information in advance. If there's something in particular that you want, go online and research the hallmarks of authentic goods so you can knowledgably inspect what's for sale. Furthermore, there are relatively simple tests that even non-experts can use to get an idea of the quality of pearls, jade, silk, and other items.

Other than knowing what you're getting into, the most important factor in successful bargaining is your attitude. Go into it with a smile and a sense of humor. If you're shy, get over the idea that you're being rude or pushy. It's all a game and everyone knows it. Even if a seller starts trying to appeal to you with statements like, "You're making me lose money!" or "I guess my family won't eat tonight," know that they are never going to sell something at a loss. Most of the vendors you'll encounter deal with foreigners all the time and speak good enough English to conduct the transaction. However, you'll still probably go back and forth with your offers by punching them into a calculator so that

there's no confusion (but most importantly so others don't hear the price).

Chinese people also have a unique set of hand signals, where the position of your fingers will resemble the Chinese character for the numbers of six through ten. You may often see these flashed during bargaining sessions and it can be very confusing if you've never had it explained. It's pretty straightforward from one to five, and then:

The sign for #6 (liù; 六) looks like the old "Hang Loose" sign, where you make a fist but then extend your thumb and pinky.

The sign for #7 (qī; 七) is made by touching your thumb to the tips of your middle finger and forefinger (keep your other two fingers curled up tight).

The sign for #8 (bā; 八) is the finger gun. This can be confusing since you might assume they mean "2" or "7."

The sign for #9 (jiǔ; 九) is made by holding up a fist and then curling your forefinger into a hook shape.

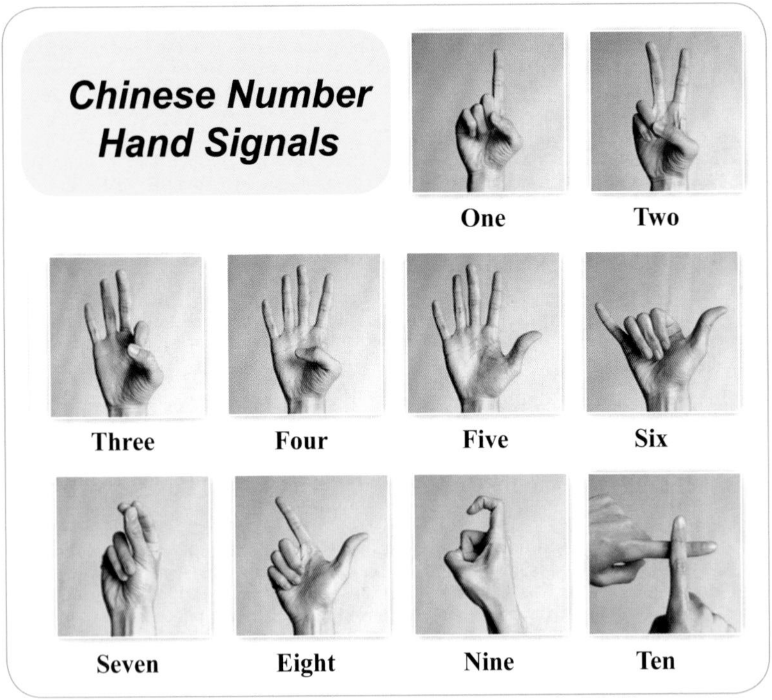

Chinese Number Hand Signals

One	Two
Three	Four
Five	Six
Seven	Eight
Nine	Ten

The sign for #10 (shí; 十) is shown by making a cross with your forefingers. So now you know they aren't mistaking you for a vampire, they just want ¥10.

The general strategy practiced by bargaining ninjas is this:

1. Look at the item and decide how much you're willing to pay for it. Keep that number in mind throughout the process and don't go over, no matter how much the seller stresses you out.

2. When the seller asks you what you're willing to pay, avoid offering a specific number right away. Try to stall and dramatically inspect the item, pointing out any flaws or signs of low quality.

3. When it's time to name your price, DO NOT start with how much you're willing to pay. Offer 1/3 of it and slowly work your way up. So, if a pair of shoes is worth ¥100 to you, start at ¥30 and go up in small increments.

4. If the seller refuses to go low enough, just say thank you and walk away. Nine times out of ten they'll chase you down and make a better offer. And if they don't, you've avoided overpaying.

Here's an example of a successful bargaining transaction:

YOU: (Admiring a wool sweater, thinking you'd pay ¥200)

SELLER: How much you pay?

YOU: I'm not sure. . . it seems a little low-quality. . .

SELLER: No, it is very high-quality, very nice. . . how much you pay?

YOU: How about ¥70?

SELLER: Ha! No way. ¥400, final offer.

YOU: 75

SELLER: 350

YOU: (With a smile on your face) 80

SELLER: ¥80 I lose money! Final price ¥280.

YOU: (Walking away) No, thanks. . .

SELLER: Ok ok, 250!

YOU: 100.

SELLER: 220.

YOU: 110.

SELLER: 200, final price!

YOU: I'll take it.

You did it! Of course you'll never know how much that ¥200 sweater was actually worth, but if you pay what you wanted to pay, you've done alright for yourself.

Where Can I Shop in Shanghai?

Shopping Malls

If you are looking for a standard shopping experience filled with name brand items from shops like Mango, H&M or Uniqlo, then make your way to one of the city's seven-kajillion malls. These places are very Western in their designs, offering multi-level, climate controlled, name brand shopping. Most malls will also have a food court in the basement in case you need a snack break during your spree. An interesting phenomenon is that malls here are also usually home to at least a few full-on sit down restaurants, and some even contain booming nightclubs. While malls are seeded all around the city, they are especially clustered around major subway stops like **Zhongshan Park** (中山公园), **Xujiahui** (徐家汇) and even **Hongkou Stadium** (虹口体育馆). They also line the major downtown streets of **Nanjing West Road** (南京西路) and **Huaihai Middle Road** (淮海中路). Most shopping centers open between 9:00 and 10:00 and usually close between 21:00 and 22:00

Huaihai Road Commercial Street (Huáihǎi Lù Shāngyè Jiē; 淮海路商业街)

This cool, fresh, modern and stylish shopping road connects the trendy French Concession to the fashionable Bund. While Nanjing Road has blown up and become too big for its britches, often inundated with a tsunami of tourists and scammers, Huaihai is kind of what Nanjing Road used to be before all the chaos. There is still a sense of charm along the narrow-ish road, and it seems that you could walk for an eternity and never run out of shopping options. You can find just about anything here, from luxurious, top notch name brand designers to knock offs sold street side, and everything in between. There are also plenty of dining options, especially on the fringes of Huaihai Road at the chic Xintiandi.

Hours: Most shopping centers open between 9:00 and 10:00 and usually close between 21:00 and 22:00
Address: Huaihai Middle Rd, Huangpu District (黄浦区淮海中路)
Transport: Subway – Line 1, Huangpi South Rd Station or Shaanxi South Road Station

Han City Flea Market (Hánchéng Tiàozǎo Shìchǎng; 韩城跳蚤市场)

This is a big one, smack dab in the heart of downtown. Enjoy four floors of countless stalls hawking everything from luggage and purses to football (international and American) jerseys and cocktail dresses. Several stores also have the classic Chinese souvenirs of chopsticks, table runners and parasols, too. Usually you can find watches, sunglasses, ties and belts in one store, shoes in another, and jewelry in another, but there is a good deal of overlap as well as redundancy in what is available throughout the market. If the vendor doesn't want to come down to your price, don't worry: you can probably find it on sale further on in the maze of shops.

Hours: 10:00-22:00
Address: 580 Nanjing West Rd (南京西路 580 号), near Chengdu North Rd (成都北路)
Transport: Subway – Line 2, Nanjing West Rd (南京西路) Station

Science & Technology Museum Fake Market (Shànghǎi Kējìguǎn Shuǐhuò Shìchǎng; 上海科技馆水货市场)

This market is not as big as the one on Nanjing West Road, but it has almost all the same things. Located directly under the Science & Technology Museum and directly around the metro station of the same name, it makes for a good shopping choice on a rainy day, as you don't even have to go outside. If Pudong seems like a big schlep to you, you could make the most out of your shopping trip by combining it with a visit to the museum to see a few different sides of Shanghai culture in the same day.

Hours: 10:00-20:00 daily
Address: 2000 Century Avenue, near Jinxiu Rd, Pudong (世纪大道 2000 号 . 近锦绣路)
Transport: Subway – Line 2, Shanghai Science & Technology Museum (上海科技馆) Station

Qipu Road (Qīpǔ Lù; 七浦路)

The aptly named Qipu Road is the epicenter of Shanghai's discount clothing industry. It would be difficult to find cheaper clothes anywhere in the city, even if you went straight to the factories on the outskirts of town. In fact, Qipu is particularly famous among foreigners because Qipu sounds suspiciously similar to that all important word in shopping: cheap. But there is still a price to pay for your financial savings: your sanity. Consisting of about eight large "malls" that flank a stretch of two city blocks (not to mention all the racks and carts set up on the pedestrian streets), it represents either your shopping dream or your worst nightmare (maybe both if you stay there long enough). It is congested with huge crowds of people not just selling, but also buying: it is the wholesale source for many of the city's boutiques and shops.

On slow days, vendors here can be especially aggressive, following you around long after you've said "no" in many different languages. A trip to any of the ATM's is like watching sharks sniff blood in the water: crowds form to see where you will go next. Women are the clear winners here, as 90% of the stores focus exclusively on women's fashion and the remaining 10% are unisex stores. Still, there's enough variety here that anyone can find something they like…if they have the patience to keep looking.

Hours: Vary by store, but for shopping, between 7:00 and 19:00 is best
Address: 168 Qipu Rd (七浦路168号), near Henan North Rd (河南北路)
Transport: It's about a five-minute walk north from Tiantong Rd (天潼路) Station (Line 10) or 20 minutes north of Nanjing East Rd (南京东路) Station (Lines 2, 10)

Traditional Shanghai qipao garments

The Fabric Market (Nán Wàitān Qīngfǎng Miànliào Shìchǎng; 南外滩轻纺面料市场)

Everybody talks about doing this when they get to Shanghai, so why not you? Head to the fabric market, a five-story cluster of seamsters and fabric merchants who

will make you a tailor made outfit of your choosing. For the best results, be prepared to make more than just one return visit here. Often your "finished" product will need considerable tweaking before it is truly prêt-à-porter. The reason is simple: no matter who measures you and takes all your custom details in regards to buttons, liner, pleats, cuffs, etc, they will simply pass it off to the next person in the chain who passes it to the next and so on, until it reaches the old lady in the basement who actually cuts and sews your clothes. It's a bit like that childhood game, "Telephone." There are many other places in town where you can get bespoke suits made, but this one has by far the biggest selection of both material and tailors to get the job done. This is also a great place for off the rack items like pashminas or silk duvet covers.

Hours: 9:00 – 18:00.
Address: 399 Lujiabang Rd (陆家浜路399号), near Nancang St (南仓街)
Transport: A five or ten-minute walk from either Nanpu Bridge (南浦大桥) Station (Line 4) or Xiaonanmen (小南门) Station (Line 9)

Dongtai Rd Antiques Market (Dōngtái Lù Gǔdǒng Shìchǎng; 东台路古董市场)

We've already warned you about shopping for antiques in this city, but if you're still looking for that old-timey souvenir, this is the place to be. The vast majority of items for sale are not in fact true antiques but reproductions that have been distressed to give them that weathered look. Even if you choose not to make any major purchases, it's an interesting place to do some window shopping. It's also very close to Yu Garden, so you can make a day of exploring Old Shanghai.

Yu Garden itself is also surrounded by different souvenir shops. Most of these will be completely full of Chinese tourists, as Yu Garden is a major landmark in the country. Some of the interesting things you can buy here are hand-painted reproductions of famous works of art. They'll offer to frame them for you (for a big charge), but really the deal is to just buy the canvas and roll it up into your backpack or suitcase.

Hours: Vary, but generally 9:00 – 18:00
Address: Dongtai Rd (东台路), enter from Xizang Rd (西藏路) into Liuhe Rd (浏河路)
Transport: A 20-minute walk from Yu Garden (豫园) Station (Line 10) or a 10-minute walk from Laoximen (老西门) Station (Lines 8, 10)

Metro City (Měi Luó Chéng; 美罗城)

Over in Xujiahui, Metro City is an iconic landmark with a five-story glass sphere at its front door that lights up with laser graffiti and LEDs when the sun goes down. Inside is a modern tech mall where you can find almost any type of computer peripheral and accessory known to man. They've got plenty of places selling cameras, mobile phones, computers and tablets, but knowing whether you are getting the real deal or not is an exceptionally difficult thing to determine. It's not recommended for big ticket tech purchases, but if you want a Hello Kitty webcam or you forgot your camera's charging cable, here is where you'll find it.

Hours: 10:00 – 22:00
Address: 1111 Zhaojiabang Rd (肇嘉浜路 1111 号), near Tianyaoqiao Rd (天钥桥路)
Transport: Xujiahui (徐家汇) Station (Lines 1, 9)

Huanlong Camera Market (Huánlóng Zhàocái Chéng; 环龙照材城)

A photophiles paradise, the top three floors of this otherwise crummy mall are devoted to all things photographic. There are stores that stock nothing but filters while others focus (haha) entirely on lenses. Need some sort of a bizarre tripod? How about a specialized flash? All this and more is available, including a huge selection of antique cameras, especially those hard to find commie models that came out of the Soviet Union.

Hours: 7:00 – 18:00 daily
Address: Huanlong Mall, 360 Meiyuan Rd, near Moling Rd (梅园路 360 号. 火车站对面)
Transport: Subway – Lines 1, 3, 4, Shanghai Railway Station (上海火车站)

Glasses Markets (Yǎnjìng Chéng; 眼镜城)

Maybe you don't feel like getting a custom three-piece suit or a silk qípáo made at the fabric market, but that doesn't mean you can't still get customized. For anyone who wears glasses, this will be a mind-blowing experience as you can choose from floor after floor after floor of "designer" frames. Even with the lenses (which can be customized by tint or finish) you'll still end up paying about 20% of what you would back home. So if you're ready for a new pair, why not stop here and get five instead - one for each day of the work week? Even if you don't need glasses you can stop by and create a pair of custom fit sunglasses to be prepared for the next stop on your travel itinerary.

Hours: 9:00 – 19:00 daily
Two Locations:

1) 3 Ye Optical Glasses Market (三叶眼镜市场); Shanghai Train Plaza, South Square 4/F & 5/F, 360 Meiyuan Rd, near Moling Rd (梅园路 360 号. 近抹陵路)
2) International Glasses City (国际眼镜城): Railway Station North Plaza, 1688 Zhongxing Rd, near Henfeng Rd (闸北区中兴路 1688 号. 近上海火车站)
Transport: Subway – Lines 1, 3, 4, Shanghai Railway Station (上海火车站)

Nanjing East Road (Nánjīng Dōnglù ; 南京东路)

No visit to Shanghai would be complete without a visit to Nanjing East Road, China's version of Times Square. Go at night to experience it in all its neon glory. Chances are you probably won't buy anything here, but there are tons of shops to browse, and it is a sight to behold. Once again, this is one of the biggest tourist attractions in Shanghai, a site that is famous all across China, so you can expect to find "the masses" wandering the streets and posing for photos. Look out for pickpockets and avoid any friendly locals who invite you to join them for tea (see Scams on pg 294). Also keep in mind that even though Nanjing East Road is a pedestrian street, there are plenty of intersections all along it that are not. Cars and motorcycles will suddenly cross your path, so keep an eye out.

Hours: 10:00–22:00
Address: Nanjing East Rd (南京东路), from

Xizang Rd to the Bund (Wàitān)

Transport: While there is an Nanjing East Rd (南京东路) Metro station (Lines 2, 10), your best bet is to get out at People's Square (人民广场) Station (Lines 1, 2, 8) and walk east until you reach the Bund.

Street Shopping

As we've said many times, Shanghai is China's most commercial city and there is something to buy in every possible place here. It is the home of the original pop-up shop, with merchants sporting fast-fold table/suitcases that offer everything from sunglasses to earrings to hats to insoles. You can find these items (and many more) outside parks, on pedestrian overpasses, under overhead highways, in the middle of a random sidewalks, and pretty much any place they can park their wares away from a vigilant police officer. A narrow stairway to the metro that has to be used by thousands of people? Seems like a good idea to set up a display of all your fake Swarovski crystals right on the stairs. Out late at night and aren't winning your sweetheart a teddy bear at the amusement park? Don't worry, even at midnight you'll still be able to find the biggest teddy bear you can carry.

Online Shopping

Before you head out to do any shopping whatsoever, you might want to familiarize yourself with **www.taobao.com**. This website is a shopaholic's best friend, with its endless supply of dirt cheap fashions, home supplies, and design pieces all delivered right to your door, guaranteed. It's so popular that some studies have named it as the country's worst drain on productivity, because so many employees are sneakily wasting office hours so they can order that new pair of sneakers. It can be a little complicated to figure out (you need to have an account and even then you might have to go to the post office and buy "taobao dollars" to spend on the site). As we mentioned before, even if you never make a purchase here, use it to find out the average lowest price for the product you want. It can be your greatest ally when bargaining to say, "Well, I can get that on Taobao for ..."

Buying English Books in Shanghai

The last thing you want to do is fill your precious luggage allowance with heavy books, so chances are you came to Shanghai with only your Panda Guides book and perhaps one other to pass the time. But if you find yourself looking for something to read on that upcoming train trip or bus ride, Shanghai's got you covered.

Garden Books

Part bookstore, part café, Garden Books has everything you need when you're pining for some literature (or fashion or pop culture magazines) from home. One warning though, these books are not fake, so you're paying the cover price and sometimes even more. It might seem like a bit of a shocker when a new paperback winds up costing you over ¥300. They've also got a lot of other foreign language books, as well.

Address: 325 Changle Rd, near Shaanxi South Rd (长乐路325号，近陕西南路)

Phone: 5404 8728

Xinhua Bookstore (Xīnhuá Shūdiàn; 新华书店)

With branches all across Shanghai, this is primarily a Chinese bookstore, but every year their collection of English books gets bigger and bigger and the prices are quite reasonable. Look for their red and white sign with black writing.

Website: www.winxuan.com (in Chinese)

Street Book Carts

Yes, more street shopping. Some of the most popular street vendors in Shanghai will always be the book sellers. Keep an eye out for a crowd and then go peruse the giant wooden wheelbarrow's English section of shrink-wrapped books. There won't be a ton of English selections, and many of them will be of the "how to succeed in business" variety, but you can usually find a few classics and new best sellers in the mix. Prices are set by your bargaining skills and more on the weight of a book than by its content. Expect to pay between ¥10-30, depending on your choice.

Shanghai's Top 10 Souvenirs

You've scrimped and saved for months to take this trip. You've endured countless sugary drinks at the city's many ladies nights just to save a few more *jiao*. It's time to treat yourself with a classic Shanghai souvenir that will always remind you of this amazing trip.

Say Cheese!

Shanghai is home to hundreds and hundreds of photo studios where you can do a quick portrait session in period costumes (from 500 BCE royalty to a 1950s Revolutionary Guard). If you feel this is a little too touristy for you, fear not: locals (especially kids and young women) get portraits like this done maybe once a year. So go ahead, put on that *qípáo* or that Confucian robe, and strike a pose in front of the plum blossom backdrop. Your friends and family will all love the pictures.

You can also take things a step further and have those pics (or any of your own photos) printed onto T-shirts, mugs, tote bags – even blown up onto huge canvases for a fraction of what it would cost you back home.

Shanghai Paraphernalia

Shanghai is a city that is proud of its past and its landmarks. Whether it is playing cards with pictures of Old Shanghai's cigarette girls on them or a crystal model of the Oriental Pearl Tower, you can find a souvenir that will tell everyone that you were in Shanghai. One of the newest items to hit the block is a keychain-bottle opener in the shape of the International Finance Center… the skyscraper everyone lovingly refers to as "the Bottle Opener."

Go Tailor Made

Hit the Fabric Market (pg 223) or any of the city's other fine tailors and have yourself a custom-made outfit. Even if it seems steep for a souvenir, it is something that is dramatically out of reach back home. So get that "Armani" suit made or that "Prada" ball gown. Or, go crazy and play with it. Widen the lapels and get a classic zoot suit from the 1930s. A wedding dress. Michael Jackson's red leather jacket from the Thriller video.

If you've got a photo and the patience to explain it, they can sew it.

Tea Time

Tea is everywhere in China and after trying some here you might wonder how you were ever satisfied with a soggy bag on a string back home. If you know nothing about tea, don't worry, all the nice tea shops (and there are plenty on every street in the city) will offer you a tasting and a tutorial, enlightening you on the "proper" way to brew the perfect cup of tea. Whether your preferences run towards jasmine, oolong, green, or pu'er, you'll find something you love, along with all the necessary equipment and paraphernalia of cups, trays and pots.

We recommend picking up a clear glass teapot and some "flower ball" tea. These are hand-stitched, egg shaped balls of tea that unfold into a beautiful flower when they are steeped in hot water for an amazing (and delicious) surprise.

Out "Hipster" the Hipsters

Returning from Shanghai will make you the envy of the PBR community in your town. Chinglish shirts that make absolutely no sense whatsoever, lensless glasses and other ironic gems can be found in almost every corner of the city. In fact it's almost too easy… **www. accidentalchinesehipsters.tumblrcom**

Clothes, Clothes, Clothes

Who says the souvenir has to be all about Shanghai? This is your vacation, isn't it? If you're a clothes horse, go nuts! There is probably more shopping to be done in Shanghai than in any other place in the world right now. Chances are if you find a really nice shirt or dress or shoes or hat, you'll always remember where you got it, even if it doesn't say, "I ♥ SH" on it. (Note: You really can get shirts that say I ♥ SH on them.)

Be Hollywood's Worst Enemy

All around Shanghai there are still countless shops that specialize in pirated DVDs. Just about every movie you can think of is available along with boxed sets of TV shows from every nation and era and genre. Occasionally there are crackdowns, where the government puts a "stop" to this illegal behavior. In these times those same stores will only have DVDs of old public domain films and Chinese movies – until of course they guide you through a secret door into the back room and unveil the regular modern offerings as though they were a 1930s speakeasy. Be forewarned, though, some tourists have spent hard-earned souvenir money on movies only to have them confiscated when they go through customs on their return home.

Classic Propaganda

Whether it is Mao's Little Red Book or any one of the posters mass printed throughout the 20th century, there is a lot of artistic appeal in those classic images of the ideal citizen and worker. If you've got a thing for the Chairman himself, you can find images of Mao on everything from ashtrays to wristwatches where each second ticking by causes Mao to wave to the crowd.

Chug-a-lug

Báijiǔ (literally translated as "white liquor") is the original "I dare you" drink. Bring a bottle or two back home and pass it around for your friends to try and expect the standard response of, "Dude, are you serious?" Yes. Even your grandma will say that after she's tried this fiery rice (or sorghum or wheat) brew that ranges anywhere from 18% to a liver-dissolving 72%. The good kinds can cost pretty hundreds of dollars, but you can find them at your local 24-hour convenience store starting at ¥10 for a 750 ml bottle. Use caution when drinking around open flames.

Play that Funky Music…

Or classical, or jazz, depending on your style. Shanghai is home to a large number of music stores that offer well-crafted instruments for far less than you would pay back home. Violins, guitars, saxophones, trumpets – you could pretty much start your own orchestra here. A major tip is to only buy what you can already play (not something that is a gift for someone back home). This will allow you to fully test out the instrument in the store and determine if it's worth buying that electric violin or acoustic guitar. If you're happy with the sound, then great, you'll be the life of the party at every hostel and hotel across China, not to mention on the train itself. For the best shops, look around the Shanghai Conservatory of Music (Shànghǎi Yīnyuè Xuéyuàn; 上海音乐学院) at 20 Fenyang Road, near Huaihai Road (凤阳路 20 号．近淮海路), or across town on Jinling East Road near Guangxi Road (金陵路，近广西路).

Fabric Market Misadventures: Shop at Your Own Risk!

By Sam

It is something that almost every visitor does in Shanghai at least once: go to the Fabric Market for a tailor-made outfit. This is understandable, as doing the same thing back home would probably cost a month's wage or more. It's also a big selling point in a city where your average off-the-rack clothing might not fit your average Westerner in size or style.

Female friends of mine often complain about going to fake markets and being teased by the multitude of fashions all around them only to discover that the store only stocks size zero. Ask for a bigger size and they'll tell you, "Oh, one moment" and then scurry off to see if one of the neighboring stores has any in stock. Often their selection isn't much better.

For guys, the story is very much the same. Walking through a shop you might be impressed that you can find jeans for US$6, but nothing is ever that easy. After trying them on you'll have the shopkeeper happily try to convince you that having six inches of sock showing is really the style of those jeans, and that nobody really does up the top button anyway.

So it's understandable that foreigners look at the Fabric Market as a sort of a mythical Promised Land of fashion with endless opportunities. And they're not wrong, because getting exactly what you want here can often feel like a 40-year exodus through the desert, albeit with fabric bolts instead of cacti.

On my first visit to the Fabric Market I was more of an observer. It was late October and my friend had to pick up a winter coat she had ordered. I myself needed a couple of yards of cheap liner for a Halloween costume (Halloween is a big deal with the foreigners in Shanghai), so we went together. It is a confusing building with about 14 entrances and a whole maze of tiny little stalls that all sell fabric and/or custom clothing. In truth there might be a little over 50 of these shops on each floor, but because of the confusing layout and visual overload, it can feel like a lot more.

My friend had been there a couple of times before to begin the process of having her coat made, so we weren't wandering too aimlessly. She also had been wise enough to take the name card of the shop that she had chosen, so we were able to find it very easily. I was impressed. She got a heavy cashmere coat in the cut and shape she had asked for and it fit her well. I found the fabric I needed a couple of stalls over and we both left, happy with our purchases.

The next time I went was in June, when I decided to get a few short-sleeved shirts made. I found one shop that seemed to have a number of well-stitched menswear and negotiated a price for three shirts. I had bought some patterned fabric from a couple

of other stalls, so I didn't have to leave a deposit with my tailor. I did give them one of my own shirts though, so they could model the new ones in the same design.

When I returned a week later, the results were not great. I don't know what they did because all three of the shirts they made were done in slightly different cuts, even with different button placements. And all of them fit poorly, jamming into my armpits and spreading open at the collar like it was disco night. Since there didn't seem to be anything else they could do to fix them, I accepted them as is, but was not pleased.

I returned a few months later when my girlfriend needed some things made and her friend had to pick up a skirt. We went first to do this, in case any changes had to be made. She had ordered a very basic office skirt, plain beige polyester, nothing fancy. When she tried it on behind the held-up-sheet that qualified as the fitting room, you could see a big bulging bubble near the zipper. Her Chinese was excellent, so she had no trouble explaining the problem to them. "Ah," they said, "don't worry. Come back in an hour and we'll have it fixed."

An hour later we went back and she tried it on again, only to see that nothing had actually been fixed. "No," they said, "we fixed it. It's just like that." But, they agreed they would try again to make her happy. Two hours later (and believe me, two hours is a long time to kill at the Fabric Market) we returned to a very similar skirt, with a zipper that still bubbled and bulged. Now the shopkeepers were starting to get angry at my friend for being too demanding. Voices started rising and tempers started flaring. After one particularly vicious exchange the man who owned the shop grabbed the skirt from my friend and threw it on the floor.

Keep in mind that I couldn't understand anything that was being spoken. I could tell that neither party was happy, that much was obvious, but all I heard was progressively louder yelling.

My girlfriend picked the skirt up off the floor and said, "Fine, if you won't fix it, I don't want it. Give me back my deposit."

The woman running the shop scoffed at her and said, "No! You still owe me money for the fabric and for the zipper!"

Things progressed pretty quickly at that point, with the skirt being thrown around a few more times and a stack of fabric samples getting knocked over. By this point a huge crowd of tailors, shoppers and sales people had gathered to watch the action. Here was a *laowai* going toe-to-toe with one of their fellow merchants. Fortunately before things got too out of hand, a security guard came over to the stall and broke it up. He brought my girlfriend, myself, our friend and the woman up to the security office (her husband had silently vanished as soon as the security guard came in to the picture).

There we sat for the next hour while the manager of the Fabric Market sat behind his desk and acted as judge and mediator in the dispute. The woman running the shop was virulent, calling us garbage and spitting in our direction in disgust, especially when the management deemed her to be at fault. Though she had demanded that my friend pay for the skirt in full, in the end, she was required to pay my friend's deposit back. She did this at a rate of one curse per RMB, refusing to look us in the eye the entire time.

Your experience at the fabric market might be entirely different. Many people I know have had amazing results there, and continue to go back for more and more complicated clothing. However at some point in China you might very well have a similar run-in, whether it's at a restaurant, in a taxi, or at a "Western" establishment.

Many times the money at stake will be a relatively small amount. Is "the principle of the thing" worth losing a half a day and getting all worked up? Maybe. Chances are whatever you're arguing for will be something that Chinese people find equally annoying but have no voice to express. Many of them might be silently cheering you on, hoping that this will lead to a change in customer service or corporate or personal responsibility.

It will be up to you to decide if the debate is worth your time and energy. Choose your battles and know when to just give up and chalk up your loss to a "learning experience." If you can avoid any sort of comments or actions that will make your opponent "lose face," they will be more likely to concede the point to you.

But always remember that no matter what your reasons are for coming to China, you are now an official ambassador of your nation, your language, your ethnicity, etc. (Congratulations.) So how you comport yourself during these conflicts will affect how your fellow countrymen, nation and society as a whole are viewed by the Chinese people. Try not to create a negative stereotype for other foreigners to have to overcome!

Distractions

The tourist's life is exciting but tiring. Take a break from it all and enjoy the city in the way a local would: in pursuit of relaxation and simple fun. The following distractions from a stressful life are all popular with residents of Shanghai, and tourists may find them a welcome change of pace from a busy schedule of sightseeing.

Massage – Dragonfly Retreats (Yōutíng; 悠庭)

You can find foot massages all over Shanghai, but quality and cleanliness are never assured, and yes, some parlors are primarily concerned with providing "other" services. Dragonfly is a safer bet than whatever massage place you found near your hotel and has nine different locations in Shanghai, whose addresses you can find on the website. It's more expensive than what you could find elsewhere, but it's still very reasonable and completely worth it for the professionalism and atmosphere.

> Website: www.dragonfly.net.cn
> Fee: ¥125 for standard one hour massage (less for foot massage)

Blind Massage – Yilin Blind Massage (Yìlín Mángrén Ànmó; 艺林盲人按摩)

If you want a more uniquely Chinese experience, you can try this cheap and clean establishment of blind masseuses, a traditional trade for the blind in China. The massages can be a little rough (though that can be a plus for some) and the masseuses talk as they please throughout, but that's the price of authenticity and the staff is very friendly. For other blind massages, please visit **www.happymassage.com/wiki/Blind_Massage_Center_in_Shanghai**.

> Address: 1, Lane 100, Nandan East Rd, near Tianyaoqiao Rd (南丹东路100弄1号, 近天钥桥路)
> Fee: ¥68 for standard one hour massage (less for foot massage)
> Phone: 6464 3786
> Hours: 10:00 – 1:00

Korean Spa – New Star Spa

New Star is a favorite among both expats and locals. As with all Korean Spas, all you need to do is walk in the door, take off your shoes and get a wristband that has a key for your locker. Then head off to the gender-divided baths, which include multiple pools of different temperatures as well as steam and dry saunas. The real experience begins when you leave the baths, put on the orange pajamas provided to every guest, and partake in the numerous entertainments of the spa's communal area. There's a small theater showing movies throughout the day, an outdoor pool, hot rooms, foot and full body massages, snacks and drinks, a reasonably priced Korean restaurant on the upper level and individual beds outfitted with their own TV screens (these are very popular so it may be hard to find a free one). Really, New Star is designed more for fun with friends or family than peace and quiet. Bring your own book or a game to play with your group if you go, and you can spend as much of the day there as you want for ¥88. Massages and food, of course, cost extra. You can even spend the night if you show your passport at the front desk and pay a little extra, but this isn't recommended as there are often more guests than beds, which means a night on the floor.

> Address: 1900 Tianshan Rd, near Yan'an West Rd (天山路1900号. 近延安西路)
> Fee: ¥88 base charge (open 24 hours)
> Phone: 6259 7779

Cooking Classes – The Kitchen At

Nevermind that oddly-placed preposition in the title, The Kitchen At is a great little cooking school located in a beautiful lane house that caters to foreigners as well as local Chinese. Actually, the classes teach a variety of different cuisines, but there's sure to be at least two Chinese cuisine classes per week. Check on the website to see their schedule of classes. You'll have to make reservations at least two days in advance.

Address: 3/F, 20, Lane 383, Xiangyang South Rd, near Yongjia Rd (襄阳南路383弄20号 . 近永嘉路)
Fee: ¥300 for one class
Website: www.thekitchenat.com

Swimming Pool – Mandarin City Pool (Míngdūchéng Yǒngchǎng ; 名都城泳场)

The Mandarin City Pool is incredibly popular among expats for its size as well as its pool-side bar. That means that during summer weekends, you'll have to contend with quite a bit of the young and drunk to find a nice place by the pool. However, the pool is large enough that many families also attend and can comfortably find a place away from the ongoing party scene. The pool is on the grounds of a hotel complex, which makes for a pleasant lack of city noise but also means you may have to walk a bit to find it.

Address: 788 Hongxu Rd, near Huaguang Rd (虹许路788号 , 近华光路)
Fee: ¥100 adult, ¥60 child
Hours: 7:30-20:00

Theater – Shanghai Repertory Theater

The Shanghai Repertory Theater is always consistent in its variety. Shakespeare is a mainstay, but the troupe also stages avant-garde pieces, crowd pleasers, and many contemporary plays from around the world. Visit their website to see what they're offering during your visit.

Address: Ke Center for Contemporary Arts (Home Stage) – 613 Kaixuan Rd, near Yan'an West Rd (凯旋路613号 , 近延安西路)
Email: shanghai.repertory.info@gmail.com
Website: www.shanghairep.com

Bowling – Orden Bowling Alley (Ōudēng Bǎolíngqiú Guǎn; 欧登保龄球馆)

The only problem with this very popular 16-lane bowling alley is that there can be a wait for an open lane during peak times, usually on weekend evenings. However, it's open 24/7 so you can go anytime. There's a small arcade and pool tables as well, along with cheap beer, naturally.

Address: 10 Hengshan Rd, near Gao'an Rd (衡山路10号 . 近高安路)
Fee: ¥35 for a game on evenings and weekends,

else ¥16
Phone: 6474 6666

Ice Skating – Champion Rink (Guànjūn Liùbīngchǎng; 冠军溜冰场)

Located on the sixth floor of New World Department Store (新 世 界 城), this rink is about as centrally located as you can get and a favorite of the teenage set. The rink is a little small, but the facilities are well-maintained. Finding the right size of shoe will definitely be a process, but the staff is helpful and you can always just give them your shoe to serve as a reference.

Address: 68, Lane 2, Nanjing West Rd, near Xizang Middle Rd (南京西路2弄68号 . 近西藏中路)
Fee: ¥60 for two hours
Phone: 6359 6692
Hours: 10:00-22:00
Transport: Subway – Lines 1, 2, 8, People's Square (人民广场) Station

Archery – Daoshun Archery (Dàoshùn Shèjiàn Guǎn: 道顺射箭馆)

This South Korean-owned establishment is more than willing to give amateurs a few lessons in archery before shooting up the targets. The place is never too crowded, and if you go there during the late hours you'll often have the place to yourself, which means free rein over the ping pong tables, badminton court, and pool tables that are also onsite.

Address: 3/F, 699 Fuxing East Rd, near Henan South Rd (黄浦区复兴东路699号3楼,近河南南路)
Fee: ¥12 for 12 arrows
Phone: 6473 6819
Hours: 9:00-1:00

Spa Etiquette

The Chinese have a mini obsession with spas and massages. In fact, you'll spot hundreds, if not thousands of spas, massage parlors and foot massage booths during your stay here; so kick back and relax to unwind from a long day of traveling. Here are a few pointers to keep in mind while at a Chinese spa.

Types of spas

Budget – Many hair salons also advertise themselves as spas since they'll wash your hair and even give you a massage. There are also small massage parlors and foot massage booths everywhere in this country, and they're easily spotted on every corner.

Price: These lower end joints provide a decent service for a cheap price. Depending treatment and duration, expect to pay anywhere from ¥30-200.

Etiquette: These places are pretty casual and you're not expected to remove your clothing.

Mid-range – These are usually larger than the budget options and may have extra amenities such as saunas, hot tubs, steam rooms, restaurants, bars, etc. Look for the big colorful signs that say "SPA" and ask to look at their treatment list; it should be translated into English.

Price: Around ¥200-500, again depending on which treatment you choose.

Etiquette: Some of these places will require you to take off your clothes, especially if you're hopping into the hot tub (nude areas are divided by gender). They will often give you a locker to store your belongings in and will give you a robe. You may or may not leave the robe on during the massage, depending on whether it's an oil massage or not.

High-end – You can certainly find some glamorous spas out there, especially in Shanghai, Beijing and Hong Kong. They offer massages, haircuts, hot tubs, saunas, steam rooms, work out facilities, restaurants, bars, nail treatments, pedicures, makeovers, movie rooms, KTVs… whatever. You can even spend a day or two in your own room inside the compound! The treatment is top notch, the service is impeccable, and the décor is glitzy; just remember that you get what you pay for.

Price: You'll pay more than ¥500… easily!

Etiquette: Like the mid-range establishments, you'll have to be nude to use the spa, but they'll give you a locker (or room) and a robe. They may also take the robe off for a massage, depending on the treatment.

Spa tips

· You'll never be expected to tip.

· The staff should tell you what to do, but if you don't know whether to remove your clothing or not, try asking or look to see what others are doing. If you don't want to remove your clothing for a massage, just leave it on.

· For the higher end places, you may want to book in advance, especially on the weekends and holidays. Speak with your hotel concierge for reservations.

· During a massage, they'll often ask about the pressure. If you want it harder, say *zhòng yīdiǎn* (重 一点); if you want it lighter, say *qīng yīdiǎn* (轻一点).

· Beware that there are many brothels in China and they come in all shapes, sizes and price ranges. They can mirror anything from the budget to the high-end, so it may be hard to tell what is legitimate and what isn't. If they offer a service you don't want, simply decline and walk away; no harm done.

Side Trips

Despite (or because of) the city's fame, there's one aspect of Shanghai tourism that remains largely unknown to foreign tourists. Namely, the city is surrounded by others of such reputation that Chinese tourists often take an entire holiday to explore them. If you've already seen what you really wanted to see in Shanghai, you may find the best way to spend the rest of your time is taking a day or two to see one of these cities. Suzhou is the most convenient, Hangzhou the most beautiful, Nanjing the most historical, and Mt Huangshan is in a league of its own, but there are others that are of great interest. In addition, traveling to any of these cities includes the experience of seeing the countryside of the Yangtze River Delta – or at least its ever-growing urban sprawl – on one of China's high-speed trains.

A Note on Trains

Read the Transportation section on page 44 for general information about buying tickets. The following are details specific to train rides for these cities.

As with all trains, foreigners can't buy tickets online, though your hotel may be able to buy tickets for you. You could buy them through an online travel agency, but that's complicated (they'll have to buy the tickets in person, then mail them to you) and expensive since all of the places listed here have trains each day. This is true even during holidays, as these are basically commuter routes.

However, you will have to wait in line to get your tickets, especially if you plan on leaving that day to a closer destination like Suzhou, so arrive about an hour before the time of departure if you're very set on a particular time. For the longer ones like Huangshan, you may want to buy your ticket a week in advance. For more info **www.chinatrainguide.com** has specific times in English.

While train travel is by far the most convenient way to reach Shanghai's nearby destinations, we have listed a few good bus routes available when the distance isn't too great.

Sūzhōu 苏州

Nobody going to Suzhou from Shanghai fails to notice the markedly more relaxed and leisurely feel of the city. Historically one of the richest and most sophisticated cities in China, Suzhou now plays a sleepy second fiddle to Shanghai, albeit one that still maintains its historic charms in the form of its three most famous features: canals, silk, and gardens. Small waterways still thread their way beside city streets, and throughout the city proper are classical gardens that rank among the best in all of southern China, from which we have chosen the three most notable and conveniently located. The ancient silk factories that were once synonymous with the city's name are gone, but you can still see the actual process that was used for centuries at the Silk Museum. In addition, the city is surrounded by water towns. If you only have time for one daytrip outside of Shanghai, it should be to Suzhou.

 **Attractions**

Silk Museum

Chinese name: 丝绸博物馆 (Sīchóu Bówùguǎn)
Admission: ¥15
Hours: 9:00–17:00 (ticket sold until 16:30)
Website: www.szsilkmuseum.com/english
Address: 2001 Renmin Lu (人民路 2001 号)
Transport: Bus – 游 1 or 游 4, get off at Pingmen (平门) Stop

The Silk Museum is located south of the train station on Renmin Road (人民路). It has all the history, displays and artifacts at the level of quality you'd expect from a smaller Chinese museum, but it also has real silk worms eating mulberry leaves and silk weavers making silk fabric. Of course, it also has a large gift shop. Right across the street and to the south is one of Suzhou's more famous pagodas.

Suzhou Museum

Chinese name: 苏州博物馆 (Sūzhōu Bówùguǎn)
Admission: FREE
Hours: 9:00-17:00 (Tue-Sun) (admission before 16:00)
Website: www.szmuseum.com (English option)
Address: 204 Dongbei Jie (东北街 204 号)
Transport: Bus – 游 2, 112 or 202, get off at Suzhou Bowuguan (苏州博物馆) Stop

Two blocks to the west of the Silk Museum following Xibei Road is one of Jiangsu's best provincial museums. It's very well

regarded for its collections, but what really deserves mention is the building itself. It was designed by I M Pei, who is China's most famous modern architect and the creator of the glass pyramid on the Louvre. He grew up in Shanghai and had a particular love for the gardens of Suzhou, where his family had ancestral roots. The museum he designed for the city is a fascinating modern interpretation of Suzhou architecture, surrounding a pond with abstract representations of the elements of classical gardens. The museum usually has a line on weekends and holidays, but it's worth it – and it's free.

Humble Administrator's Garden

Chinese name: 拙政园 (Zhuōzhèng Yuán)
Admission: ¥50 (Oct 31-Apr 15)/¥70 (Apr 16-Oct 30)
Hours: 8:00-17:30
Recommended time for visit: 1-2 hours
Website: en.szzzy.cn
Address: 178 Dongbei Jie (东北街 178 号)
Transport: Bus – 游 1, 游 2, 游 5, 202, 313, 923, 529, 40, 78, get off at Zhuozhengyuan (拙政园) Stop, then walk east 100 m (328 ft)

Near the Suzhou museum is the town's largest classical garden, a place you could easily spend an hour in. The desired effect of a classical garden is to cultivate within its walls a miniature world of novelties, and this one contains numerous ponds, some with islands and pavilions, a hill topped by a pagoda, a pathway lined with bamboo, expansive rockeries with caves, a mandarin duck pond, glass-walled buildings, a maze of bridges, serene gardens of bonzai trees and plants, and so on. To put it bluntly, it's a ¥50-70 admission, but you get more than your money's worth.

Pingjiang Road (Píngjiāng Lù; 平江路)

This may be the most charming canal street in the entire delta region. Walk west from the Humble Administrator's Garden to the unassuming beginning of Pingjiang Road. Continuing south between houses, the street eventually runs alongside a canal and becomes lined on one side with cafes, stores, food stalls, and tea houses, all of them full of character, while the other side remains a network of canals and residences. The street is always crowded but never hectic. Gondola

rides can be had at various points on the canal, and food vendors sell a variety of local snacks. It's the best water town experience you can have without ever having to travel outside the city.

Lion Grove Garden

Chinese name: 狮子林（Shīzǐ Lín）

Admission: ¥20 (Oct 31-Apr 15); ¥30 (Apr 16-Oct 30)

Hours: 9:00-17:00

Website: www.szszl.com/en

Address: 23 Yuanlin Lu（园林路 23 号）

Recommended time for visit: 1-2 hours

Transport: Bus – 游 2, 112 or 202, get off at Suzhou Bowuguan（苏州博物馆）Stop, then walk south 300 m (984 ft)

Somewhere along Pingjiang Road you'll see a sign pointing down a street to the west that leads to this garden. Lion Grove is definitely the most unique classical garden you'll find in Suzhou. At the time of its building, taking rocks from the nearby Tai Lake and molding them into immense and intricate rockeries was something of a craze among the Chinese aristocracy. This garden took the fad to another level, and the effect is, quite frankly bizarre, almost alien. The rocks, which are porous, contorted and white, form walls and spires that make the grounds seem less like a garden than some kind of termite metropolis interspersed with human buildings and a surrounding pond.

Shiquan Street, Suzhou's bar street, is a ways south of the end of Pingjiang Road. If you take a taxi, a good cross-street to go towards is Wuqueqiao Road（乌鹊桥路）. At this intersection is a favorite expat haunt, **the Bookworm**. It's a combination café/bar/restaurant/bookstore, with a beautiful patio overlooking a canal and a surprisingly large selection of English and foreign books. A canal runs the length of Shiquan Street on its north side. Walk east from the Bookworm and you'll encounter the bars and shops that Shiquan is known for. Walk that same direction on the alley just to the north of the street and you'll find many quiet cafes with views of the canal.

Master of the Nets Garden

Chinese name: 网师园（Wǎngshī Yuán）

Admission: ¥20 (Oct 31-Apr 15); ¥30 (Apr 16-Oct 30)

Hours: 8:00-17:00

Recommended time for visit: 2 hours

Website: www.szwsy.com/en

Address: 11 Koujietou Xiang（阔街头巷 11 号）

Transport: Bus – 55 or 202 and get off at Wangshiyuan（网师园）Stop

There's a small alley that branches off from Shiquan Road called Wangshi Xiang（网师巷）that ends at this garden, which is the smallest in Suzhou, but also one of the best. The garden is a perfectly balanced succession of interconnected spaces, each defining itself with carefully wrought moments of aesthetic surprise. True for any classical garden but

especially this one, attention to the detail and order of all these finely tuned elements is rewarded with beauty.

Tiger Hill

Chinese Name: 虎丘 (Hǔ Qiū)

Admission: ¥40 (Oct 31–next Apr 15); ¥60 (Apr 16–next Oct 30)

Hours: 7:30–17:30

Recommended time for visit: 2-3 hours

Website: www.tigerhill.com/en

Address: 8 Huqiu Hill, Suzhou (苏州市虎丘山门内8号)

Transport: Bus – 游 1, 游 2, 146, 949, get off at Huqiao Stop to arrive at South Gate; or take 32, 快线 3, get off at Huqiao Stop to arrive at North Gate

The Song Dynasty Scholar Su Dongpo said, "It would be a pity if you had been to Suzhou but didn't get to visit the Tiger Hill." It was the burial place for King Hélǔ in 496 BCE, and with the construction of the 47.5 m (156 ft) octagonal Tiger Pagoda (Hǔqiū Tǎ; 虎丘塔) in 961 CE it became one of the earliest tourist attractions in the region. It is characterized by its pronounced

"lean" and has become one of the most notable features of Suzhou. The other most prominent feature is Sword Pond (Jiàn Chí; 剑池), a deep rectangular pool that is reputed to have a collection of swords buried beneath it, leading to the name. Just 5 km (3 mi) from the city center, Tiger Hill is visited by nearly 1.5 million tourists each year and is connected to the city by Shantang Canal, initially so that tourists could arrive at the mountain by boat (there are still boats taking tourists to the hill). There is also a walking path that offers a pleasant stroll to the mountain with tourist shops lining the way.

Jinji Lake

Chinese name 金鸡湖 (Jīnjī Hú)

Admission: FREE; ¥80 for Ferris wheel.

Hours: 9:30 -17:30 (Ferris wheel)

Recommended time for visit: 2-4 hours

Website: english.sipjinjilake.com

Address: Jinji Lake, Jinjihu Lu, near Xingzhou Jie (金鸡湖, 近星洲街)

Transport: Subway – Line 1 to Cultural Expo Center (文化博览中心) Station

Jinji Lake, or literally Golden Rooster Lake, is the centerpiece of the Sino-Singapore joint venture – the Suzhou Industrial Park. An artificial lake, the 1.4 km (0.9 mi) dam Ligong Di (李公堤) is where you can find a waterside leisure area with trendy nightclubs, Western restaurants and spas. Take a ride on the lakeside 120 m- (393 ft)-high Ferris wheel for a bird's-eye view of Jinji and this modern area of Suzhou. The lake also hosts a multi-media evening musical fountain show every weekend, with the tallest water columns reaching over 100 m (328 ft). Free of charge, the show takes place at Jinji Lake's West City Plaza on weekends and public holidays.

Believed to be China's last land-water gate (1355 CE), nowadays it is one of the last places in town where you can walk along Suzhou's ancient city wall. Also here are the Ruiguang Pagoda (¥6) that was constructed in the 3rd century CE, and the Gold Gate, which hasn't been restored. Boat rides are available for a water tour along the city moat.

Suzhou Opera Museum

Chinese name: 苏州昆曲博物馆 (Sūzhōu Kūnqǔ Bówùguǎn)

Admission: FREE

Hours: 10:00-17:30 (late night for certain performances)

Recommended time for visit: 2-3 hours

Address: 14 Zhangjia Xiang, near Daru Xiang (张家巷14号, 近大儒巷)

Transport: Bus – 9, 32, 68, 89, 112, 146, 178, 200, 261, 307, 518, get off at Xiangmen (相门) Stop

This city is a Chinese cultural mecca for opera. Suzhou is the home of Pintan Opera, a unique operatic style sung in the Suzhou dialect. It's typically narrated and features stories about historical romances and epic heroes. The city is also rich in Kunqu Opera, one of the oldest forms of Chinese Opera and one that influenced the famous Beijing Opera style. It's rumored to have originated in Suzhou's Kunshan suburb. Some classical gardens, such as the Lingering Garden (Liú Yuán, 留园), feature free opera performances during the afternoon in the main courtyard. Fuxi Qinguan (伏羲琴馆) offers a traditional opera show plus tea. The performers are in full makeup and elaborate ancient-style Chinese robes. The most in-depth exploration into this Chinese art-form treasure is the Suzhou Opera Museum with exhibitions on the evolution of Chinese opera styles.

🛏 Sleeping

Hostel – **Mingtown-Suzhou Youth Hostel** (Sūzhōu Míngtáng Qīngnián Lǔshè; 苏州明堂青年旅舍)

This hostel is right in the middle of Pingjianng Road and has its own nearby restaurant and bar. The location alone is enough to recommend it.

> Address: 28 Pingjiang Lu (平江路28号)
> Phone: (0512) 6581 6869

Mid-range – **Bamboo Grove Hotel** (Zhúhuī Fàndiàn; 竹辉饭店)

The hotel is about a block east of Shiquan Road and the Master of Nets Garden. It's notable for its use of traditional Suzhou architecture and has its very own Chinese Garden in the front. ¥300 and up.

> Address: 168 Zhuhui Lu (竹辉路168号)
> Phone : (0512) 6520 5601
> Website: www.bamboogrovehotelsuzhou.cn

Splurge – **Garden Hotel** (Sūzhōu Nányuán Bīn'guǎn; 苏州南园宾馆)

This hotel is on Shiquan Road and in the middle of an enormous and perfectly preserved classical garden. It has luxury and character to spare. ¥500 and up.

> Address: 99 Daichengqiao Lu (沧浪区带城桥路99号)
> Phone : (0512) 6778 6778
> Website: www.gardenhotelsuzhou.com

✈ Getting In & Out

Shanghai – Suzhou

Trains leave from Shanghai Station and Shanghai Hongqiao Station throughout the day at intervals of less than half an hour. The first train departs at 6:00 (5:56 at Hongqiao), and the last train going to Shanghai from Suzhou Station is at 22:30 (aim for the multiple 22:00 trains just to be safe).

Shanghai Railway Station to Suzhou Railway Station (¥39.5; about half an hour)

Shanghai Hongqiao Railway Station to Suzhou North Railway Station (¥24.5; about half an hour)

Shanghai Hongqiao Railway Station to Suzhou Railway Station (¥25.5; about half an hour)

Around Suzhou

"Around Suzhou" may be a little misleading since the other two water towns listed below are technically an hour or so away from Suzhou and actually lie directly in between it and Shanghai. Nonetheless, either Tongli or Zhouzhuang can be a perfect stopover destination when returning to Shanghai from Suzhou or vice versa, and they can also make great day trips from either Shanghai or Suzhou.

Tongli

Chinese name: 同里古镇 (Tónglǐ Gǔzhèn)

Admission: ¥100

Hours: 7:30- 21:30

Recommended time for visit: 1 day

Website: www.tongli.net

Location: Wujiang District (吴江区)

Transport: There are buses at Suzhou North Bus Station to Tongli that leave every 30 minutes, beginning at 7:25 and ending at 17:25 (1 hour; ¥8). From Shanghai, you can purchase a round trip bus ticket which includes admission to all of Tongli's sights for ¥130. Buses regularly depart the Shanghai Sightseeing Bus Center starting at 8:30 and take less than 2 hours.

Tongli is a nice little water town most obviously distinguished from others by its **Sex Museum** (Zhōnghuá Xìngwénhuà Bówùguǎn; 中华性文化博物馆 ; ¥20; 9:00-17:30). The museum has exhibits about sex culture through the ages in China and many artifacts that you can safely assume you won't see in any other Chinese museums. Other than that, Tongli is a bit smaller than other water towns but consequently less crowded. There is an admission fee of ¥100 for the quiet and beautiful **Old Town** (Gǔzhèn; 古 镇), which covers entrance to various small historical sites around the area.

You can see the entire city, old town, attractions and Sex Museum within a few hours, but if you want to stay the night, try the upscale choice of **Zhengfu Caotang** (正福草堂 ; address: 138-58 Xinmingqing Jie, 新明清街 138–58 号 ; phone: 0512 6332 0576; email: zfctmjkz@163.com; ¥1,380) or the budget option **Tongli International Youth Hostel** (Tónglǐ Guójì Qīngnián Lǚshè; 同理国际青年旅舍 ; address: 210 Zhuhang Jie, 竹行街210号 ; phone: 0512 6333 9311; dorms start at ¥45). Note: there is another branch of the hostel right next to Taiping Bridge.

Zhouzhuang

Chinese name: 周庄古镇 (Zhōuzhuāng Gǔzhèn)

Admission: ¥100 (7:00–16:00);¥80 (16:00–21:00)

Hours: 7:00- 21:00

Recommended time for visit: 1 day

Website: www.zhouzhuang.com (in Chinese)

Location: 38 km (23.5 mi) southeast of Suzhou city.

Transport: There are buses at Suzhou North Bus Station to Zhouzhuang leaving every 30 minutes, beginning at 7:05 and ending at 17:05. (1.5 hours; ¥17.5). From Shanghai, buses depart regularly starting at 7:00 in the morning from the Shanghai Sightseeing Bus Center (1.5 hours; ¥140 return ticket).

Zhouzhuang is one of the biggest, oldest, prettiest, and unfortunately most crowded water towns in the area. Its fame ensures there are many things to do and see, including small museums, historical sites, etc, so a comprehensive tour could take the better part of a day. This is also the best place to take a gondola ride (¥100), as the area is so large that the trip won't seem like a repeat of places you've already seen while walking. You can even take a **speed-boat ride** (¥80), which departs from Baoen Bridge (Bào'ēn Qiáo; 报恩桥) to take a tour of South Lake. Admission covers many of the attractions inside the town, including Zhang's House and Shen's House, both incredible displays of ancient Ming and Qing designed architecture.

If you need a place to crash, there is a wide selection of guesthouses to choose from, but we'd recommend the **Zhouzhuang International Youth Hostel** (Zhōuzhuāng Guójì Qīngnián Lǚshè; 周庄国际青年旅舍 ; address: 86 Beishi Jie, 北市街86号 ; phone: 0512 5720 4566; dorms start at ¥45 on weekdays and ¥100 on weekends) or, for something a little more classy and expensive, the **Zhengfu Caotang** (正福草堂 ; address: 90 Zhongshi Jie, 中市街90号 ; phone: 0512 5721 9333; rooms start at ¥480).

Hángzhōu 杭州

To understand Hangzhou, one must first know that for most of China's history, it, and not Shanghai, lied at the mouth of the Yangtze River. So it's no surprise that at one point it was the richest city in China and, at certain times, the largest city in the world, a metropolis that astonished Marco Polo with its sophistication, beauty, sheer size and wealth. Then, the harbor silted up and Hangzhou quieted down a bit, but it kept its reputation for beauty largely because of West Lake, which was famous throughout ancient China as a playground for the leisure class. Hangzhou is also the home of China's most famous type of green tea, Longjing (龙井), and the fields are not far off from West Lake. Hangzhou also offers the opportunity to hike around in something close to a wilderness setting in the form of the hills surrounding the lake. You could easily spend two days here.

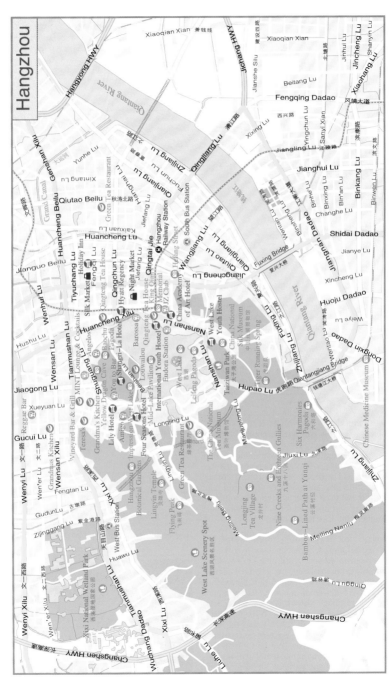

Hangzhou

Xiaoqian Xian 萧钱线

Xiaoqian Xian

Qianshang HWY

XMH Bung

Jiehong Lu

Jinhui Lu

Jincheng Lu

Shanyin Lu

Jianshe Silu

Beitang Lu

Fengqing Dadao 风情大道

Qiangyong HWY

Qiantang River

Yunhe Lu

Xintang Lu

Zhijiang Lu

Qingtang Lu

Xixing Lu

Yingchun Lu

Sanyi Xian

Zhiling Lu

Changsheng Lu

Grand Canal

Genshan Xilu

Qiutao Beilu

Jianguo Beilu

Huancheng Beilu

Green Tea Restaurant

Qiutao Lu

Jiangling Lu 江陵路

Jiangling Lu

Jiangnan Dadao

Binhe Lu

Jianghui Lu

Binxing Lu

Bin'an Lu

Binkang Lu

Binwen Lu

Hushu Lu

Wenhui Lu

Jianguo Beilu

Huancheng Lu

Tiyuchang Lu

Holiday Inn

Fenglai

Silk Market

Qingteng Tea House

Qingchun Lu

Hyatt Regency

Night Market

Hangzhou Railway Station

Qingtai Jie

Jiefang Lu

Hangyang Street

Wangjiang Lu

South Bus Station

Fuxing Bridge

Jiangcheng Lu

Xincheng Lu

Shidai Dadao

Jianye Lu

Huoju Dadao

Weiye Lu

Qiantang River

Jiangnan Dadao Wenzao Lu

Dongxin Dadao

Wensan Lu

Jiaogong Lu

Wensan Xilu

Snuguang

Tianmushan Lu

MINT Lounge & Cocktails

Angeloes

Yellow Dragon Cave

Xiaocui

Pagoda

Huancheng Xilu

Barossa

Von to Bar

Shangri-La Hotel

Louwailou

China Academy of Art Hotel

West Lake Youth Hostel

West Lake 西湖

China National Silk Museum

JZ Club

Nanshan Lu

Gucui Lu

Reggae Bar

Xueyuan Lu

Vineyard Bar & Grill

Teresa's

Grandma's Kitchen

Xixi Lu

Amy's

Impression West Lake

Lily Hotel

Four Seasons Hotel

Mid-Lake Pavilion

International Youth Hostel

Qingteng Tea House

Eudora Station

Leifeng Pagoda

Taiziwan Park

Nanshan Lu

Tiger Running Spring

Hupao Lu

Zhijiang Lu Qiantangjiang Bridge

Qiantangjiang Bridge

Wenyi Lu 文一路

Wen'er Lu 文二路

Grandmas Kitchen

Wensan Xilu

Fengtan Lu

GudunLu 古墩路

Zijinggang Lu

Hangzhou Botanical Gardens

Lingyin Temple 灵隐寺

Flying Peak

Longjing Lu

Green Tea Restaurant

Meiling Lu

The China National Tea Museum 茶叶博物馆

Longjing Tea Village 龙井村

Nine Creeks and Eighteen Gullies 九溪十八涧

Bamboo-Lined Path at Yunqi 云栖竹径

Jiuxi Lu 九溪路

Six Harmonies Pagoda 六和塔

Meiling Nanlu 梅灵南路

Chinese Medicine Museum

Zhijiang Lu

Qingqu Lu

Wenyi Xilu 文一西路

Wen'er Xilu 文二西路

West Bus Station

Huawu Lu

Tianmushan Dadao

Wuchang Dadao

Xixi National Wetland Park 西溪国家湿地公园

Xixi Lu 西溪路

West Lake Scenery Spot 西湖风景名胜区

GudunLu

Luhe Lu

Changsheng HWY

Changshen HWY 长深高速

Wuchang Dadao 长深高速

Attractions

West Lake (Xī Hú; 西湖)

West Lake has been famous for its beauty for centuries; you could call it one of the world's oldest tourist attractions. It inspired countless poems and works of art in ancient China and is especially important as a much-replicated ideal of Chinese garden design. It was made a **UNESCO World Heritage Site** in 2011, and was described as having influenced garden design within China as well as Japan and Korea. Said to reflect an idealized fusion between humans and nature, the lake was continuously modified over the years in order to create a harmonious landscape filled with both natural and man-made features. Now, the entire area is like one enormous classical garden, with numerous parks, pagodas, villas, pavilions, three man-made causeways (Sūdī [苏堤], Báidī [白堤], and Yánggōng Dī [杨公堤]), and artificial islands. Tourist cruises around the lake are one way you could take it all in, but even better is to travel around its perimeter and discover for yourself what this mesmerizing lake has to offer.

Before you begin your circumnavigation of West Lake, which can take a full day, you need to decide: walk or bike? Walking requires no preparation, but biking is almost as easy, thanks to Hangzhou's incredibly extensive bike rental network. To get a card (which requires showing your passport), go to **Orioles Singing in Willows Park** (Liǔlàng Wényīng; 柳浪闻莺) near the West Lake Museum on the eastern side of the lake. They should also give you a map that shows where all the other rental stations are. There are too many gardens, small museums

and restaurants around West Lake to list, so take some time to explore whatever seems interesting on your trip. Also remember that the east side of the lake is more developed and even features a Xintiandi-style cluster of restaurants, so you might want to plan your trip to end there for dinner. Boat rides are available on the east side of the lake.

Leifeng Pagoda

Chinese name: 雷峰塔 (Léifēng Tǎ)
Admission: ¥40
Hours: 8:00-17:30
Recommended time for visit: 2 hours
Address: 15 Nanshan Lu (南山路 15 号)
Transport: Bus – K4, K504, K514 or Y1, 2, 3, 6, 7 and 9, get off at Jingsi (净寺) Stop

An eclectic mix of modernity and mysticism, Leifang Pagoda, situated next to West Lake, is a replica building set on the ruins of the original. It has an escalator and lifts which take you to the most spectacular views around. If on the way down you fancy a tale or two, then check out the drawings and calligraphy that adorn the walls (they explain the legend of how Leifang fell down). History actually has it that the temple collapsed in 1924 because the locals were stealing bricks! A tall tale, but a historical one too.

Lingyin Temple

Chinese name: 灵隐寺 (Língyǐn Sì)
Admission: ¥30 for temple; ¥45 for Flying Peak
Hours: 7:00-18:00
Website: www.lingyinsi.org (English available)
Address: 1 Fayun Nong (法云弄 1 号)
Transport: Bus – 7/k7, K807, K837, Y1, Y2, Y13, get off at Lingyin (灵隐) Stop

One of the ten most famous Buddhist temples of China, Lingyin Temple was founded in 328 CE as one of the most important monasteries in Hangzhou. Once upon a time under the Kingdom of Yue (907-978), there were more than 70 halls and 18 pavilions inhabited by more than 3,000 monks. Today☐ it is still an active temple, and though many of its original halls are gone (the temple now houses only five), it still retains a good deal of its magnificence through giant statues of heavenly kings, arhats, intricately painted ceilings and forests boasting many ancient trees.

Flying Peak (Fēilái Fēng; 飞 来 峰) is an amazing limestone peak located at the front of Lingyin Temple. Hundreds of Buddhist sculptures are carved into the rocks dating back to the 10th and 14th centuries.

Many more carvings can be found in the caves and grottos nearby. Some of the best are in the main cave, which is dedicated to the goddess of mercy and bears a crack in the ceiling that reaches up to the surface. If you are lucky then you may see a sliver of sunlight known as the "one thread of heaven" peaking in.

Six Harmonies Pagoda

Chinese name: 六和塔 (Liùhé Tǎ)
Admission: ¥10
Hours: 7:00-17:30
Address: 84 Zhijiang Lu (西湖区之江路 84 号)
Transport: Bus – 190, 202, 280, 291, 308, 354, 4, 504, 808, Y5, get off at Liuheta Stop

On the northern shore of the Qiantang River stands a charming octagonal pagoda known as Liuhe Temple. First built in 970 CE, the temple today provides the most spectacular views of Hangzhou.

Hefang Street

Chinese name: 河坊街 (Héfāng Jiē)
Address: Hefang Jie
Transport: Bus – 8 or 155

For those wanting to take home a little piece of China, a trip to Hefang Street, a long pedestrian street, is a must. This colorful street is lined door to door with shops selling what Hangzhou is most renowned for: silk scarves, paper cuttings, chop sticks, personalized calligraphy and sesame snacks.

Not only renowned for modern knick-knacks, Hefang Street can also give you a taste of what Hangzhou was like in the days of the Song Dynasty, particularly at the Museum of Traditional Chinese Medicine. Situated in a side alleyway off of Hefang Jie, this fascinating place showcases the area's medicinal history and still serves as an old-style pharmacy selling modern day prescriptions.

Museum of Traditional Chinese Medicine

Chinese name: 中药博物馆 (Zhōngyào Bówùguǎn)
Admission: ¥10
Hours: 9:00-17:00
Address: 95 Dajing Xiang, Hefang Jie(上城区大井巷 95 号)
Transport: Bus – 8/K8, get off at Gulou (鼓楼) Stop

The Museum of Traditional Chinese Medicine is the only state-level professional

Chinese medicine museum in the country. It is seated at the foot of Wu Hill in the restored Hu Qingyu Tang, an ancient Chinese pharmacy opened in 1874 and regarded as the "King of Medicine" by the people of southern China. Hu Xueyan, the first boss of the pharmacy, was not only a successful businessman, but also a high-class official in the imperial court. In China's feudal society, people doing business were widely looked down upon, whereas state officials were highly respected. Many tourists go to the Hu Qingyu Tang Museum to not only appreciate the treasures of Chinese medicine, but also to admire its magnificent architectural complexities and to learn more about Hu's legendary stories.

The museum takes up two floors. The second floor is dedicated to the history of Huqingyu Tang and Chinese Medicine, and through pictures and artifacts you will learn all there is to know about Traditional Chinese Medicine. The ground floor displays a variety of specimens – there are jars preserved with all sorts of concoctions and you can witness pills being moulded and herbs being sliced in preparation for prescriptions.

China National Silk Museum

Chinese name: 中国丝绸博物馆 (Zhōngguó Sīchóu Bówùguǎn)
Admission: FREE
Hours: 9:00-17:00
Website: www.chinasilkmuseum.com (English available)
Address: 73-1Yuhuangshan Lu (皇山路 73-1 号)
Transport: Bus – 12, 42, 271, Y3, get off at Sichou Bowuguan (丝绸博物馆) Stop

Hangzhou, or the House of Silk as it is otherwise known, is home to the China National Silk Museum, located south of West Lake.

It has four main halls for you to weave in and out of, and each displays a number of informative and interesting exhibits on the history and production of silk.

There are a number of ancient silk fabrics on show, some of which are over 2,000 years

old. The museum also displays all kinds of traditional looms, and inside the workshop you will find two modern versions to experiment with.

Weaving and dyeing demonstrations are given by experts, so if you want to experience the many processes of silk making first-hand, don't worm yourself out of a visit to Hangzhou's National Silk Museum.

Tea Museum

Chinese name: 茶叶博物馆 (Cháyè Bówùguǎn)
Admission: FREE
Hours: 8:30- 16:30; closed on Mon
Website: english.teamuseum.cn
Address: 88 Longjing Lu (龙井路 88 号)
Recommended visiting time: 1 hour
Transport: Bus – K27 or 游 3, get off at Shuangfeng (双峰) Stop

The Tea Museum resides on the southwest side of West Lake in the middle of a sea of tea fields; the aroma alone is enough to recommend the place. It has exhibits on tea history and tea-making techniques, and it also has enormous bricks of compacted tea molded into various shapes and a spacious and beautiful design that's a pleasure to walk through. However, if you accept the free tea tasting that's offered to you by pretty girls roaming throughout the museum, be advised that you'll be subjected to soft but insistent encouragement to buy things from a tea shop when the tasting is over.

Longjing Tea Fields & Hiking in the Western Section (Lóngjīng Chátián; 龙井茶田)

Just behind the Tea Museum, take a hike up the hills for one of the most amazing experiences in Hangzhou. Stretching many kilometers to the west of the lake is an area made up largely of wilderness, with tea fields, small temples and farming villages hidden amongst its hills. It's hard to get lost for long, as a road and a bus stop are never too far off, but you should probably buy a

hiking map from one of West Lake's many tourist stalls to guide you. Notable locations include the actual "**Dragon Well**" (龙井) for which Longjing tea is named and numerous villages where you can drink tea fresh from the fields. Remember to find a hill close to West Lake for a picture: the view of West Lake with Hangzhou city in the background is stunning.

Guo Villa

Chinese name: 郭庄 (Guō Zhuāng)

Admission: ¥10

Hours: 8:00- 17:00

Transport: Take bus 游 1 or 游 2 and get off at Hangzhou Huapu (杭州花圃)

Of the many little places to take a rest around West Lake, this one deserves special mention. The villa has a very nice classical garden, and it also has a patio shaded by trees that looks out on the whole of the western part of the lake. After exploring the garden, sit down here for some tea or a lunch and enjoy the serenity of the surroundings.

Baoshi Mountain (Bǎoshí Shān; 宝石山) & Guapai Mountain (Guàpái Shān; 挂牌山)

These two are on the north side of West Lake and present an hour or so of non-strenuous hiking. The views are beautiful: caves and historical sites are scattered around, and there's a particularly eerie abandoned restaurant on one of the paths. It's a nice experience of a little slice of wilderness for those who don't want to spend a whole day lost in the western stretches of the scenic area. Signs are posted at every fork in the path, so getting lost is impossible, and a map is unnecessary.

🛏 Sleeping

Hostel – Hangzhou Hofang International Youth Hostel (Hángzhōu Héfāng Qīngnián Lǚshè; 杭州荷方青年旅舍)

It's very close to West Lake in Hangzhou's historic district and very clean and professional.

> Address: 67 Dajing Xiang, Shangcheng District (上城区河坊街大井巷 67 号)
> Phone: (0571) 8707 9290; 8706 3299
> Email: lotushostel2010@gmail.com

Midrange – Shenanbei Boutique Hotel (Shěnánběi Jīngpǐn Jiǔdiàn; 舍南北精品酒店)

A very cute and perfectly located little hotel in the southwest nature area of West Lake. It's run by expats.

> Address: 87 Manjuelong Lu (满觉陇路四眼井 87 号 , near Hangzhou Zoo)
> Phone: (0571) 8998 8558
> Website: www.shenanbei.com.cn

Splurge – **Hyatt Regency Hangzhou** (Hángzhōu Kǎiyuè Jiǔdiàn; 杭州凯悦酒店)

All the amenities you'd expect from a luxury Hyatt hotel with great views of West Lake.

Address: 28 Hubin Lu (湖滨路 28 号)
Phone: (0571) 8779 1234
Website: www.hangzhou.regency.hyatt.com

Getting In & Out

Shanghai – Hangzhou

Trains leave every 30 minutes from Shanghai Hongqiao Station starting at 6:38 every. The last train to Shanghai from Hangzhou is at 21:10.

Only take the high-speed D and G trains. Other trains beginning with T or K might take you five hours or more.

Shanghai Hongqiao Railway Station to Hangzhou Railway Station (¥77.5; about 1 hour)

Shanghai Hongqiao Railway Station to Hangzhou East Railway Station (¥73; about 1 hour)

Suzhou – Hangzhou

Trains to Hangzhou from Suzhou Railway Station begin at 8:08 and end at 19:10.

Suzhou Railway Station to Hangzhou Railway Station (¥117.5; about 2 hours)

Suzhou Railway Station to Hangzhou East Railway Station (¥72.5; about 2 hours)

Around Hangzhou

If you just can't get enough of those picturesque water towns and you've already marked all those in Shanghai and Jiangsu off your list, don't worry, Zhejiang has two off-the-beaten-track ones that will quench your desire.

Wūzhèn 乌镇

Like the other water towns of the region, Wuzhen rose to prominence about 1,300 years ago after the construction of the Grand Canal, becoming an important hub in the cross-continental silk trade. After renovation and modernization efforts, some of this history and charm can still be found in the hundreds of little wooden houses and stone-clad buildings that stand proud in this up-market town. These days it's a bit touristy but still packs a ton of charm, making it a great stop en route from Shanghai to Hangzhou or vice versa. Alternatively, it can be a fun day trip from either Shanghai or Hangzhou.

There are two parts to this town: the east and the west. From the east you can either take a free shuttle bus or a short ride on a wooden gondola. While the latter will set you back ¥80 per boat, it will give you a quick ride through history whilst witnessing the locals living their life in modern day society. Following the boat ride, a 20-minute walk or a fun ride on a tricycle through the back streets is all you need to take you to the best part of town.

The west has a very modern ticket office which also serves as a booking center for many of the guest houses inside. Like stepping back in time, leaving the ticket hall will deposit you in an ancient town full of splendor and wonder. **Xizha Street** (Xīzhā Dàjiē; 西栅大街) greets you as you depart the free wooden ferry boat. It's a street renowned for numerous guest houses, restaurants, spas and museums.

At the end of this street you will find **Bar Street,** which is made up of a row of bars sitting on the water's edge. From the outside, these bars appear as tranquil as the water that flows beneath, but at night they come alive, playing loud music and flashing with neon lights.

Crossing any one of the bridges in this town takes you to another long stretch of charming architecture and beauty; parallel streets adorned with little boutiques selling everything from hand lacquered musical boxes to tie-dyed children's clothes are common.

A truly remarkable place that shines as bright at night as it does during the day, Wuzhen is decked with lanterns and fairy lights to make it a magical place. Staying the night here is really a necessity if you want to appreciate its true splendor, and any one of the guesthouses in the West Wuzhen Scenic area will offer you a warm and welcoming place to rest your head while also guaranteeing you the best waterside views around.

Getting In & Out

From Shanghai South Bus Station (Shànghǎi Chángtú Kèyùn Nánzhàn; 上 海 长 途 客 运 南 站) on 666 Shilong Rd (石龙路 666 号), buses depart every hour (¥46; 90 minutes; 11 shifts daily).

Wuzhen

Nanxun

Nánxún 南浔

For a side trip from a side trip, travel 20 km (12.5 mi) from Wuzhen to the quaint town of Nanxun. It's much smaller than many other water towns and has archetypical small alleys, traditional white-washed houses and, yes, lots of winding canals. But it's different in the sense that alongside Chinese buildings stand European-designed ones; a mixture of Eastern and Western structures around whispering streams that makes for a truly relaxing day.

There are many ancient courtyard houses around town, and some have even opened their doors to tourists as hotels. Nanxun never gets too packed, so it should be easy to find accommodations.

Getting In & Out

Ten buses a day leave Hangzhou's North Bus Station (¥40); and there are numerous buses connecting Wuzhen and Nanxun. Regular buses (¥47; 2.5 hours) also connect Shanghai and Nanxun daily.

Pǔtuó Shān 普陀山

Admission: ¥160 (Feb-Nov); ¥140 (Dec-Jan)
Website: www.putuoshan.gov.cn (in Chinese)

On a small island only 5 km (3 mi) from Zhoushan Islands (Zhōushān Qúndǎo; 舟山群岛) stands one of China's four sacred mountains. A pilgrimage site for more than 1,000 years, Mount Putuo (aka Putuo Shan) became the center of Chinese Buddhist of Guanyin (the goddess of mercy) during the Tang Dynasty. As such a sacred mountain, it welcomes millions of people for the celebration of the birth of Guanyin every year in February, June and September.

The peak of Mount Putuo can only be reached by stone steps – 1,088 to be precise. This spiritual staircase takes you on a journey to more than 30 ancient Buddhist temples and monasteries, where today monks and nuns still come from all over China and the world to live and practice Buddhism. Some of the mountain's most famous sights include:

Beaches – There are two near the main hotels

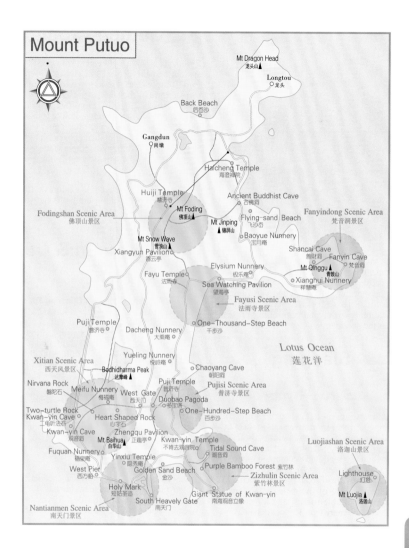

Mount Putuo

Mt Dragon Head
龙头山

Longtou
龙头

Back Beach
后岙沙

Gangdun
岗墩

Haicheng Temple
海澄禅院

Huiji Temple
慧济寺

Ancient Buddhist Cave
古佛洞

Mt Foding
佛顶山

Fanyindong Scenic Area
梵音洞景区

Fodingshan Scenic Area
佛顶山景区

Mt Jinping
锦屏山

Flying-sand Beach
飞沙岙

Mt Snow Wave
雪浪山

Baoyue Nunnery
宝月庵

Xiangyun Pavilion
香云亭

Shancai Cave
善财洞

Fanyin Cave
梵音洞

Elysium Nunnery
极乐庵

Mt Qinggu
青鼓山

Fayu Temple
法雨寺

Sea Watching Pavilion
望海亭

Xianghui Nunnery
祥慧庵

Fayusi Scenic Area
法雨寺景区

Puji Temple
普济寺

Dacheng Nunnery
大乘庵

One-Thousand-Step Beach
千步沙

Lotus Ocean
莲花洋

Xitian Scenic Area
西天风景区

Yueling Nunnery
悦岭庵

Chaoyang Cave
朝阳洞

Bodhidharma Peak
达摩峰

Puji Temple
普济寺

Pujisi Scenic Area
普济寺景区

Nirvana Rock
磐陀石

Meifu Nunnery
梅福庵

West Gate
西天门

Duobao Pagoda
多宝塔

Two-turtle Rock
二龟听法石

Kwan-yin Cave
观音洞

Heart Shaped Rock
心字石

One-Hundred-Step Beach
百步沙

Kwan-yin Cave
观音洞

Zhengqu Pavilion
正趣亭

Mt Baihua
白华山

Kwan-yin Temple
不肯去观音院

Luojiashan Scenic Area
洛迦山景区

Fuquan Nunnery
福泉庵

Yinxiu Temple
隐秀庵

Tidal Sound Cave
潮音洞

West Pier
西万船

Golden Sand Beach
金沙

Purple Bamboo Forest
紫竹林

Lighthouse
灯塔

Zizhulin Scenic Area
紫竹林景区

Mt Luojia
洛迦山

Holy Mark
短姑圣迹

Giant Statue of Kwan-yin
南海观音立像

South Heavenly Gate
南天门

Nantianmen Scenic Area
南天门景区

---

on Putuoshan: One-Hundred-Step Beach (Bǎibù Shā; 百步沙) and One-Thousand-Step Beach (Qiānbù Shā; 千步沙). One-Hundred-Step beach gets a little more crowded, but has better facilities and activities (like banana boating), while One-Thousand-Step Beach is less touristy with little infrastructure.

Fayu Temple (Fǎyǔ Sì; 法雨寺 ; ¥5) – At the foot of Foding Hill (Fódǐng Shān, 佛顶山), just north of the One Thousand Step Beach.

Huiji Temple (Huìjì Sì; 慧济寺 ; ¥5) – Near

the top of Foding Shan. You can either take the cable car (¥40) or do as the pilgrims do and climb to the top (it takes about one hour for the average person). Ironically, there is some old PLA army equipment dotting the path up this holy mountain, a good contradiction that can only be seen in China.

Puji Temple (Pǔjì Sì; 普济寺 ; ¥5) – In the middle of the island, it's the most accessible and famous temple on Putuo Shan. Every morning around sunrise you can see the

monks chant, but many visitors flock to the scene, so get there early (around 4:00 or 4:30 in the morning) to get a good view. Luckily, around Puji there are many cafes and restaurants, so consider grabbing breakfast after the ceremony.

Sleeping

Haishan Xianguan Inn (Hǎishān Xiān'guǎn Kèzhàn; 海山仙馆客栈)

A small guesthouse situated opposite a fishing port that sports views of the sea, boats and luscious green mountains, this fine inn is run by a very friendly staff and the owner is extremely kind and accommodating. They also serve up some delicious local dishes as well as an array of fresh fish. It will cost ¥300 to sleep in one of their clean, modern and very comfortable rooms, and a hearty meal will cost no more than ¥30 per person.

Address: 46 Liwan Cun (朱家尖镇里湾村 46 号)
Phone: (0580) 603 5207

Putuoshan Hotel (Pǔtuóshān Dàjiǔdiàn; 普陀山大酒店)

Situated in an excellent location for nearby shops and restaurants, this is a well-looked-after hotel offers guests a comfortable stay. Rooms start at ¥635.

Address: 93 Meicen Lu (普陀山梅岑路 93 号)
Phone: (0580) 609 2828

Getting Around

Putuo Shan has a convenient transportation system and the central bus stop is close to Puji Temple. Bus 1 takes you to the main ferry terminal, then afterwards south to the giant statue of Guanyin. From there you can walk to the Guanyin Temple, Purple Bamboo Temple and the Holy Mark. Bus 2 goes to the same ferry terminal but then goes north to the Fayu Temple. From Fayu Temple you can get another bus to the ropeway up to the Huiji Temple.

Putuoshan is small enough to explore on foot, and you can stroll along the paths between the temples, beaches and the village.

✈ Getting In & Out

By Bus

Take the bus from Shanghai Huangpu Tourist Station near Nanpu Bridge (address: 1588 Waima Rd – 外马路 1588 号 ; phone: 021 3376 5128; trasport: Subway Line 4, Nanpu Bridge Station, Exit 2, walk south about 80 m [262 ft]). Buses depart at 7:00, 8:00, 9:00, 10:20, 13:00, 14:00, 15:00, 16:00, 17:00. The journey takes 4.5-5 hours and costs ¥138.

By Ferry

Take the bus from Shanghai Huangpu Tourist Station at 8:00. An hour and a half later it arrives at a wharf in Luchaogang (芦 潮 港) where a hoverferry will take you to Putuo Shan. The ticket is ¥258.

A second combination, which is cheaper but longer (about 13 hours, departing at 19:30, and arriving next day at 8:00), leaves from Wusong Port (吴淞港 ; address: 251 Songbao Rd – 淞宝路 251 号). Price varies from ¥139 (4th class) to ¥499 (VIP).

Nánjīng 南京

Nanjing has a singular place in Chinese history for many reasons. Its name means "Southern Capital" and it has been the capital for many Chinese rulers, often because Beijing ("Northern Capital") was controlled by another faction. The most recent example of this was at the beginning of the 20th century, when Sun Yat-sen made Nanjing the capital of the Republic of China since Beijing was still possessed by the Qing Dynasty. It would remain the capital of General Chiang Kai-shek's Republic until World War II, when it was captured by the Japanese and underwent one of the greatest atrocities of the war, the Nanjing Massacre. Nanjing was also the capital of the Taiping Heavenly Kingdom, the product of a pseudo-Christian revolt that may be one of the oddest chapters in China's history. Now it leads a quieter existence as the provincial capital of Jiangsu Province. Remnants and memorials of these events exist throughout the city, and seeing them all could require a multi-day tour.

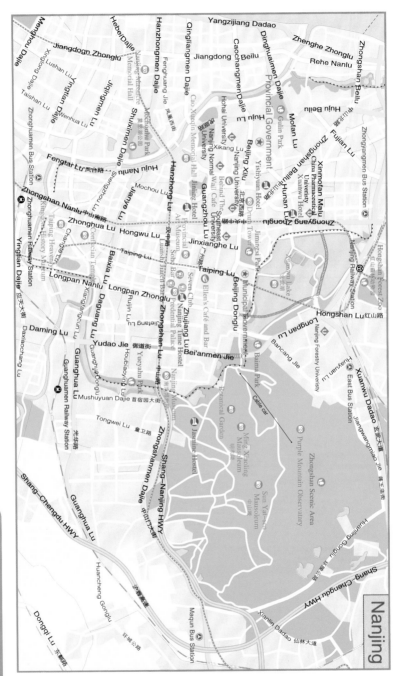

Nanjing

254

Attractions

Sun Yat-sen Mausoleum

Chinese name: 中山陵 (Zhōngshān Líng)
Admission: FREE
Hours: 8:30- 17:00; closed Mon
Recommended time for visit: 2-3 hours
Website: en.zschina.org.cn
Address: 7 Shixiang Lu (中山门外石象路 7 号)
Transport: Subway – Line 2, get off at Xiamafang (下马坊) Station

Sun Yat-sen was the George Washington of China's Republic and the destroyer of the Qing Dynasty. He's the only man that is venerated by every Chinese no matter what country they live in or political affiliation they subscribe to, and his mausoleum in Nanjing is fit for an emperor and surrounded by an enormous scenic area with many other attractions. Come here and brace yourself for the crowds - and the glory. You could spend hours in the scenic area, but one attraction you don't want to miss is the **Purple Mountain Observatory** (Zǐjīnshān Tiānwéntái; 紫金山天文台), which is fully functioning and contains some very cool ancient Chinese astronomical instruments. As if that isn't enough, just to the south of Sun Yat-sen's mausoleum is the mausoleum complex for the emperor who founded the Ming Dynasty, called the **Ming**

Xiaoling Mausoleum (Míngxiào Líng; 明孝陵). It's as grand as you'd expect.

Presidential Palace

Chinese name: 总统府 (Zǒngtǒng Fǔ)
Admission: ¥40
Hours: 8:00-17:00
Recommended time for visit: 2-3 hours
Website: www.njztf.cn (in Chinese)
Address: 292 Dong Changjiang Lu (东长江路 292 号)
Transport: Bus – 29, 304, 44, 65 or 95 and get off at Zongtongfu (总统府) Stop

A few blocks southwest of this scenic area is the former seat of the republican government and Taiping Kingdom. The massive complex is now a modern history museum with some great artifacts of the Republican era. A few blocks east are the remains of the Ming Palace, which was the model for Beijing's Forbidden City.

City Wall (Chéng Qiáng; 城墙)

The Nanjing City Wall was for most of its history the largest city wall in the world. It still stands today, and there are multiple gates along it that you can climb, usually after paying a fee. However, you can't walk along the wall itself in most parts, so you might just want to take in its enormity for free on the west or south side of the very beautiful **Xuanwu Lake** (Xuánwǔ Hú; 玄武湖).

Nanjing Massacre Memorial Hall

Chinese name: 侵华日军南京大屠杀遇难同胞纪念馆 (Qīnhuá Rìjūn Nánjīng Dàtúshā Yùnàn Tóngbāo Jì'niàn'guǎn)

Admission: FREE

Hours: 8:30- 16:30; closed Mon

Recommended time for visit: 1-2 hours

Website: www.nj1937.org/english

Address: 418 Shuiximen Dajie (水西门大街 418 号)

Transport: Subway – Line 2, get off at Yunjin Rd (云锦路) Station

The historical event that looms largest in Chinese memory whenever the word "Nanjing" is mentioned is the mass slaughter and rape of Chinese civilians by Japanese soldiers in World War II. It remains one of the most contentious issues between Japan and China today; denial that the massacre was large enough to merit the term or even that it happened at all is still a depressingly common opinion in some parts of Japanese society, and the Chinese government has been accused of inflating the death toll for propaganda purposes (the memorial unquestioningly uses the official Chinese estimate of 300,000 deaths). Sane voices on both sides agree that it was one of the great atrocities of World War II, and the Nanjing Memorial has become something of a pilgrimage of remembrance for many in China. This makes the memorial one of the most heavily attended attractions in Nanjing.

Taiping History Museum

Chinese name: 太平天国历史博物馆 (Tàipíng Tiānguó Lìshǐ Bówùguǎn)

Admission: ¥30 (¥70 at night)

Hours: 8:00- 23:00

Recommended time for visit: 2 hours

Website: www.njtptglsbwg.com (in Chinese)

Address: 128 Zhanyuan Lu (瞻园路 128 号)

Transport: Bus – 2, 16, 26 or 33, get off at Changlelu (长乐路) Stop

In the middle of the 19th century, the son of poor peasants declared himself the son of God and brother of Jesus, then lead a rebellion against the Qing government that would become the bloodiest civil war in world history, culminating in the founding of the "Taiping Heavenly Kingdom," which at its height ruled over more than 30 million people. That doesn't even begin to describe the profound strangeness of the Taiping Rebellion, but this small museum offers a nice summary of the events, aided by many historical artifacts and documents.

Confucian Temple

Chinese name: 夫子庙 (Fūzǐ Miào)

Admission: ¥30

Hours: 8:30- 22:00

Website: www.njfzm.net (English option)

Address: Zhonghua Rd on north bank of Qinhuai River (秦淮河北岸中华路)

Recommended time to visi: 2 hours

Transport: Bus – 4, 7, 40 or 44, get off at Fuzimiao (夫子庙) Stop

Nanjing's Confucian Temple and its surroundings are less a historical site than a tourist district. The temple used to hold the massive testing grounds for provincial level imperial examinations, but the current, smaller complex was completely reconstructed in 1984 after its destruction in World War II. Now, this crowded tourist center is filled with souvenir shops, outdoor restaurants, tea rooms and the like. The area is divided by a confluence of canals, and gondola rides are also available throughout the day. It may not be the appropriate place to serenely contemplate the vagaries of Confucian thought, but it is full of energy and fun, and the best time to visit may be at night, when you can eat dinner outside surrounded by the colorful lights that festoon the entire district. The temple is located on the southern side of town next to Zhonghua Gate (Zhōnghuá Mén; 中华门) and the Taiping History Museum.

🛏 Sleeping

✈ Getting In & Out

Hostel – **Jasmine International Youth Hostel** (Nánjīng Guójì Qīngnián Lǚshè; 南京国际青年旅舍)

Well-located, stylish, and clean, it's one of the better known hostels in the city.

Address: 7 Hequn Xincun, near 83 Shanghai Lu (上海路 83 号合群新村七号)
Phone: (025) 8330 0517

Midrange – **Sheraton Nanjing Kingsley Towers** (Nánjīng Jīnsīlì Xǐláidēng Jiǔdiàn; 南京金丝利喜来登酒店)

Right in the city center and boosting all the quality you'd expect from an international hotel.

Address: 169 Hanzhong Lu (汉中路 169 号)
Phone: (025) 8666 8888
Website: www.starwoodhotels.com

Splurge – **Kayumanis Nanjing Private Villa & Spa (**Nánjīng Xiāngzhānghuápíng Wēnquán Dùjià Biéshù; 南京香樟华苹温泉度假别墅)

This hotel is a bit far from the city center, but that only means its closer to more scenic landscapes. It has the feel of a Pacific Island getaway, and the free-standing villas are as luxurious as they are expensive.

Address: 12 Wenquan Lu, Tangshan Town (江宁区汤山街道温泉路 12 号 , close to Meiquan Lu, 美泉路)
Phone: (025) 8410 7777
Email: nanjing@kayumanis.com

Shanghai – Nanjing

Trains leave from Shanghai Hongqiao and Shanghai Station about every 15 minutes (sometimes longer from Shanghai Station). Nanjing Station and Nanjing South Station are both conveniently located and linked by a metro, so get a ticket to either one. Trains begin at 6:15 at Shanghai Station and 6:30 at Hongqiao. The last train from Nanjing South to Hongqiao is at 22:00.

Shanghai Hongqiao Railway Station to Nanjing South Railway Station (¥134.5, 100 minutes)

Shanghai Railway Station to Nanjing Railway Station (¥139.5; 100 minutes)

Suzhou – Nanjing

Trains start at 6:56 and end at 20:52 at Suzhou North Railway Station.

Suzhou North Railway Station to Nanjing South Railway Station (¥64.5 / ¥99.5; 1 hour and 15 minutes / 50 minutes)

Hangzhou – Nanjing

Trains start at 6:45 and end at 21:06 at Hangzhou East Railway Station.

Hangzhou East Railway Station to Nanjing South Railway Station (¥117.5; about 100 minutes)

Wúxī 无锡

It's known as "Little Shanghai," even thought this city of five million doesn't even come close to competing with Shanghai in... well, just about anything. In fact, Wuxi is nowhere near as famous as the other cities on this list, but it lies on the banks of Tai Lake, the large body of water that dominates the Yangtze delta region. Apart from its booming economy and constant development, Wuxi has some lovely canals scattered around town, a few pleasant parks and one incredibly gigantic Buddha. If you need a stopover in between Nanjing and Shanghai, put Wuxi on your docket and maybe you'll really end up liking this little big city.

Attractions

When the various sections of the Grand Canal were connected in the 6th century CE, it became the largest artificial river in the world, a title it still retains, stretching from Beijing to Hangzhou. It also runs right through Wuxi, and the local government has recently made an effort to build up a tourist area around it. The best place to experience the canal is near the Qingming Bridge (Qīngmíng Qiáo; 清明桥), not far from where the ticket stands for tourist cruises up the canal can be purchased.

Tai Lake (Tài Hú; 太湖)

Tai Lake is massive, and its adjacent scenic area is too. You could walk for hours along the banks that are closest to Wuxi, but a better way to tour the lake would be to first see **Li Garden** (Lí Yuán; 蠡园), the premier classical garden in the area, then walk a short distance to the east to find the main dock for tourist cruises. Besides being a nice way to see the lake in comfort, some of the cruises also go to the following two attractions, which are a ways away.

Three Kingdoms City

Chinese name: 三国城 (Sānguó Chéng)
Admission: ¥90 (through ticket of ¥150 including Shuihu Cheng – 水浒城)
Hours: 7:30-18:00
Recommended time for visit: 1 hour
Website: www.ctvwx.com (in Chinese)
Address: 1 Dafuqitang Lu (大浮漆塘路 1 号无锡影视中心内)
Transport: Bus – 82 and get off at Sanguo Cheng (三国城) Stop

This theme park consists of a large reconstruction of an ancient Chinese city whose main draw is a film set where many historical costume dramas are filmed for television. As you'd expect, the architecture is not exactly historically authentic, but it is suitably entertaining. The park has many activities that resemble a Renaissance Fair, though obviously this is a completely different slice of idealized history. There are historical battle reenactments throughout the day, and some actual theme park rides as well. Two other film set theme parks are adjacent to Three Kingdoms City, and you can buy combined tickets if one really isn't enough for you.

Lingshan Great Buddha

Chinese name: 灵山大佛 (Língshān Dàfó)
Admission: ¥120
Hours: 7:00- 17:00
Recommended time for visit: 2 hours
Transport: Take bus 88 and get off at the terminal Lingshan Shengjing (灵山胜境) Stop

First and foremost, there's a big Buddha. The statue is more than 80 m (262 ft) tall and one of the largest in China, but it should be mentioned that the correspondingly large temple complex where this Buddha is located resides a good deal to the west of the other attractions, across the lake. Also worth noting is an enormous and ornate hall built on the grounds in 2006, which doesn't seem to have much purpose beyond being an object of amazement for tourists.

Sleeping

Mid-range – **Juna Hubin Hotel** (Wúxī Jūnlái Húbīn Jiǔdiàn; 无锡君来湖滨酒店)

Located right next to Li Garden and the tourist docks, this hotel is the perfect base for an in-depth exploration of the lake side.

Address : 1 Huanhu Lu (环湖路 1 号)
Phone: (0510) 8510 1888
Website: www.hubinhotel.com (in Chinese)

Getting In & Out

Shanghai – Wuxi

Trains that go from Shanghai to Wuxi all go to Nanjing as well, so stations, intervals, and earliest departure times are the same as for Nanjing. The last train to Shanghai from Wuxi is at 22:40.

Shanghai Hongqiao Railway Station to Wuxi East Railway Station (¥34.5 / ¥38.5; 50 minutes)

Shanghai Railway Station to Wuxi Railway Station (¥59.5; about 1 hour)

Suzhou – Wuxi

Trains begin at 6:23 and end at 22:14 at Suzhou Railway Station.

Suzhou Railway Station to Wuxi Railway Station (¥12.5 / ¥19.5; 15-20 minutes)

Suzhou North Railway Station to Wuxi East Railway Station (¥9.5; 10 minutes)

Hangzhou – Wuxi

Trains begin at 9:30 and end at 19:20 at Hangzhou East Railway Station.

Hangzhou East Railway Station to Wuxi Railway Station (¥85.5; about 2.5 hours)

Hangzhou Railway Station to Wuxi Railway Station (¥87.5; about 2.5 hours)

Nanjing – Wuxi

Trains begin at 6:22 and end at 21:32 at Nanjing Railway Station.

Nanjing Railway Station to Wuxi Railway Station (¥53.5 / ¥79.5; 1 hour and 20 minutes / 55 minutes)

Huángshān 黄山

One of China's most spectacular attractions, this UNESCO World Heritage Site has been written about by literary superstars like Lǐ Bái (李白), has been depicted on rice paper canvases of famed artists, and has even been the inspiration for classical melodies by some of the nation's top musicians. Mt Huangshan, in many ways, isn't a must see attraction; it's required for anyone yearning for the best of what China has to offer.

The sharp granite peaks jutting out of the mountain were formed about 100 million years ago and were chiseled by powerful glaciers over the centuries. Along with this one-of-a-kind rock formation, it's also famous for scratching the floors of heaven (visitors will literally be above the cloud line), and for the rare Welcome Pine (Yíngkè Sōng; 迎客松) that magically graces the rocky expanse and the legendary sunsets and sunrises.

Depending on your physical health, time constraints and preferences, choose wisely how and where you'd like to explore Mt Huangshan. At the time of research, there were 140 sections open for visitors, but in all honesty it'd take several days to see the entire complex, so plan accordingly and read this chapter carefully before taking off. Also, keep in mind that it's nearly impossible to treat Mt Huangshan as a day trip from Shanghai. Reserve at least two days and three nights for this trip: one night on the overnight train to get here, one night sleeping on top of the mountain, and one night on the overnight train back to Shanghai.

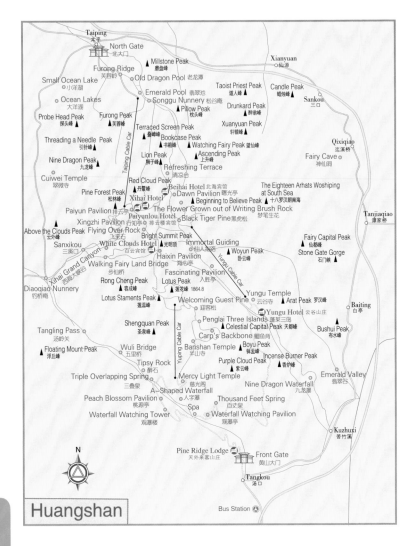

Taiping 太平

North Gate 北大门

Millstone Peak 磨盘峰

Xianyuan 仙源

Furong Ridge 芙蓉岭

Small Ocean Lake 小洋湖

Old Dragon Pool 老龙潭

Taoist Priest Peak 道士峰

Candle Peak 蜡烛峰

Sankou 三口

Ocean Lakes 大洋湖

Emerald Pool 翡翠池

Songgu Nunnery 松谷庵

Drunkard Peak 醉翁峰

Probe Head Peak 探头峰

Furong Peak 芙蓉峰

Pillow Peak 枕头峰

Xuanyuan Peak 轩辕峰

Threading a Needle Peak 引针峰

Terraced Screen Peak 叠嶂峰

Bookcase Peak 书箱峰

Watching Fairy Peak 望仙峰

Qixiqiao 迄溪桥

Taiping Cable Car

Lion Peak 狮子峰

Ascending Peak 上升峰

Fairy Cave 神仙洞

Nine Dragon Peak 九龙峰

Refreshing Terrace 清凉台

Cuiwei Temple 翠微寺

Red Cloud Peak 丹霞峰

Beihai Hotel 北海宾馆

The Eighteen Arhats Woshiping at South Sea 十八罗汉朝南海

Pine Forest Peak 松林峰

Dawn Pavilion 曙光亭

Xihai Hotel

Beginning to Believe Peak 始信峰

Paiyun Pavilion 排云亭

The Flower Grown out of Writing Brush Rock 梦笔生花

Tanjiaqiao 潭家桥

Paiyunlou Hotel 排云楼宾馆

Black Tiger Pine 黑虎松

Xingzhi Pavilion 行知亭

Above the Clouds Peak 云外峰

Flying Over Rock 飞来石

Bright Summit Peak 光明顶

Immortal Guiding 仙人指路

Fairy Capital Peak 仙都峰

Sanxikou 三溪口

White Clouds Hotel 白云宾馆

Woyun Peak 卧云峰

Stone Gate Gorge 石门峡

Yungu Cable Car

Haixin Pavilion 海心亭

Xihai Grand Canyon 西海大峡谷

Walking Fairy Land Bridge 步仙桥

Fascinating Pavilion 入胜亭

Diaoqiao Nunnery 钓桥庵

Rong Cheng Peak 容成峰

Lotus Peak 莲花峰 1864.8

Yungu Temple 云谷寺

Arat Peak 罗汉峰

Baiting 白亭

Welcoming Guest Pine 迎客松

Yungu Hotel 云谷山庄

Lotus Staments Peak 莲蕊峰

Penglai Three Islands 蓬莱三岛

Bushui Peak 布水峰

Shengquan Peak 圣泉峰

Celestial Capital Peak 天都峰

Tangling Pass 汤岭关

Yuping Cable Car

Carp's Backbone 鲤鱼背

Boyu Peak 钵盂峰

Incense Burner Peak 香炉峰

Floating Mount Peak 浮丘峰

Wuli Bridge 五里桥

Banshan Temple 半山寺

Purple Cloud Peak 紫石峰

Emerald Valley 翡翠谷

Tipsy Rock 醉石

Triple Overlapping Spring 三叠泉

Mercy Light Temple 慈光阁

Nine Dragon Waterfall 九龙瀑

Peach Blossom Pavilion 桃源亭

A-Shaped Waterfall 人字瀑

Spa

Thousand Feet Spring 百丈泉

Kuzhuxi 苦竹溪

Waterfall Watching Tower 观瀑楼

Waterfall Watching Pavilion 观瀑亭

Pine Ridge Lodge 天外来客山庄

Front Gate 黄山大门

N

Tangkou 汤口

Bus Station

Huangshan

The Ascent

Buses from Huangshan City will drop you off in the town of Tāngkǒu (汤口) at the base of Mt Huangshan. In Tangkou, before your ascent, stock up on supplies at the markets, have a good meal at some of the local restaurants, and find a hotel for the night. There is also a nearby hot springs (wēnquán; 温泉; ¥240) where you can bathe in a coffee, alcohol and/or wine infused luxury hot spring, or get a massage.

The mountain is divided into two halves: the Eastern Steps (the easiest climb, but still no cake walk) and the Western Steps (much steeper and more challenging). From Tangkou, take the shuttle bus to Yungu Station (Yúngǔ Zhàn; 云谷站) for the eastern route entrance, or the Mercy Light Temple Station (Cíguānggé Zhàn; 慈光阁站) for the western route entrance.

There are also cable cars at both of these entrances that will beam you up to the summit faster than you can say Scotty: the Yungu Cable Car (Yúngǔ Suǒdào; 云谷索道; ¥80) is on the east side, and the Yuping Cable Car (Yùpíng Suǒdào; 玉屏索道; ¥80) is on the west. Once on the summit, a third called Taiping Cable Car (Tàipíng Suǒdào; 太平索道) will bring you right past Purple Cloud Peak at 1,700 m (5,577 ft).

Eastern Steps

The Eastern Steps are just a wee bit easier than the Western steps. A hike from the base at Yungu Station to the top at White Goose Ridge (Bái'é Fēng; 白鹅峰) at 1,770 m (5,807 ft) will take the average person just under three hours. While the Eastern Steps are easier and quicker, they lack the breathtaking beauty seen on the western slope.

The east is where the majority of tourists prefer to trek, so during peak season the crowds can create a real traffic jam. There are plenty of rest stops for food, drinks and even a siesta along the way, making it much more convenient than the west.

Western Steps

The sheer, stunning, and at times, staggering

ascent on the western side begins at the Mercy Light Temple Station, from where the paths fork off in various directions all clearly marked by signs. Some of the peaks you can reach from the western slope are:

Lotus Flower Peak (Liánhuā Fēng; 莲花峰) 1,873 m (6,145 ft) – Usually closed off to the public.

Heavenly Capital Peak (Tiāndū Fēng; 天都峰) 1,810 m (5,938 ft) – Sometimes closed.

Aoyu Peak (Āoyú Fēng; 鳌鱼峰) 1,780 m (5,839 ft) – It actually kind of resembles two turtles (so they say).

Bright Summit Peak (Guāngmíng Dǐng; 光明顶) 1,841 m (6,040 ft) – Offers the best views of distant Aoyu Peak.

Lianrui Peak (Liánruǐ Fēng; 莲蕊峰) 1,776 m (5,826 ft) – A summit that's named after significant animals in Chinese folklore.

The Summit

Once you have reached the top (either by cable car or by walking up the eastern or western routes), the hardest part is over. From there on out, the mountain turns into a mix of various trails leading you to different peaks, lakes, forests other pristine natural wonders. Some recommended sites on the summit are:

The Refreshing Terrace (Qīngliáng Tái; 清 凉 台) close to Beihai Hotel is the best place to view Mt Huangshan's one of a kind sunrise, sunset and signature sea of clouds over the horizon. The sunsets and sunrises over this cloudy phenomenon are a once in a lifetime spectacle and present excellent photo opportunities to make all your Facebook friends jealous.

If **Beginning to Believe Peak** (Shĭxìn Fēng; 始 信峰) doesn't make you a believer of Mt Huangshan's grandeur, nothing will.

Purple Cloud Peak (Dānxiá Fēng; 丹霞峰) is best seen from the Taiping Cable Car.

Cell Phone Rock (Shŏujī Shí; 手机石) is a millennium old rock formation that eerily resembles that thing in your pocket that you need to turn off so you can truly appreciate every second of Mt Huangshan.

Take the hike for 9 km (5.5 mi) in the **Xihai Gorge** in the West Sea Canyon (Xīhăi Dàxiágŭ; 西海大峡谷 , aka Illusions Scenic Area) and check out the exquisite turquoise **Heavenly Sea** (Tiān Hăi; 天海), surrounded by a gigantic granite peak backdrop. There are two entrances: the northern one is near the Pianyunlou Hotel and the southern one is by the Baiyun Hotel (see below).

🛏 Sleeping

There's no shortage of sleeping options, (both budget and blow-out) to choose from in or around Mt Huangshan. We've listed our favorite ones in each of the three main sections: Tangkou, the Western Steps and on top of the peak.

In Tangkou – **Huangshan Hot Springs Youth Hostel** (Huángshān Wēnquán Guójì Qīngnián Lǚshè; 黄山温泉国际青年旅舍)

A no-frills hostel conveniently located in Tangkou. There are dorms for the backpackers on a budget and basic singles for a slight jump in price. Beds start at ¥38.

Address: Donghou Jie, Tangke He (黄山风景区 汤口河东后街)
Phone: (0559) 556 2478

In Tangkou – **White Clouds Hotel** (Báiyún Bīn'guǎn; 白云宾馆)

You'll find all sorts of people here under all budget ranges. This fancy hotel has nice rooms for over ¥1,000, mid-range rooms for around ¥400, and even dorm rooms for a discounted price at under ¥200. The luxury suites are suitable though overpriced for what you get, while the dorms on the other hand are a step up, with TVs and private showers.

Address: Around Heavenly Sea
Phone: (0559) 558 2708

The Peak – **Xihai Hotel** (Xīhǎi Fàndiàn; 西海 饭店)

Similar to the other establishments on Mt Huangshan, Xihai has dorms, doubles and luxury options. You can get a bed in the dormitory or a cozy double, or consider a room in the brand-spanking-new five-star wing that will cost you an arm and a leg.

Address: Purple Cloud Peak
Phone: (0559) 558 8888
Website: www.hsxihaihotel.cn/en

✈ Getting In & Out

As mentioned, you need at least three nights and two days to successfully pull off a side trip from Shanghai, so plan wisely and book your tickets well in advance. Train is by far the most convenient travel option, so grab one from Shanghai Railway Station to Huangshan Railway Station (Huángshān Huǒchēzhàn; 黄山火车站). After getting off at the train station, take a bus to Mt Huangshan (¥16).

Train number	From – To	Departing – Arriving	Duration	Price
K8418/K8419	Shanghai – Huangshan	21:24 – 09:00	11 hr 36 min	seat/sleeper: ¥93/¥174
K782/K783	Shanghai – Huangshan	12:28 – 00:11	11 hr 43 min	seat/sleeper: ¥93/¥174
K8420/K8417	Huangshan – Shanghai	20:45 – 08:52	12 hr 076 min	seat/sleeper: ¥93/¥174
K784/K781	Huangshan – Shanghai	21:57 – 10:33	12 hr 36 min	seat/sleeper: ¥93/¥174

Christmas in Shanghai

By Trey Archer

I had just arrived in Beijing, my final destination on my trip via the Trans-Siberian Express. It was a long one, marked by the onset of Russia's winter, fatigue from being cramped in a tiny train cabin for countless nights, and getting mugged on the streets of Ulan Bator. It was always my dream to visit China because it seemed like such a mysterious place, one where ancient culture meets the future, and after spending a few nights in Beijing, I quickly realized that I didn't just want to tour this intriguing land; I wanted to live in it.

That was December 2008, and getting a job teaching English was a breeze. Back then, there were no regulations and no need to have prior work experience or even know anything about teaching (things have changed drastically since then, however). Shanghai seemed like an interesting place, so I looked for jobs there on the internet, and sure enough, seemingly overnight, I had found one. It was exciting to know that I'd be living in China, learning the language, interacting with the locals and immersing myself in the culture.

After a long overnight train ride in a hard seat alongside farmers, factory workers, and the rest of China's proletariat, I arrived in the suburbs of Shanghai – the place I would call home for the next year. I have to admit, at first I was flabbergasted. The sky was painted with dark brushes of soot and all the buildings were aligned in perfect blocks, standard communist form. Alucard (whose name spells Dracula backwards), was the Chinese representative of the school who met me at the train station. He, with spiky hair, an oily face, and one lone long fingernail creeping off of his right middle finger, had the personality of a conch, and really didn't answer any of the millions of questions I had concerning my new life. My fantasy vision of China was fading quickly.

Soon, we jumped in a taxi, and Alucard brought me to my apartment. The outside was just as soulless as the others, and it radiated a profoundly negative vibe. But the inside was quite cozy, with new appliances, bedding, furniture and a TV. I knew that after several days I'd make this place my very own and suit it to my needs. Alucard left as quickly as he had arrived, and there I was alone in my new home in a strange foreign city. After flipping on the TV and hearing nothing but strange rapid tones, a voltage of culture shock pricked my spine, and the reality that I'd be in that place for a year made me tremble.

The next day I went to the school and met some of the other foreign teachers: Adam, Anna, Leo, James, Jacob and many others from all corners of the English speaking world. It was nice to meet other foreigners since it blunted the all-powerful culture shock that was slicing through me like a hot knife. A few days and a few friends later, some of the crew said that they planned to travel to the Shanghai city center (since we lived on the outskirts of town) the following week to celebrate Christmas. The plan was to get several hotel rooms so that we could be close to the action and all be together for our secret Santa gift exchange, as well as use our time off to have a non-stop party. Psyched to be able to actually celebrate Christmas, explore more of the city proper and discover

My first view of the Bund back in 2008 - no Shanghai Tower yet. How times have changed!

essence of Shanghai, I agreed to go with them.

After work on the 23rd of December, we hopped on the short train and arrived right in the middle of Shanghai. Upon exiting the train station, I noticed that things were a lot different than in the suburbs. The buildings were towering on all sides, just like New York, seemingly scraping the very floor of space. Things were bright, vibrant and alive, while people and cars zipped by in every direction, and horns squealed through the smell of exhaust, street food and construction. The city pulsed with life as adrenaline charged through my veins – it felt good. I instantly noticed that Shanghai was no joke; it was a real city, and I was ready to tackle it from all corners.

That night we went straight to the bars and started the party. Our first stop was Hengshan Bar Street, one of the oldest in the city. Since it was only my first night out in China (I had only been in the country for three weeks by that point), I was expecting to see the venues packed only with Chinese people. But this was Shanghai, one of the world's most international cities. Americans, Europeans, Latinos, Africans, Asians, Chinese – it seemed like I had walked into a UN meeting with so many countries represented. The only difference between the bar and the UN was that the bar's "ambassadors" were just a bunch of thirsty clients looking to let loose, enjoy some good music and start celebrating the Christmas holidays. And celebrate we did, until the wee hours of the morning.

With only a few hours of sleep, we awoke the next morning to actually get some sightseeing done. I was 24 at the time – the age where hangovers don't affect the body too much – so I, along with everyone else in our six person entourage, got ready to go. Our hotel was on Nanjing West Road, and we decided to walk it on through to Nanjing East Road for some shopping and eating, then hit up the Bund, cross over on the Bund Sightseeing Tunnel to Pudong, and strike out to the top of the newly constructed Shanghai World Financial Center.

Nanjing East Road was pretty cool. While Anna from England was busy buying cheap souvenirs for her friends back home, Adam and I used that opportunity to eat the time away. There were plenty of food stalls and restaurants all over the area featuring local Shanghai fare, regional Chinese cooking from different provinces and even Western fast food like KFC.

Night view of the Bund from above

Next, we strolled down the Bund and gawked at the classic bank buildings from the former European powers. They were impressive in their own right, but walking down the Bund, we couldn't help peering at what was on the other side of the river. Glorious Pudong, with its magnificent skyscrapers and futuristic feel, is something else. The Pearl Oriental TV Tower looked like a rocket ship from the year 2142, and the Jinmao Tower, bottle opener-like Shanghai World Financial Center, and the other sleek and brightly lit neon behemoths surrounding it were truly breathtaking. Still to this day, after much traveling, I'd say Shanghai's Pudong has one of the most impressive skylines in the world. I was anxious to cross over and get up close and personal with these giants.

To do that, we went the fashionable way: through the Bund Sightseeing Tunnel. The tunnel was a little immature, and used tacky lighting and props to try to fool you into believing you were cutting the fabrics of space-time. Corny, to be sure, but in some way it was entertaining, and we all had a good laugh along with all the other strangers in our carriage.

Finally, we made it to the base of the World Financial Center after passing by the Pearl Oriental TV Tower and the other monsters. The Financial Center was even bigger than I had thought, and I quickly discovered why it was one of the tallest buildings in the world. The elevator warped us to the observation deck at the top, presenting us a view of Shanghai at sunset: a miraculous mix of reds and oranges in the sky and millions of lights from the towers.

But no matter how high we were, and how big Shanghai had already been built up, the city still seemed to be growing. Leo pointed to a construction project on the ground and explained that the site would be the future Shanghai Tower, which would be even larger than the building we were surveying the city from at that moment (which was the tallest in the city in 2008).

Looking back on that moment six years later, it's hard to believe that the Shanghai Tower is in its final stages of construction. From that tiny pile of rubble to the king of Shanghai's biggest and brightest, in many ways it parallels my time in China, first working as an English teacher and now working the job of my dreams.

Once we descended back to ground level, we were all starving, and James had the wonderful idea of grabbing a big fat juicy burger with all the trimmings that Christmas Eve. The idea sounded delicious, but I was skeptical that we could find a good burger in the heart of Pudong. James told me he knew a good place, and not to worry. A 20-minute walk later, we arrived at James' bright idea: Hooters.

Really man??? Just like at every Hooters in the world, the beer is flat, the chicken thighs are a bit overcooked, and the buns are soggy. But the entertainment and waitresses always seem to keep a smile on the patrons' faces. *I wonder how they do that?* We enjoyed our Christmas Eve Hooter's feast while our servers Sunny, Happy and Hott (those are the names they told us at least) hoola-hooped in the background. I even got a picture with the crew before taking off and made it my new Facebook pic. (These were the days when Facebook still worked in China; just like the Shanghai Tower, so much has changed since then.) A Hooters in China is definitely an interesting experience to say the least, especially when it's on Christmas Eve. I also love the comment my good buddy Travis wrote under the caption of me posing with

four Hooter girls: "God Bless Communism." The whole thing for me (sarcastically) describes China perfectly: an anti-religious communist country that allows Hooters to set up shop but shuts down Facebook the next day.

That night, we painted the town red again and made it another late (or early, depending on how you look at it) night. The next morning we woke up and congregated in Leo's room to exchange our secret Santa gifts. My secret Santa was Jacob, and he gave me an atrocious puke yellow, dark green scarf. I was forced to wear it the rest of the day out of kindness, but in a way I did appreciate the thought... even though I never touched the thing again.

Later, we had a late lunch at a tapas restaurant in Xintiandi. Inflatable Santas, cardboard cutouts of reindeers and fake snow decked the halls of Xintiandi, and we enjoyed several bottles of red wine and dozens of small platters of *carnes, calamares, chorizo, quesos, boquerones, croquetas, jamon crudo, pulpo, tortilla, pan* and *aceitunas*. After our Spanish feast, we returned to the suburbs that night, ready to start work up again the following day.

On the fast train ride back, I couldn't help thinking how good of a time I had: new friends, a new city and a new country all during one of the happiest times of the year. A smile slipped across my face, and I was content knowing that I had made the decision to a) move to China, b) choose a place that was close enough to Shanghai, and c) perhaps the most important of them all, eat at Hooters on Christmas Eve!

Shanghai – so full of quirky surprises that never seem to run out. I love this city!

First Days in Shanghai
By Sam Gusway

My requisite Bund photo portrait

Whether you move here or you're just visiting, one of the first things people will ask you is, "What brought you to Shanghai?" My standard response to this is, "My parents sold their house so I had to move out of the basement."

There is far more than just a kernel of truth to this joke, though. Back in 2006 my parents were finishing their third teaching contract in China, and I was house sitting for them, minding my own business in a small town on Vancouver Island while I worked a disappointingly boring job at the local radio station.

Each time my parents returned from one of their teaching gigs in China they would rave about it and encourage me to go. "You would love it!" they'd say. "I think it would be easy for you there. With your skills, you'd be able to find a job, no problem!"

Upon their final return they really did

decide to sell the house, so I was left with a dilemma: rent an apartment in a town I hated so I could continue working a job I disliked? Or take a leap and see what would happen on the other side of the world, in a place I had no clue about, and where I couldn't speak the language.

The choice was clear, and with my parents' experiences to guide me I narrowed down my destinations to only a few cities. I then started researching those cities and perusing job listings. Before long I was receiving lots of responses to my applications and finally accepted one of the offers from a school in Shanghai. It was to teach 16 hours a week for about ¥13,000 a month. They faxed me a contract, I faxed back a signed copy and then applied for my Chinese visa. The day it arrived I booked my plane tickets and I was set. The whole process had taken less than 3 weeks.

While I waited for my departure day, I started

networking. Back then MySpace was king, and I reached out to several friendly expats who offered all kinds of great advice about the city (one would go on to be my roommate for over three years).

I arrived in Shanghai at about 18:00 on a Friday night. The school I had agreed to work for sent someone to pick me up from the airport and drop me off with a friend of my parents. It took about three hours fighting through weekend traffic for us to finally get to his place. I had gone from a town of 5,000 to this monstrous city, where a flood of 5,000 cyclists would rush out of an intersection when the light changed.

When we finally got to my friend's housing compound it was dark. I had his address, but it wasn't much help as it was almost impossible to see which building in the compound was which. Numbers were small, and lighting was non-existent. Once I found his building, I ran into another problem. It was pitch black inside. I had no idea that in China the lighting in most apartment halls and stairways is audio activated, much like "The Clapper." Fortunately, as I was mulling my options, someone else came in and stomped his foot and the lights flickered to life, letting me see the stairs and find my friend's door.

The next day I took the bus to the Bund and then walked a very circuitous route back through the city, enjoying the sights. Even though it was late September, it was ridiculously hot, so I was grateful that there seemed to be a convenience store every ten feet where I could get a drink.

I bought myself a cheap phone and then went to meet my online contacts to see if we could be real life friends instead of just virtual ones. We all got along well but I went home early because Sunday was going to be a big day. Even though I had a contract to start work on Monday, I had set up some interviews at other schools and tutoring companies. I figured this way, if things didn't work out at the school, I would have some other options.

Good thing, too, because when I went to the school first thing Monday morning for orientation and to sign the official contract, I was thoroughly disappointed. When they showed me my schedule, the "16 working hours" were split up through the week in a way that had me at the school all day from Monday to Friday. When I told them that this wouldn't work for what they were offering, they were surprised, not knowing that I had met with other schools over the weekend.

Still, as I walked away from the contract back to where I was staying, I couldn't help but feel nervous. Maybe all the contracts I would be offered would be "too good to be true." How long would it be until I found a job?

Not long at all. As I was walking I passed a table set up on the sidewalk that was advertising some sort of language school, so I asked the person manning it, "do you need English teachers?" They couldn't understand me, but brought me upstairs to meet the manager. After looking at my resume, she told me that they would only be hiring new teachers in a few weeks, but in the meantime I could do promotions for the school. So at 18:00 that night I started my first shift with the company, standing on the corner and encouraging passersby to come up on stage and try playing a little English game.

I had a microphone and a whiteboard, and a few assistants would drag people over to play hangman or solve a rebus or say a tongue-twister. My job was just to ramble in English, even though nobody could understand what I was saying. It was great. From the stage I could see throngs of people on the way home or off to dinner after their busy days of work, and all around us the city lights came on, filling the street with color.

Over the next few weeks I developed more games and activities for the promotion, much to the delight of the big boss. I also started teaching some classes, which began my first interactions with the local population.

Many of my friends in Shanghai have reported similar experiences with work: just being in the right place at the right time, just by asking around and telling people what they can do, doors opened up and things fell into place. The economy has gotten a little tougher in Shanghai over the years, and some bubbles have burst, but it is still a place that offers phenomenal opportunities to anyone who's got the courage to step up and put their talents (proven or imagined) to the test.

The classics

Shanghai World Expo 2010:
The Contradictions of a Rising Superpower

By Ansel Klusmire

We are surrounded mostly by things that are meant to be profitable. At least, they are supposed to be worth their cost. It's so intrinsic a fact that we are mostly oblivious to it, and when said it seems a little trite. But when travel is good, it offers a new perspective along with its experiences, and formerly obvious things seem less so. China is now a country of such wealth and so little say by its citizens in how it should be spent that the constraint of cost no longer seems to apply, and the result is a strange phenomenon rarely seen except in those instances when, for example, two superpowers have a pissing contest in space or a pharaoh builds his grave.

In Inner Mongolia, a city for one million people has been expanding for five years and still has almost no residents. The largest mall in the world is located in Guangzhou and is almost completely vacant. Shanghai has a sleek and powerful maglev train at Pudong Airport that doesn't even take its passengers all the way to the city, and even has it's own English-themed ghost town with its own unused cathedral and yacht dock. Much of this is attributable to sloppy planning encouraged by opportunities for corruption (graft and construction naturally attract), as well as the government's decision to evaluate officials solely by GDP improvement, whether what they're producing makes any sense economically or not. But China also disregards cost in the pursuit of glory, and here the results can be spectacular. The world saw this during the 2008 Olympics, and I experienced it firsthand at the 2010 Shanghai Expo.

Everyone I met at the Expo agreed that it was amazing, but for reasons they couldn't always express. Everyone also agreed that the tedium of the lines for each pavilion almost always canceled out the coolness of their interiors. For the more popular attractions, the wait could easily be six hours. But the outsides made up for it. France had a stylish and abstract pavilion, perfectly white; Spain had a pavilion of undulating wicker panels; Britain's pavilion was a cube of quills exploding outward; Japan's looked like a purple blob with dimples and tendrils or a globed and purple graph of gravity wells. North Korea gamely slapped together an exhibit hall fit for one of Shanghai's smaller museums in which it installed a fountain and sold some of its then Dear Leader's books on economics, aesthetics, morality, etc. I regret to say that my country's pavilion looked like a corporate headquarters with some pointless modernist curves, but it tried to make up for it by being very big – classic USA! There were trees on top of buildings and all that because "eco-friendly" touches are forever in vogue at the Expo (2008 Expo theme: Water and Sustainable Development, 2010 Expo theme: Better city—better life, 2015 Expo theme: Feeding the planet, energy for life). It was the most unique theme park in the world, and everyone agreed that apart from the attractions, the Expo was amazing because it had happened at all. Where else would something like this ever happen again in China? Who knows?

But underlying all this international good-will was another emotion, which I think

added to the frisson at least as much as anything else: awe. Shanghai had built an entire city of architectural confections on two sides of the Huangpu River, ferries running back and forth all day, that totaled more than five square kilometers in size. Giant, multi-storied, canopied walkways ran the length of the park, with enormous funnel-shaped objects spreading out above them at fixed intervals. Multiple buildings were as large as airplane hangars. Everything – restaurants, parks, restrooms – had been specially designed and fabricated for the fair. Not only China, but Chinese cities and even the various branches of its military had constructed their own pavilions. The money the Chinese government spent for the whole thing was US$55 billion. And all of it ran like clockwork, a product of maniacally meticulous planning. And all of it, from beginning to end, would last for six months, after which time almost everything would be dismantled or left to decay. This is what made the immensity and the money and the planning awesome in a nearly unreal way. The flimsiness of the construction when you looked closely reminded you that this entire effort, whose every detail was thought out and showered with money, was not even meant to exist for a year. Nine billion dollars a month.

That the Chinese government was willing to spend so much for so transient a splendor, a half-year theme park, shocked me, coming from a country where no government project is too small or too important to escape a battle over funding (by the way, the US pavilion was entirely sponsored by corporations; the government contributed not one cent). When people go to other countries, they immediately notice the things that look and taste different. But small details can be just as deserving of attention, like the fact that in China's most prosperous city, most malls can't find any businesses to fill their top stories and that Pudong Airport never has enough people to not seem too big. This massive amount of spending, seemingly divorced from any worries about cost or

any reasonable expectations of profit, may one day justify itself as people continue to move to cities, or it may be the sign of a bubble economy that's about to pop. Certainly, no one cares enough to stop it as long as everyone's getting rich, and the way it shapes, or distorts, the country is part of what makes present day China a truly singular place to visit. Whether it is moral for the government to take part in this frenzy – and for nothing more than publicity's sake – is no trivial question. Whether the result is sometimes wondrous is beyond dispute.

Now, all but five of the 246 buildings have been taken down or left to rust, and tall grass grows behind the fences that have been put up everywhere in the site to discourage exploration. The China Pavilion and an old power station have been turned into regular museums, and each struggles to fill its massive spaces, whose size didn't seem so ridiculous when the buildings were surrounded on all sides by equal excess. Their only company is an 18,000-seat stadium made to look like a golden flying saucer, some smaller buildings maintained for whatever purpose the government can find, the naval pavilion, which looks like the ribcage of another spaceship, and a section of the giant, multi-storied, canopied walkway, which now comes from and goes to nowhere. A ghost town, but this one at least has the Huangpu River, which still rolls quietly along, undisturbed by the brilliant city that rose and disappeared in a flash just a few years ago along its banks. The park beside it, and just outside the Power Station of Art is a nice place to sit and think about whether hubris can be justified when it's done so right.

Sample Itineraries

Shanghai gives Reno a run for its money since it's probably the biggest little city in the world. It's compact enough that you can explore nearly all of it in a (very long) day, as you'll see with the One Day in Shanghai tour or the Puxi One Step at a Time tour, but as you can imagine, it's certainly better to give yourself several days or more to savor each destination for what it's worth.

The following itineraries can each be completed in several hours, and some will leave you a lot of time in the afternoon to do whatever you wish. Feel free to mix and match them with other itineraries, or get distracted and get lost in the concrete jungle to discover your own personal adventure. If this region really is the Pearl of the Orient, then let Shanghai be your oyster.

As mentioned, these are only suggestions, and many of the places listed on these itineraries are very close to other attractions that you might want to go to, so it also might be a good idea to read through this guide for other things that look especially interesting and add them to these itineraries. Look at the individual articles for these sites to find more specific information, as well as addresses, admission fees, etc. Also keep in mind that each itinerary, except for Puxi One Step at a Time (a walking tour), assumes metro use except when it's not convenient.

One Day in Shanghai

Yu Garden→ People's Square Museums (Shanghai Museum, Shanghai Museum of Contemporary Art (MOCA), Urban Planning Exhibition Hall)→ Nanjing East Road→ The Bund→ World Financial Center→ Xintiandi→ Tianzifang

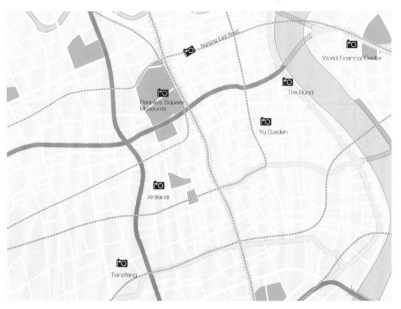

If you want to knock off all the big hits of the city in one day on both sides of the river, this is it. You're going to need a lot of time and energy, so wake up early, grab a greasy bag of *xialongbao* for the road, and get movin'!

First visit **Yu Garden**, which is near the Yu Garden metro station and opens at 9:00, and pay respect to the **City Gods Temple** near the garden exit for good measure. Next, take a taxi to **People's Square** (the metro is not very convenient from here). People's Square has three museums to choose from, so decide at your own discretion which ones you want to go to. **MOCA** closes at 18:00; the **Shanghai Museum** closes at 17:00; and the **Urban Planning Exhibition Hall** stops admitting at 16:00. Note that even if you finish everything at 15:00, you'll still have enough time to see most of the things on this list, so don't push it too hard.

After you've browsed as many museums as you can handle, walk down **Nanjing East Road**, starting at the east side of People's

Park, for shopping, eating, and more shopping and more eating. Beware not to fall for any phony scams in this neighborhood! (see pg 294). At the very end of Nanjing East Road lies **the Bund**, whose classical buildings you should take the time to look inside (see page 62). Then take the **Bund Sightseeing Tunnel** over to Lujiazui, where you'll find the **World Financial Center** and its top floor observation deck for a bird's eye view of flashy Shanghai. The last admission for this deck is 22:00.

From the Lujiazui metro stop, cross back over to Puxi on Line 2, then transfer to line 10 and go three stations over to the heart of the former French Concession, **Xintiandi** (metro stop has the same name). Explore a bit of the area's wonderful architecture, then after travel south by taxi to **Tianzifang** to end your night with historic architecture, dinner and drinks.

Shopaholics Anonymous

Nanjing West Road→ Huaihai Middle Road→ Xintiandi→ Dongtai Road Antique Market

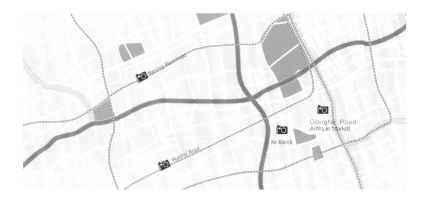

This is Shanghai, a shopper's heaven! This tour was made by the shopahlic, for the shopaholic, so get those credit cards oiled up and let your bank know that no one has hacked into your account; it's going to be a long, long day.

Start your spree at the Jing'an Temple Metro Station (while you're here, you may want to stop by the temple for a quick blessing, so that the shopping gods may acompany you on this pilgrimage) going east on **Nanjing West Road** – famed for its shopping centers and malls. Renowned for its designer name brands and knock off "Made in China" brands, Nanjing West Road starts off strong, but just remember that you have a lot of shopping left to do, so don't exhaust yourself.

Walk east on Nanjing West Road all the way to the Nanjing East Road Metro Station (while hitting up as many shops as possible), then take Line 2 from that station toward People's Square, then change to Line 1, going towards South Huangpi Road and South Shaanxi Road. If you get off at South Shaanxi, you can walk towards Huangpi Station and catch the small shops along this stretch on **Huaihai Middle Road** in the French Concession. The area around Huangpi Road Station has some of the city's biggest and best modern malls, and in many ways it's making its name as the next Nanjing Road.

Directly south from Huangpi Road Station

and a few blocks down on Madang Road is **Xintiandi**, which features more high end shops and many places to eat and drink. Here in Xintiandi, you can grab any kind of food imaginable, from tapas to teppanyaki, or unwind a bit with a foot massage. Try one of the two Xintiandi locations of **Green Massage** (www.greenmassage.com.cn), but make sure to book a reservation since this upscale parlor is always backed up (phone: 5386 0222; 6384 1356).

Walking east on Zichong Road on the southern edge of Xintiandi gets you to the start of **Dongtai Road Antique Market,** which sells authentic (and some fake) souvenirs. With all those LV bags in your hand, it'll be a nice change of pace here at this dusty yet fascinating outdoor market.

When it's all said and done, it might be a good idea to return to your hostel or hotel to drop all your loot off and take a rest. But don't get too comfortable, the night is young and we're sure you'll be ready to show off your new look to the world. See page 198 for Nightlife & Drinking.

The Pu-Jersey Shore

Oriental Pearl Tower→ World Financial Center→ Science and Technology Museum→
Century Park

Pudong is affectionately known as Pu-Jersey by many Shanghai expats. Even though it's part of the city proper and boasts some of the most jaw-dropping skyscrappers in the universe, it, like the real Jersey, is separated by a river and connected by a few tunnels, bridges and trains. Many Shanghai expats don't venture off into this "outer burrow" for entertainment, but that doesn't mean it's not worth a token of your time. In fact, there are some really cool sights, and we're not just talking about the skyscrapers.

The Oriental Pearl Tower, which serves as the city's most iconic tower, is the first stop from Lujiazui Station, and while its observation deck tour is pointless if you're going to the World Financial Center, it's surrounded by a large park that offers great views of the west bank. It's also home to the **Shanghai History Museum** which, honestly, is a lot more fun than it sounds.

Next, walk southeast through the forest of skyscrapers on Lujiazui East Road to the **Shanghai World Financial Center,** which is without question the world's biggest bottle opener, and take the speedy elevator to the top for an observation deck with incredible views of the city. Also, don't forget that there are a few good (and expensive) places to eat on its lowest levels and around its front entrance.

Also, by the time you read this, the colossal Shanghai Tower should be completed. You'll definitely notice it since it is the the tallest building in town (and one of the tallest in the world). Even if it's not open to the public, it'll still make you whisper "Oh my God."

After, take Line 2 at Lujiazui Station to the **Science and Technology Museum** next to the station of the same name. Have fun playing around with the gizmos, gadgests, robots and all the other surprises this spunky, space-age museum has to offer. It's a very fun museum and perfect if you're bringing the kids along.

For your last stop, walk a block east and you can't miss the enormous **Century Park**, one of the biggest and nicest parks in the city. It's a great place to relax and unwind after a long day of sight-seeing, and it's the only place on this side of the Huangpu that puts the garden back in Jersey.

Since all of Pudong's biggest attractions lie along Line 2, you could start this itinerary with a visit to numerous attractions on the west side of the river (like the museums of People's Square, for example) or, better yet, combine it with the power walking tour Puxi One Step at a Time to get the full blown, all out Shanghai experience.

The Crosstown Art Tour

Long Museum of Art→ Shanghai Museum of Contemporary Art (MOCA)→
Moganshan Road (M50)

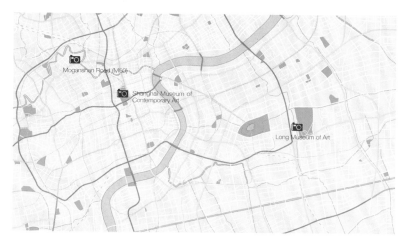

From one side of the Huangpu to the other, this Crosstown Art Tour is not only a great way to check the city's finest collections of art, but also experience both Puxi and Pudong. It's going to be a long one, so consider bringing some snacks and water along for this day trip.

It's best to start your day in Pudong at the **Long Museum of Art** (take Line 7 to Huamu Road Station), the largest privately owned art gallery in all of China. Check out their website **www.thelongmuseum.org/en/** to see if any special exhibits are being showcased during your stay; they've always got fresh work from Chinese and international artists passing through their doors.

After the Long Museum of Art and a few cappucinos, hop back on the metro at Huamu Road Station and travel one stop to Longyang Road Station to transfer to Line 8, then enjoy the ride all the way to People's Square, where you can knock off the **Shanghai Museum of Contemporary Art (MOCA)**. As with many art galleries in the world, be sure to check their website (**www.mocashanghai. org**) to see what big hits they're showing off. The MOCA is one of the nicest museums in Shanghai, but as the name suggest it focuses almost entirely on contemporary art, which is a blessing for some and a curse for the classical realist. It would also be a good idea to grab some lunch in or around People's Square since there's no shortage of eateries; People's Park is not a bad place to relax and catch your breath before moving on to the next destination.

As for **Moganshan Road (M50)**, take Line 1 from People's Square to the Shanghai Railway Station then transfer on to Line 3 or 4 for one more stop to Zhongtan Road station (taking a taxi from People's Square might be easier). Once in M50, you have several galleries to choose from: Shanghart, EastLink Gallery, Island6, Biz Art, M97, Pantocrator Gallery and plenty of graffiti art sprayed on the walls of the surrounding district. These galleries and others specialize in a wide range of art, from photography to fine art to contemporary. To end your day, find one of the many restaurants in the area for wine and dinner.

The Parisian

Fuxing Park→ Changle Road→ Arts and Crafts Museum→ Yongkang Road

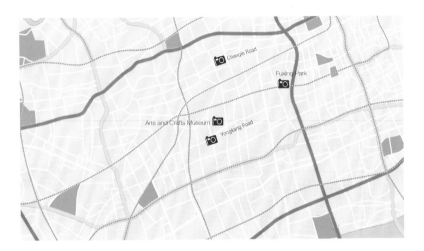

As you may have already guessed, this tour focuses on the sights inside the former French Concession. Complete with European style villas, parks, cafes and luxury hotels, it's definitely one of the finer areas of town and the perfect retreat if you're overdosing on all things Chinese. A comprehensive overview of the old French Concession can be found on page 80, but this itinerary gives you the quick low-down in case you only have time to scratch the surface.

All in all, this is just a particularly nice walking route. Start at **Fuxing Park** (Huangpi South Road is the closest station), which is one of the most pleasant patches of tranquility within Shanghai's overpowering steel canopy, and exit the park from the west side to see the orthodox basilica and Sun Yat-Sen's villa.

After exploring these two historic sights, walk north past Huaihai Road to the intersection at **Changle Road,** right after the multiple art deco hotels, and take a left on Changle to enjoy its charms. Changle Road is kind of the younger, hipper side of the French Concession, and you'll spot plenty of lens-less glasses, fixies and old-school Reeboks. Follow Changle all the way to Xiangyang Road then turn left and walk back to Huaihai, taking a look at the other orthodox basilica and Xiangyang Park on the way.

At Huaihai, turn left and walk about 60 m (197 ft) to Fenyang Road, which starts from Huaihai and goes south. Take this street down to find the **Arts and Crafts Museum** right before the street bends. This is an interesting little display; you'll find pieces of jade, ivory woodcarvings and other folk crafted trinkets. You can also watch the artisans create their treasures and purchase some wonderful souvenirs.

Right below the museum is an intersection from which Dayang Road goes straight south. Take that road to **Yongkang Road** about a block down and turn right. A few blocks away are the small restaurants and cafes that the street is known for. Actually, it's more than just a few "small restaurants and cafes" – any local partier knows well that this is one of the funnest bar streets in all of Shanghai.

Note that since this tour ends on a bar street it might be best to start it during the afternoon on a Friday or Saturday so that you can finish just after sunset when things start heating up.

The Wild West

Jade Buddha Temple→ Jing'an Temple→ Zhongshan Park→ Changfeng Park (Matchbox and Brand Museum)→ Foreigner Street

OK, it's probably not that wild. Nonetheless, there is a loose collection of attractions united by their location in the less trafficked west side of the city center. This itinerary is recommended for the jaded Shanghai traveler who has seen it all and is looking for something off the beaten tourist trail.

First, get your daily dose of harmony and follow the Eightfold Path. Start at the **Jade Buddha Temple** (you may want to take a taxi directly to here since it's a bit out of the way, but if not, it's close to Line 7 Changshou Road Metro Station). Next, take the metro from Changshou Road to Jing'an Temple station just a few stops down to see the famous **Jing'an Temple**, one of the city's finest.

After seeing Jing'an, make your way out west and take Line 2 to **Zhongshan Park**, one of the few parks in Shanghai that's big enough to

feel legitimately park-like.

One stop to the west on Line 2 is Shuicheng Road, north of which is **Changfeng Park** and its strange little **Matchbox and Brand Museum**. It's a quirky exhibit that you can see fairly quickly, but if you make it all the way out here, you might as well... especially since you may never be back in this part of town ever again.

From the Matchbox Museum, it's easiest to take a taxi south to **Foreigner Street** and have a drink or something to eat. True to its name, there are many foreign (i.e. non Chinese) restaurants to choose from, along with many bars and live music shows.

The Shanghai Pub Crawl

Captains Bar→ Windows II→ Café des Stagiares→ Tap House→ Sliders→ Shelter→ Flamingo

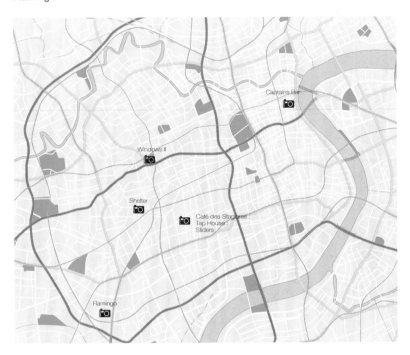

If Beijing is known for its historic monuments, then Shanghai is most certainly renowned for its nightlife. The city never sleeps and runs on all cylinders every day of the week, making it party central for many expats and locals alike. If none of the other itineraries quench your thirst, don't despair, the Shanghai Pub Crawl might be exactly what the doctor ordered for an unforgettable (or perhaps forgettable) bar and club hopping extravaganza. Follow the Panda through the night to Shanghai's coolest nightlife venues, and get ready to party hard!

The Panda starts early, and so should you. Head to **Captains Bar** around 17:00 to get your night rolling. You'll catch an amazing glimpse of the Pudong skyline at sunset, a sight that's sure to get you psyched for the evening and ready to pull an all-nighter. Have a drink or two, then jump in a taxi to your next destination.

Windows Too off Nanjing West Road is a great pre-gaming destination and not a bad idea for dinner either. Purchase some beers and some of their ¥15 burgers, and watch some sports or play some darts afterwards to let your food digest. By this time, it should be around 20:00, and time to move on to your next spot.

Take a taxi while you're still sober enough to give directions down to Yongkang Road. There are plenty of bars to choose from on this up-and-coming bar strip, but we'd recommend hitting up **Café des Stagiares** and the **Tap House** – both of which have a wide range of good beers. However, we would note that you should probably hit up **Sliders** before 22:00 for sliders and other greasy snacks that will give you the fuel needed to blast you on to tomorrow. Sliders also has great beers and good mixed drinks to wash it all down. By 23:00 on Yongkang

Road, things start flatlining, so use your time wisely and try to check off as many bars as possible here before making your way deep underground.

Chances are by around 00:00, you'll be well on your way to drunkenness, and if you're mingling on Yongkang Road you'll most definitely run into some other people that are heading to **Shelter** – one of Shanghai's coolest clubs that's inside an old Cold War-style bomb shelter. You can either follow the masses here on foot with a few street beers along the way or take a taxi in which you can also drink. Be prepared to dance your face off, but once things start getting a little too sweaty at around 3:00 in the morning, it'll definite be time to move on.

It'll be late, and you'll likely be inebriated, but don't worry, so will everyone else at **Flamingo**, one of Shanghai's primier after-

hours venues. It'll be hard to keep yourself off the poles to show off your own pole-dancing skills, but try to refrain because you'll definitely regret it the next morning (especially if and when you fall). By 5:00, there will still be some people still going hard, but for the most part the majority of the troopers will have surrendered.

From Flamingo, you can either a) go home or b) head back to the Bund if you still have the energy to watch the sun rise over Pudong and the Huangpu. Grab a few beers from 7-11 and sit out on one of the benches facing the river for an immaculate sunrise, and catch a look at the old timers' morning exercises and tai chi routines. All the little breakfast joints will start popping up around this time as well, so grab a bite to eat if you're feeling hungry. It's a fitting end to your pub crawl and an awesome way to wrap up any night out in Shanghai.

Sweet Songjiang

Songjiang Mosque→ Zuibaichi Park→ Thames Town

For another far westward excursion, try checking out Sweet Songjiang. Similar to the Wild West tour, there's nothing extraordinarily sweet about this place, except for maybe the fact that it's off the tourist trail and away from the herds of tour buses. Give it a shot and check out this off-beat part of town – you might just like it!

This place is about an hour and twenty minutes away from Shanghai by metro Line 9. Get off at Zuibaichi station and go north to find the **Songjiang Mosque** – the oldest mosque in Shanghai, built during the 14th century.

Then head back to that same station and visit **Zuibaichi Park** for some R&R. Next, get back on the metro and head two stops north to Xinjiang Xincheng station, the closest station to **Thames Town**, one of the quirkier sides of Shanghai.

Like Foreigner Street, Thames Town has a foreign face (a replica of an English town) with a Chinese style (it's virtually a ghost town). It's a hillarious ending to your day, and we swear you will get a laugh out of this one.

Puxi One Step at a Time: The Power Walking Tour

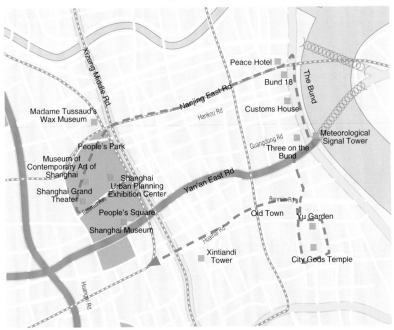

Start: People's Square
Finish: French Concession
Top Attractions: People's Park, Shanghai Museum, Shanghai Urban Planning Exhibition Hall, Nanjing East Rd, the Bund, Yu Garden, Xintiandi, French Concession
Time: 6-8 hours (including a lunch break)

Shanghai is one of the world's biggest cities, but that doesn't mean you have to spend a fortune on taxis to get around. If none of the other itineraries fit your form and you'd rather be out on the street experiencing Shanghai, lace up your Nikes and limber up, we've got the perfect power walking tour for you right through the heart of Puxi. By starting at People's Park, then working your way through Nanjing East Road, the Bund, Yu Garden, Old Town and finishing up in the French Concession, you can capture the soul of Shanghai all while getting a bit of exercise and a breath of fresh (well… semi fresh) air.

1. (1-2 hours) Get off at **People's Square** (Rénmín Guǎngchǎng; 人民广场) Metro Station Exit 1 and take a quick stretch at the fountain to get those legs nice and warm. Take a lovely stroll around the square south of Renmin Ave (Rénmín Dàdào; 人民大道) and check out the city's finest museum: the **Shanghai Museum** (Shànghǎi Bówùguǎn; 上海博物馆). Next, head north on Renmin Avenue into **People's Park** (Rénmín Gōngyuán; 人民公园) and pop into the **Museum of Contemporary Art of Shanghai** (Shànghǎi Dāngdài Yìshù Bówùguǎn; 上海当代艺术博物馆) or the **Shanghai Grand Theater** (Shànghǎi Dàjùyuàn; 上海大剧院). However, we recommend the **Shanghai Urban Planning Exhibition Hall** (Shànghǎi Chéngshì Guīhuá Zhǎnshìguǎn; 上海城市规划展示馆) for a glimpse into the city's bright future.

2. (1 hour) Head to the north of the park and follow **Nanjing West Road** (Nánjīng Xīlù; 南京西路) to the east until you reach

Madame Tussaud's Wax Museum (Dùshā Fūrén Làxiàng Guǎn; 杜莎夫人蜡像馆) at the intersection of Nanjing East Road (Nánjīng Dōnglù; 南京东路). If you're into wax figurines of famous international characters then step in, otherwise continue east on Nanjing East Road, one of the city's most popular streets. You can buy anything here, from knock-offs to top-notch swag, and there are plenty of options for delicious Shanghai snacks and fast food along the way.

3. (1 hour) If you follow Nanjing East Road all the way to the end, you'll reach the banks of the Huangpu River and **the Bund** (Wàitān; 外 滩), not only one of the most iconic spots of Shanghai, but also one of the most famous in all of China. Take a quick left and walk 100 paces to the **Jardine Matheson Bank** (Yíhé Yángháng; 怡和洋行): one of the city's finest examples of traditional housing. After a quick look around, turn around and head south along the Bund to the original **Bank of China Building** (Zhōngguó Yínháng Dàlóu; 中国银行大楼), which was commissioned in 1936 (you'll spot the blue roof and funky lion statues) and the **Peace Hotel** (Hépíng Fàndiàn; 和 平 饭 店 ; originally called the Cathay), which was the ritziest hotel in all of Asia when it was first constructed in 1929.

Continue south along the Bund for 50 m (164 ft) and notice **Bund 18** (Wàitān Shíbāhào; 外 滩 十 八 号), formerly the Chartered Bank of Australia, India and China. For a drink, head up to **Bar Rouge** (phone: 6339 1199) on the 7th floor. Its immediate neighbor is the former **North China Daily News** (Zìlín Dàlóu; 字林大楼) edifice. It's one of the oldest buildings of the Bund, built in 1864, giving it the nickname "Old Lady of the Bund."

Keep on truckin' after Hankou Road (Hànkǒu Lù; 汉 口 路) and check out the **Customs House** (Hǎiguān Dàlóu; 海 关 大 楼), topped with a massive clock, and the old **Hong Kong Shanghai Bank** (**HKSB**; Huìfēng Yínháng; 汇丰银行), which was established in 1923. The HKSB is perhaps the most attractive structure of the Bund and it was even considered one of the the of the largest banks in the world at that time.

Make sure that compass needle is still on S as you walk the length of a football pitch to the extravagant **Three on the Bund** (Wàitān Sānhào; 外滩三号), which, in their own words, "is a leading lifestyle destination blending gastronomy, art, culture, music, fashion, and retail in an elegant, sophisticated gathering place for vibrant people and stimulating ideas." Feel free to enter, but it's a little pompous if you're not a millionaire. Fittingly by its side is the **Shanghai Club** (Shànghǎi Zǒnghuì; 上 海 总 会). Built in 1911, this is where top hat tooting British businessmen used to hang out, smoke cigars and sip G&Ts.

4. (1 hour) The Bund comes to an end at the corner of Yan'an East Road (Yán'ān Dōnglù; 延安东路). On the left by the river is the 1908 **Meteorological Signal Tower** (Qìxiàng Xìnhào Tái; 气象信号台), which stands at a height of nearly 50 m (164 ft). The inside is pretty cool; it has old black and white photos of the Bund from decades ago and there's even a café called **Atanu** (phone: 6350 7649) with a tremendous view. We recommend grabbing some lunch here and taking a long rest to reenergize; you still have a lot of exploring left!

5. (1-2 hours) Now it's time to digest and walk off the calories. Take a right on Yan'an East Road, but make a quick detour (see the map) and go south on Yong'an Road (Yǒng'ān Lù; 永 安 路). If you stomp 500 m (1,640 ft) further you'll eventually reach **Yu Garden** (Yù Yuán; 豫 园). This gorgeous park is the best in Shanghai, and you should make sure to visit the **City Gods Temple** (Chénghuáng Miào; 城隍庙) and the **Chenxiangge Nunnery** (Chénxiāng Gé; 沉 香 阁) while here. Sipping a bit of tea at **Huxinting Teahouse** (Húxīntíng Chálóu 湖心 亭茶楼 ; phone: 6373 6950) will also make for a nice break.

6. (1 hour). Next, head north from the park's entrance and veer left on Renmin Road (Rénmín Lù; 人民路). Saunter to the west and pass through the **Old Town** (Lǎo Chéng; 老 城) for some authentic Chinese architecture, then keep going straight until you reach East Huaihai Road (Huáihǎi Dōnglù; 淮海东路).

Soon you'll pass **Xīntiāndì** (新 天 地) on the left hand side, right before the intersection of Huaihai Middle Road (Huáihǎi Zhōnglù; 淮 海 中 路) and Chengdu South Road (Chéngdū Nánlù; 成 都 南路). There're tons of shopping and upscale dining options here, and it's also nice for a quick walk around, or "cool down" from your mega power walk.

Huangpi South Road (Huánpí Nánlù; 黄陂南路) metro station is right across from Xintiandi, so you can call your walking tour to an end if needed, or stay on Huaihai Middle Road to pass through the heart of the **French Concession** (Fǎguó Zūjiè ; 法国租界) for some quaint European architecture, hip cafes and trendy shops. Huaihai Middle Road is lined with various metro stations, so you can call it quits at any time, but if you've still got some fuel in the tank, fill 'er back up at one of the French Concession's many bars.

Air Pollution in Shanghai

If your trip to Shanghai was inspired by colorful photos of Pudong on a blue-sky day, be prepared for the unfortunate reality: many days in Shanghai don't look like that. In fact, if you're following the news, you've surely encountered some less appealing images of the city, like people sporting futuristic face masks commuting through thick smog and the sun hidden behind a grimy haze. While Shanghai may not be as bad as Beijing – where reports of Beijing's pollution problem swept the globe in 2013 when air quality soared from bad to levels beyond any existing index – this is still a massive Chinese city, and there are definitely problems concerning the air quality.

Travelers on a tight schedule may fret over canceled flights when heavy smog cuts down visibility at Pudong International Airport, while those with children may worry about the impact of polluted air on their little ones' health. Pollution can have a real impact on your travel plans, but the air quality index doesn't have to make or break your trip. Below, we'll outline what you need to know about air pollution in Shanghai and what you can do to minimize its impact on your travel plans and health.

What are the causes?

Shanghai's toxic air is the product of a number of factors, with coal-burning industrial operations as the leading cause. Coal provides 80% of China's electricity, and much of the coal used here is a type that is particularly high in sulfur. When residents, especially of those in rural communities, wish to keep warm during the damp and bitter winter months, guess what they turn to. Coal, and lots of it too. For this reason, you can bet the most polluted months of the year are December, January and February.

Another factor is simply the number of cars and people living in this city. Shanghai is considered the biggest city in China, and that's saying a lot since a city of five million people is considered a third-tier backwater town in this country. In fact, Shanghai, according to some accounts, is one of the most populous cities in the world! It's hard to put an exact number on it, but most estimates put the total count of people over the 23 million mark (and that's only taking into account the number of residents living in the megalopolis legally). Basically, there are a lot of people in Shanghai, and that creates a lot of pollution.

Actually, one of Shanghai's greatest claims to fame is also one of its biggest polluters. The city has been in a non-stop construction boom since the early '90s. Nowadays, there are hundreds of big and small construction projects all around the city, and each and every one of them is contributing to higher levels of hazardous particles being released into the air.

The good news for Shanghai is that it's situated right on the ocean (unlike its rival Beijing), meaning a nice sea breeze can come in at any time and wipe all that smoggy air out. The bad news, unfortunately, is that when Shanghai used to laugh at Beijing's air pollution problem, Shanghai's has gotten substantially worse within the past year or two.

How is air quality measured?

There are two types of air pollution measurements in China: PM10 (particles less than 10 microns in diameter) and PM2.5 (particles less than 2.5 microns in diameter). The United States Consulate and the Shanghai government each maintain equipment that provides hourly readings, and both publish their own air quality index that incorporates both PM2.5 and PM10 data. Their hourly readings are reported on a 1-500 scale. Depending on the source you're consulting, the same reading may be described differently, as you can see in the chart below.

The efforts to monitor pollution in China have not been without controversy. Previously, the Chinese Ministry of Environmental Protection's index did not include data for the smaller PM2.5 pollutants. When it comes to air quality, smaller particles are considered more harmful because they are small enough to penetrate the lungs and enter the bloodstream. After public outcry and pressure, the MEP began including PM2.5 data in their measurements as of January of 2012. Even after that adjustment, observers have noted that the US Consulate's readings are frequently higher than the Chinese readings, a discrepancy that has only made deciphering air quality more complicated. One possible explanation for the discrepancy is the fact that the US and Chinese pollution monitoring locations are in different parts of the city from one another. Another argument is based on political grounds, with CCP officials saying the US is artificially inflating numbers, while the US says China is downplaying them.

AQI Range	Chinese Ministry of Environmental Protection (MEP)	American Environmental Protection Agency (EPA)
0-50	Excellent	Good
51-100	Good	Moderate Unusually sensitive people should consider reducing prolonged or heavy exertion.
101-150	Lightly Polluted	Unhealthy for Sensitive Groups People with heart or lung disease, older adults, and children should reduce prolonged or heavy exertion.
151-200	Moderately Polluted	Unhealthy People with heart or lung disease, older adults, and children should avoid prolonged or heavy exertion; everyone else should reduce prolonged or heavy exertion.
201-300	Heavily Polluted	Very Unhealthy People with heart or lung disease, older adults, and children should avoid all physical activity outdoors. Everyone else should avoid prolonged or heavy exertion.
301-500	Severely Polluted	Hazardous Everyone should avoid all physical activity outdoors; people with heart or lung disease, older adults, and children should remain indoors and keep activity levels low.

of exertion than do adults. But children are considered more at risk mostly because their lungs are still developing. For girls, lungs finish developing at 18, while a boy's lungs mature by their early 20s. Luckily, the steps you can take to prevent exposure for children are the same as for adults (see below).

Travelers planning a long-term stay in Shanghai face more intense, but still manageable, risks. Long-term exposure to polluted air is the number one cause of lung cancer, which is the leading cause of death in China. Extended exposure to pollutants is associated with depressed lung functions even in healthy people. Studies have tied premature births, birth defects and low-weight babies to pollution. Overall, the World Health Organization estimated in 2007 that 656,000 Chinese were dying prematurely every year from health conditions caused by indoor and outdoor air pollution. Holy cow!

What can you do about it?

Short-term travelers

Time your visit wisely. Unfortunately, it's difficult, if not impossible, to forecast air quality in advance. But, certain seasons are reliably cleaner than others, so if you're serious about avoiding pollution, shoot to visit Shanghai in spring or autumn. The weather is nicest then, anyway.

Check the web or download apps to monitor air quality. You can't make wise decisions about pollution unless you have information. (A sunny nice-looking day in Shanghai isn't always an indicator of great air quality, so it's best to consult an official reading). Navigate **aqicn.org/city/shanghai/** for real-time data from a number of locations in Shanghai, or download one of the many Shanghai air quality apps available for iPhones, Androids, and other smartphones

As a rule of thumb, take the measurement from the US and China and meet somewhere in between and that will probably give you a more accurate pollution reading. Also, trust your body – if you're coughing and feeling the burn, it might be a good idea to stay indoors that day.

What are the health effects?

Depending on the timing of your visit, you may be facing a string of hazardous air days or a week of beautiful blue skies. (Remember that Shanghai isn't polluted every day.) If the air is polluted while you're here, take heart that the health effects of short-term exposure to polluted air are likely to be limited. On a heavily polluted day, it's possible to develop irritation of the eyes, nose, and throat, coughing, phlegm, chest tightness, and shortness of breath, or to simply feel sluggish and under the weather. Travelers with heart conditions should note that air pollution has been associated with an increased risk of heart attack and an increase in blood pressure.

Travelers with children may be especially concerned about pollution, and research does seem to suggest that children are more vulnerable. For starters, children take in more air per unit of body weight at a given level

Stay away from heavily-trafficked areas. Harmful pollution is concentrated around Shanghai's busy roads and highways. When you're exploring the city on foot, opt to walk on smaller roads and streets (they tend to be a lot more interesting, anyway). If you're trying to maintain an exercise routine while on vacation, practice caution: never go running outside without checking the air quality first, and if you choose to run, again, avoid busy streets.

On a heavily polluted day, limit outdoor activity. You may get lucky and have beautiful weather during your stay in Shanghai. If you don't, don't fight it. On heavily polluted days, plan indoor activities, like trying your hand at cooking classes or visiting one of the city's many excellent museums or art galleries. Your lungs will thank you. Chances are the pollution will clear in a few days, so you'll be able to tackle your outdoor activities later.

Long-term travelers

Invest in an air purifier or find accommodation that provide them. If you're going to be in Shanghai long-term, make an effort to stay somewhere as pollutant-free as possible by keeping an air-purifier in your bedroom. You'll find a wide variety of models of all sizes and prices, but no matter which one you choose, it should have a HEPA filtration system and use activated carbon. IQ Air is the most reputable brand on the market, but can run as much as US$6,000.

Fill your home with green plants. Household plants are inexpensive and have been shown to purify air indoors. In fact, according to experiments conducted by NASA, having several plants six to eight inches in diameter is enough to combat toxins floating around in a small room.

Drink clean water and eat fruits and vegetables. If you can't avoid being exposed to pollution from the air, minimize your exposure from other sources. Shanghai tap water contains heavy metals and other chemicals that can't be eliminated by boiling. Choose bottled water instead, and get it from a reputable supplier (more on water safety in the next chapter). Help your body fight the harmful effects of pollution by eating plenty of fruits and vegetables, which contain antioxidants and enzymes that counteract pollution damage. These steps sound simple, but every antioxidant helps.

(see pg 291). You'll find Shanghai to be very wifi equipped, so check the air quality early and often during your visit. If you're interested in the Chinese Ministry of Environmental Protection data, you can find it at **www.cnemc.cn** (in Chinese).

Buy a face mask. Inexpensive pollution masks can be had at 7-11s and other chain convenience stores throughout the city and some upscale hotels even provide them for you in your room. Simple cloth surgical-type masks will provide a limited amount of protection, but for a short stay they're better than nothing. "N95" type masks are also widely available – search for an "N95" face mask online and you'll get a number of results. Purchasing these at home before you leave is wise, though again they are available once you arrive. If you're looking for something a little more heavy-duty, try to purchase a mask in advance: one commonly recommended model is a Totobobo (**www.totobobo.com**), which filters PM10 and PM2.5 and can be easily adjusted to fit a child. On the high end, masks such as a 3M brand 8812 industrial facemask will remove more than 95% of pollutants.

Hot Topics

Water & Food Safety

Water Safety

Unlike in most Western countries, the tap water in Shanghai is undrinkable before it is boiled. In addition to pollution at and near the reservoirs that provide Shanghai's water, the underground pipes that deliver water throughout the city are often in terrible shape, allowing groundwater, bacteria, and other contaminants to seep into the supply. Many cases of "food poisoning" are actually the result of food being washed or prepared with contaminated water.

It's very important to avoid drinking tap water during your visit, but you shouldn't go thirsty. So what are your options for staying healthy and hydrated in Shanghai?

Boiled and Bottled Water. Hotel rooms often feature an office-style water cooler which delivers both cool and hot purified drinkable water. Other hotels offer a water heater or thermos that you can use to boil water. In some cases, four- or five-star hotels may supply high-quality mineral water for free or for a minimal charge. If you're thirsty in a restaurant but don't want to pay sky-high prices for bottled water, ask for boiled water: *kāishuǐ* (开水).

Boiling water will prevent you from getting acutely sick, but your glass will still contain high concentrations of heavy metals and other chemicals. Your healthiest bet in Shanghai is bottled water, which is ubiquitous and inexpensive. Several popular brands of bottled water, such as Wahaha (Wáhāhā; 娃 哈 哈), Nestle (Quècháo; 雀巢), Ice Dew (Bīnglù; 冰露 ; produced by Coca-Cola) and Nongfu Spring

(Nóngfū Shānquán; 农 夫 山 泉), are available in many street stands, shops, supermarkets, restaurants and hotel stores for ¥1-2 per bottle. Check to be sure that the bottle is properly sealed before you drink it.

Other Things to Consider. Order your drinks without ice cubes: they could be made with tap water. Luckily, the Chinese prefer to drink warm or hot water, even on the hottest summer day, so you're unlikely to be served ice water.

Using a minimal amount of tap water is generally OK for brushing your teeth. Alcoholic drinks and drinks made with boiled water, like coffee or tea, are also safe to drink, unless of course your Tequila Sunrise is made with fake alcohol (see pg 299 for more in this scam).

Food Safety

Forget about General Tso's chicken and fortune cookies. Thanks to the amazing diversity of Chinese cuisine, dining can be one of the most thrilling aspects of your time in Shanghai. As with any international destination, however, you're probably worried about what is safe and what will make you sick, and how you'll be able to tell the difference. It doesn't help that China seems to be in the news every month with a new food safety scandal, from glow-in-the-dark pork and melamine-laced baby formula to exploding watermelons and fake eggs, and not too long ago thousands of dead pigs were discovered mysteriously floating in a nearby river. Yuk!

China undeniably lags behind much of the West when it comes to food safety regulation and enforcement. Why? China's massive population means a massive number of companies are involved in producing food, ranging from small mom-and-pop operations to mega farms, which makes accountability and enforcement tough. And until the State Food and Drug Administration was created in early 2013, oversight was conducted by a haphazard list of different ministries and agencies. What's more, as a rapidly-growing, still-developing country, China finds itself in a similar position to the United States around the turn of the 20th century, when exposes like Upton Sinclair's book *The Jungle*

revealed the horrific standards at meat-production plants caused a public outcry over food safety standards.

Despite some high-profile scandals and room for improvement, eating in Shanghai can be completely safe and fun, with a little knowledge and preparation. Below, we'll outline some basic precautions and common-sense suggestions to keep an eye-opening culinary experience from becoming a painful one

There are a few things you can do before you leave home that will pave the way for a safe eating experience in Shanghai. It's not a bad idea to put together a mini-medical kit stocked with Immodium, Pepto Bismol, Tums and other over-the-counter stomach aids. These medicines may be available in Shanghai, but could be hard to find and expensive.

Next, ask your doctor to prescribe an antibiotic such as Ciprofloxacin (Cipro) that is effective against traveler's diarrhea. In the event that you do eat something you regret, antibiotics can seriously cut down on the duration of your suffering.

Also, consider bringing a supply of hand sanitizer, soap and hand driers are relatively rare in Shanghai public restrooms, and you'll be out in the streets encountering all kinds of new germs. Keeping your hands clean will go a long way toward keeping you healthy.

For vegetarian travelers or travelers with food allergies, consider learning how to express your special requirements in Mandarin. Or, print out a small card that states your allergies in both English and Chinese: you can show this card to waiters and waitresses. Be aware that it can sometimes be difficult to tell when a dish contains meat or other ingredient you're trying to avoid, but most restaurants will be reasonably cooperative with special requests.

Restaurants

There are a number of factors to help you judge whether a restaurant is safe to visit. An old rule of thumb says that if a place is busy and packed, especially with locals, you can probably trust it. A bigger restaurant or a chain, likewise, may have more standardized food safety practices. Locations that have been reviewed in this guidebook are also a safe bet, unless of course we mention otherwise. If you're an adventurous eater, feel free to venture off the beaten path to explore lesser-known spots, but keep your eyes open for obvious red flags like a filthy dining room or food that has been sitting out at room temperature.

Once you've chosen a restaurant, there are things you can do to minimize your risk of food poisoning. If a dish arrives at your table and it seems undercooked, rotten, or just slightly "off," trust your gut. Ask for a replacement or don't eat it.

Markets & Shops

If you're hoping to do some self-catering during your trip, keep in mind that not all markets and shops are created equal. In Shanghai, you'll see small fruit and vegetable carts and mini-markets popping up anywhere and everywhere. Some of these will be more organized outdoor set-ups, while others may simply be a man standing next to a pile of cabbages on the sidewalk. Most likely, the pineapple or peppers you buy from a roadside stand will be just fine, and interacting with hawkers and vendors is definitely part of the China experience. But if you're really concerned about food safety, the rule "bigger is better" applies when buying food on your own.

That means that sometimes you might be better off getting groceries at a big well-known, usually foreign-based chain such as Tesco (UK), Carrefour (France) or Walmart (US). These stores have better-developed supply chains, more standardized food storage, and food safety practices. Just use caution and common sense and wash your purchases very thoroughly with purified water.

Toilets in Shanghai

The Chinese toilet experience is one of contradictions – amusing to some, horrifying to others. For starters, the Chinese are credited with inventing toilet paper way back in 1391 CE when the Bureau of Imperial Supplies began producing 720,000 sheets of 6.5 m X 10 m (2 ft X 3 ft) sheets of toilet paper a year for use by emperors. Good luck finding a few squares in Shanghai when you need them today! And although the high-end toilet market is booming in China, with 5% of toilets purchased in 2010 costing between US$150 and US$6,000, you'll see plenty of Chinese infants relieving themselves not in diapers but freely on the ground, through split pants designed exactly for this purpose.

So, you could say that Chinese bathroom culture is in transition. The good news is that toilets in China's major cities, Shanghai included, have improved dramatically in recent years, and your experience will likely be just fine. Shanghai is home to everything from glass-and-marble restrooms with fresh flowers and classical music piped in to grungy side-by-side squat toilets in public restrooms.

How can I locate public toilets in Shanghai?

Public toilets are more common in some places than others. In airports, train stations, subway stations, hotels, shopping centers, chain restaurants like KFC or McDonalds, tourist attractions, and grocery stores, you'll find them everywhere. Feel free to walk confidently into these places and go right for the bathroom – most places are very permissive about non-customers using their facilities (there's a bit of foreigner privilege at play, too). Wherever you are, the ladies' and mens' rooms will probably be marked with the Chinese characters 女 (*nǚ* for female) or 男 (*nán* for male). Learn to recognize these characters. If the location of the bathroom isn't obvious, you can ask *Xǐshǒujiān zài nǎli?* (洗手间在哪里 ?) which means "Where is the toilet?" If you'd rather rely on English, choose "toilet" or "WC" instead of "restroom," "bathroom," or "washroom" – it's more likely to be understood.

Western-style toilets are becoming more and more common in public restrooms, and you'll sometimes see just one or two next to a row of squat toilets. Keep your eyes peeled for a sign or a picture on one of the stall doors with a picture of a Western toilet.

What is a squat toilet and how do I use it?

A squat toilet looks more or less like the photo on the following page. Stand with your back to the wall and place your feet on the grooved areas. Squat over the hole, doing your best to aim. Used toilet paper should always be placed in the small wastebasket to the side of the toilet to avoid backing up the plumbing and making an already-messy situation even worse. Squat toilets usually flush at the press of a button or by stepping on a foot pedal on the floor. That's all there is to it, really – it can be an intimidating process at first, but you'll get the hang of it.

Some public restrooms will have private stalls dividing the toilets, while others may have only waist-high dividers with no doors or partitions at all. Some toilets have splash guards to keep you and your pants legs from getting caught in the crossfire. Try to relax and take care of business as quickly as possible – eventually you'll be as accustomed as the locals and expats, who shrug and count their blessings when they find a clean decent place to pee.

Advanced toilet tips: how can I survive my Shanghai bathroom experience?

Want to squat with the best of 'em? Here are some tips for ensuring a smooth squatty potty experience.

Never go anywhere without TP. The number one tip is to always, always carry a small supply of toilet paper with you. A bottle of hand sanitizer can't hurt, either.

Know the rules of lining up. Unlike other Western countries, people tend to line up outside one specific stall rather than forming one big line and taking the next one that becomes available.

Hand off bags and purses to a friend before venturing in. There may not be any hooks to hang a bag, and the floor might be covered in something you'd rather not carry around with you all day.

the same seat. Think of your squatting experience as a new trend in hygiene. Or, consider that some studies suggest that squatting to use the bathroom is healthier than sitting, because sitting constricts some of the muscles used for evacuation. It's believed that sitting on the toilet is a factor in the higher rates of hernias, hemorrhoids, and gastroesophageal reflux disease (GERD) in the West.

There's no way I can use a squat toilet. What's my alternative?

You can use the bathroom before you leave your hotel in the morning and try to plan the rest of your pit-stops at places where you know there's likely to be a nice clean bathroom (think international hotels or upscale restaurants and shopping malls). If you have a tour guide, ask him or her to suggest good opportunities to use the restroom throughout the day – they're usually very well-acquainted with the quality of the facilities in popular tourist areas.

Ditto for phones and keys. It's better to approach the squat with nothing in your pockets – at least nothing that you don't want to lose down the black hole from which there is no return.

Roll up your pants. Public restrooms can be very wet, sometimes because they're frequently mopped, and sometimes because they're not.

Get in the Chinese mindset. To the Chinese, it's Western-style toilets that are unsanitary, since everyone's bare butt touches

Smart-phone Apps for Traveling Shanghai

Technology is making traveling easier by the day. Not too long ago suitcases and backpacks alike would be jammed with maps, language dictionaries, guide books, reservation confirmations, plane/train tickets, cameras, video recorders and other travel items. Nowadays all you need is your smart-phone and your Panda Guides book or e-book and you're set for the trip of a lifetime! For your convenience, we've made a list of the best smart-phone apps that will make your journey through the Middle Kingdom as hassle free as possible. Type the bold heading in the app store and your desired app will appear.

Weather, Date & Time

China Air Quality Index (FREE) – Due to the notorious clouds of smog covering the country, this app provides an up to date air quality index for every city in China and serves as a great way to avoid places with high levels of pollution.

The Weather Channel (FREE) – Though not limited to Chinese cities, it's still probably the most professional and accurate weather app available. It literally has everything you need to know about the weather conditions in every city in the world.

World Clock- Time Zones (FREE) – China technically only has one time zone (don't tell the people of Xinjiang that since they created their own unofficial individual time zone), but this app is still beneficial for contacting those on other side of the globe.

Calendar Conversion (FREE) – With so many festivals in China, and with those like Spring Festival (aka Chinese New Year) greatly affecting transportation comfort and pricing, you'll definitely need to know which days local holidays fall on. Calendar Conversion does just that and can help you avoid hectic travel seasons throughout the year.

Top 10 Most Used Apps in the World (Weixin/WeChat is the only Chinese app listed).

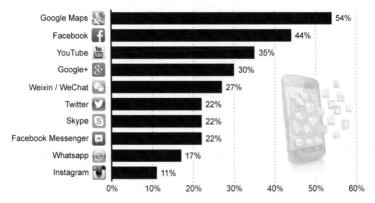

App	Percentage
Google Maps	54%
Facebook	44%
YouTube	35%
Google+	30%
Weixin / WeChat	27%
Twitter	22%
Skype	22%
Facebook Messenger	22%
Whatsapp	17%
Instagram	11%

Currency & Unit Converter

Convert Free (FREE) – As straight forward as it comes, this one converts currency and every other international unit of measurement.

XE Currency (FREE) – XE is better than Convert Free if you're solely looking to convert currencies rather than other units of measurements. It has over 80 international currencies and gives an instant update with the shake of a phone.

Transportation

Drive Me To ($1.99) – This app is a virtual address book with all the major points of interest in Mainland China and Hong Kong. Upon selecting your destination, a polite request note with the address written in Chinese will appear on your screen to show your driver.

Driving in China ($1.99) – In case you're tired of using overcrowded public transportation, get a car, go your own way and be prepared to face massive traffic jams. This app quizzes and prepares you for the national Chinese driving test that's required for both locals and foreigners looking to obtain a local's driver's license.

Aibang Trains (Àibāng Lièchē; 爱 帮 列 车 **) (FREE)** – Despite requiring an internet connection, Aibang is still useful for checking out national train times, information regarding specific train routes and departing/arrival stations. It is even updated for the speedy new D-trains (aka bullet trains) for those in a hurry.

Explore Shanghai (FREE) – Shanghai's metro map is constantly upgrading, so make sure to stay up to date with this one in order to never get lost.

Mandarin

Pleco Chinese Dictionary (FREE) – Pleco is perhaps the best Mandarin/English electronic dictionary out there. You can write in English or pinyin for a translation or upgrade some add-ons at a cost to get flashcards, a camera based optical Chinese character recognition device, full touch screen handwriting and other tech-savvy accessories.

HanZi Card ($5.99) – An electronic flashcard system coupled with a voice pronunciation feature for the top 3,000 most used words in the Chinese language. You can even personalize your list to narrow down your trouble words. This one is recommended for anyone serious about learning Mandarin.

Nemo Chinese Phrases (FREE) – Nemo is a user friendly app for the short-term traveler that has the 50 most used phrases in Mandarin. It's also compatible with English, pinyin, Chinese characters and an audio voice device.

Waygo Chinese Translator (FREE) – In case you don't want to purchase a camera-based character recognition device on Pleco, get Waygo's for free. Though it's mostly aimed towards menu vocab and simple phrases, it's still extremely useful. All you have to do is take a picture of the characters on your phone and Waygo will translate them instantly into English.

Google Translator (FREE) – Just like everything else Google makes, this is another popular app. Type English, pinyin or simply draw the character with your finger on the touch screen to get an instant translation. You can also use the voice translation function which is fairly accurate.

China Travel Guide by Triposo (FREE) – A complete travel guide for all major Chinese cities with the latest info concerning everything from nightlife, entertainment, hotels/hostels, leisure activities to tours, tourist attractions, restaurants/cafes, outdoor activities, parks and shopping. It also includes maps, pictures, recommendations, prices and operating hours.

World Travelpedia Nightlife ($5.99) – The app a party animal can't live without, this displays the hottest parties, nightclubs and bars from every major city in the world. There's even a map to show you the best spots closest to you in case you get drunk and lost from one club to another.

City Weekend (FREE) – This app lists all the popular listings such as bars, restaurants and other popular venues by category and area in the Shanghai metropolitan zone. It also provides a map, directions, reviews and contact information of each place.

Shanghai FashionNomad ($2.49 + $0.99 for the Shanghai app)- Perfect for the shopper, this creative app lists shopping addresses, areas and boutique listings, and has maps to get your spree started.

Shanghai City Guide (FREE) – Has info concerning all the hot spots in Shanghai, from accomodations, bars, tourist sites, etc.

Communication & Social Media

QQ (FREE) – QQ is China's favorite instant messaging portal and is used by everyone from students to businessmen. In fact you may hear the signature QQ *beep beep beep* for incoming messages hundreds of times a day while in China. It's fantastic for keeping in touch with local friends or meeting new ones.

WeChat/Weixin (FREE) – Another popular Chinese instant messaging program, WeChat (known as Weixin in Chinese) allows you to send voice messages, share photos, and meet new friends with the shake of the phone or a "messages in a bottle."

WhatsApp (FREE) – Though more popular in the West, WhatsApp is growing quickly in China and the rest of Asia. It's another great instrument for keeping in touch with those back home, chatting with your local friends and meeting new people.

Skype (FREE) – Skype is without a doubt one of the cheapest and easiest ways to contact loved ones from afar. There's also a video chat feature so you can actually show them all the fun you're having.

News

China Daily News (FREE) – Stay informed with one of China's premier English news services. Here you can get the inside scoop for all the latest news happening across China.

Accommodation

Hostelworld (FREE) – Handy for booking hostels within and outside of China.

Booking.com (FREE) – Another accommodation app similar to Hostelworld, Booking focuses more on hotels than hostels

History

Chinese History Timeline (FREE) – This one can help the confused traveler digesting 5,000 years of history make sense of all the dynasties and historic relics found all over the country.

Maps

iMaps+ for Google Maps ($1.99) – With Google's classic street view, road maps, GPS and directions, this is a wonderful gizmo to get you from point A to point B. However, it must be noted that Google is frequently "unavailable" in China.

百度地图 **(Bǎidù Dìtú) (FREE)** – This might be a better option for the traveler who can read Chinese. It's similar to Google Maps but better with walking, driving and public transportation directions.

Other

Sit or Squat (FREE) – A potential life saver, especially if you haven't learned how to say the most important travel phrase out there, "Where's the bathroom?" Sit or Squat shows you the closest public restrooms near your current location and even rates them on cleanliness. You've got to love technology!

Tudou (土豆) (FREE) – Sites like Youtube are blocked in China unless you have a VPN. If you don't, try Tudou – the Chinese equivalent to Youtube – which has many Chinese and Western videos, movies and TV shows. It also has many of the viral videos seen on Youtube for those who can't live without them.

Scams

Though Shanghai is one of the safest cities in the world, scammers can truly make a meal out of some of the top tourist sites. Buzzing like bees, they hover around places like the Bund, Guyi Garden and (especially) Nanjing East Road, looking for those unwitting and unaccustomed to their land. While they are pesky and persistent, for the most part they are nothing to fret about, just be aware and avoid them. This section describes the scams you will certainly encounter at some point if you plan to see the big attractions. With a quick read you will be well-armed to deal with or avoid the cons.

Black Taxis

Black Taxis are ubiquitous all over the city. Update your knowledge on them first and foremost.

The scam: Hēichē (黑车), or black taxis, troll the streets for gullible tourists to bite on their unlikely stories. These taxis will overcharge unaccustomed tourists, take detours, or jack up the agreed price at the end of the trip.

How to avoid it: Only take metered taxis. The most conspicuous of the *heiche* are the private taxis, civilian cars with (often) small red lights below the rear-view mirror. Such operations are usually accompanied by a man, or men, who accost travelers to jump in their cars. Do not take these cabs, plain and simple.

The first thing to be aware of when grabbing a cab is the placard on the top of the car. These are government sanctioned (official) taxis, and you should only hail them; no placard, no go. Taxi drivers are required by law to use their meter, so say *dǎbiǎo* (打表) to make them turn it on. Some official taxi drivers may have a story about their meter being broken, or some other hoodwinking reason for why theirs is a set price. If this happens, forget that taxi; get out and find a new one.

Note: Pudong and Hongqiao Airport are crawling with these illegal private operations, and they are likely to be your first encounter upon arrival. Fervently deny them, and get in the official taxi lines. Don't let a long taxi line daunt you, they are fast moving.

Personal Account

I've lived in China for years and know all about the black taxis, and still, I fell for their dirty games. I'm an English teacher from the US who lives in Chengdu, and I returned home one April to visit my family and friends. It had been two years since I'd seen them! On my return leg, I had a 24 hour layover in Shanghai, but having been to the city many times, I decided to explore Hangzhou, a place I had never visited before.

We landed in Pudong right on time and I took the four hour shuttle straight to Hangzhou. It passed a tremendous time around West Lake, then returned to Shanghai the following morning to catch my flight back to Chengdu. The only problem was I caught the shuttle to the Shanghai city center and not Pudong airport, but I figured that'd be OK since I could just take a taxi.

Well, as luck would have it, the bus was delayed, and when I arrived in Shanghai I only had a little more than an hour before my plane was departing. Frantically, I tried hailing down taxis, but to no avail. I was sure I was going to miss my flight until a regular car pulled up and asked me where I needed to go. I knew it was a black taxi, but at this point, I had no other option. He charged me ¥300 (a major rip off, but that's as low as I could get him and I needed to catch that flight), but he actually zipped me to the airport in record time.

When I pulled out my money to pay, I was short ¥100, but I did have a 100 dollar bill leftover from my trip home. I gave him that and told him to give me ¥300 in change and we'd call it even. He grinned, slipped the Benjamin in his pocket, and said, "No change." He knew time was against me, and I argued for a bit until I realized I had 35 minutes left. I grabbed my belongings, jumped out of the car and ran toward the gate, leaving the black taxi with an outrageous ¥600 fare. FML.

Taxi Drive-offs

Easy to avoid if you have a heads up, a new scam hitting the market in early 2013 is the drive-off.

The scam: China Daily covered two January police reports where taxi drivers claiming to have a dead battery asked passengers to exit the car and help push the car or help to close the trunk. With the passengers removed from the car the drivers quickly hit the gas, in one instance making off with ¥17,000 ($2,700) and a laptop.

How to avoid it: Never exit a cab with your articles still inside. The obvious response to any driver who requests your assistance (before you have reached your destination and have all your belongings) is to give a firm "No!" Do not exit a vehicle without all your personal effects, and do not be afraid to firmly refuse an insistent driver; eventually they will want to get on with life and will drop the issue. If you arrive at your destination and have removed all your possessions from the car, feel free to lend a neighborly hand to a friendly driver if he needs one.

Tea Houses

Many international youth hostels and large hotels are now warning of the Tea House scammers. Originating in Beijing, the scam became so profitable for the scammers that they spread like wildfire throughout the country. In Shanghai, they have become quite prolific around the Nanjing East Road area, but you have a chance to encounter them elsewhere.

The scam: Nearly always encountered as well-spoken locals or domestic tourists, these friendly and charming crooks invite naïve and unaccustomed travelers to absurdly priced tea houses and proceed to foot the unfortunates with bills often exceeding US$100. Though the teahouse is the most prominent type of this scam, drinks, meals, and coffees might also be offered. These scammers often prey on men by using pretty girls as their representatives.

How to avoid it: Be suspicious of any stranger on the street offering to take you somewhere. Obvious tourists (i.e. with an open guidebook, map, or a foreign face) are major bait for these scammers, so be on high alert at tourist hot spots. The key word in this scam is "stranger." The friendly Chinese you met having breakfast at your hostel that wants to share a day out with a new friend is one thing, the stranger that approaches you on the street to take you to a food or drink venue is totally different.

Strangers who insist on choosing the venue raise another big red flag. Conversations started randomly by strangers offering to take you for food or drinks are almost always a scam. They can be persistent as well, offering to walk you to your destination. Quite simply, do not agree to go anywhere with strangers if it doesn't feel right.

Personal Account

I love Shanghai and everything about it. The architecture, the clubs, the lights and the action… everything! Unfortunately, I lived in Wuxi in Jiangsu Province when this scam hit me, just an hour train ride away, but that gave me the chance to come here on the weekend. I checked into Captain Hostel just like I always do, and got the warning from the staff about not accepting offers from strangers to drink tea, practice English or check out an art gallery… just as they always do. I told them I had been to Shanghai countless times and was pretty much a local.

While doing some shopping along East Nanjing Road, I got approached by a hip girl with perfect English. I instantly knew what was up. When she invited me for tea, I told her, "I'm not interested in getting scammed today, so I'll be on my way. BYE!" The girl called me a bitch and walked away.

Later that night, I was at Perry's with two of my friends who had just gotten off work. My friends are actually boyfriend and girlfriend, so I was kind of the third wheel, but a handsome guy from Spain made his way into our conversation. Alejandro was backpacking and had just arrived in Shanghai the previous day. We got to talking, and he explained that his three-month trip to China had been amazing up until the point he got scammed that afternoon off Nanjing East Road. A bell rang in my head, and I asked if the girl was tall, skinny, wore a purple shirt and spoke perfect English.

Alejandro screamed, "Yes! But how did you know that?" I smiled and simply told him that she almost got me too. He explained that the scammer, Jessica, invited him for tea and ordered some meager snacks, and when the bill arrived, it came out to ¥2,000! She then told him that the tea was very special and that's why it was so expensive (even though it was probably Wal Mart brand Oolong). In the end, he ended up paying ¥1,500, which is still a lot, but not nearly as much as other people I know have paid.

Art Students

Very similar in nature to the Tea House scams, pesky "art students" patrol the big tourist spots, in particular Nanjing East

Road, striking up friendly conversations with strolling tourists.

The scam: How many of them are actually art students remains uncertain, but what ensues is a trip to an overpriced art gallery where a high pressure buying situation can sour your mood quickly. Certain foreigners may enjoy the friendly chitchat, but keep in mind that if they feel they have hooked you, it will not be easy to get rid of them.

How to avoid it: Identify the situation and just say "No!" Avoiding this one is almost exactly the same as the teahouse scam above. Strangers approaching you are big red flags. Our advice is to give them a friendly brush-off.

Personal Account

My wife and I had two weeks in China, so we planned to have one week in and around Shanghai, then one week in Beijing. Our first stop was Shanghai, and having amazingly conquered jetlag, we hit the streets thr first morning to explore the city. Our hotel was located near the French Concession, so that's naturally where we started off first. It didn't take long, however, for a young female to come up to us and start chatting with us, asking us where we were from and what we thought of China. After a quick introduction, she told us that she was an art student and had a gallery she wanted us to check out. My wife, being an art teacher, jumped at the chance, and we were on our way.

Once we got there, we met her boyfriend (who was also supposedly an art student) and toured the gallery (which wasn't much of a gallery). They showed us a few pictures and claimed they painted them, though my wife who has an eye for art knew they were all prints. We were just about to walk out the door when they began asking us which ones we wanted to buy. I politely told them we weren't interested, but they persisted. They then began to give the line about being "poor, humble, art students just trying to make a living," but we weren't having any of that.

Finally, we had enough, so I gave them ¥200 for a cruddy picture just to get them off my back. We left, frustrated and ¥200 in the hole, but at least we had a valuable lesson the rest of the trip not to trust the so-called art students. Actually, this bit of inside info paid off when we went to Beijing and got approached by both tea scammers and art students in the same day! We blew them off, feeling like true China experts.

Pickpockets

Theft, on the surface, may not seem like a scam, but those pickpockets who work in teams are akin to con artists.

The scam: In public areas it is not uncommon for partnered rogues to play the bump and cut combination. That is, one may distract you (ask a question, bump into you, photo op, etc) while another slits your bag or pocket with a razor and nimbly extracts your valuables.

How to avoid it: Keep your valuables as close to your body as possible and within your field of vision. The best way to guard against this is to keep your money and other valuables in a money belt under your shirt, or otherwise close to your body, and right where you can see them. Items that may not fit so closely to your body should be kept inside a snug interior pocket of your bag, one that is hidden and inaccessible from the bag's exterior. When riding public transportation, it is advisable to wear your bag on the front of your body where you can easily see it.

Bag Snatching

Not exactly a scam, and definitely not unique to China, but very pertinent.

The scam: Some tourists have become the unfortunate victims of the drive-by bag-snag, where a running thief snatches an unfastened, unattended, or otherwise vulnerable bag at full sprint. Because the thief hits at full speed, the dazed victims are unprepared, and by the time it dawns on them what has happened, the quick bandit is long gone.

How to avoid it: Keep your bags away

from the open. When dining or relaxing in public areas, always keep your bags close and away from the road; the backs of chairs or places adjacent to trafficked areas are especially vulnerable. Good spots to place your bag include the seats of chairs that are between you and the interior (i.e. the wall or window) of your dining environment or on the floor (if it seems clean enough) between your legs.

Massage

It goes without saying that many massage parlors in Shanghai double as brothels, or at least have a seedy side.

The scam: Unsuspecting patrons have found their relaxing massages taking sudden and unwelcomed erotic turns, and the embarrassed victims shell out for the extortionate bill in lieu of causing a scene.

How to avoid it: Only use patron massage parlors that are suggested by a reliable source. A good general rule to follow is avoiding massage parlors with tasteless red neon signs or those that staff only women. Your best bet is to check with your hostel or hotel, or search our recommendations in Disctractions (pg 230).

Counterfeit Bills

One of the less common scams but one of the more difficult to spot, counterfeit cash in China is limited to ¥50 and ¥100 bank notes, and they are dealt out by dishonest taxi drivers and small shops. There are two ways you may be given a fake bill.

The scam (1): The scam is played out when you pay for your goods or transport with a ¥100 (or less often with a ¥50) note and the driver or shopkeeper "inspects" it, often outside your field of vision. They then inform you that the bill is fake, return it to you, and ask for another one. This may happen several times, and when you suspect something is amiss and check your bills later you will realize that the bills they returned to you were switched out for fakes by their crafty hands. It is a sleight of hand parlor trick.

The scam (2): Sometimes the attempt to pass you a bogus bill occurs when the driver or shopkeeper tries to give you a large bill as change, claiming they have no small change. Maybe your cab fare was ¥60 and they try to give you a ¥50, using the "no change" excuse and even saying they'll give you a slight discount. What they are actually doing is passing you a fake note. If they truly don't have change, they will go to another shop and exchange for it.

How to avoid it: Pay attention to your large bills and watch the driver and shopkeeper's hands very carefully. To beat this scam, first keep one thing in mind: banks are masters at screening for fake bills, which means that whether you exchanged for Chinese RMB at a bank back home or grabbed some from a Chinese ATM, you can be 100% sure that your bank issued 100s are not fake. When paying a suspicious taxi driver or shop owner with a large bill, watch their hands very carefully, and feel free to make a fuss if they try to examine the note out of sight, even if it's just behind the counter. The extra cautious will check the serial number on the bank note and write it down in view of the recipient to discourage any funny business. If they manage to pull one over on you, and you are close enough to your hotel, grab one of the staff to come out and get the driver's information.

Personal Account

My sister was visiting from New York and took a cab directly from the airport to my apartment. She called me when she arrived, so I ran downstairs to help bring her bags up. After a big hug, she told me that she thought the ATM had given her fake bills since the taxi driver wouldn't accept them. Astonished, especially knowing that the ATMs will NEVER dispense fake notes, I examined her ten 100 bills and saw that several of them were indeed fake.

I asked, "Did you give the bills you got from the ATM to the driver, and did he hand them back saying they were fake?"

She exclaimed, "Yeah, he did that with a few of my bills." Case closed – I explained to her that she had just fallen for one of the oldest tricks in the book.

"Welcome to Shanghai, sis!" I patted her on her back, carried her bags up to my room and brushed the incident off into the wind.

Beggars

Beggars are not as bad in Shanghai as in some second or third-tier cities, but you will likely encounter some, especially on the fringes of tourist areas.

The scam: Shanghai has a phenomenon of the professional beggar. Though it's not

unique to the city, one of its characteristics (which is less common in the West) is that many beggars make more money than white-collar office workers. Some statistics suggest that 85% of beggars are not actually poor and beg professionally. If you give money to some of these people, they may hound you for more, or you may be subject to a train of beggars who have quickly caught word of the "generous foreigner." There are also those children who sadly beg for money and are almost 100% of the time kidnapped and forced by a crime syndicate to beg for money, which of course goes to the unscrupulous bosses.

How to avoid it: Don't give money to those you can't be sure are legitimate. Ignore them, plain and simple. Some may pester you for a bit, such as an old woman clutching a few small bills and making gracious gestures while murmuring *xiexie* (thank you). Just ignore them. Looking through your phone or chatting with others is a good way to snub these panhandlers.

Do not give money to child beggars; it only promotes their tragic situation, and the money you would give them will not stay in their hands. If you really feel the urge to help, give them some food to eat in front of you. Then you know that what you gave truly went to them. Be warned, however: if you do this you may be subject to a spree of children who have heard of your generosity.

Note: Sometimes you will see those with shocking disfigurements, or those affected by terrible accidents (such as people who have obviously been severely burned or lost limbs). It can be heart wrenching (so be prepared), and many of these people actually cannot work to pay for large medical bills. They are far less likely to hound you, because their need is often genuine. If you feel the urge to give, these people are far more legitimate (and gracious) recipients.

KTV Scam

This one is not terribly common, but it is one that can really ruin what begins as a fun-filled and jovial night.

The scam: Usually happening to lone travelers, but can also happen to a couple of friends or gullible groups, the scam usually begins when you meet a friendly Chinese man (who often gussies up the role to look like a businessman) while out to dinner. He invites you to eat with him and a couple of very pretty ladies who have just come to meet him. He's so friendly in fact, that he pays for the whole meal, yours included, and invites you to come sing some songs at the local karaoke joint. Before you know it, the alcohol is flowing, dishes of fruit and snacks are being brought out, and you end up left with an outrageous bill – often in the thousands of dollars – that you never imagined you'd suddenly be muscled into paying. Bad end to a great night.

How to avoid: Don't run off with strangers you meet. Your mother told you this one, didn't she? There are endless friendly and honest locals who would love to be your friend, but it's very unlikely that these are the kind of people who invite random strangers out for a night of drinking and karaoke on their tab. Meeting friends at your hostel is a different story; just be very wary of random people wanting to show you a high-priced good time.

Bar Tab Scam

Having some kicks out at the bars is for many an integral part of the traveling experience. Just remember that alcohol impairs your judgment and memory, and there are some places who may try to take advantage of you in your inebriated state.

The scam: You're having a good time drinking with some friends. The time is flying by, and the beers are going down. The servers have a tab running for you, or maybe they suggest just leaving the bottle caps on the table to tally up when you are done. The problem is, you've been having too much fun to keep track, and they may even slyly snuck a few extra caps onto your table from departed patrons. When all is said and done, your tab is much higher than it should be, but you're in no position to argue now.

How to avoid: Pay for every drink as you order. Easy enough, right? It really is. You buy a beer, you pay for it. Get a round of shots, pay before the server leaves the table. By consistently paying each round there is no way they can throw on extras at the end, and you can easily stand your ground if they try to say otherwise.

Fake Alcohol

China has a problem with fake alcohol. Be aware of it and try to avoid it, it's not something you want to mess with.

The Scam: A bar will use rubbing alcohol or some other potentially dangerous alcohol "substitute" (like ethylene glycol) to refill or fill their alcohol containers. Sometimes this will be done by the distributor and then sold to bars looking to cut costs; fake alcohol is cheaper than the real deal.

How to avoid it: Taste your drinks carefully. This scam isn't so common that you need to be paranoid about having some drinks in Shanghai, and there isn't any foolproof way to avoid it. The best things you can do are stick to alcohol brands you know well (i.e. know their taste and feel) and stop drinking anything that seems, tastes or feels amiss. Oftentimes you will notice that a drink, or especially a shot, just doesn't taste right and isn't making you feel the way you normally do. These are signs to pack up and find a new place to drink.

Personal Account

You know it's bad when you have a two-day hangover that came from one drinking session and both were two of the worst hangover days of your life! I'm not going to lie, I'm a big buy and can throw back my shots, and my buddies and I always seem to kill a few bottles when out on the town (the perfect remedy after a long week of teaching kindergarteners the colors of the rainbow and greetings in English). But last Friday, after going to a bar and having a mere three shots of Tequila and a few beers, I started throwing up and became extremely dizzy. My drinking buddies felt the same, and we called it quits to return home, where I slept the rest of the weekend. When I finally came to around Sunday afternoon, we all realized that we had been served fake booze.

Restaurant Scams

There are two scams that you should watch out for in restaurants. They are not terribly common, but they do happen to domestic and international tourists, so be aware of them.

The scam (1): Many restaurants will keep separate English and Chinese menus. When a foreigner comes in, the owner will immediately provide them with an English menu, and while the prices may seem approximately equivalent to those in the West, in China they are steep and actually much higher than those on the Chinese menu.

How to avoid it: This one may be a bit harder to avoid than others, but fortunately it's less common. The big red flag to look out for is if you are immediately greeted with an English menu. If this happens, request a Chinese menu. If they refuse you can be pretty sure they are up to something; choose a different place to eat. Also, if you order from the Chinese menu be sure they do not try to charge inflated prices in the end, this can happen as well and you should make a stink about it until they give you the original prices from the menu you ordered from.

The scam (2): One that happens to domestic tourists and foreigners alike, a restaurant will have two menus that look identical except one has significantly inflated prices. They first give you the menu with reasonable prices to order from, then when the bill comes at the end of the meal it's higher than it should be. When you protest, they bring out the menu with higher prices and try to make you out to be the fool.

How to avoid it: Beating this one is simple. Using a smart-phone or camera, simply take pictures of the items on the menu and their prices, and if they try to show you a different menu at the end, simply pull out your picture and you've got them red-handed.

Culture Shock

Language Barrier

Travelers may be surprised to find that English isn't widely spoken in Shanghai, despite the impression in the West that everyone in China is furiously studying it. That impression is true to some extent – English is a requirement in high school curriculums across the country – but most people learn just enough to pass the test and then rarely use it again. Tour guides, hotel staff, and others who work with tourists on a regular basis are likely exceptions.

Think about your own language skills in this context. Even if you studied Spanish in high school back in the day, if a Central American tourist approached you in your hometown speaking native-level *español*, you'd probably be pretty startled and might not have a clue what to say. Here are a few tips to ease the language barrier during your stay.

An English sign outside doesn't mean English is spoken inside. Plain and simple, just because the name of a business is in English (it seems just about everywhere in Shanghai these days has an English name) it doesn't necessarily mean the staff speaks English. While most locals don't speak English fluently, it is said by many Chinese that the Shanghanese have a better command of English than the residents of most other major Chinese cities. Whether that's true or not, most of the English speaking natives will probably be in the downtown area, around the former French Concession, People's Square, the Bund and Nanjing Road. The further you get away from the center, the less English you'll encounter.

Don't be shy about gesturing. When ordering from a menu or buying things in a store, don't hesitate to simply point at what you want. No one will be offended. Likewise, don't be afraid to use your fingers to show how many you want. You might feel a little silly, but it's a language everyone can understand. That being said, before you head out on your trip, it can't hurt to:

Learn a little Chinese. Even if you only learn a few phrases and numbers, your effort will be recognized and appreciated. Your basic Mandarin may not always get your point across, but it will always earn a little goodwill from whoever you're interacting with. See pg 30 for an overview of basic Mandarin.

Download some helpful language apps. If you have a smart-phone, there are a number of apps that you can use to ease the language barrier. Some apps simply provide Chinese phrases on your phone that you can point to when instructing a taxi driver or alerting a waitress to your food allergies. Others have cool tools like the ability to trace a Chinese character on the screen with your finger and get an instant English translation. See pg 291 for an overview of helpful apps.

Behavior

When you imagine Shanghai, do you picture a super-crowded street with hordes of people fighting their way down the street en masse? If so, you might be pleasantly surprised by the elbow room in many parts of the city, though downtown is extremely dense, and there are definitely different norms for public behavior here that you should be aware of.

Forget your "personal space" bubble. Maybe it's a natural consequence of growing up in a country with 1.4 billion people, or maybe it's China's emphasis on a communal society, with multiple generations often living under one roof. Whatever it is, it means that you won't have nearly as much personal space as you're probably used to. On a crowded subway car, you can be pressed up against a stranger in a way that you wouldn't expect until after your third date. An elevator will be crammed with twice as many people as you imagined could ever fit in it. People passing you in the street will brush up against you and not acknowledge it. Try to take it in stride.

Cutting in line – if there is a line at all – is common. You probably haven't thought about someone "skipping" you in line since kindergarten, but be prepared to battle it again during your visit. An orderly, formal line is something you probably won't encounter here. Assert yourself and don't be afraid to stand very close to the people in front of you – what might seem like a respectable distance to you looks like an opening to someone else.

You're going to get a lot of curious looks and stares. Foreign tourists and expats have become a common sight, but Shanghai is still a very homogenous city, and anyone who looks "different" will be an object of curiosity.

Look out for spitballs. Expect to see people spitting on the ground, even indoors, in Shanghai. Often it can transcend mere spitting, becoming an elaborate hacking and coughing routine that produces a phlegm wad the size of a golf ball (air pollution and high smoking rates may be partly to blame). Not everyone does it, but don't be shocked when you do see (and hear) it.

Casual littering is accepted. Despite garbage cans and anti-littering posters, you will see garbage on the streets of Shanghai. It can be surprising to see a grown man unwrap a Snickers bar and let the wrapper fall to the ground, but there's simply a different set of expectations. You may also notice the orange-clad sanitation workers with brooms and dustpans scouring each block for trash – perhaps that explains why locals seem so casual about littering. Don't add to the problem by joining in!

Regular conversation volume is much louder. After a few hours in Shanghai, you may start to wonder why everyone is yelling. It's not in your imagination. Former NBA superstar and Chinese native Yao Ming even coached his fellow countrymen to try to speak more softly in order to be good hosts during the Olympics. It's hard to say why shout-talking is so prevalent here – some people tend to speak up to demonstrate authority, make a point or simply show energy and friendliness.

Food & Eating

*T*hey will eat everything that swims except a submarine, everything that flies except an airplane, and everything with four legs except the table. That's a famous saying about the people of Guangdong Province in southern China. Shanghai doesn't have quite the same reputation for culinary adventurousness, but you're likely to encounter foods – or part of animals – being served here that would be totally alien in your culture. Think turtle soup, chicken feet, pig hooves, fish heads, and stinky tofu. Western culture is actually unique in its refusal to eat many animal parts, so either say a polite "no thank you" or give it a shot! 1.4 billion people can't be too wrong.

Chinese food in China isn't like Chinese food at home. If you come to Shanghai expecting to feast on crab Rangoon, egg rolls, and fortune cookies, you're in for a letdown. None of these dishes are common here; they're mostly Americanized versions of Chinese food created by immigrants from southern China. There's a huge and delicious variety of real Chinese food waiting for you, though, so don't be disappointed.

Chinese restaurants can be crowded, noisy and smoky. Depending on where you eat during your trip, you may encounter restaurants that aren't exactly what you're used to in terms of ambience: diners are often crowded around small tables and seated on stools, a TV might be blaring in the corner, people smoke heavily and ash their cigarettes on the floor, and shouting to get the waiter or waitress's attention is perfectly normal. None of these things mean the restaurant won't be delicious – in fact, it might be a good sign that you've found a popular local spot.

All my drinks are warm! The Chinese believe that drinking too many cold beverages is unhealthy and throws your body out of balance. You might be frustrated to find that everything you order, including soda, juice, water, and beer, arrives at your table room temperature, or in the case of water, steaming hot! Try to have a "when in Rome" attitude about this one – you shouldn't consume ice since it's likely made from tap water.

You call this breakfast?! The foods that locals prefer for breakfast, from hot rice porridge and deep-fried dough to hot soymilk and fluffy meat dumplings, might not exactly scream "breakfast" to your Western tastes. Coffee is becoming more popular, but is not reflexively served with breakfast the way it is in other places. It can be had at cafes and coffee chains like Starbucks and Pacific Coffee, but it's relatively expensive here, usually costing upwards of ¥25 (about US$4).

Eating dogs and cats is acceptable in China. Well, yes, you may find dog and cat on the menu in China, but it's much more common in very rural areas and in the south, not in large metropolitan cities. Protests and public outcry have increased, however, and public opinion has started to turn against this custom, especially when it comes to cats. As a tourist in Shanghai, you're very unlikely to end up in any restaurants serving either. Again, it's basically unheard of in the West, but not totally uncommon in other areas of the world.

Out & About

The air is hazy and polluted. We've already mentioned this, but if the pollution is high during your trip, it can take your breath away. See our section on air pollution (pg 284) for more details on how to keep gray days from ruining your trip.

Smoking is very common, and seems to be allowed everywhere. Smoking rates have fallen off in most Western countries, but in China, over 50% of men are smokers. (The rate for women is much lower, as in most societies). And not only are there more smokers, they seem to have free reign to smoke indoors, outdoors, in restaurants, offices, elevators, and hospitals. A "no smoking" sign on the wall is usually no indication that the air will be smoke-free.

Salesmen and scammers can be very aggressive with tourists. Everyone from fake handbag sellers to rickshaw drivers sees a tourist as a potential money-making opportunity, so don't be surprised if you find yourself being constantly approached or followed by them in touristy areas. If you're not interested, just keep walking and don't make eye contact. A few choice Chinese words like *bú yaò* ("don't want") can be helpful as well.

Many girls are carrying umbrellas, but it's a sunny day. Maintaining very white skin is considered desirable among Chinese women, so they take sun protection seriously. You'll see plenty of girls carrying frilly and cute umbrellas to stay in the shade, and you might want one yourself if you're visiting Shanghai in the height of summer.

It seems like everyone's face is buried in a smart-phone, whether they're walking, biking, riding the subway or even driving! Personal computer ownership rates are much lower in China than in most Western countries, but most people in Shanghai own some type of

When you consider that non-computer owners have to do all their email, gaming and chatting on their phones, it makes more sense. On top of that, instant-message programs called QQ and Wechat are massively popular in China, and many people remain logged in all day to keep in touch with friends. One study even showed that white-collar office workers in China spend an average of 6.72 hours a day on their phones. That may seem like a shocking number, but many people spend as much as three hours a day commuting back and forth to work – and unlike many subway systems elsewhere in the world, cell phones get reception even when you're underground – you can see how the time begins to add up.

Others

Bargaining is the rule when shopping **at markets.** There are good deals to be had in Shanghai on everything from DVDs to dresses, but you may have to bargain for them. Haggling might be unfamiliar to you and make you feel rude or cheap, but rest assured that it's expected here. See page 220 for tips on successful bargaining.

Websites like Facebook, The New York Times, Blogspot, and YouTube are blocked in China. If you were expecting to keep in touch with family and friends on your Facebook account or your blog, you're out of luck. Many common websites are inaccessible in China thanks to what some call the "Great Firewall" put up by the Chinese government. The list of blocked sites is long and ever-changing. If it's very important to you, you can set up a VPN (Virtual Private Network) to get around the restrictions during your travels, but for most people it's most practical to just close the computer and go see more of the city.

Nobody wants to tell you "no." You might not notice this right away or at all, but it's an aspect of Chinese culture that you should keep your eye out for, partly because it's fascinating and partly because it could save you a lot of headaches. Chinese people are often reluctant to tell someone "no" or deliver disappointing news, because to do so would mean a loss of "face." The meaning of "face" in this context is related to the English phrases "saving face" or "losing face" – face refers to some social status or dignity that we all try to preserve for ourselves.

In Chinese culture, the context of one's words – like actions, attitude, and body language – bear more weight than the actual words being spoken. For example, when asked a direct question by a Westerner, a Chinese person might say "yes" but act as if they have said "no." This confusing communication is a red flag to alert the Westerner that the real answer is no, but that they value the relationship and do not want to offend you. Westerners place far more emphasis on the literal meaning of spoken words and can become upset when they feel like they're being lied to or given the run-around.

See the next page for more on losing and saving face.

Etiquette & Taboo

When it comes to taboo and etiquette in China, there's good news and bad news for foreigners. The bad news is that China is a 5,000 year-old culture that has developed completely apart from Western civilization, so there are a lot of rules and habits that can be confusing and not at all intuitive to outsiders. But the good news is that with a little preparation, you can easily learn to make a good impression. Plus, the Chinese give foreigners (lǎowài; 老外) a lot of leeway when it comes to local customs and are unlikely to be offended if you break any rules.

When considering manners it's important to note that "politeness" doesn't have the same implication that it does in the west. In Chinese, kèqi (客气) means polite, but to be kèqi is not necessarily a good thing. Kèqi implies that by being polite, you are hiding your true feelings and keeping a formal distance from others. As Chinese people become closer friends, they drop the kèqi to the extent that it's perfectly acceptable for good friends to make the most honest and critical remarks to each other. This is not considered rude; it's a sign of trust. If the people at the next table in the restaurant sound like they're having a huge fight, they're not. Losing one's temper in public would be shameful in China. Those people are just bantering, exchanging opinions, enjoying each other's company, and not being overly kèqi.

After a few days in Shanghai, you might be thinking, "Chinese manners? What a joke! Some guy just cut me in line, everyone's yelling, and I can't even count how many have spit on the sidewalk right next to me!" The reality is that many Chinese apply a double standard when implementing etiquette rules. They divide the world into two groups: people they know, and everyone else. They may practice impressive manners when it comes to their circle, but when dealing with strangers on the street, it's every man for himself. Take China's history: in a country that as recently as a generation ago was facing wars, famines, political repression, and countless other hardships, families survived by sticking together, which often meant being indifferent to the anonymous masses.

Below, we've outlined some basic etiquette rules. Apart from helping you put your best face forward, they offer interesting insights into Chinese culture.

Losing & Saving Face

The concept of face has been extremely important in Chinese culture for a very long time. Though it's quite difficult to translate, it basically means something along the lines of "honor," "prestige" or "reputation." So if you hear someone say "lose face" (diūliǎn; 丢脸) it means they "lost honor" or, in layman's terms, "got embarrassed." On the contrary, saving face is what Chinese people do to avoid losing face or to keep from making a fool of themselves.

A boss can lose face when he makes a false statement in front of his subordinates, especially if one of his subordinates corrects him. However, this scenario is very unlikely since it's understood in the unwritten social contract never to correct your superior and to just keep your mouth shut to ensure he or she doesn't lose face (unless of course it's a life or death situation). Indeed, if you make your boss lose face, you'll be in the hot seat!

One can also lose face if they lose their temper in public. If you see an open dispute, bystanders, cars and mopeds will stop in their tracks to watch. After the quarrel is over, the ones involved will most certainly place their hands on their face and run off for losing face. You can also lose face if you get too drunk, trip while walking up the stairs, make a ridiculous comment or do something else humiliating.

In regards to saving face, if the Chinese side in a business negotiation no longer wishes to pursue the deal, they may not tell you. In an attempt to save their own face, they may become increasingly inflexible and hard-nosed, forcing you to be the one to break off negotiations. This way they can avoid any direct blame for the failure.

In another attempt to save face, the Chinese avoid saying "no" as much as possible and instead opt for nonchalant phrases such as "unfortunately it's not convenient" or " "that may cost a little too much money" or "give me some time to think about it." In this manner, both parties – the one making the invitation and the one declining the invitation – save face.

Remember, in the end the best way to behave in China is in a manner that allows you and the people around you both to never lose face.

Conversations

There are a number of conversation topics that are best avoided by foreigners in China. Do not bring up these issues unless your host does first:

· **Sino-Japanese relations** The two countries have been fighting or at odds for much of the 20th century and are constantly walking on thin ice, so never compare the two neighbors.

· **The Three "T's"** – Taiwan, Tibet and the events that took place at Tian'anmen Square on June 4th, 1989. There's a lot of national sentiment that can be aroused by the first two and frankly many people don't know much about the Tian'anmen Square incident.

· The **Falun Gong** or religious and human rights in general.

· Anything negative about Chinese cleanliness or manners, or anything **comparing China negatively** to another country.

· **The Cultural Revolution**, or what someone's family went through during any of Mao's campaigns. Just like any country, there are liberals and conservatives, so it's best just to keep politics out of it because the conversation can get heated fast.

· Asking someone "How many children do you have?" There's still a **One Child Policy** for most Chinese, and calling attention to it could make for awkward small talk.

Greetings

· Punctuality is considered a virtue in China. Being on time shows respect for others.

· Always stand up or remain standing when being introduced.

· Handshakes are the most common form of greeting. Unlike what you may have heard, Chinese people usually don't bow when greeting someone. They also don't hug or kiss on the cheek when meeting someone for the first time.

· The oldest person is always greeted first as a sign of respect.

· Use family names and appropriate titles until specifically invited by your Chinese host or colleagues to use their given names.

· Chinese family names are placed first with the given name (which usually has one or two syllables) coming last. So in the Chinese name Chén Ruì, Chén is the family name and Ruì is the given name.

· Amongst more casual acquaintances, a common greeting is "Have you eaten?" (Nǐ chī le ma? 你吃了吗?).

· Do not overreact when asked personal questions regarding marital status, family, age, job or income. This is very common and is done to seek common ground, not to be nosy.

Body Language

· The Chinese dislike being touched by strangers. Do not touch, hug, lock arms, back slap or make any body contact.

· Clicking fingers or whistling is considered rude.

· Never put your feet on a desk or a chair. Never gesture or pass an object with your feet.

· To get the attention of a Chinese person, face the palm of your hand downward and move your fingers in a scratching motion. Never use your index finger to get anyone's attention.

· Sticking your pinkie up is an ugly gesture, so avoid doing it. They also know all about the ole middle finger, so don't flip the bird either.

Gifts

· In general, gifts are given at Chinese

New Year, weddings, births, and birthdays. Bringing a gift is also a good idea when you're invited to someone's home, and a small gift is expected when meeting a business acquaintance for the first time.

· Food and a nice basket of fruit make great gifts.

· Do not give scissors, knives or other sharp objects as they indicate that you want to cut off the relationship.

· Do not give clocks, handkerchiefs or straw sandals since they are associated with funerals and death.

· Do not wrap gifts in white, blue or black paper. Choose red, pink, or a colourful pattern.

· Never give gifts in groups of four since it's an unlucky number. It's better to give them in groups of eight since it's the luckiest number.

· Always present gifts with two hands.

· Gifts are usually not opened immediately in front of the giver – but if you're unsure, ask "Should I open it now?"

· The Chinese, especially older people, may try to refuse a gift several times before finally accepting it. Just smile and keep insisting that they accept it.

Visiting a Home

· Since Chinese people often live in small homes or apartments, many people prefer to entertain in public places rather than in their homes, especially when entertaining foreigners.

· If you are invited to their house, consider it a great honor. If you must turn down such an honor, explain the conflict in your schedule so that your actions are not taken as an insult and cause them to lose face.

· Arrive on time. Unlike in the West, when you're invited to a dinner party at 19:00, the food is likely to be on the table at 19:00 sharp.

· Remove your shoes before entering the house. Your host may offer you a pair of house slippers when you arrive – wear them, even if they don't fit perfectly.

· It's always polite to bring a small gift for the host or hostess. Chocolates or fresh fruit are good choices.

Eating

· In China, there is no such thing as going Dutch. If you are invited to dinner, your dinner will usually be paid for by the host. It's considered polite to offer to pay, but if you actually do pay, it will embarrass your host.

· Learn to use chopsticks, period.

· Wait to be told where to sit. The guest of honor will be given a seat facing the door.

· The host begins eating first, and the host offers the first toast.

· Be prepared to make a small toast various times throughout the meal.

· When cheers-ing the host or someone older, always keep the rim of your glass lower than theirs.

· It is not necessary to always drain your glass after a toast, although hosts should encourage it.

· You should try everything that is offered to you.

· Never eat the last piece from the serving tray. Leave some food on your plate during each course of a meal to honor the generosity of your host. It is bad manners for a Chinese host not to keep refilling guests' plates or teacups.

· Be observant to other peoples' needs; if you want to pour yourself more tea, first ask if anyone else would like more. Serve them first, then fill your own cup.

· Do not be offended if a Chinese person makes slurping or belching sounds; it merely indicates that they are enjoying their food.

· Never leave your chopsticks stuck in a bowl of rice sticking upwards. Doing so wishes a bad curse on the proprietor since it resembles sticks of incense used at funerals and/or dead ancestors shines.

Business Etiquette

· As mentioned, punctuality is especially important in business. Being late is considered very rude and meetings always begin on time.

· Business cards are exchanged upon meeting and should be printed in English on one side and Chinese on the other. Make sure the

Chinese side uses simplified characters and not traditional characters, which are used in Taiwan and Hong Kong. Also be sure to use two hands when handing out or receiving a business card.

· Be prepared for the possibility of long meetings and lengthy negotiations with many delays.

· The Chinese will enter a meeting with the highest-ranking person entering first. They will assume the first member of your group to enter the room is the leader of your delegation.

· Seating is very important at a meeting. The host sits to the left of the most important guest.

· There may be periods of silence at a business meeting. As uncomfortable as it may seem to you, do not feel the need to break the silence.

· If the Chinese side no longer wishes to pursue the deal, they may not tell you. To save face, they may become increasingly inflexible and hard-nosed, forcing you to break off negotiations. In this way, they may avoid direct blame for the failure.

Numbers

Lucky Numbers

The number 2 (èr; 二) is good since the Chinese often use it to amplify the meaning of positive feelings, like double happiness.

The character and sound of 3 (sān; 三) is lucky because it looks and sounds like the word birth (shēng; 生).

6 (liù; 六) is pronounced the same as "smooth" (liù; 溜) and "to flow" (liú; 流), and is considered good for business. Therefore, you will see the number 6 at many business functions, and 666, contrary to the West, is extremely lucky in China.

As in the West, 7 (qī; 七) is important, especially when dealing with relationships because it's similar to the word together (qǐ; 起) and life (qì; 气).

8 (bā; 八) is by far the luckiest number because it sounds similar to fortune (fā; 发). Many people like to use 8 in their telephone number, when pricing items and the time/date of special events (e.g. the Beijing Olympic Games began on 8-8-2008 at 8 seconds and 8 minutes past 8:00 pm local time. In 2003, Sichuan Airline acquired the phone number 028 8888 8888 at the cost of over ¥7 million.

A good number to use for future relationships is 9 (jiǔ; 九) since it phonetically sounds like long lasting or time (iiǔ; 久). The pronunciation of the number 9 is also identical to the word for alcohol (jiǔ; 酒), so if you see a bar with 9 in its name, it probably represents booze and not that they wish to build a future relationship with you.

Unlucky Numbers

0 (líng ; 零) is bad because it represents emptiness. Therefore, when giving money the traditional way in red envelopes, it's best to give an amount that doesn't end with zero. For example, it'd be better to give ¥88 instead of ¥90 for two reasons: eight is a lucky number so it's better to use it as much as possible, and 90 ends in zero, which is unlucky.

4 (sì; 四) is the most unlucky number mainly because it sounds like the word death (sǐ; 死). It's best to avoid using the number four whenever logically possible and you won't see it in many elevators.

The number 4 is omitted in some Chinese buildings

Internet & Phone Access

Internet Access

Hotels

Most mid-range and high-end hotels provide wired broadband internet access for guests with their own laptops, though there may be a daily fee (it tends to be more expensive in the fancier hotels). Many hotels and almost all hostels will have wireless internet free of charge: sometimes it's only available in common areas like the lobby, however. In youth hostels you can often find a PC or two in the lobby either for free or for a small hourly fee.

Wifi cafes

More and more people are choosing to travel with their laptops, and a café with wireless internet can be a good place to have a quick lunch and check your email. Shanghai is full of Western-style cafes and bars that offer wifi, especially in popular expat zones like Pudong, the French Concession, and the Jing'an District. You'll know you're on the right track when see a small "wifi" sticker in the window or notice that many of the patrons are on their laptops.

Internet cafes

If you're not traveling with a computer, internet cafes are an easy way to get online. They might not be obvious at first, but once you keep an eye out for the characters 网吧 (wǎngbā; internet café) you'll start seeing them all over town. (You can remember the characters easily because the *wǎng* looks like a net.) These cafes can be dark and smoky, but they offer PCs for public use at a cheap rate of ¥3-6 per hour (US$0.5-1). The price may vary depending on when you visit and they're often open 24 hours. You'll need to provide your passport before getting web access, and the café may hold on to it until you're ready to leave. Be aware that your visit may be monitored in one way or another. Your picture may be taken at the front desk before you're given a card with a user number and password that you use to log in with. One caution: if you're hoping to be able to print something out, make copies or burn a CD, internet cafes aren't your best option. They tend to cater to gamers and online-chatters and probably won't be set up to provide those services. Try a Kodak

Express store instead: the chain is quite common throughout Shanghai.

Censorship & VPNs (Virtual Private Networks)

No matter how you're getting online in China, surfing the web will be different than it is in your home country. You may or may not feel like the connection is slower than you're used to, but you'll definitely notice that many of your favorite sites are not accessible: Facebook, YouTube, Twitter, Flickr, Blogspot, Wordpress, Wikipedia (sometimes), The New York Times, and many more. Because of a spat between Google and the Chinese government in 2010, Google products like Gmail and Google Search can be unreliable. Unfortunately, these blocked sites are useful for travelers for keeping in touch with friends and family, keeping up with the news back home, organizing pictures or writing blog updates.

Internet censorship in China is a government operation. Some sites may be blocked for political reasons – they may include content that is not favorable to the Chinese government. In other cases, Chinese websites lobby the government to block their international counterparts so that they can corner the domestic market. Whatever the reasons, this so-called "Great Firewall" is inconvenient and upsetting to travelers who are used to complete internet freedom. For some, the best solution is just to put away the computer and enjoy a trip spent offline. But for those who prefer or need to access the web freely, there is a relatively simple solution: Virtual Private Networks, or VPNs.

Simply put, a VPN is a program that allows you to hop over the Great Firewall by connecting to a proxy server outside of Mainland China, which allows you to access the internet as if you were in that location instead of in Shanghai. Ironically, the websites for VPN providers are often blocked in China, so if you're determined to use one, it's smart to set it up before you leave home. Some reliable and popular VPN providers include Astrill (astrill.com, from $29.95 for 3 months), StrongVPN (strongvpn.com, from $21.00 for 3 months) and Witopia (witopia.net).

Telephone Access

Public phones

You may have a phone in your room if you're staying at a hotel or hostel. Local calls are usually free, but long-distance and international can be quite pricey. Check with the staff for rates before you start dialing. When you're out and about in the city, public phones are everywhere: you can usually make calls from newspaper stands and small hole-in-the-wall shops for less than ¥1. There are also pay phones in many locations, but they take phone cards, not change.

Mobile phones

You may be able to use the mobile phone you use in your home country, unless it has been locked by your network – check with your phone company before you go. If your phone is locked, you can buy an inexpensive cell phone here for about ¥200-300. Either way, you'll need to purchase a local SIM card: these can be found in China Unicom and China Mobile outlets all over town, as well as in many grocery stores and some convenience stores. A SIM card will set you back between ¥40 and ¥100, usually with ¥50 of credit to start. When your initial credit runs out, you can recharge your minutes with credit-charging cards that you can buy practically on every corner.

Phone cards

No matter what phone you're calling from, phone cards offer the cheapest rates. There are two kinds of phone cards you should be aware of: IC cards and IP cards. You can buy both of these cards in convenience stores, newspaper stands, supermarkets, hotel lobbies and other retail outlets throughout China. The Chinese word for "card" is *kǎ* (卡) so ask for an IC or IP *kǎ*. But note that they often only work in the region/province of purchase and also have an expiration date.

IC (Integrated Circuit) cards: These are prepaid cards you can use to make calls from payphones.

IP (Internet Phone) cards: For international calls on a mobile phone or a hotel phone, use one of these. IP cards offer a rate of ¥1.8 per minute to the United States and Canada and ¥3.2 to all other countries; domestic long-distance calls are ¥0.3 per minute. IP cards usually work like a calling card in the West: you dial a number and input a PIN before dialing. Your card will have dialing instructions on the back side, and English-language service is usually available.

Dialing

To make an international call from China, dial: 00 + country code + area/region code + phone number.

International country dialing codes

US & Canada: 1	Australia: 61
China: 86	Hong Kong: 852
Macau: 853	New Zealand: 64
UK: 44	Taiwan: 886

Area/Region calling codes

Beijing: 10	Changsha: 731
Chengdu: 28	Chongqing: 23
Fuzhou: 591	Guangzhou: 20
Guilin: 773	Hangzhou: 571
Hefei: 551	Ji'nan: 531
Kunming: 871	Lhasa: 891
Nanchang: 791	Nanjing: 25
Shanghai: 21	Shenyang: 24
Shenzhen: 755	Tianjin: 22
Urumqi: 991	Wuhan: 27
Xiamen: 592	Xi'an: 29

Traveling with Kids

Let's face it: taking your kids to China isn't quite like packing up the minivan and driving down the road. But if the thought of long international flights, unfamiliar foods, crazy traffic and rumors of stifling air pollution weren't enough to deter you from visiting with kids, congratulations! You'll find that not only is it cleaner and safer than what you've heard, it's a fascinating and kid-friendly destination. Thanks in part to the country's One Child Policy, the Chinese shower attention on children, and in all likelihood, you and your family will be happily accommodated wherever you go (and maybe asked to pose for more pictures than a celebrity on the red carpet – but more on that later).

But what does the city even offer for kids? In this section, we'll first highlight some kid-pleasing Shanghai attractions, then get into common concerns and how you can best prepare for a worry-free trip.

Kid-Friendly Attractions

You don't necessarily need to tailor your entire itinerary to your kids. Many of Shanghai's sights are visually exciting and offer huge open spaces for kids to run around and explore. But some won't appreciate the nuances of architecture or history the same way you will, and after a few days, boredom might become an issue. The key to successfully touring Shanghai with kids is to balance out the more adult-centric visits with something that the kids will love. For example, spend a few hours exploring the famous and beautiful Yu Garden as a family, then zip over to the zoo and awesome aquarium to please your child.

Your kids may surprise you with their ability to take interest in what they observe in a foreign culture. But for those temper tantrum moments when you really need a kid-oriented activity, check out one of our top five recommended kid-friendly attractions below.

The Bund Sightseeing Tunnel (pg 62)
This is the perfect winning combo for mom and dad and your child. On one side of the Bund Sightseeing Tunnel is the Bund with Shanghai's oldest buildings and historical monuments, and on the other side is Pudong with the city's newest, tallest and most striking sky-scrapers. Tell your kid that you have to walk to the length of the Bund in order to get to the flashy futuristic time-warp of the sightseeing tunnel, and explain to him or her that it's going to blast you from 20th century Puxi to 21st century Pudong. Once there, let the tunnel do the rest; you might actually enjoy it yourself.

Pudong's Skyscrapers (pg 56)
The spiky Jinmao Tower, the bottle-opener shaped Shanghai World Financial Center, the monstrous Shanghai Tower (which should be completed in 2014) and the spaceship-like Shanghai Oriental Pearl TV Tower (kids under 1 m free entry) are all exciting sights for the whole family. In fact, the Pearl TV tower is a highlight since the Science Fantasy World with the Laser Theater, 3D Screen and other cool trademarks never fail to impress any child. Kids and parents will love being blasted up to the top floor of some of the world's tallest sky-scrapers, and everyone in your family will enjoy the view and amazing architecture exhibited by these modern feats.

Shanghai Aquarium (pg 151), Shanghai Wild Animal Park (pg 153) and the Shanghai Zoo (pg 154).
Though located in different locations throughout the city, you can easily tackle two of them within the same long day. If you only have room for two on your docket, the aquarium and the wild animal park are the two best of the trio. The zoo is standard and on par with many international zoos, but the aquarium is standout and particularly outstanding. Sharks, jelly fish, live shows… this place has got it all. The only thing you have to worry about is your kid wanting to jump in the hammerhead tank with the scuba diving staff! Put a leash on them. The wild animal park is more like a safari, where you take jeeps around the vast "Shanghai Serengeti" to explore the creatures in their "natural" habitat. It's a little plastic, but still a lot of fun.

Shanghai Happy Valley (pg 148)
A theme park with rides, roller coasters, fast food, goofy characters putting on live shows, and enough cotton candy to float them to the moon, this "Disney World of China" is a real treat for both your child and your inner child. Use this place as a great bargaining tool: tell

them that if they're good and don't misbehave during your tour of the MOCA, you'll bring them to Happy Valley. It works every time!

Zhujiajiao Ancient Town (pg 124)
Less action packed than some of the other attractions listed above, so it may be better for the non-ADHD-ers. The canals of this quaint river town are splendid. Just as many kids enjoy a gondola ride through Venice, they might very well enjoy a peaceful and relaxing float through some of China's finest canal villages. Note: Zhujiajiao is a bit far from the Shanghai city center, so bring enough snacks for your little one for the commute.

Before You Go:
How to Prepare

Time your trip wisely. Travel during Chinese holidays? Forget about it. China's 1.4 billion people all seem to travel at the same time: during Lunar New Year every January or February and during the National Day holiday in October. Lines for tourist attractions can stretch on for hours. Train stations are a mess. Adults can deal with it, but children may not be able to. Consider visiting in the spring or fall when extreme weather is less likely to be a factor. Bundling kids up to face the cold every time you go out will be a hassle, and likewise, the summer heat and humidity can sap the little ones' energy.

Get healthy before you go. Try to ensure that everyone is getting their vitamins and is in good shape before you embark on a long trip. If you're already prone to illness, 12 hours on a packed airplane can do you in.

Prepare in advance for medical issues. Check with your pediatrician or travel clinic to see if kids need extra vaccines. Many pharmacy staples that are easily available in your home town are tough to find in China, so pack accordingly. Also note emergency contacts for a major hospital – preferably an international one.

Examples of good things to bring include oral hydrating salts or electrolyte solution, hand sanitizer, Aspirin or Tylenol (or whatever anti-fever/pain meds you usually use), anti-itch cream, hydrocortisone cream, Benadryl syrup, and children's sunscreen and mosquito repellent.

Figure out what to bring with you and what to buy in Shanghai. It's smart to bring your own infant formula when traveling abroad anywhere, since switching brands suddenly can upset a baby's stomach. But if your luggage is lost or you run out while in China, don't panic: family doctors in Shanghai regularly advise their patients that buying international brands, such as Nestlé, Similac and Enfamil, is safe. Ditto for diapers – unless your baby is very sensitive or has particular needs, you'll find imported diapers with little trouble in Shanghai. Plus, many brands have Chinese counterparts, like Huggies and Pampers. They're not exactly like the ones back home, but pretty much OK.

As for food, if your kid is picky, you're better off bringing his or her favorite snacks with you, as they might be hard to find and expensive here. If your kid is a little more easygoing, there's a wide range of treats that they'll probably love. Heinz brand baby food is widely available, though the flavors may be a little unfamiliar. If you're looking for no-sugar-added or organic baby food, it's better to pack it with you. There's a wide variety of safe bottled water brands to give to kids or mix with formula, and a brand called Great Lakes makes 100% apple, orange and tomato juice that is widely available in small bottles and sometimes juice boxes.

Learn a little bit about Shanghai before you leave. Rent movies that take place in China and watch the newspaper and TV for stories from Shanghai (see our movie, reading and TV list on pg 27-28 in the Overview). Have your kids think up questions they have about China and try to find the answers on Google. Basically, anything you can do to build excitement and curiosity for the trip will pay off.

Try to pick up a few phrases in Mandarin. Becoming fluent is obviously not a reasonable short-term goal, but learning a few key words can be fun. You might even find a Chinese language camp or class in your neighborhood that your kids could take before you go. Children pick up new languages much more easily than adults, and they might surprise you! An adorable seven-year-old with a few phrases in Chinese is an excellent bargaining tool in the markets of Shanghai.

Give Chinese food a test run. The good news is that most Chinese restaurants have kid-friendly choices – it's hard to go wrong with pork dumplings or fried rice. But it's smart to hit up a few Chinese spots in your town before the trip. You'll find that Western Chinese food doesn't necessarily resemble Chinese food in Shanghai, but it's a good warm-up for your kids' taste buds and can help them feel more adventurous.

Pack comfort food. Bring the peanut butter, Nutella, chips, crackers, cookies, and whatever other favorite snacks your kids like from home along with you. Just because they are giving Chinese food a try doesn't necessarily mean they'll like it, and these snacks can do wonders in preventing grumpy attitudes.

Time to Travel: The Flight

Time your flight wisely to maximize sleep. It's bound to be a grueling overnight flight to Shanghai, but you can try to minimize the disruption to your kids' sleep schedules by choosing a flight that leaves later in the evening, when they're likely to be asleep.

Check in early to select good seats. Online check-in becomes available 24 hours before departure, so make a point of logging on to check in and choose your family's seats. Try to avoid sitting near the restrooms, where a lot of foot traffic and doors opening and closing can disturb sleep. The ultimate score for traveling with kids is to be seated in the bulkhead, the row of seats with nothing in front but a wall. There's more legroom (or crawl room) and you won't have to worry about your kids kicking the seat in front of them.

Use the time to read about China. Reading about where you're going when you're actually on your way only adds to the excitement. Whether you choose our guidebook, history books, or even Chinese children's stories in English, books can provide hours of entertainment.

Go high-tech. Even if you try to limit your kids' use of electronics at home, now is not the time to take away the DVDs, iPads or the Game Boy. You can confiscate the gadgets once you land and only pull them out again on long bus rides or for the flight home. Older kids might even have homework they need to keep up with if you're traveling during the school year, and the flight is a perfect opportunity to take care of it.

On the Ground: Once You've Arrived

Treat jet lag with patience. The first three nights are the most difficult and the second night is probably the worst. The best advice is to take it slow and sleep when they do. This might mean slowing down your sightseeing activities for the first couple of days. Don't push everyone too hard. There's a lot to see in Shanghai, but you can't see it all in two weeks anyway. The time difference is a big adjustment, especially for the little ones. Being tired and run down can lead to sickness so make sure everyone gets rest and try to adjust slowly to the time difference.

Hope for the best, plan for the worst. Give your children our Emergency Card to carry in their pocket (pg 43).

Don't leave home without tissues. Toilet paper is not provided in most bathrooms, and you never know when you'll need it. Likewise for Kleenex when you need to blow your nose or wipe your hands.

Plan for toilet drama. If you stay in nicer hotels and restaurants in Shanghai, you may never see a squat toilet. But odds are you'll encounter one eventually. See our toilets section (pg 290) for more information on how to make using a squat toilet a relatively painless experience. Odds are, small children probably won't care, though older kids might.

Keep hands clean. That's good advice for all the travelers in your group, no matter their age. Bring along hand sanitizer and wet wipes (wipes are readily available in China too). Wash your hands and your kids' hands whenever you get a chance – it'll go a long way toward keeping you healthy.

Be prepared to face the paparazzi. This is less true in Shanghai, where foreigners are a more regular sight, but foreign kids can attract a lot of attention in China. Notions of personal space are different than what you're used to. Some people might try to touch or pick up your baby. If you'd rather they didn't, just be polite and firm.

Watch the traffic. It's extremely important to keep an eye on your little ones when you're out and about, and little kids will be better off in an infant carrier, in your arms or in a stroller. It's not a good place to learn how to walk.

Engage your kids in their cultural surroundings. Take the time to point out cultural differences that you notice and explain the reasons behind them. With a little guidance, kids tend to appreciate them, rather than become grossed out or upset. Remember that it's good to step out of your comfort zone, no matter how old you are.

Shanghai on a Budget

Shanghai has numerous billionaires and an average income that is far below those of Western countries, which is merely to say, there are ample opportunities to live very cheaply or spend a small fortune in one day. The prices below will always err on the high side, but they're a pretty good guideline of what you can expect to pay in Shanghai, depending on what choices you make. The following only encompasses what every tourist will be spending on an average day in Shanghai. If you plan on shopping, going out to the bars every night, etc, obviously you'll need to add in more for your budget.

Attractions &Transportation

The Shanghai World Financial Building is roughly ¥150 for the observation deck. Most other attraction in the city cost less than that, but we'll go a little high and say you should set aside ¥150 each day for admission fees, but you probably won't even reach this if you don't go to a lot of museums.

If you're busy, you'll take the subway or a taxi about six times a day. Again, this estimate might even be a little high, but if you assume ¥30 per taxi, the daily total is ¥180. Subway trips are ¥3-4, so the daily total for this mode of transportation would be ¥21. Shave off ¥9 from this if you take only the bus (with no transfers), but this should just go to show how incredibly cheap the metro is.

Food

You could eat for ¥15 a meal if you only eat at noodle shops and steamed bun stands. ¥50 per day is perfectly doable for the very cost conscious. A meal at a Western fast food restaurant or a dish at a mid-range Chinese joint will cost around ¥30. Add in a nice dinner and snacks, and you could be pushing ¥150. There are, of course, many restaurants in China where you could spend that before even getting to the main course; ¥500 per day might be a good budget for higher end eating.

Bars in Shanghai commonly charge around ¥70 for a good drink. ¥200 for a trip to the bar is reasonable unless you plan to indulge.

Accommodations

Very nice hotels can be ¥1,000 a night or more. Good hotels can easily be had for ¥500 or less. Budget hotels cost around ¥200. These are very much rough estimates so check online to see exactly what quality you can get at what price. Be advised that cheaper hotels can have rock-hard beds (Chinese people like their beds a lot firmer than Westerners), so you may want to check before booking. A bed at a hostel is around ¥50.

Per Day Price List

Item	Chinese Yuan (RMB)	US Dollars
Admission fees	¥150	$25
6 trips by taxi	¥180	$30
6 trips by metro	¥21	$3.5
Meals – Budget	¥50	$8.3
Meals – Mid-range	¥150	$25
Meals – Splurge	¥500+	$83+
A trip to the bar	¥200	$33.3
Hotel –Budget	¥200	$33.3
Hotel – Mid-range	¥500	$83
Hotel –Splurge	¥1,000+	$167+
Hostel Bed	¥50	$8.3

Hot Topics

All the Single Ladies

So you've decided to make a bold choice and take a trip by yourself to the edge of the Orient. Congratulations! Chances are, in between the moments of excitement, you have an occasional worry or fear. So here are some of the things you should know about traveling as an unaccompanied woman in China.

Shanghai is extremely safe. There are crowds of people everywhere, all of whom make excellent witnesses, and there are security cameras all over downtown. This is not a city that sees a lot of violent crime, especially directed at foreigners: the most common danger is pickpocketing or taxi drivers taking the long way. Foreigners and locals alike routinely walk down dark streets and alleys alone at all hours of the night without any hint of fear, true, but that being said, there are 23 million people in this city, and it would be foolish to think every single one of them has your best interests at heart. So by all means, be cautious, but there's no need to be paranoid.

Shanghai is a fantastic city with all kinds of amazing opportunities and friendships waiting for you around each corner, but it can also be an intimidating place with a difficult language standing as a barrier between you and the good times. Here are some of the biggest complaints from foreign women in Shanghai:

1) *"All the foreign guys here have 'Yellow Fever' and Chinese guys are intimidated by Western women."* Many women coming to China are surprised when they try to work their magic and find that the fish are not biting. It's true that many foreign guys find

a special appeal with the local girls, but keep this in mind: not all the expats here are exclusively into Chinese girls and many avoid them like the plague. For them, you as a foreigner can be a rare jewel, an exotic flower. However, don't expect the rules of dating and seduction to be the same.

The men you encounter here will come from all over the English speaking world, Asia, Europe, South America, Africa, and the Middle East. A typical nightclub will also have a much broader range of ages than one back home. You'll meet fresh faced 18-year olds with milk on their breath and worldly men of 50 with white in their beards. Keep an open mind and an upbeat attitude and you'll meet some interesting males of all ages, nationalities and occupations.

2) *"I'm so fat."* You're not really, but a short time in Shanghai can make you feel that way. First of all, Chinese girls are notoriously skinny (though the new generation with its diet of KFC and dairy is changing that), so the fashions presented to you in the shops might be discouraging, unless you're used to wearing size zero. Secondly, Chinese people will tell you straight up that you're fat. As in, *"Wow! You so fat!"* Some of them are doing it to cut you, but most people in China don't really see this as a major insult or emotionally scarring statement. Just the same way that they have no qualms about asking your age or your income, they'll tell you that

you're a little fat. End of story.

The only way to win in this case is to be confident in yourself. It is human nature for people to want what they don't have, so many Chinese girls will be envious of your curves. It might take a bit of work, but you'll be able to find clothes that flaunt your figure, even if you have to look in a few shops or ask, *"Yǒu méi yǒu dà yī diǎn de?"* (有没有大一点的 ? Do you have a little bigger?)

3) *"People stare at me all the time."* For sure. You can dress as low key as you want, and there will still be some grubby dude on the subway, three knuckles deep in his nose, staring at you open mouthed like you were some kind of alien. Well, guess what. You are. Fortunately this will happen less in Shanghai than in other parts of the country, but there's still a big part of the population here that has just arrived off the farm; they are going to stare. The good news is they'll most likely look but won't touch. It's still not perfect, but at least you will very rarely find a physical threat from any of your oglers. If someone does get too close to you, just cuss him out as loudly and as viciously as you can. Chances are he won't understand what you're saying and neither will anyone else, but everyone will know what's going on, which is usually enough to make the dude back off entirely.

4) *"The toilets and tampons. WTF?!"* Women

who have been camping and are familiar with the act of squatting in the woods will have an easier time here. Sure, more and more places offer good old-fashioned Western toilets (including some places with high-tech remote control Japanese seats), but you will definitely run into places where there is not a throne in sight. Get ready to meet the squatter. Actually, you should start practicing your posture at home to make sure your technique won't stain your pants as it can take a bit of practice to get used to.

However, there are many, Westerners included, who prefer the squatter. They claim it is physically more effective than sitting upright, and that it is more hygienic since you're not actually touching that grimy seat. This is all true, but conversely not too many people fall over when using a Western toilet while a little tipsy... Oh, and at all costs, avoid touching the mop that graces every stall in the nation, but you don't need us to tell you that.

The final toilet tip is, unless you enjoy wiggling and shaking, always bring your own tissues. Buy a big bulk bag of the individual sized ones and keep a packet in your purse at all times. It'll come in handy both at the table, since few (if any) restaurants offer free napkins, and in the restroom since you'll never, ever find toilet paper.

Moving on to "feminine hygiene"... Although more and more foreign brands arrive in China all the time, the vast majority of tampons in China are of the applicator-free variety. If you're not used to this environmentally friendly style of protection, then you need to either get used to it or bring a supply from back home with you. That's no big deal if you're staying for two weeks, but if you'll be here for a few months you'll probably want that luggage space for something more important. If you're OK with the applicator-free, then keep in mind that just as Chinese restrooms almost never have toilet paper, they almost never have soap. Bring your own Purel and/or wet wipes.

5) *"Can I just find some normal lotion?"* No. You can't. Well, you can but it's rare. Almost every lotion, sunscreen, toner and soap you buy here will be filled with bleach, helping your skin look whiter and therefore (according to this antiquated Chinese notion) more beautiful. Read everything carefully before you use it. If you have a friend who reads Chinese, bring them along to the store and ask them to read every bottle. If it doesn't have whitening, it still might have bird vomit or some other folk remedy in it, so it's good to know for sure what you're getting. To play it safe, just buy more expensive Western brands. Problem solved!

Don't let these things deter you from having a great trip to Shanghai. This city is actually an awesome place for women and here are a few reasons why:

1. **Shopping** – Of course, not all women love shopping or fashion, but if you're in the "tiny" percentage that does, then Shanghai is a paradise for you. From shoes to bags to belts to dresses, all kinds of new and even crazy fashions come out every day, and they can be found in all corners of the city for dirt cheap, especially once you hone your bargaining skills. A warning here though: you might run the risk of buying far more than you can actually wear, so pace yourself.

2. **Ladies Nights** – Speaking of pacing yourself... Shanghai nightlife is ridiculous with its Ladies Nights. From Monday to Friday you can go out drinking and dancing till your heart's content, and it won't cost you a dime. You don't even have to tip or pay cover, just rock up to the bar and they'll fill your cup. The options range from high class clubs that give you free champagne, candy, manicures and massages, to the lowest gutter bars that serve sugary fruity cocktails with barely a drop of real alcohol in them. The crowds at each of the places differ greatly too, from a "girls night out" atmosphere to something more reminiscent of Pamplona's Running of the Bulls. The fun you have will mostly depend on the group of crazy girlfriends you head there with. Which brings us to...

3. **Friends** – Shanghai's expat community is extremely generous with its advice, its friendships and its contacts. Even if you're staying alone in a hotel you can walk into almost any bar and strike up a conversation with some foreigners and find someone you click with. You can also do this with Chinese people, but it can be much harder to communicate if you can't hurdle the language barrier.

If you're in a hostel there will probably be a whole slew of like-minded adventurers gathering in the lobby, ready to head out in search of excitement. The key in any case is to be brave and bold about who you are and what you want; be open and adventurous and Shanghai will give you an experience you'll remember for the rest of your life. You are woman. Let China hear you roar!

Shanghai vs Beijing

Fighting out of the blue corner is Shanghai: China's business Mecca, and arguably the most international and most productive city in the country. In the red corner is Beijing: China's political capital, cultural center and most historic city. It's a heavy-weight title for the quest to be China's #1, a power struggle amongst the nation's two biggest contendors.

First and foremost, the biggest distinction between these two metropolises is that Beijing is the capital of the nation. As with other capitals, a good deal of the city's resources and attention are focused on the bureaucracy of government. Generally speaking, the closer you get to the seat of power in a country, the stricter and more uptight things will be. However, this often leads to a bit of a backlash in many national capitals, and for this reason there is a thriving punk scene in Beijing, especially in regards to live music.

Shanghai on the other hand likes to consider itself distant and independent from the decrees of the central government. But sometimes the city crosses the line and goes a-stray, as was the case in 2010 when former Shanghai mayor and local Party chief Chen Liangyu was forced to step down amidst a storm of corruption allegations. Corruption was the official reason, but blogosphere chatter made it clear that most people believe the scandal arose from Shanghai becoming too autonomous under Chen's leadership.

Another major difference is in the layout. Shanghai is proud of its upward expansion with chic modern skyscrapers, while Beijing is steeped in history, hutongs and heritage. In other words, Beijing (as the center of China for centuries) is inward looking and home to some of the country's finest museums, galleries and UNESCO sites. Shanghai is outward looking, and it's the place where you would go to get a view of the future and the world outside of China.

Geographically speaking, both cities are flat as a pancake, but Shanghai is a lot easier to get around. Beijing is sprawling: its neighborhoods are vast and its streets are wide. Shanghai is condensed, for rather than showing its greatness by expanding outwards, it went upwards. Streets are narrow, which

forces traffic to move a little slower, creating a surprisingly relaxed pace of life in one of the world's most industrious cities. True, you still risk your life when crossing many of the city's streets, but most of us can handle sprinting 15 meters if need be. In Beijing, you'd better be Usain Bolt to make the 100 meter curb-to-curb dash.

In regards to mentality, Shanghai and Beijing are where millions of Chinese (and foreigners) go for a shot to make money and possibly make it big, but the paths to success are defined differently within these two megalopolises. In the old days, if you weren't from a wealthy family (and often even if you were), the only way to advance your career was to ace the Imperial Examination and enter the government or bootstrap yourself up through careful business strategies. In many ways, this mindset still represents one of the big differences between the two cities. Today in Beijing, there is a clear administrative structure, a hierarchy that can be followed to achieve greatness or even comfortable mediocrity. In Shanghai, it's the quest for the almighty Yuan, and the sky is the limit.

Weather-wise, Shanghai seems a bit more extreme than Beijing. While Beijing is technically a few degrees colder in the winter, it's a dry cold so it is more tolerable. Meanwhile, Shanghai is cold and damp, and Shanghai buildings don't really seem to worry about frivolous things like "insulation", "centralized heating" or "windows that seal," so locals constantly feel cold for the entire winter even when indoors. In Beijing, pop inside and you'll instantly feel snug as a bug since everywhere blasts efficient heating systems in air-tight rooms.

Once summer rolls around, Beijing's arid climate helps out again, keeping hot temperatures more reasonable, but the city does get a bit muggy and rainy during June and July. Heading outdoors in Shanghai between May and September, however, will leave you stewing in your own juices, feeling as if it were a humid, tropical rainforest.

So while the weather is more tolerable in Beijing, the air quality is not. Beijing is surrounded by desert and factories, so the only thing a breeze sweeps in is sand,

The Bund in Shanghai

Forbidden City in Beijing

dust and pollution. This is not to say that Shanghai's air is like a virgin alpine forest, but at least the city will get a sea breeze once in a while to clear out the smog and grime.

Of course, this is in a perfect world. The reality is that Shanghai has sort of shot itself in the foot with constant construction. When every street corner is being dug up to lay new pipe, and every building is being renovated, restored or demolished, it goes without saying that grit is in the air. Some days you can actually taste the progress, and it brings tears to your eyes. City officials are trying (ineffectively) to deal with this mess though, so you will see some construction sites covered with a fine mesh while others are constantly being hosed down to keep the dust from rising.

Beijing seems to have a more vibrant, modern arts scene than Shanghai. It's not that Shanghai has no art, it's just that this city seems to attract those who wish to commoditize their visions. A visit to a "gallery" in Shanghai might consist of the artist showing you dozens of very similar paintings of a horse running through a foaming ocean, with calligraphy scribbled down the side. They all look the same, with slightly different color schemes so that you can buy the one that matches your couch the best. But all is not lost. Shanghai has a more vibrant expat art scene, which is starting to inspire the locals. There are also a few outdoor sculpture spaces that have opened up in recent years, showcasing some huge, amazing pieces from foreign and local artists alike.

Continuing with art, fashion is one of the biggest creative outlets in Shanghai and it puts the Beijing look to shame, and we're not talking about the expat population. No, it's the locals who truly push the boundaries of fashion with extreme looks from head to toe: crazy boots, bedazzled skin-tight jeans, low-cut tops and swoopy spiky bleach-blonde

hair are just a few of the styles, and that's just the guys! Whether or not you like the fashion is beside the point, what matters here is that people go all out with a look rather than just wearing one nice or crazy article of clothing. And the hair... the hair! The hair is a culture all on its own, with salons across the city that are open until midnight and staff that do warm-up line dancing to Lady Gaga before work.

With food, Beijingers are lucky. True, the sheer size of Shanghai and its foreign population means that there are tons of high quality restaurants of every conceivable cuisine, but deep down, it's the local food that matters, and Shanghainese cuisine, quite frankly, isn't the best. This is not to say that there aren't some incredibly tasty Shanghainese dishes out there (*xialongbao* rocks!), but the formula for Shanghai food seems to follow four simple steps: 1. Take any dish from another part of China. 2. Add a pound of sugar and a gallon of oil. 3. Be sure to add some vinegar to balance out that oil. 4. Serve.

In the end, it's all according to your own personal tastes. If you want a place that feels a little more genuine (even to the point of avoiding the modern world), a place where the art scene is a little grittier, a place where life seems more "real" somehow, where people are in touch with their history, then Beijing is the place for you. But if you're looking for the best and the brightest, the biggest and the newest, a place where life flashes by and is beginning to define a new type of global culture, a place that offers you a rocket ship to financial glory, then try Shanghai.

When it's all said and done, you should visit both, because after all the facts and figures, cities have a feel and a spirit that you can't numerize. See for yourself which one of them is best for you. Enjoy!

	Beijing	Shanghai
Layout		Winner
Weather	Winner	
Air Quality		Winner (barely)
Appreciation of History	Winner	
Museums & Galleries	Winner	
Financial Opportunity		Winner
Fashion		Winner
Architecture	Tie	Tie
Globalism		Winner
Nightlife		Winner

Hot Topics

Mandarin Phrasebook

Introduction

Chinese is one of the world's oldest and most unique languages. Though Chinese actually has a vast number of dialects and language varieties, it's the nationally standardized variety known as Mandarin – which is based off of the Beijing dialect – that you will encounter the most in Shanghai. Mandarin is called Pǔtōnghuà (普 通 话), and is currently the official language of the People's Republic of China and is widely spoken in Taiwan, Singapore and somewhat in Hong Kong, Macau, Thailand, Malaysia and Indonesia. Since many in the PRC still don't speak fluent English, knowing a bit of Mandarin will most certainly make your trip much easier, so it's recommended to remember some key phrases and characters. But before you start memorizing countless strokes and confusing tones, there are a few other things about the language that are worth noting.

First, more than one billion people, or roughly 12.5% of the world's population, speak Mandarin as their native tongue, making it the most widely spoken language (in terms of native speakers) in the world today. Second, although there are more than 80,000 Chinese characters, most of them are not commonly used. Nonetheless, you still need to know about 3,000 to fully comprehend a newspaper, while an educated Chinese person knows more than 6,000. Third, Mandarin is a tonal language with four distinct tones (1. flat, 2. rising, 3. falling and rising, 4. falling) and one neutral tone. Since many of the words in Mandarin sound alike, the only way to differentiate them is with tones. For example, if you say the word "ma" it can mean either mother (pronounced mā in the first tone) or horse (pronounced mǎ in the third tone); it's quite easy to call your dear mother a horse! Fourth, though most Chinese speak Mandarin, accents vary greatly from province to province and

even village to village, making it extremely difficult to understand those with different regional pronunciations. Many times, locals even speak local languages, like Cantonese in Hong Kong, which can be very different from Mandarin and unintelligible by other Chinese not from that particular province or city. Fifth, with so many twisting tones and a never ending list of characters, Mandarin is considered by many linguistic experts to be one of the hardest languages for a native English speaker to learn.

But wait, there's more. You'd still better be careful when speaking Mandarin since your meaning may not always translate well into the ears of native speakers. One expat with little knowledge of Mandarin traveled to the coast with his Chinese colleagues to watch the incoming high tide. Upon seeing the rushing current, his colleagues asked, "What do you think of the tide?" He responded, "I've never experienced such a high tide (gāocháo) before." He used the correct translation of gāo which means "high" and cháo which means "tide," but the crowd went silent followed by a long moment of awkwardness. After asking a Chinese friend, he discovered that the words gāocháo (高 潮) when put together literally mean "orgasm", not "high tide," which should be pronounced as dàcháo (大 潮), or "big tide." This man had told every single one of his colleagues that he had never experienced such an orgasm before!

Another traveler in a restaurant wanted to know how much for a bowl of dumplings, so he asked, *"Xiǎojiě, shuìjiào yīwǎn duōshǎo qián?"* The humiliated waitress ran away with her face planted in her hands. He later discovered that although his words were 100% correct, his tones were off. Instead of saying, "Miss, how much is one bowl of dumplings?" which should be pronounced *"Xiǎojiě, shuǐjiǎo yīwǎn duōshǎo qián?"* he asked the waitress, "Miss, how much does it cost for one night?" The waitress was mortified because he used two fourth tones in *shuìjiào*, which means "to sleep," instead of two third tones in *shuǐjiǎo*, which means "dumplings." To make matters more difficult, phonetically the words *yīwǎn* mean both "one night" (一晚) and "one bowl" (一碗) even though they are two different characters.

There are also other nuances in Chinese that can be confusing for foreigners. When one fellow we know first got to China, he went to a bar and realized that bartenders kept calling him *shuàigē* (帅哥) which means "handsome guy." He even checked the dictionary to make sure he understood them correctly, which he did. At first he had quite a nice confidence boost, but he soon noticed that not only were both men and women calling him handsome guy, they were also saying it to everyone else at the bar. Furthermore, all the waiters and waitresses were calling the women customers *měinǚ* (美 女) which means "beautiful lady." Despite the compliments he thought he was receiving, his confidence deflated when he discovered that "handsome man" and "beautiful woman" are common terms loosely used to address someone you don't know, not to indicate how physically attractive one is.

Since it takes years of practice to master one of the world's most difficult languages, don't be discouraged if you embarrass yourself a couple of times, because it's going to happen at some point during your Mandarin career. For the beginner, we've provided some useful information, words and phrases to help get you around town.

Pronunciation

There are four distinct tones and one neutral tone in Mandarin (see the diagram to the right). The first tone is high and flat (e.g. 妈 or mā for "mother"), as if you're singing a single note. The second tone starts at a middle pitch and rises to high (e.g. 麻 or má for "hemp"), as in a question like "Really?" The third tone starts low, dips even lower and then slightly rises (e.g. 马 or mǎ for "horse"). The fourth tone starts high and rapidly shoots down (e.g. 骂 or mà for the verb "to scold"), as if you're giving a command to your dog (like "Sit!"). The fifth tone is neutral and pronounced without any intonation (e.g. 吗 or ma used as a question tag). Although tones are extremely important and can change the entire meaning of your sentence, sometimes the native speakers will be able to understand what you mean even if your tones are atrocious.

Pinyin

Pinyin is the romanized alphabetical system used for Chinese, and it's a great tool for foreigners learning how to pronounce a character. Many letters are pronounced the same way they are in English and the tonal markings (see the diagram below) are placed over the vowel in every syllable to indicate one of the four tones. Listed below is the phonetic guide for pinyin letters.

Vowels
a   – as in "father"
ai – as in "aisle"
ao – as in "now"
e   – as in "her"
ei – as in "weight"
i   – as in "see"
ian – as in "yen"
ie – as in "yeah"
o   – as in "more"
ou – as in "oh"
u   – as in "flute"
ui – as in "spray"
uo – as in "whoa"
yu -as in "new"
ǔ   – as in "new" but with closed lips

Consonants
The consonants *b, ch, d, f, hard g, h, j, k, l, m, n, p, s, sh, t, w,* and *y* are all pronounced the same as they are in English.

However, there are several exceptions:
z – as in the "ds" in "suds"
c – as in the "ts" in "bits"
q – as in the "ch" in "chase" but with tongue touching the teeth
x – a combination of the English pronunciation of "s" and "ch"
zh – as in the "dge" in "judge"

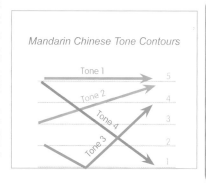

Mandarin Chinese Tone Contours

Basic Phrases

Hello!	Nǐhǎo!	你好!
Goodbye!	Zàijiàn!	再见!
How are you?	Nǐhǎo ma?	你好吗?
I'm fine, and you?	Wǒ hěnhǎo, Nǐ nē?	我很好,你呢?
Excuse me (When speaking)…	Qǐngwèn…	请问……
Excuse me (When passing through)	Láojià…	劳驾……
I'm sorry.	Duìbùqǐ.	对不起。
Yes.	Shì.	是。
No.	Búshì.	不是。
Please!	Qǐng!	请!
Thank you!	Xièxiè!	谢谢!
You're welcome!	Bùkèqi!	不客气!
What's your name?	Nǐ jiào shénmē míngzi?	你叫什么名字?
My name is…	Wǒ jiào…	我叫……
Nice to meet you!	Jiàndào nǐ hěn gāoxìng!	见到你很高兴!
I (can't) speak Chinese.	Wǒ (bù) huì shuō zhōngwén.	我(不)会说中文。
I (don't) understand.	Wǒ (bù) míng bái.	我(不)明白。
Can you speak English?	Nǐ huì shuō Yīngyǔ ma?	你会说英语吗?
I (don't) want…	Wǒ (bù) yào…	我(不)要……
I like…	Wǒ xǐhuān…	我喜欢……
I don't like…	Wǒ bù xǐhuān…	我不喜欢……
Do you have…?	Nǐ yǒu méiyǒu?	你有没有……?
I don't know.	Wǒ bùzhīdào.	我不知道。
No problem!	Méi wèntí!	没问题!
Good (morning/evening)!	(Zǎoshang/Wǎnshang) hǎo!	(早上/晚上)好!
Good night!	Wǎn'ān!	晚安!
See you soon.	Yīhuì'er jiàn.	一会儿见。
See you tomorrow.	Míngtiān jiàn!	明天见!

Travel, Transport & Directions

taxi	chūzūchē	出租车
train/train station	huǒchē /huǒchēzhàn	火车 / 火车站
bus/ bus stop	gōngjiāo /gōngjiāozhàn	公交 / 公交站
airplane/ airport	fēijī /jīchǎng	飞机 / 机场
car	qìchē	汽车
metro/metro station	dìtiě /dìtiě zhàn	地铁 / 地铁站
Where is the…	…zài nǎ lǐ?	……在哪里?
Please take me to…	Qǐng dài wǒ qù…	请带我去……
How to get to…	…zěn me zǒu ?	……怎么走?
I'd like to buy a ticket.	Wǒ xiǎng mǎi piào.	我想买票。
turn left/right	zǒu zhuǎn /yòu zhuǎn	走转 / 右转
go straight	zhí zǒu	直走
north/south/east/west	běi /nán /dōng /xī	北 / 南 / 东 / 西
stop	tíng	停
map	dì tú	地图
I'm lost!	Wǒ mí lù le!	我迷路了!
Where's the bank/ATM?	Yínháng zài nǎlǐ ?	银行在哪里?

Famous Dishes

hot and sour shredded potato	suān là tǔdòu sī	酸辣土豆丝
stir fried bean curd with chili	mápó dòufǔ	麻婆豆腐
tomato and egg soup	xīhóngshì jīdàn tāng	西红柿鸡蛋汤
kung pao chicken	gōngbǎo jīdīng	宫保鸡丁
stir fried pork	dōngpō ròu	东坡肉
double cooked pork slices	huíguō ròu	回锅肉
sweet and sour pork	tángcù lǐjǐ	糖醋里脊
steamed stuffed bun	bāozi	包子
thin pancake	jiānbǐng	煎饼
wonton	húntún	馄饨
dumpling	jiǎozi	饺子
steamed rice	mǐfàn	米饭
fried rice	chǎofàn	炒饭
BBQ	shāokǎo	烧烤
deep fried breadstick	yóutiáo	油条
kebab	ròuchuàn	肉串
hot pot	huǒguō	火锅
noodles	miàn	面
fried noodles	chǎomiàn	炒面

Shopping

supermarket	chāoshì	超市
shop/store	shāngdiàn	商店
Where is the nearest store?	Zuìjìn de shāngdiàn zài nàlǐ?	最近的商店在哪里?
Where can I buy…?	Zài nǎlǐ kěyǐ mǎi…?	在哪里可以买……?
How much is this?	Zhège duōshǎo qián?	这个多少钱?
Too expensive!	Tài guì le!	太贵了!
I want it cheaper.	Wǒ yào piányí yìdiǎn.	我要便宜一点。
Can you give me a discount?	Nǐ kěyǐ dǎzhé ma?	你可以打折吗?
No, I really don't want it.	Bù, wǒ zhēnde bùyào.	不, 我真的不要。
OK, I'll buy it.	Hǎode, wǒ yào mǎi.	好的, 我要买。
clothing	fúzhuāng	服装
furniture	jiājù	家具
art	yìshù	艺术
bicycle	zìxíngchē	自行车
jewelry	zhūbǎo	珠宝

Question Words

Who?	Shuí?	谁?
What?	Shénme?	什么?
Where?	Nǎlǐ?	哪里?
When/What time ?	Shénme shíhòu?	什么时候?
Why?	Wèishén me?	为什么?
How?	Zěnme?	怎么?

Restaurant & Bar

I don't eat (peanuts).	Wǒ bù chī (huāshēng).	我不吃（花生）。
What's your specialty?	Nǐmen de tèsè shì shénme?	你们的特色是什么？
What do you recommend?	Nǐ tuījiàn shénmē?	你推荐什么？
Table for (two/four)	liǎng wèi / sì wèi	两位 / 四位
Waiter, check please!	Fúwùyuán, mǎidān!	服务员，买单！
Cheers!	Gānbēi!	干杯！
one bottle of (beer/water)	yīpíng (píjiǔ / shuǐ)	一瓶（啤酒 / 水）
breakfast	zǎofàn	早饭
lunch	zhōngfàn	中饭
dinner	wǎnfàn	晚饭
knife	dāo	刀
fork	chā	叉
spoon	sháo	勺
chopsticks	kuàizi	筷子
bowl	wǎn	碗
glass	bēizi	杯子
menu	càidān	菜单
I don't want it spicy.	Bú yào là.	不要辣。
I want it very spicy!	Wǒ yào hěn là!	我要很辣！
restaurant/bar	cāntīng / jiǔbā	餐厅 / 酒吧

Emergency

Leave me alone!	Búyào dǎrǎo wǒ!	不要打扰我！
I don't want it.	Wǒ búyào.	我不要。
Don't touch me.	Bùyào pèng wǒ!	不要碰我
Call the police!	Jiào jǐngchá ba!	叫警察吧！
Thief!	Xiǎotōu!	小偷！
It's an emergency!	Jǐnjí qíngkuàng!	紧急情况！
Call a doctor!	Jiào yīshēng ba!	叫医生吧！
I've been injured.	Wǒ shòushāng le.	我受伤了。
Help!	Jiùmìng!	救命！

Accommodation

hotel	jiǔdiàn / bīn'guǎn	酒店 / 宾馆
hostel	qīngnián lǚshè	青年旅舍
room	fángjiān	房间
single room	dānrén jiān	单人间
double room	shuāngrén jiān	双人间
dormitory	duōrén jiān (sùshè)	多人间（宿舍）
deposit	yājīn	押金
(private/public) bathroom	(sīrén / gōnggòng) yùshì / cèsuǒ	（私人 / 公共）浴室 / 厕所
I would like to check in.	Wǒ yào dēngjì.	我要登记。
I would like to check out.	Wǒ yào tuìfáng.	我要退房。
I have a reservation.	Wǒ yǒu yùdìng.	我有预订。

Drink

beer	píjiǔ	啤酒
coffee	kāfēi	咖啡
(green/black) tea	(lǜ / hóng) chá	（绿 / 红）茶
(hot/cold) water	(kāi / bīng) shuǐ	（开 / 冰）水
(orange) juice	(chéng) zhī	（橙）汁
milk	niúnǎi	牛奶
(red/white) wine	(hóng / bái) pútáo jiǔ	（红 / 白）葡萄酒
Chinese liquor	báijiǔ	白酒
cola	kělè	可乐
soy milk	dòujiāng	豆浆

Telephone & Internet

Where is the internet café?	Nǎlǐ yǒu wǎngba?	哪里有网吧？
Can I make a (international) call?	Wǒ kěyǐ dǎ (guójì) diànhuà ma?	我可以打（国际）电话吗？
How much is it for one hour?	Yīxiǎoshí duōshǎo qián?	一小时多少钱？
Do you have wi-fi?	Yǒuméiyǒu wúxiàn xìnhào?	有没有无线信号？
telephone number	diànhuà hàomǎ	电话号码
Internet	wǎngluò	网络
cell phone	shǒujī	手机
computer	diànnǎo	电脑

Shanghai Popular Sights

Lujiazui	Lùjiāzuǐ	陆家嘴
City Gods Temple	Chénghuáng Miào	城隍庙
The Bund	Wài Tān	外滩
Jade Buddha Temple	Yùfó Sì	玉佛寺
Nanjing Road	Nánjīng Lù	南京路
Shanghai Museum	Shànghǎi Bówùguǎn	上海博物馆
Tianzifang	Tiánzǐfāng	田子坊
Xintiandi	Xīntiāndì	新天地
Yu Garden	Yù Yuán	豫园
Jing'an Temple	Jìng'ān Sì	静安寺
Longhua Temple	Lónghúa Sì	龙华寺
Shanghai Ocean Aquarium	Shànghǎi Hǎiyáng Shuǐzúguǎn	上海海洋水族馆
Shanghai Science & Technology Museum	Shànghǎi Kējìguǎn	上海科技馆
People's Square	Rénmín Guǎngchǎng	人民广场
shikumen	shíkùmén	石库门

Wishes & blessings

Happy birthday!	Shēngrì kuàilè!	生日快乐！
Happy New Year!	Xīnnián kuàilè!	新年快乐！
I love you!	Wǒ ài nǐ!	我爱你！
Good luck!	Zhù nǐ hǎoyùn!	祝你好运！
Have a good trip!	Yīlù shùnfēng!	一路顺风！
Congratulations!	Gōngxǐ!	恭喜！

Numbers

one	yī	一
two	èr	二
three	sān	三
four	sì	四
five	wǔ	五
six	liù	六
seven	qī	七
eight	bā	八
nine	jiǔ	九
ten	shí	十
eleven	shíyī	十一
twelve	shí'èr	十二
thirteen	shísān	十三
fourteen	shísì	十四
fifteen	shíwǔ	十五
sixteen	shíliù	十六
seventeen	shíqī	十七
eighteen	shíbā	十八
nineteen	shíjiǔ	十九
twenty	èrshí	二十
thirty	sānshí	三十
forty	sìshí	四十
fifty	wǔshí	五十
one hundred	yìbǎi	一百
one thousand	yìqiān	一千
ten thousand	yíwàn	一万
one million	yìbǎiwàn	一百万

Time & Date

January	Yī yuè	一月
February	Èr yuè	二月
March	Sān yuè	三月
April	Sì yuè	四月
May	Wǔ yuè	五月
June	Liù yuè	六月
July	Qī yuè	七月
August	Bā yuè	八月
September	Jiǔ yuè	九月
October	Shí yuè	十月
November	Shíyī yuè	十一月
December	Shí'èr yuè	十二月
Monday	Xīngqī yī	星期一
Tuesday	Xīngqī èr	星期二
Wednesday	Xīngqī sān	星期三

Time & Date

Thursday	Xīngqī sì	星期四
Friday	Xīngqī wǔ	星期五
Saturday	Xīngqī liù	星期六
Sunday	Xīngqī rì / Xīngqī tiān	星期日 / 星期天
yesterday	zuótiān	昨天
today	jīntiān	今天
tomorrow	míngtiān	明天
one o'clock	yīdiǎn	一点
two fifteen	liǎngdiǎn shíwǔ fēn	两点十五分
three thirty	sān diǎn bàn	三点半
four forty-five	sìdiǎn sìshíwǔ fēn	四点四十五分
What time is it?	Xiànzài jǐdiǎn?	现在几点?

Signs

entrance	rùkǒu	入口
exit	chūkǒu	出口
open	yíngyè / kāimén	营业 / 开门
closed	xiēyè / guānmén	歇业 / 关门
toilets	cèsuǒ	厕所
man	nán	男
woman	nǚ	女

Food

chicken	jīròu	鸡肉
beef	niúròu	牛肉
pork	zhūròu	猪肉
duck	yāròu	鸭肉
lamb	yángròu	羊肉
seafood	hǎixiān	海鲜
fish	yú	鱼
fruit	shuǐguǒ	水果
apple	píngguǒ	苹果
banana	xiāngjiāo	香蕉
orange	chéngzi	橙子
mango	mángguǒ	芒果
watermelon	xīguā	西瓜
pineapple	bōluó	菠萝
vegetable	shūcài	蔬菜
green beans	biǎndòu	扁豆
mushroom	mógū	蘑菇
cucumber	huángguā	黄瓜
onion	yángcōng	洋葱
radish	luóbo	萝卜
egg	jīdàn	鸡蛋

Food

tofu	dòufu	豆腐
bread	miànbāo	面包
salt	yán	盐
soy sauce	jiàngyóu	酱油
vinegar	cù	醋
sugar	táng	糖
pepper	hújiāofěn	胡椒粉
MSG	wèijīng	味精

Nationality

What country are you from?	Nǐ shì nǎguó rén?	你是哪国人?
I'm from…	Wǒ shì…rén.	我是……人。
America	Měiguó	美国
Canada	Jiānádà	加拿大
Mexico	Mòxīgē	墨西哥
Brazil	Bāxī	巴西
Ireland	Ài'ěrlán	爱尔兰
Great Britain	Yīngguó	英国

Nationality

Spain	Xībānyá	西班牙
France	Fǎguó	法国
Germany	Déguó	德国
Italy	Yìdàlì	意大利
Sweden	Ruìdiǎn	瑞典
Russia	Éluósī	俄罗斯
Turkey	Tǔ'ěrqí	土耳其
South Africa	Nánfēi	南非
Egypt	Āijí	埃及
India	Yìndù	印度
Australia	Àodàlìyà	澳大利亚
New Zealand	Xīnxīlán	新西兰
Japan	Rìběn	日本
Korea	Hánguó	韩国
Vietnam	Yuènán	越南
Thailand	Tàiguó	泰国
Singapore	Xīnjiāpō	新加坡
Malaysia	Mǎláixīyà	马来西亚

Provinces & Cities

Provinces	Cities
Ānhuī 安徽	Héféi 合肥;Huángshān 黄山;Wúhú 芜湖
Běijīng 北京	
Chóngqìng 重庆	
Fújiàn 福建	Fúzhōu 福州;Xiàmén 厦门;Pútián 莆田;Quánzhōu 泉州
Gānsù 甘肃	Lánzhōu 兰州;Jiāyùguān 嘉峪关
Guǎngdōng 广东	Guǎngzhōu 广州;Dōngguǎn 东莞;Zhūhǎi 珠海;Shēnzhèn 深圳
Guǎngxī 广西	Nánníng 南宁;Guìlín 桂林;Běihǎi 北海;Bǎisè 百色
Guìzhōu 贵州	Guìyáng 贵阳;Ānshùn 安顺;Zūnyì 遵义
Hǎinán 海南	Hǎikǒu 海口;Sānyà 三亚
Héběi 河北	Shíjiāzhuāng 石家庄;Chéngdé 承德
Hēilóngjiāng 黑龙江	Hā'ěrbīn 哈尔滨 (Harbin)
Hénán 河南	Zhèngzhōu 郑州;Kāifēng 开封;Luòyáng 洛阳
Hong Kong Xiānggǎng 香港	
Húběi 湖北	Wǔhàn 武汉;Jīngzhōu 荆州;Yíchāng 宜昌;Shénnóngjià 神农架
Húnán 湖南	Chángshā 长沙;Xiāngtán 湘潭;Zhāngjiājiè 张家界
Inner Mongolia Nèiměnggǔ 内蒙古	Hūhéhàotè 呼和浩特 (Hohhot);Bāotóu 包头;Hūlúnbèi'ěr 呼伦贝尔 (Hulunbuir);E'ěrduōsī 鄂尔多斯 (Ordos)
Jiāngsū 江苏	Nánjīng 南京;Sūzhōu 苏州;Wúxī 无锡;Chángzhōu 常州;Yángzhōu 扬州
Jiāngxī 江西	Nánchāng 南昌;Jǐngdézhèn 景德镇
Jílín 吉林	Chángchūn 长春;Yánbiān 延边
Liáoníng 辽宁	Shěnyáng 沈阳;Dàlián 大连
Macau Àomén 澳门	
Níngxià 宁夏	Yínchuān 银川
Qīnghǎi 青海	Xīníng 西宁
Shāndōng 山东	Jǐnán 济南;Qīngdǎo 青岛;Tài'ān 泰安;Wéifāng 潍坊;Wēihǎi 威海;Yāntái 烟台
Shànghǎi 上海	
Shānxī 山西	Tàiyuán 太原
Shǎnxī 陕西	Xī'ān 西安;Yán'ān 延安
Sìchuān 四川	Chéngdū 成都;Lèshān 乐山;Zìgòng 自贡;Yíbīn 宜宾
Táiwān 台湾	Táiběi 台北 (Taipei)
Tiānjīn 天津	
Tibet Xīzàng 西藏	Lāsà 拉萨 (Lhasa);Rìkāzé 日喀则 (Shigatse)
Xīnjiāng 新疆	Wūlǔmùqí 乌鲁木齐 (Urumqi);Tǔlǔfān 吐鲁番 (Turpan);Ākèsū 阿克苏 (Aksu);Hétián 和田 (Hotan);Kāshí 喀什 (Kashgar)
Yúnnán 云南	Kūnmíng 昆明;Lìjiāng 丽江;Dàlǐ 大理;Xīshuāngbǎnnà 西双版纳
Zhèjiāng 浙江	Hángzhōu 杭州;Níngbō 宁波;Shàoxīng 绍兴;Wēnzhōu 温州

Glossary

A

arhat (luóhàn; 罗汉) – Sanskrit for a Buddhist, especially a monk, who has attained enlightenment and is freed from the cycle of rebirth

B

bāguà (八卦) – literally "the eight trigrams"; a set of broken (yin) and solid (yang) lines formed into eight sets of three and used for divination practices and to describe the nature of universal events in Taoist philosophy

bīn'guǎn (宾馆) – tourist hotel

Bodhisattva (púsà; 菩萨) – Buddhist who has reached nirvana but remains on earth to help others achieve enlightenment

bówùguǎn (博物馆) – museum

C

CAAC (Zhōngguó Mínháng; 中国民航) – Civil Aviation Administration of China

cān'guǎn (餐馆) or **cāntīng** (餐厅) – restaurant; cafeteria

CCP (Zhōngguó Gòngchǎndǎng; 中国共产党) – Chinese Communist Party

chēpiào (车票) – train or bus ticket

Chiang Kai-shek (Jiǎng Jièshí; 蒋介石) (1887-1957) – anti-communist leader of the Kuomintang and head of the nationalist government from 1928 to 1949

CITS (Zhōngguó Guójì Lǚxíngshè; 中国国际旅行社) – China International Travel Service

Confucius (Kǒngzǐ; 孔子) (551-470 BCE) – legendary thinker, philosopher and scholar who developed the philosophy of Confucianism, a system of rules, moral values and code of conduct for civil and obedient society

cūn (村) – village

D

dàfàndiàn (大饭店) – large hotel

dàjiǔdiàn (大酒店) – large hotel

dàshà (大厦) – hotel; building; mansion

dàxué (大学) – university; college

Dèng Xiǎopíng (邓小平) (1904-1997) – paramount leader of the Chinese Communist Party from 1978 to 1992.

diàn (殿) – hall

dìtiě (地铁) – subway

dòngwùyuán (动物园) – zoo

E

erhu (èrhú; 二胡) – the Chinese fiddle; a two-stringed bow instrument originally used in folk music and now being applied to a spectrum of musical genres

F

fāpiào (发票) – receipt, usually from a restaurant, taxi or department store

fàndiàn (饭店) – hotel; restaurant

fēngjǐngqū (风景区) – scenic area

fēng shuǐ (风水) – also called geomancy, literally "wind and water"; the ancient art of arranging a space (i.e. buildings and objects) to maximize the flow of qi and harmonize humans with the surrounding environment

G

gé (阁) – pavilion; temple

gōng (宫) – palace

gōngyuán (公园) – park

guàn (观) – hall; temple

gùjū (故居) – former residence

gǔzhèn (古镇) – ancient town

H

hǎi (海) – sea

hé (河) – river

hú (湖) – lake

Huí (回) – a Chinese Muslim ethnic group

huǒchēzhàn (火车站) – train station

J

jiǎo (角) – a unit of Chinese currency; 10 jiao equals 1 yuan

jiàotáng (教堂) – church

jīchǎng (机场) – airport

jiē (街) – street

jié (节) – festival; celebration

jīn (斤) – a unit of weight; 1 jin equals 500 g

jì'niàn'guǎn (纪念馆) – memorial hall

jiǔdiàn (酒店) – hotel

kuài (块) – in spoken Chinese, the colloquial term for the currency yuan

Kuomintang (Guómíndǎng; 国民党) – the Nationalist Party under Chiang Kai-shek who were dominant for a time after the fall of the Qing Dynasty

kung fu (gōngfū; 功夫) – western word for the Chinese martial arts

lǐ'nòng (里弄) – alleyway

lóu (楼) – tower; building

lù (路) – road

lǚdiàn (旅店) or **lǚguǎn** (旅馆) – guesthouse

lǚshè (旅舍) – hostel

mahjong (májiàng; 麻将) – a hugely popular Chinese game that involves engraved tiles and rabid gambling

mén (门) – door; gate

ménpiào (门票) – entrance ticket

miào (庙) – temple

mù (墓) – tomb

nánzhàn (南站) – south railway (or bus) station

nòng (弄) – alleyway

Pīnyīn (拼音) – the official system for transliteration of Chinese characters into Roman script

PSB (gōng'ānjú; 公安局) – Public Security Bureau, the branch of the police force that manages foreigners in China

qiáo (桥) – bridge

qìchēzhàn (汽车站) – bus station

qìgōng (气功) – exercises and meditation to channel and nurture qi

qípáo (旗袍) – also known as *cheongsam*, one-piece figure-hugging dress worn by Chinese women

rénmín (人民) – the people; the people's

rénmínbì (人民币) – literally "the people's currency"; the official name of Chinese currency

RMB – abbreviation of renminbi

sānlúnchē (三轮车) – non-motorized three-wheeler

shān (山) – mountain; hill

shāngdiàn (商店) – shop; store

shěng (省) – province; provincial

shì (市) – city

shìchǎng (市场) – market

shíkùmén (石库门) – stone gate house; it blends a Chinese courtyard home style with English terraced homes

shòupiàochù (售票处) – ticket office

sì (寺) – temple; monastery

Sun Yat-sen (Sūn Zhōngshān; 孙中山) (1866 -1925) – first president of the Republic of China; considered by many to be the father of modern China, he is adored by communists and republicans alike

tǎ (塔) – pagoda

tai chi (tài jí; 太极) – a slow-moving martial art that also functions as a moving meditation

tíng (亭) – pavilion

wǎngba (网吧) – internet bar

wēnquán (温泉) – hot springs

wǔshù (武术) – Chinese word for martial arts, today it mostly refers to martial-based performance acrobatics

xiàn (县) – county

xīzhàn (西站) – west railway (or bus) station

yáng (阳) – outward, giving, light and masculine energy; complimentary force to yin

yīn (阴) – inward, accepting, dark and feminine energy; complimentary force to yang

yīn yáng (阴阳) – as a whole, the complimentary forces of the universe that act in harmony to create existence

yóujú (邮局) – post office

yuán (元) – basic unit of Chinese currency

yuán (园) – garden

zhāodàisuǒ (招待所) – guesthouse

zhíwùyuán (植物园) – botanical gardens

Zhōngguó (中国) – China

Travel Resources

Consulates

Wether you have a problem, lose your passport, or are looking to continue your trip and need a visa into another country, all roads lead to the consulate. Even though Shanghai isn't the capital of China and doesn't have any embassies, it's big enough and important enough to host an array of national consulates, which can do all the work an embassy can do. Listed below are the names, locations, telephone numbers, emails and websites for the consulates of Shanghai.

Argentina, Consulate General of

Address: Suite 1202-1203, Golden Finance Tower, 58 Yan'an East Rd (延安东路 58 号高登金融大厦 1202-1203 室)
Phone: 6339 0322
Website: www.cshan.mrecic.gov.ar/en
Email: cshan@mrecic.gov.ar; consu_cshan@mrecic.gov.ar

Australia, Consulate General of

Address: 22/F, Citic Square, 1168 Nanjing West Rd (南京西路 1168 号中信泰富广场 22 楼)
Phone: 2215 5200
Website: www.shanghai.china.embassy.gov.au
Email: acgshang@public.sta.net.cn

Austria, Consulate General of

Address: 3A, Qihua Bldg, 1375 Huaihai Middle Rd (淮海中路 1375 号启华大厦 3 楼 A 座)
Phone: 6474 0268

Belgium, Consulate General of

Address: 127 Wuyi Rd (武夷路 127 号)
Phone: 6437 6579
Website: www.diplomatie.be/shanghai
Email: Shanghai@diplobel.fed.be

Brazil, Consulate General of

Address: 7/F, ASA Bldg, 188 Jiangning Rd (静安区江宁路 188 号亚盛大厦 703 室)
Phone: 6437 0110
Website: xangai.itamaraty.gov.br/en-us
Email: visa.xangai@itamaraty.gov.br

Bulgaria, Consulate General of

Address: Unit K, 7/F, Hongqiao Business Center, 2272 Hongqiao Rd (虹桥路 2272 号虹桥商务大厦 7 楼 K 座)
Phone: 6237 6183
Email: bulconshan@yahoo.com

Cambodia, Consulate General of

Address: A/12 Floor, Sapphire Tower, 267 Tianmu Middle Rd (天目中路 267 号蓝宝石大厦 12 楼 A 室)
Phone: 5101 5857
Email: camcg.sh@mfa.gov.kh

Canada, Consulate General of

Address: 8/F, ECO City Bldg, 1788 Nanjing West Rd (南京西路 1788 号国际中心 8 楼)
Phone: 3279 2800
Email: shngi@international.gc.ca

Chile, Consulate General of

Address: Suite 2501, Shanghai Mart, 2299 Yan'an West Rd (延安西路 2299 号世贸商城办公楼 2501 室)
Phone: 6236 0770

Cuba, Consulate General of

Address: Suite 502, 55 Loushanguan Rd (娄山关路 55 号新虹桥大厦 502 室)
Phone: 6275 3078
Email: cgeneralsg@embacuba.cn

Czech Republic, Consulate General of

Address: Suite 808, New Town Center, 83 Loushanguan Rd (娄山关路 83 号新虹桥中心大厦 808 室)
Phone: 6236 9925
Email: shanghai@embassy.mzv.cz

Denmark, Consulate General of

Address: Suite 701, International Trade Center, 2200 Yan'an West Rd (延安西路 2200 号国际贸易中心 701 室)
Phone: 6209 0500
Email: shagkl@um.dk

Egypt, Consulate General of

Address: 19A & 19B, Qihua Bldg, 1375 Huaihai Middle Rd (淮海中路 1375 号启华大厦 19A.19B)
Phone: 6433 1020
Email: egyconsh@sh163.net

Finland, Consulate General of

Address: Suite 2501-2505, CITIC Square, 1168 Nanjing West Rd (南京西路 1168 号中信泰富广场 2501-2505 室)
Phone: 5292 9900
Email: sanomat.sng@formin.fi

France, Consulate General of

Address: Suite 201, Haitong Securities Bldg, 689 Guangdong West Rd (广东路 689 号海通证 券大厦 201 室)
Phone: 6103 2200
Website: www.consulfrance-shanghai.org

Germany, Consulate General of

Address: 181 Yongfu Rd (永福路 181 号)
Phone: 3401 0106

Greece, Consulate General of

Address: Suite 3501, 989 Changle Rd (长乐路 989 号世纪商贸广场 3501 室)
Phone: 5467 0505
Email: greekconsulate@126.com or; grgencon.sha@mfa.gr

Hungary, Consulate General of

Address: Suite 2810-2811, Haitong Securities Bldg, 689 Guangdong Rd (广东路 689 号海通证 券大厦 28 楼 2810、2811 室)
Phone: 6341 0564; 6341 1003
Website: shanghai.hungary-china.com
Email: mission.shg@mfa.gov.hu

India, Consulate General of

Address: Suite 1008, Shanghai International Trade Center, 2201 Yan'an West Rd (延安西路 2201 号国际贸易中心 1008 室)
Phone: 6275 8885
Website: www.indianconsulate.org.cn
Email: cgisha@public.sta.net.cn

Iran, Consulate General of

Address: 17 Fuxing West Rd (复兴西路 17 号)
Phone: 6433 2998
Website: shanghai.mfa.ir (English available)
Email: iranconsulate.sha@mfa.gov.ir

Ireland, Consulate General of

Address: 700A, Shanghai Centre, 1376 Nanjing West Rd (南京西路 1376 号上海商城 700A 室)
Phone: 6279 8729

Email: shanghai@dfa.ie

Israel, Consulate General of

Address: Suite 703, New Town Mansion, 55 Loushanguan Rd (娄山关路 55 号新虹桥大厦 703 室)
Phone: 6126 4500
Email: shanghai@dfa.ie

Italy, Consulate General of

Address: 19/F, 989 Changle Rd (长乐路 989 号 世纪商贸广场 19 楼)
Phone: 5407 5588
Email: conitsha@public4.sta.net.cn

Japan, Consulate General of

Address: 8 Wanshan Rd (万山路 8 号)
Phone: 5257 4766
Website: www.shanghai.cn.emb-japan.go.jp

Kazakhstan, Consulate General of

Address: Suite 1005, 85 Loushanguan Rd (娄山 关路 85 号东方国际大厦 A 座 1005 室)
Phone: 6275 2838

Luxembourg, Consulate General of

Address: Suite 907-908, ECO City Bldg, 1788 Nanjing West Rd (南京西路 1788 号国际中心 907-908 室)
Phone: 6339 0400

Malaysia, Consulate General of

Address: Suite 01 & 04, 9/F, Block B, Dawning Center, 500 Hongbaoshi Rd (红宝石路 500 号东 银大厦 B 栋 9 层 01、04 室)
Phone: 6090 0360
Website: www.kln.gov.my/web/chn_shanghai
Email: shanghai@imi.gov.my

Mexico, Consulate General of

Address: 10/F, Block A, Dawning Center, 500 Hongbaoshi Rd (红宝石路 500 号东银中心 A 座 10 楼)
Phone: 6125 0220

Monaco, Honorary Consulate of

Address: Suite A-11, 2/F, Tomson Commercial Bldg, 710 Dongfang Rd (东方路 710 号汤臣金融 大厦 2 楼 A-11 室)
Phone: 5831 4008

Mongolia, Consulate General of

Address: Suite 3001, City Gateway Bldg, 398 Caoxi North Rd (漕溪北路 398 号汇智大厦 3001 室)
Phone: 6128 9520

Nepal, Consulate General of

Address: 16/F, Bldg A, 669 Beijing West Rd (北京西路 669 号 16 楼 A 座)
Phone: 6272 0259

Netherlands, Consulate General of

Address: 10/F, Tower B, Dawning Center, 500 Hongbaoshi Rd (红宝石路 500 号东银中心东塔 10 楼)
Phone: 2208 7288
Website: shanghai.nlconsulate.org
Email: sha@minbuza.nl

New Zealand, Consulate General of

Address: 16/F, 989 Changle Rd (长乐路 989 号世纪商贸广场 16 楼)
Phone: 5407 5858
Website: www.nzembassy.com/home.cfm?c=19

Norway, Consulate General of

Address: Suite 1701, Bund Center, 222 Yan'an East Rd (延安东路 222 号外滩中心 1701 室)
Phone: 6039 7500
Website: www.norway.cn/Embassy/Shanghai
Email: cg.shanghai@mfa.no

Pakistan, Consulate General of

Address: 7/F, Hongqiao Business Center, 2272 Hongqiao Rd (虹桥路 2272 号虹桥商务大厦 7 楼)
Phone: 6237 7000
Website: www.pakconsulateshanghai.org.cn
Email: pakrepshanghai@yahoo.com

Peru, Consulate General of Peru

Address: Suite 2705, Kerry Centre, 1515 Nanjing West Rd (南京西路 1515 号嘉里中心 2705 室)
Phone: 5298 5900
Website: www.conpersh.com
Email: conperu@conpersh.com

Philippines, Consulate General of

Address: Suit 301, Metrobank Plaza Bldg, 1160 Yan'an West Rd (延安西路 1160 号首信银都广场 301 室)
Phone: 6281 8020
Website: www.philcongenshanghai.org
Email: pcg@philcongenshanghai.org

Poland, Consulate General of

Address: 618 Jianguo West Rd, near Gao'an Rd (建国西路 618 号 , 近高安路)
Phone: 6433 9288
Website: www.shanghai.mfa.gov.pl/en
Email: shanghai.info@msz.gov.pl

Portugal, Consulate General of

Address: 16C-D, Crystal Century Tower, 567 Weihai Rd (威海路 567 号晶采世纪大厦 16C-D)

Phone: 6288 6767

Romania, Consulate General of

Address: Suite 502, Honi International Plaza, 199 Chengdu North Rd (成都北路 199 号恒力国际大厦 502 室)
Phone: 6270 1146
Website: shanghai.mae.ro
Email: romania.cg.sh@gmail.com

Russia, Consulate General of

Address: 20 Huangpu Rd (黄浦路 20 号)
Phone: 6324 2682
Website: www.rusconshanghai.org.cn/english
Email: gkshanghai@mail.ru

Serbia, Consulate General of

Address: Suite 801, 1 Lyon Garden, Lane 60, Ronghua East Rd (荣华东道 60 弄 1 号里昂花园 801 室)
Phone: 6208 1388

Singapore, Consulate General of

Address: 89 Wanshan Rd (万山路 89 号)
Phone: 6278 5566
Website: www.mfa.gov.sg/shanghaichi
Email: singcg_sha@sgmfa.gov.sg

Slovakia, Consulate General of

Address: 4/F, Qihua Tower, 1375 Huaihai Middle Rd (淮海中路 1375 号启华大厦 4 楼)
Phone: 6431 4205

South Africa, Consulate General of

Address: Suite 2706, The Bund Center, 220 Yan'an East Rd (延安东路 220 号外滩中心 2706 室)
Phone: 5359 4977
Email: embassy@saembassy.org.cn

South Korea, Consulate General of

Address: 60 Wanshan Rd (万山路 60 号)
Phone: 6295 5000

Spain, Consulate General of

Address: Suite 301-303, 12 Zhongshan East 1st Rd (中山东一路 12 号 301-303 室)
Phone: 6321 3543

Sri Lanka, Consulate General of

Address: 5/F, Unit E, Shanghai Hongqiao Business Center, 2272 Hongqiao Rd (虹桥路 2272 号虹桥商务大厦 5 楼 E 座)
Phone: 6237 6797

Sweden, Consulate General of

Address: Suite 1521-1541, Shanghai Central

Plaza, 381 Huaihai Middle Rd (淮海中路 381 号
中环广场 1521–1541 室)
Phone: 5359 9610
Email: generalkonsulat.kanton@foreign.
ministry.se

Switzerland, Consulate General of

Address: 22/F, Block A, 319 Xianxia Rd (仙霞
路 319 号远东国际广场 A 幢 22 楼)
Phone: 6270 0519; 6270 0516

Thailand, Consulate General of

Address: 15/F, Crystal Century Mansion, 567
Weihai Rd (威海路 567 号晶采世纪大厦 15 楼)
Phone: 6288 3030
Website: www.thaishanghai.com

Turkey, Consulate General of

Address: 13/F, Qihua Tower, 1375 Huaihai
Middle Rd (淮海中路 1375 号启华大厦 13 楼)
Phone: 6474 6838

Ukraine, Consulate General of

Address: Suite 502, West Tower, Sun Plaza, 88
Xianxia Rd (仙霞路 88 号太阳广场西塔 502 室)
Phone: 6295 3195

United Kingdom, Consulate General of Kingdom

Address: Suite 301, Shanghai Centre, 1376
Nanjing West Rd (南京西路 1376 号上海商城西办
公楼 301 室)
Phone: 3279 2000
Website: www.gov.uk/government/world/
organisations/british-consulate-general-
shanghai
Email: consular.shanghai@fco.gov.uk

United States of America, Consulate General of

Address: 1469 Huaihai Middle Rd (淮海中路
1469 号)
Phone: 6433 6880
Website: shanghai.usembassy-china.org.cn
Email: shanghai_acs@yahoo.com

Uruguay, Consulate General of

Address: Suite 2403, Hong Kong New World
Tower, 300 Huaihai Middle Rd (淮海中路 300 号
香港新世界大厦 2403 室)
Phone: 6335 3927
Website: www.conurushang.com
Email: info@conurushang.com

Uzbekistan, Consulate General of

Address: Suite 801, Yaojiang Development
Center, 258 Wusong Rd (吴淞路 258 号耀江发展
中心 801 室)
Phone: 6307 1896

Vietnam, Consulate General of

Address: Suite 304, Huachen Financial
Mansion, 900 Pudong Avenue (浦东大道 900 号
华辰金融大厦 304 室)
Phone: 6855 5871

Expat Websites

In such a diverse, vibrant city, there are new places
popping up by the day, and various shows, concerts
and special events glitter every night of the week.
To stay up to date with the best Shanghai has to
offer, surf through some of these English language
expat websites.

eChinacities
www.echinacities.com/Shanghai

City Weekend
www.cityweekend.com.cn/Shanghai

Time Out Shanghai
www.timeoutshanghai.com

Shanghai Expat
www.shanghaiexpat.com

Shanghaiist
www.shanghaiist.com

Smart Shanghai
www.smartshanghai.com

Shanghai Daily
www.shanghaidaily.com

iDealShanghai
www.idealshanghai.com

Useful Telephone Numbers

Emergency calls

Police: 110
Fire: 119
Ambulance: 120
Police service for traffic accidents: 122

Calling codes

Country code: 86
City code: 21

Other useful numbers

Local telephone number inquiry: 114
Weather forecast: 12121
Shanghai tourism hotline: 962020
Flight inquiry: 96990
Free hotline for railway tickets booking:
95105105
Shanghai Call Center: 962288

Index

Notes

Notes

Behind the scenes

This is the first edition of Panda Guides *Shanghai* and it was written by a team of expert Shanghai expat writers who come from all corners of the English speaking world. Apart from their writings, this book was produced in Panda Guides' Beijing office with assistance from the Panda Guides headquarters in Toronto, Canada. It was produced by the following:

Commissioning Editor - **Trey Archer**

Managing Editors - **Robert Linnet, Grant Dou**

Managing Layout Designers - **Liu Qingli, Alice Harris**

Coordinating Cartographer - **Yan Laiyong**

Managing Cartographers - **Ding Zhicheng, Jessie Li**

Assistant Cartographers - **Feng Lili, Paul Taylor**

Proofreaders - **Jessica Suotmaa, Elmer Chen, Douglas Smith, Tina Johnson**

Internal Image Research - **Ellen Wong, Aaron Clarke**

Mandarin Content - **Xue Xue**

Office Assistant - **Suriguga, Li Lan, Zhang Qin**

Writers - **Brendan P O'Reilly, Trey Archer, Sam Gussway, Ansel Klusmire**

Other Contributors - **Cecilia Garcia, Emily Umhoefer, Natalie Manning**

A special thanks also goes out to **Chang Zhengong, Ellen Hou, Jason Yu, Han Fei, Liu Quanzu, Zhao Yong, Li Weixing, Yang Haibin, Wang Lei, Abel Thompson, Jeffery Scott, Lawrence Anderson** and **Jackie Lee.** Your work and help are greatly appreciated.

And last but not least, thank you to everyone along the way who helped us research this book. From the farmer on the street who pointed us in the right direction to the business man who gave us a ride when it was raining outside; none of this would have been possible without the people of China. 谢谢你们! *Xia Xia Nong!*